studies in jazz

Institute of Jazz Studies
Rutgers—The State University of New Jersey
General Editors: Dan Morgenstern and Edward Berger

1. BENNY CARTER: A Life in American Music, *by Morroe Berger, Edward Berger, and James Patrick, 2 vols., 1982*
2. ART TATUM: A Guide to His Recorded Music, *by Arnold Laubich and Ray Spencer, 1982*
3. ERROLL GARNER: The Most Happy Piano, *by James M. Doran, 1995*
4. JAMES P. JOHNSON: A Case of Mistaken Identity, *by Scott E. Brown;* Discography 1917–1950, *by Robert Hilbert, 1986*
5. PEE WEE ERWIN: This Horn for Hire, *as told to Warren W. Vaché Sr., 1987*
6. BENNY GOODMAN: Listen to His Legacy, *by D. Russell Connor, 1988*
7. ELLINGTONIA: The Recorded Music of Duke Ellington and His Sidemen, *by W. E. Timner, 1988; 4th ed., 1996*
8. THE GLENN MILLER ARMY AIR FORCE BAND: Sustineo Alas / I Sustain the Wings, *by Edward F. Polic;* Foreword *by George T. Simon, 1989*
9. SWING LEGACY, *by Chip Deffaa, 1989*
10. REMINISCING IN TEMPO: The Life and Times of a Jazz Hustler, *by Teddy Reig, with Edward Berger, 1990*
11. IN THE MAINSTREAM: 18 Portraits in Jazz, *by Chip Deffaa, 1992*
12. BUDDY DeFRANCO: A Biographical Portrait and Discography, *by John Kuehn and Arne Astrup, 1993*
13. PEE WEE SPEAKS: A Discography of Pee Wee Russell, *by Robert Hilbert, with David Niven, 1992*
14. SYLVESTER AHOLA: The Gloucester Gabriel, *by Dick Hill, 1993*
15. THE POLICE CARD DISCORD, *by Maxwell T. Cohen, 1993*
16. TRADITIONALISTS AND REVIVALISTS IN JAZZ, *by Chip Deffaa, 1993*
17. BASSICALLY SPEAKING: An Oral History of George Duvivier, *by Edward Berger;* Musical Analysis *by David Chevan, 1993*
18. TRAM: The Frank Trumbauer Story, *by Philip R. Evans and Larry F. Kiner, with William Trumbauer, 1994*
19. TOMMY DORSEY: On the Side, *by Robert L. Stockdale, 1995*
20. JOHN COLTRANE: A Discography and Musical Biography, *by Yasuhiro Fujioka, with Lewis Porter and Yoh-ichi Hamada, 1995*
21. RED HEAD: A Chronological Survey of "Red" Nichols and His Five Pennies, *by Stephen M. Stroff, 1996*
22. THE RED NICHOLS STORY: After Intermission 1942–1965, *by Philip R. Evans, Stanley Hester, Stephen Hester, and Linda Evans, 1997*
23. BENNY GOODMAN: Wrappin' It Up, *by D. Russell Connor, 1996*

24. CHARLIE PARKER AND THEMATIC IMPROVISATION, *by Henry Martin, 1996*
25. BACK BEATS AND RIM SHOTS: The Johnny Blowers Story, *by Warren W. Vaché Sr., 1997*
26. DUKE ELLINGTON: A Listener's Guide, *by Eddie Lambert, 1998*
27. SERGE CHALOFF: A Musical Biography and Discography, *by Vladimir Simosko, 1998*
28. HOT JAZZ: From Harlem to Storyville, *by David Griffiths, 1998*
29. ARTIE SHAW: A Musical Biography and Discography, *by Vladimir Simosko, 2000*
30. JIMMY DORSEY: A Study in Contrasts, *by Robert L. Stockdale, 1998*
31. STRIDE!: Fats, Jimmy, Lion, Lamb and All the Other Ticklers, *by John L. Fell and Terkild Vinding, 1999*
32. GIANT STRIDES: The Legacy of Dick Wellstood, *by Edward N. Meyer, 1999*
33. JAZZ GENTRY: Aristocrats of the Music World, *by Warren W. Vaché Sr., 1999*
34. THE UNSUNG SONGWRITERS: America's Masters of Melody, *by Warren W. Vaché Sr., 2000*
35. THE MUSICAL WORLD OF J. J. JOHNSON, *by Joshua Berrett and Louis G. Bourgois III, 1999*
36. THE LADIES WHO SING WITH THE BAND, *by Betty Bennett, 2000*
37. AN UNSUNG CAT: The Life and Music of Warne Marsh, *by Safford Chamberlain, 2000*
38. JAZZ IN NEW ORLEANS: The Postwar Years Through 1970, *by Charles Suhor, 2001*
39. THE YOUNG LOUIS ARMSTRONG ON RECORDS: A Critical Survey of the Early Recordings, 1923–1928, *by Edward Brooks, 2002*
40. BENNY CARTER: A Life in American Music, Second Edition, *by Morroe Berger, Edward Berger, and James Patrick, 2 vols., 2002*
41. CHORD CHANGES ON THE CHALKBOARD: How Public School Teachers Shaped Jazz and the Music of New Orleans, *by Al Kennedy*, Foreword *by Ellis Marsalis Jr., 2002*
42. CONTEMPORARY CAT: Terence Blanchard with Special Guests, *by Anthony Magro, 2002*
43. PAUL WHITEMAN: Pioneer in American Music, Volume I: 1890–1930 *by Don Rayno, 2003*
44. GOOD VIBES: A Life in Jazz, *by Terry Gibbs with Cary Ginell, 2003*

Good Vibes

A Life in Jazz

Terry Gibbs

with
Cary Ginell

Studies in Jazz, No. 44

The Scarecrow Press, Inc.
Lanham, Maryland, and Oxford
2003

SCARECROW PRESS, INC.

Published in the United States of America
by Scarecrow Press, Inc.
A Member of the Rowman & Littlefield Publishing Group
4501 Forbes Boulevard, Suite 200, Lanham, Maryland 20706
www.scarecrowpress.com

PO Box 317
Oxford
OX2 9RU, UK

Copyright © 2003 by Terry Gibbs

All rights reserved. No part of this publication may be reproduced, stored in a retrieval system, or transmitted in any form or by any means, electronic, mechanical, photocopying, recording, or otherwise, without the prior permission of the publisher.

British Library Cataloguing in Publication Information Available

Library of Congress Cataloging-in-Publication Data

Gibbs, Terry, 1924–
 Good vibes : a life in jazz / Terry Gibbs with Cary Ginell.
   p. cm. — (Studies in jazz ; no. 44)
 Includes index.
Discography: p.
 ISBN 0-8108-4586-5 (hardcover : alk. paper)
 1. Gibbs, Terry, 1924– 2. Jazz musicians—UnitedStates—Biography.
I. Ginell, Cary. II. Title. III. Series.
ML419.G5 A3 2003
781.65'092—dc21
                                                         2002151153

∞™ The paper used in this publication meets the minimum requirements of American National Standard for Information Sciences—Permanence of Paper for Printed Library Materials, ANSI/NISO Z39.48-1992.
Manufactured in the United States of America.

For Rebekah

Contents

Editor's Foreword	ix
Foreword	xi
Preface	xiii
Acknowledgments	xv
1. A Real Go-Getter	1
2. Dizzy, Bird, and a Bebop Breakdown	27
3. Fifty-Second Street	39
4. My Three Minutes with Tommy Dorsey	47
5. "Shooby Yockson" in Sweden	55
6. Buddy Rich: Mr. Nice Guy	63
7. Woody Herman and the Four Brothers Band	79
8. Bellson, Shavers, and Dorsey (Again?)	111
9. Benny Goodman: El Foggo	117
10. Finally, a Full-Time Bandleader	125
11. El Foggo Rides Again	147
12. Terry G. and Terry P.	155
13. California, Here I Come!	179
14. The Dream Band	187
15. The Coltrane Connection	227
16. What's a Regis Philbin?	233
17. Operation: Entertainment	241
18. Hi-Ho, Steverino!	259
19. Phil Spector: Mr. Overtime	275
20. Three Women–Four Marriages	279
21. My Friend, Buddy D.	283
22. Goodbye for Now	297
Terry Gibbs Discography	301
Index	319

Editor's Foreword

As anyone who has seen him in action will know, Terry Gibbs is a study in time and motion. His time is impeccable: no tempo is too fast for him, and he never fails to swing. And when he plays, he is in constant motion; the vibraphone is a very physical instrument, with sound being made by striking its bars with mallets. Even when he isn't playing, Terry moves around on the bandstand, responding to the music with his body and his voice. After more than sixty years of making music, he still can't contain his enthusiasm when the band is swinging—and with him at the helm, it always is.

And he's as fast with words as he is with notes—a champion talker. When he talks and when he plays, Terry Gibbs tells us stories, and in these pages, he's told his best one yet: his own. It is a fascinating tale that covers many of jazz's greatest years and features a multitude of its greatest players, and it unfolds like a great Gibbs solo, with never a dull moment.

Terry has seen much and heard much, and he has perfect recall and perfect pitch. The voices you hear ring true, as do the stories—and what stories they are! Some are hilarious, others are harrowing, others still are deeply moving. Terry tells it like it was, pulling no punches, as frank about himself as about others. And throughout, the music is always in view. Terry doesn't lecture or pontificate, but in telling a story that never fails to hold the reader's interest, he sheds much light on the many facets of the great American music we call jazz. This is not a scholarly work, but it offers to the serious student of jazz great insights of the music and entertainment businesses—and of twentieth-century America.

From start to finish, *Good Vibes: A Life in Jazz* strikes the right note and stays in tune. Terry has captured the true sound of his voice and transposed it to the page. (And as a fringe benefit, this is a great primer in Yiddishisms.) It is a pleasure to add this authentic American autobiography to Studies in Jazz.

Dan Morgenstern
Director, Institute of Jazz Studies
Rutgers University

Foreword

What a pleasure to sit down and write some true goodies about a friend that deserves much more than just "great!" That's our Terry Gibbs.

Born and raised in the New York area that houses Brooklyn, he was schooled in New York City, the boss city of the world. Consequently, I look at Terry as a post-graduate student who was taught all the magnificent New York concepts that just happened to be labeled Life.

His personality is something else. I call him "Mr. X+Y=Z." Know what that means? "X" represents his artistic talent, "Y" the fantastic way he executes that talent, and "Z" is the finished product. How he puts his know-how and talent together with a terrific sense of humor and his obvious energy makes for his wonderful personality, offstage as well as on.

He started out playing drums, then added some two-finger playing on the upper register of the piano. But then there is his winner which is called the vibraphone. He fell into a groove that showed off the vibraphone's many different sound patterns and has mastered them all.

I always enjoyed being onstage with Terry. Why? Number one, we had a ball being the first bebop band to enter Sweden. Then we both returned to America and joined "The Band" of its time known as Woody Herman's Second Herd. Terry fit so well. He never stopped creating in all of his time on Woody's bandstand.

Terry's talent was particularly obvious in his many years on *The Steve Allen Show*, as was his musically creative thinking when leading his own Dream Band. His sidemen all loved him as well as his musical charts. His version of being a bandleader is, without any doubt, the greatest.

We had trumpet player friends called Shorty Rogers and Al Porcino. Shorty and Al talked more slowly than anyone I've ever heard. When you talked to either one of them, you stayed overnight. Mister Gibbs is the absolute opposite. When Terry begins to talk, he gets to the point in a few quick seconds and then leaps into another subject with the speed of Woody's "Caldonia." WOOH-EE! That exact tempo carried over to his vibraphone playing.

To put it all together, I'm overwhelmed with our friendship and the hard driving force he employs on a bandstand or a CD. Thanks, Terry, from one New Yorker to another. In this new era, we all need more students of our Gibbs. Bless our Terry from the past, the present, and the future. He's what's known as "A Winner."

Chubby Jackson

Preface

Legendary baseball announcer Vin Scully often employs a metaphor to describe a restless player who can't stop moving. Scully says that the player "would make coffee nervous." That describes Terry Gibbs to a "T." He is living proof of Newton's first law of motion, which states, "an object in motion tends to stay in motion with the same speed and in the same direction."

Terry Gibbs' life has been like Newton's law: always moving forward at a constant speed: fast. He went from being a *wünderkind* on *Major Bowes' Amateur Hour* to one of the pioneers of bebop, and finally, as leader of his celebrated Dream Band. Terry Gibbs has witnessed and participated in over sixty years of jazz history; always driving in the fast lane and never looking back. In this book, Terry finally looks back and does so from the lofty vantage point of one of jazz's elder statesmen.

One of the few survivors remaining from the embryonic years of bebop, Terry performed with many of the legendary figures in the jazz world. From the swing era: Tommy Dorsey, Benny Goodman, Woody Herman, and Buddy Rich. From bebop: Charlie Parker, Dizzy Gillespie, Bud Powell, Stan Getz, and Oscar Pettiford. In 1959, his Dream Band revived the big band era in a big way. In the 1960s he became a familiar figure on television programs starring his friend Steve Allen.

As a master of the vibraphone, Terry has had few peers in his field. The short list of influential vibists includes Lionel Hampton, Adrian Rollini, Red Norvo, Milt Jackson, Cal Tjader, Gary Burton, and Bobby Hutcherson. Terry ranks alongside Jackson as one of the two major innovators in bringing the vibes into modern jazz. Not bad for someone who doesn't know what "wrist lifts" are.

He is an exciting musician, whether he is playing vibes or two-finger piano á la Hampton. When Terry plays, he sweats, chews gum, exhorts his fellow musicians, and above all, has a lot of fun onstage. As a bandleader, he is never quiet, always yelling, whooping, and hollering; a one-man cheering section for his band.

Terry was also a pioneer in the social development of jazz. He always felt best when he had a racially mixed group. In the early 1950s, he challenged the prejudices of the deep South by hiring the little known but immensely talented Terry Pollard to accompany him on piano. Female pianists were Terry's "bag." In addition to Pollard, Terry also hired Pat Moran and Alice McLeod; the latter Terry would introduce to her future husband, John Coltrane.

In his long career, Terry Gibbs also became an anomaly in jazz: an astute businessman who ran his own affairs with intelligence, insight, logic, and fairness. In Yiddish, the word that best describes Terry is *mensch,* someone who always does the right thing. As a Jew growing up in Brooklyn, Terry received much of his moral training from his father, a New York bandleader and musician. The rest he got on the street, playing and sometimes fighting his way toward his goal: a career in music. He learned to command respect from his musicians, to pay a fair wage, and to respect his audience. He became a songwriter, and while other composers sold their creations "for a song," Terry early on established his own publishing company and still retains the rights to his several hundred compositions.

I met Terry in 1999 while producing a documentary on his life for the NPR series *Jazz Profiles,* hosted by Nancy Wilson. While doing the interviews for the show, I became fascinated by Terry's attention to detail, amazing recall, and most of all, his infectious sense of humor. There is no better storyteller around, as you will find in many of the hilarious as well as poignant moments in this book.

We shared some things in common besides jazz. My mother and Terry are only one month apart in age and went to the same high school in Brooklyn, although they were unaware of each other. My cousin, Ira Ginsburg, who later became a professional symphonic drummer, took lessons from the very same Freddy Albright who gave Terry vibes lessons. We also share our heritage. From Terry I have learned a lot about "talking Jewish," and we shared many laughs concerning that rich language.

I've learned many lessons from Terry Gibbs in the three years I've known him. The most important of these is self-confidence. If you know what you are capable of, you should go after your dreams. That, a little luck, and a little *chutzpah* will take you far.

Cary Ginell

Acknowledgments

If I had to thank everybody for helping me write this book, I'd have to include everyone from my butcher to my rabbi to every name I mention in the book. For without these stories about them, I'd have no book at all. The idea of putting the story of my life into a book starts with everybody who ever interviewed me, whether they were disc jockeys or newspaper people. They always said the same thing after the interview was finished: "These are great stories! You should write a book!" So to them I say, thank you for the idea.

Without a doubt, I want to acknowledge my wife Rebekah, who has put up with listening to these stories for all the years that we've been married. I taught Rebekah some funny Jewish expressions, one being *bobeh meisehs,* which literally means "grandmother stories," but translates into "old wives tales." Every time we are around a bunch of people we don't know too well, if they want to hear a little about my life, I would tell them some of the stories in this book. Because she's heard them for twenty-five years, Rebekah would always say, "All right! Enough with the *bobeh meisehs!*" I know that she's happy now, for if I start to tell these stories again to anyone, she'll say, "Let them buy the book." I love her, and I thank her for being there for me.

A big thanks to Cary Ginell for teaching me how to write a book and for sitting with me for about a year-and-a-half listening to my *bobeh meisehs* as we tape-recorded them. He always laughed at each story every time I told it. He had the hard job of trying to figure out half of what I was talking about, and thank God that even though my once athletic body ain't what it used to be, my brain is still a half-hour ahead of my body. I would go from one story in 1949 to a story in 1980 and Cary had to try and figure out which was which and put it down on paper. Also, thanks to Cary for not asking me to change my Brooklynese way of telling my stories and also for teaching me where to use the word "had." Without Cary, I never would have written the book.

Also thanks to my biggest fan, Rod Nicas, who not only helped me put Volume 6 of "The Dream Band" CDs together, but who also taught me how to use a computer. I'm a complete klutz when I'm trying to learn anything except the chord changes to "I Got Rhythm." Rod made it his business to come to my house and show me what to do so that I could edit this book.

And to anybody that thinks that I may have left them out and that they either deserved to be or should be thanked, thank you.

Terry Gibbs

Chapter 1
A Real Go-Getter

This will probably be the only story in this book that was told to me that I don't remember. Everything else you read here will be something that I do remember or that I was involved in. This actually happened when I was two years old and was told to me by my mother. Every Friday night, my mother would have all of our Jewish relatives over to the house. She baked enough cakes, cookies, pies, and Russian delicacies to feed half the Jews in Brooklyn and then some. Sometimes when it rained or snowed, they'd wear galoshes, which were completely wet, and put them in the closet. Galoshes are rubber boots or shoes that fit over the shoe or boot that you'd wear when it rained or snowed to keep your shoes from getting wet. They would all sit in the living room talking Jewish or Russian. Our living room was not even ten by ten; it was that small.

While they were all talking, someone mentioned my name and somebody said, "Where is the baby?" It was at that time they realized that I wasn't there so they started looking for me. I was only two years old, where could I be? They looked all over the place, opening up every door in the house. They even looked in the Frigidaire. Finally, they opened the door to the closet where all the galoshes and shoes were, and they found me, sitting on the floor, licking the bottoms of the shoes and galoshes. Everybody thought that was kind of strange, especially my parents. And now that I think of it, it was kind of strange. I'd give anything to find out why I did that. I guess I just liked the taste of shoes and galoshes. I suppose you shouldn't knock it until you've tried it.

My father, mother, sisters Sonia (who was nicknamed Sunny), and Shirley (who later changed her name to Sherry), and brother Sol escaped from Russia in 1921. My sister Sherry, who is three years older than me, was one year old when they arrived in the USA. I was the only one born in the United States. When my mother died at the age of eighty-five, she and my father had been married for seventy years. My father passed away exactly four weeks after she died. I knew that he was going to die, and I was happy for him because I remember on the way home from my mother's funeral all he could say was "I lost my best friend."

I was born with the name Julius Herbert Gubenko on October 13, 1924. We lived at 669 Stone Avenue in Brooklyn. It was kind of a nice neighborhood. There were all kinds of vendors with pushcarts walking the streets selling everything from shoes to kosher pickles. They used to push their pushcarts, yelling in Jewish, "*Alteh zachin! Alteh shich!*" which means "old things, old shoes." There was a vendor who came around with a camera on a stand, almost like a Polaroid, that could make a picture for you in eight or ten minutes. I had a whistle and a lollipop that I put inside the whistle. This one vendor thought that I looked cute and took a picture of me like that. He then asked me if I wanted the picture and I said of course. I showed him where I lived. He took me upstairs to my mother and asked her for ten cents for the picture he took of me and she said, "What picture? Get out of here!" She actually started to push him out the door. He said, "Wait a minute, I already took the picture!" He showed it to her and she liked it. After bargaining with him for about fifteen minutes, she wound up giving him seven cents, and I was told never to do it again.

We didn't seem to be affected too much by the Depression because we always had food in the house. When we had dinner my mother had her own way of serving the meal. You would think that a normal way to serve a meal would be to put the main dish in the middle of the table and then put all the vegetables or whatever you're serving around the table, and you usually helped yourself by passing everything around. But not in my house and not with my mother. My mother would fix you your own plate, and when she fixed you a plate and put it in front of you, there was enough food there to choke a horse. It was enough for twelve people. Years later, I took Claude Williamson, a piano player who was playing in my quartet, to my parents' house to eat, and as usual, my mother fixed him a plate and put it in front of him. There must have been enough food on his plate for about eight people. He thought it was for everyone, and he pushed it into the middle of the table. She saw him do that and came over and pushed it back in front of him again. He figured it was still too close for everybody to get to so he pushed it back in the middle of the table. She said, "Vat are you doing?" Claude said, "I put it in the middle. It'll be hard for everybody to reach it over here." She said, "Vat do you mean, reach? Dey all got dere own! Dis is far you!" My mother was beautiful.

I was sort of the rebel of the family. I was very respectful and listened to my parents, but my mother really wanted me to live my life according to her old-fashioned ways of thinking. That was okay when I was in my teens, but as I got older, I didn't particularly want to live my life her way. There was a point in my life when I thought that I was at an age where I was mature enough to live my life the way I wanted to. I never married a Jewish girl. I never thought about what religion anybody was. I married whoever I wanted to marry. If I made a mistake, it was my mistake to make, whatever it was. The cliché "you make your bed, you lie in it" is what I was always told. When she tried to make me do certain things that I didn't believe in, I wouldn't do them. She was really strict and very old-fashioned, but as a mother, she was the greatest. She really lived for her children. She was like the song "My Yiddishe Momme." *Through fire and vasser*, which means that she'd go through fire and water to do anything for her children. I'd get up in the morning to go to school, and there would be two of the fattest lox or sturgeon sandwiches you've ever seen for me to eat, and I had to eat both sandwiches. If you went into the Carnegie Deli today, where they charge you twenty dollars for a sandwich and it's eight feet high, that's the kind of sandwich she made for me. And of course, I loved it!

My father used to get up early in the morning before I went to school and go out and buy fresh lox and sturgeon. It was always fresh. I was taught to respect my elders and of course, without a doubt, respect my parents. One time, I remember getting a spanking. I never got spanked ever, except for this one time. My mother told me to go to the store to get some "soupngreens" and I said I didn't want to go. When my father heard what I said, he spanked me. I was wrong. That was being disrespectful.

When I went to junior high school, my rabbi would wait for me at my house to give me my *bar mitzvah* lesson after I got home from school. He used to come to my house about three times a week to teach me what to do for my *bar mitzvah* when I turned thirteen years old. I must have been around twelve years old at the time. Studying for my *bar mitzvah* felt strange to me because the words the rabbi was teaching me to read were written in Hebrew, and I hadn't the slightest idea what I was reading. I spoke and understood Jewish, but I didn't know what the Hebrew words meant. My folks were religious Jews so I had to go along with it. I don't think that they knew what the Hebrew words meant either, except for the prayers you'd say before eating bread or drinking wine.

One time when I was in school, I had to go to the bathroom really bad. It was the end of the day, and I was too embarrassed to go while I was in school. I don't know why, but when you're a kid, you feel ashamed to tell anybody that you have to go to the bathroom, especially if you have to move your bowels. It was about twelve blocks from school to my house. It was freezing outside and my mother made me wear long underwear, long pants, eighteen sweaters, and who knows how many shirts underneath that. I was loaded with clothes. I was walking back from school and there was ice on the rocks and the street. I had to go so bad that I would sit on the rocks and rest because I was afraid I was going to crap in my pants. It took me about twenty minutes longer to get home than it usually did. When I got to my house, my rabbi was sitting in the kitchen waiting for me. I ran into the house, ran right past him to the bathroom, and by the time I got my eighteenth sweater off, boom, that was the end of that. Crapped right in my pants. My mother was most understanding. She told the rabbi that I wasn't feeling good. As a matter of fact, after I crapped in my pants, I felt great!

My father learned to speak English fairly well but with a Jewish accent. My mother learned to speak English from a black janitor. We lived in a four-family house in an all-Jewish neighborhood. Next door was an apartment house that was about three or four stories high. That was big in those days. The janitor, who lived in the basement apartment with his wife and kids, was called Charlie. My mother would always bake cakes for him, and he would teach her how to speak English. She ended up sounding like a southern black person. Pretty hip for an old Jewish lady. I didn't know what she was talking about half the time. She sounded hipper than me. In fact, I think she was getting too hip for the neighborhood.

Our neighborhood movie house, the Ambassador Theater, once gave away a set of dishes. The way you got the dishes was that if you went to the movie on Wednesday between one and four in the afternoon, you would get one dish with your movie ticket. You'd have to go every Wednesday and get your one dish until you wound up with a whole set. My mother used to go every Wednesday with my *Tanta* (aunt) Dunia. *Tanta* Dunia was really out there. She would get very excited while watching the movie and sometimes start talking to the movie picture as if it were really happening with her being in the scene. This one Wednesday, my mother couldn't go, so she made me go with *Tanta* Dunia and get the dish for her. We were watching an action movie. In this scene there was a bad guy hiding behind a door with a knife in his hand. The good guy walked past the bad guy who was hiding and as he passed him, the bad guy came out with the knife in his hand and was about to stab him in the back. My *Tanta* Dunia saw this and stood up screaming, "*Drayzach arimet, eh hut ah messer!*" which means "Turn around, he's got a knife!" When she stood up and started to scream, I hid under my seat. I was too embarrassed to get up for half the theatre stood up to see who was screaming. Dishes or no dishes, I never went to any movie again with my *Tanta* Dunia.

My father's name was Abe Gubenko. He was a very gentle person, one of the most honest people who ever lived. He was a bandleader and violinist and was very big in the Jewish club date business playing Jewish weddings, bar mitzvahs, and banquets. Sometimes he booked two or three jobs a night. I used to play these jobs with my father when I was a kid. The name of my father's band was Abe Gubenko and his Radio Novelty Orchestra. I was eleven, twelve, thirteen years old and when they were having dinner I would go out in the middle of the floor and play "Hora Staccato," "Czardas" by Monti, and a few Jewish pieces on the xylophone.

On a xylophone, there are three sharps and flats, then two, then three, and then two, just like the black keys on a piano. My father would set them up that way, and I'd just go out on the floor and play. I got up there and looked at the xylophones and thought, "Oh God, I forgot the beginning!" It looked completely different. My father had made a mistake and set them up three, two, TWO, and three. Luckily, I had enough sense to just move one bar over to the left and I went right into the song. Otherwise, I would have had a nervous breakdown right in the middle of serving the chopped liver.

There was a musician named Naftule Brandwein who was probably the greatest Jewish clarinet player who ever lived. His biggest problem was that he was an alcoholic. He was an out-and-out drunk. He made some great records in 1923 and 1924. Later on in his life, it was hard for him to get a job as a bandleader because nobody would hire him because he'd get so drunk on the job. My father hired him with the stipulation that he wouldn't drink. He drank, played great, and took care of business, but he didn't get drunk. He was a funny guy. When I went out on the floor to play my solos, he would grab a chair and sit right next to me. I'd be in the middle of the floor playing, surrounded by tables with people eating. Sometimes my father would have the piano player play the accordion and stand next to me so that I could hear the accompaniment. Naftule would come out to the middle of the floor, sit next to me and keep saying, "*Aye, goot, aye, goot!*" He was *kvelling*. He embarrassed the hell out of me.

When I was sixteen years old, Naftule told my father that he wanted me to play drums for him on his own job. He played these really tricky authentic Russian tempos, and I had all this energy, so I'd rush a little bit. I couldn't help it. As we were playing he turned around, and he was half-drunk already, looked right at me and yelled at me in front of everyone: *"Goddemmit, Gubenko, you FAUK! You're rrrrushing!"* Real loud with a Russian Jewish accent, as loud as he could say it. I told my father that I'd never play for him again, ever.

Years later, when I was working in the Catskill Mountains, Naftule came up to perform where I was working. He used to have an act where he'd wear a suit with light bulbs sewn in it. The suit would be hooked up to a cord that stretched 80,000 feet with a plug at the end. They would turn all the lights off and he'd walk around the hall playing the clarinet. While he was walking and playing, he tripped over the cord and a few of the bulbs started to short out. There was a big flash and he yelled out, "I'm on FIRE! I'm on FIRE!" ran out of the place and jumped right in the pool.

I'll tell you how honest my father was. He'd get home from playing a job around four or five o'clock in the morning and before he went to bed, he'd count all the money that the job paid. This one time he was supposed to get four hundred dollars for the whole band but when he counted the money out, there were two one hundred-dollar bills stuck together, so he had one hundred dollars too much. The father of the bride was drunk when he gave my father the money and my father was afraid that the guy would think that he had stolen a hundred dollars from him. Not everybody had telephones and there was no way to reach the man, so at four o'clock in the morning, my father got on a bus that was about two blocks from our house to get to a trolley car to get to a subway station. Then from the subway station he got another bus to get to the man's house. The whole trip took him about two hours. When he got to the guy's house, the guy was still juiced out of his bird and my father told him that he had given him a hundred dollars too much. The guy didn't even know that he had given him too much money but my father couldn't sit in the house five more minutes knowing that he had been overpaid.

My father would hire the best young musicians and groom them. Club date musicians in those days were sort of like *schnorrers*, which means they were like moochers. There was always a table set up for the musicians to sit at. In all those Jewish catering halls, the kishke was the greatest. You couldn't buy kishke like that anywhere. The musicians would take napkins, wrap up the kishke, and stuff them in their pockets. My father taught them that that wasn't the way a professional musician acts and told them that if you want to be treated with class, you have to act like you have class.

I learned a lot about being a bandleader and how to take care of business from my father; how to treat people and how to act on stage.

When you play club dates, you have to play requests, and sometimes people tip you for that. That's the nature of the club date business. When you're playing jazz, it's a completely different thing. You don't have to cater to anybody. I never played requests or took tips, but I did find a way to get to them without selling out. When I played clubs in big cities like New York or Chicago, I could play songs like "Groovin' High" and all these hip bebop songs and there was no problem because the audiences were hip. When I played in the Midwest, I would play "Whispering," which had the same chord changes as "Groovin' High." At least they recognized the melody to "Whispering." Or I'd play "How High the Moon" instead of "Ornithology." I played the melodies of the original songs instead of the bebop songs that had the same chord changes. We'd play the same type of jazz as if we were playing "Whispering" or "How High the Moon" anyhow.

My mother's name was Lizzie, and she ran the household. She lived for the family. Everything was done for the family. I don't remember my whole family ever eating dinner together in the house, except on the Jewish holidays like Passover or *Rosh Hashanah*. My older sister Sunny worked. My other sister Sherry and I could have eaten together sometimes. My father was busy booking jobs.

My brother Sol was a pussycat of a guy, but he loved to gamble. He was a great card player. After twelve cards were dealt, he could remember all the remaining cards in the deck. He was also a giant billiard player and was good at shooting straight pool. The poolroom that we went to in Brooklyn, like just about any poolroom, was considered to be like a gang hangout. That's how people thought of it. Poolrooms were considered places where bad guys would hang out. We did nothing there but play pool, but it was considered bad because sometimes you'd see guys gambling there and that was considered bad. I was fairly good at pool, not great, but good enough. My brother took me to my poolroom and spotted me twenty-five points in straight pool. Then he ran fifty balls. I never got to shoot. He really rubbed it in when on the last four or five balls, he shot with one hand. If you're that good and you gamble, there always has to be somebody better. He got in trouble gambling and owed some guys about two thousand dollars and they were going to beat him up and break his legs. Breaking a guy's legs was no big deal for a guy who was a hood. He owed them two thousand dollars and they wanted their money immediately. My mother came to me and said, "You've got to help your brother and lend him two thousand dollars." They didn't have any money and I was working with Woody Herman at the time and had saved a little money. I never thought twice about it. I had to do it, and so I gave him the money. He couldn't pay me back for years afterward and didn't until my folks died and left $10,000 to the four of us, which we split four ways. Then he paid me back. Later on, when I played on Fifty-Second Street, he wanted to come along and carry my vibes for me. He was thirteen years older than me. I said, "I can carry my own vibes!" But he actually cried and said, "I gotta help you," because he really felt so bad all those years about never being able to pay me back the money until my folks died.

I was always the best athlete on the block. At eight, nine, and ten years old, I was a great punchball player. Punchball was the game in Brooklyn. There would be a guy playing center, a first baseman, a third baseman, and one or two outfielders. The idea was to hit the ball between the first baseman and the center or the third baseman and the center. You could also punch the ball as far as you could to try to get a home run. There were sewer covers about every thirty or forty yards. I was good enough to hit the length of two sewers. I also could place the ball. I could place the ball right between the first baseman's legs. If I wanted to hit a homer real far, I'd punch it. But other times I would slap it with English, and it would hit the ground and curve so you couldn't get it. It was like baseball without a bat.

I used to go to a few games at Ebbets Field. I knew somebody who lived across the street and we'd go up on the roof and watch the Dodgers' games. But I was a New York Giants fan. A New York Giants fan living in Brooklyn. That's brave. In fact, when I moved to Los Angeles and the Giants moved to San Francisco, I rooted for them until all the guys I knew like Willie Mays and Orlando Cepeda retired. Then, when I didn't know the names of any of the new ball players, I stopped rooting for them. When I was a kid, there was a player on the Giants named Mel Ott, a left-handed batter who used to lift his right foot when he swung. I copied him but I lifted my left foot because I was a right-handed batter. I could hit pretty good that way.

I also loved boxing and always wanted to be a boxer. Street fighting, though, was not my bag. I never liked street fighting, I thought that was the dumbest thing. We were playing football. I must have been about fourteen or fifteen. We played touch tackle in the schoolyard on cement with some older guys, maybe twenty-one or twenty-two years old. We had rules like no dirty tackling, no hitting below the knees, but these guys were doing that to us. I'll never forget this one guy whose name was Jerry who was about six feet tall. I was a little guy about five-foot-two, but I had more guts than I should have had. I've never been afraid of anything in my life except a knife or a gun. Looking back, it's really stupid not to have fear because you can get yourself into situations where you can get killed. Today, forget about it. I'm afraid of a midget with or without a gun or a knife. Anyhow, we're playing this game, and this guy Jerry is playing dirty. So I said to my friends, "Here's what we'll do. You guys hit him high, stop him from running, and I'll leap at his legs and we'll knock him right off his feet and on his ass, okay?" And we did that. I probably could have broken both of his legs, I hit him so hard. He got up and wanted to fight me, and he started to swing at me. I jumped up at him, got him in a headlock, and threw him to the ground. He couldn't do much because of the headlock. My arms have always been the strongest part of my body. When he finally got out of it, he hit me in the head and knocked me down. I started to get up and was on one knee, ready to fight some more, but he hit me in the head before I could get up and knocked me down again. I was dazed because he had hit me with his fist. He said, "Get up!" I said, "Kiss my ass, I'll get up if you don't hit me while I'm still on one knee." One of the brothers of one of the guys on our side, who was also an older guy about twenty-one or twenty-two came in and beat the shit out of that guy, and he deserved it. I would have kept fighting if he had let me get up. Who knows what kind of chance I would have had with that big ape? Maybe I would have gotten hit more, but I would have gotten a few good shots in, too.

We used to play touch tackle football at night. We couldn't afford a real football so we'd take a whole gang of newspapers and tie them all together. We'd play at eight, nine o'clock at night under the streetlights. I was never afraid to run through the whole team. You had to catch me to start with; I was very fast.

This reminds me of a funny thing my mother once did. When we played in the daytime, we always played in front of my house, because one of the sewer covers was right there. My mother would get bugged because we made so much noise; we'd be screaming and yelling. At first, we lived on the second floor but later we moved down to the ground floor. What she would do is, she'd yell out the window, "C'mon! C'mon!" about four or five times and we'd all run over to her. Then she'd say, "Get outta here!" She never put the sentence together to actually say, "C'mon, get outta here!" so by the time she yelled, "get outta here!" we were all in front of her.

There was a guy called Mr. Sherman, who lived about two houses down from my house. He also used to scream at us to get away because he'd be sitting on a bench in front of his house. He got bugged when we wouldn't go away, and he grabbed our punchball. The punchball wasn't solid; it was a small rubber ball with a hole in the middle. It was made by Spalding, but in Brooklyn we called it a Spaldeen. Mr. Sherman grabbed our ball and wouldn't give it back to us. We got so mad that we went and found an old ball, cut it and made a slit in the ball, then squeezed it and made a hole in it, and then one of us would pee into it. The next time we were playing, we knew he was going to grab the ball so we purposely threw it towards him. Sure enough, he grabbed the ball and got pee all over his hand. We really laughed hard. Those things are funny when you're young. Pretty sick but funny.

We lived in a neighborhood called East New York, which was very close to Brownsville. That was where Murder, Inc. came from. We lived in a brownstone at 428 East Ninety-Third Street. When I was going to high school, the cops captured Abe Reles, who was part of Murder, Inc., a crime organization where you could get anyone killed for the right price. Later they made a movie about him. The police hid him on the top floor of the Half Moon Hotel in Coney Island because he was going to squeal on the mob. They had police on every floor guarding him in this empty hotel. Reles was the only witness and the cops were going to bust Murder, Inc. wide open. Burton Turkus was the district attorney. They finally got their only witness in Abe Reles and the newspapers said that he jumped out of a window. What jump? They got to him.

Well, to get to the point, Reles lived about four or five blocks from my house on East Ninety-Third Street. The police roped off the whole neighborhood so that in order to go to Tilden High School, I had to walk eight or ten blocks out of my way to get there.

My father was forty years old when I was born. My uncle Lovya was one of the greatest violin players in Russia, but they wouldn't let him leave the country. He couldn't escape because he was playing with the symphony and they didn't want to lose him.

My favorite uncle was my Uncle Nat who changed his name from Nathan Gubenko to Nat Gubin. He was the black sheep of the family because he liked to drink hard liquor. He was a cab driver and was the most proud of me of anyone. If somebody would get into his cab and nonchalantly start to whistle, he'd hear the music and immediately turn around and ask the person if they knew his nephew Terry Gibbs. He thought that everybody who liked music, any kind of music, knew who Terry Gibbs was. Everybody in Birdland loved him, especially PeeWee Marquette, Birdland's emcee. On Monday nights, which were my uncle's days off, he would go down to Birdland when I was playing there and buy drinks for everyone who worked there. He'd spend his whole paycheck in one night. PeeWee used to call him Uncle Nat. In fact, everybody who worked at Birdland called him Uncle Nat. I really loved him.

All Jews are given Jewish names. It's usually the name of a relative who has died. I think I was named for my grandfather. My Jewish name is Yehudi. They used to make jokes about that name because on the Bob Hope Show, Jerry Colonna used to say, "Who's Yehudi?" That was one of the famous lines on the show. From when I was about six to thirteen years old, my parents and all my relatives never called me by my English name. They didn't even call me by my Jewish name, Yehudi. Yehudi became Yahudle, which became just plain Hudle. All the kids on my block nicknamed me Poodle because they thought that I could run real fast like a dog. I remember when my friends would come to my house to look for me, my mother would come to the door, and they would ask her, "Where is Poodle?" She said, "We don't have a pudle, we don't have a dog." My friend kept saying, "You know, your son, Poodle." She didn't know what they were talking about. As they were arguing, I was walking up the stairs to our apartment. As I became visible to everybody, my friends pointed to me and said, "There's Poodle." My mother said, "What, Pudle? Dots a Pudle? Dots not a Pudle, dots a Hudle."

My folks were religious Jews who kept a kosher home. We had two sets of dishes, one for dairy (*milchik*) and one for meat (*flaishek*). They always bought chicken and meats from a kosher market. I remember when I was about sixteen, my friends and I went to a Chinese restaurant. That was the first time I ever went to a restaurant with just my friends, and that's also where I had my first piece of pork. I looked around the whole place to see if anybody was looking before I ate it. Some of my friends came from Reform Jewish families but not all of their parents kept kosher homes. When I tasted that pork, I fell in love with Chinese food. I never knew what pork looked like because we never had pork at our house. In a kosher home, you don't eat meat and dairy dishes together, so when the main meal was meat, we'd have sweet corn for dessert. It was used more as dessert than as part of the meal. According to Jewish customs, you're not supposed to have any dairy for a half-hour after you eat meat. Since I was the baby of the family, my mother would let me cheat and put butter on the corn about five minutes later.

I've got to admit that as a kid, I could have been very spoiled because I was a child prodigy and everybody was always telling me how great I was. But for some reason, it didn't affect me at all. It actually affected me in a reverse kind of way because at the age of about eleven or twelve, I had a little bit of a nervous breakdown. I think they called it St. Vitus' dance. I was very hyper, even as a kid. One of the things that made me that way was everybody always told me how great I was. I'd be playing these classical things and technical Jewish songs and would make mistakes. Even though most people didn't know it, I knew it. So I thought, "How great can I be if I'm making mistakes?" It really used to bug me when they made a big fuss over me. I'm very fortunate, for at an early age, I knew how good I was and how bad I was. Everybody usually thinks they know how good they are but they don't always know how bad they are. Sometimes when I thought that I was playing bad, it may not have been bad to the audience because in playing a visual instrument where you are always moving, they would watch me more than they would listen to me. They couldn't tell the difference, but I could.

In my younger days, when I wanted to play jazz, I played when I felt like it. Two o'clock in the afternoon, three o'clock in the morning, anytime we could get a session together. Now it's a business. Eight o'clock, get on stage and become George Gershwin. What if I hurt my finger or had a headache or had a fight with my wife or couldn't pay my rent? No matter what, you still have to create. It's what I call instant composing. Sometimes your brain won't let you be George Gershwin. Even though I could technically play the instrument well, there were times that I knew I wasn't improvising like I wanted to. I could get a standing ovation and if I didn't think I played good, I'd walk off the stage sick.

When I first started out playing, I really didn't listen to anybody but myself. That's because I was just trying to learn the song that we were playing and trying to figure out what I was hearing on the chord changes. Later on, when I got to know the song better, I'd start hearing what the drummer was doing and so on. When I used to go out and play with a quartet, I was actually doing a single because they would give me a rhythm section of musicians I never heard or played with before. The first night, I wouldn't care if the drummer wasn't that good because I was still trying to find my way and figure out the room and the sound. The second night, I'd start hearing what the rhythm section was playing and sometimes they wouldn't be playing together. That's when it was hard for me to play. But when you're a kid, you don't think about how good or bad anyone else is playing, you just go straight ahead. You don't know any better. It takes a lot of experience to get to the point where you really feel that you are playing good.

I once had a ten-day engagement in Minneapolis where they brought in a rhythm section from Chicago to play piano, bass, and drums. After playing the first song, I didn't know where the first beat, the third beat, or any beat was. The time was terrible; it was all over the place. After the first song, I said to the guys, "You know what? They do something out in California that could be fun. After we play the first chorus, which usually is the melody, the bass player plays in two instead of four." I figured that if they knew where one and three were, then they would know where two and four were. After the next song using this method, they still weren't playing together, so I said to them, "Another thing we do in California is, after we play the melody to the first chorus, hit the first beat to the next chorus, lay out, and let me play alone for a few choruses. I'll cue you guys when to come in." The ten days wound up with me playing practically all my choruses alone. At least I knew where the time was.

When I was nine years old, I went to a summer resort with my brother in the Catskill Mountains. My brother was the leader of the band. A funny thing about my brother: if he's sleeping and you walk into the room and whistle, he'll start swinging his arms, whacking pillows, walls; anything that's around him gets whacked. When I slept with him, he had me sleep near the window rather than on the other side of the bed because he was afraid that he would push me out of the bed. He was the worst sleeper I ever knew. Musicians usually slept late but some of the guys would get up early to play tennis or swim in the morning and walk by where our room was and once in a while, would purposely stand under the window and whistle. They knew my brother was going to start swinging and eventually fall out of bed. When I was in bed by the window, I saw some of the guys coming by so I knocked on the window and told them not to whistle because he was liable to start swinging and knock me out the window.

My mother was a clean freak. She would clean the house every day. We didn't have wall-to-wall carpeting; we had hardwood floors. She was cleaning under the bed where my brother was sleeping. Suddenly he grabbed her by the hair, and she started screaming. Who knew what triggered him off? He wouldn't wake up so we had to jump on him and hold him down because he didn't know he was grabbing my mother's hair. Sol was married a few times, and both of his wives had to sleep in other beds because he was liable to punch them out.

My father had two jobs on Saturday and two jobs on Sunday. He hired a drummer called Whitey Stalavitzky who played drums with him both nights. My brother Sol fronted the band on the other jobs. The job they played on Saturday was in Brooklyn and Whitey lived in the Bronx, which was about an hour-and-a half ride on the subway. The job on Sunday was an afternoon job and it was also in Brooklyn, close to where we lived, and so my father told Whitey that there was no sense in going back to the Bronx and shlep his drums on the subway. He could sleep with my brother Sol. Whitey said great; it would save him a big trip. The next morning when my father and Sol got up to get ready to go to work, there was no Whitey Stalavitzky anywhere. When my father got to the job that Whitey was playing with him, there stood Whitey with a black eye. He told my father that in the middle of the night Sol whacked him in the eye and being that his drums were out in the hall of our house, he just let himself out of the house and went back to the Bronx.

Sol was the best Jewish drummer I ever heard. Irv Cottler, the drummer who played with Frank Sinatra, used to go out of his way to go hear him play at weddings. He was the Art Blakey of Jewish drummers. He could swing you off the stage. When he was in his eighties, he'd come to visit me, and even though he hadn't played the vibes in five or ten years, he'd go over to my vibes and start playing these Jewish melodies and bend notes like clarinet players did. I'd watch him, and I still couldn't figure out how he did it. He really could have done well doing studio work, but the big drag was that he loved to gamble. Pinochle and billiards, those were his two hang-ups.

Sol had his xylophones set up in our house and when he wasn't around, I would go over and noodle on them, even though I wasn't supposed to touch them. The summer I spent with my brother in the Catskills actually started my career off. When Sol would be out playing tennis or golf, I would go into the casino where his xylophones were and fool with them. I figured out how to play the song called "The Boulevard of Broken Dreams." I really learned it well. They used to have an amateur hour night on Mondays and one time when nobody was around, I was noodling on the xylophones and this very rich lady happened to come into the casino. I didn't even know she was there. She heard me play and came up to me and said, "You've got to play the amateur night!" I got scared. I didn't know where she had come from. I said, "No! Please don't tell my brother you saw me play his xylophones because he'll get mad and he'll beat the heck out of me! Don't tell him!" She wouldn't listen to me. "You've GOT to play!" And she told my brother. He hadn't any idea that I had been playing his xylophones or knew anything about music.

That same night, my sister Sunny came up there for the weekend. Somebody told her that I was going to play in the amateur hour and she said, "What are you talking about? He doesn't know how to play! He's never played in his life!" She said later that she was ashamed to go into the casino because she'd be embarrassed. I played the xylophones in the amateur contest, and she was so impressed that when she got home, she went to the New York Philharmonic, talked to a mallet player named Harry Brewer, and asked him about getting me a teacher. He recommended Freddy Albright, who was also playing with the symphony. Freddy became my teacher when I was eleven or twelve years old.

Freddy was great. He charged my sister three dollars a lesson, which was a lot of money. He lived in New Yonkers and it would take him two hours to get to my house. He'd take subways and trolleys to our house to give me my lesson. After the lesson he would ask me if I understood what he showed me. I said yes every time and played everything right back at him. So he'd give me another lesson. Sometimes he'd give me ten lessons in a row in one sitting. He'd give me music to practice reading and I'd memorize it. One time he gave me a hard piece of music and I memorized it overnight. He'd come back the next week and I'd pull out the music and play it perfect every time. He thought I was the greatest reader that ever lived. Five lessons went by before he got wise to me. I think he may have caught me looking down at the xylophones instead of at the music and then realized that something was wrong. So he said, "Take it four bars after letter C." I said, "Lemme take it from the top!" I didn't know what was supposed to happen four bars after letter C. I couldn't read it anyhow. I didn't become a good reader until years later when I started studying conducting for TV shows. It's just a matter of seeing the same musical figures over and over. It's like reading a newspaper where you almost read a few words ahead. In reading music, you try to read a few bars ahead.

Freddy then found out that I was memorizing everything. After that, he'd bring the music with him and I'd have to sight-read it for him. That's how I learned to read music. I think that the most important thing he taught me that really helped me to play jazz was all the different scales and chords. He was a great teacher. I eventually went on to develop a system of my own. I play with short mallets, and I use a finger system that I developed on my own.

By the time I was twelve, Freddy had taught me how to play "Czardas" by Monti on the xylophones. That was my showpiece. He recommended that I try out for *The Major Bowes Amateur Hour*. This was 1936 and that was the biggest radio show in the world. Frank Sinatra was once a winner on that show. I played "Czardas" for them and they asked if I could play something shorter. I said that I didn't have anything right then but I'd come back the next day and have something then. I went home and memorized "The Flight of the Bumble Bee" overnight. The next day I played it for them in forty-five seconds and they said that was good.

The premise of *The Major Bowes Amateur Hour* was that people who were listening to the radio show would call in and vote for their favorite artist. Whoever got the most votes would be the winner. They couldn't tell you who the winner was until the next week for there was no way that anybody could vote for the last few people who performed and have it added up before the show was over. What really happened was that they picked who they thought should be the winner and didn't pay any attention to the votes. The day before the show, they told me to go back to playing "Czardas" because it was longer and that I was going to play first. Then they told me that I was going to win and that I would join one of their road shows in Pittsburgh right after the show.

They arranged it with my folks and they picked out a tutor for me for Christmas week.

Finally it came time for the radio show. I have a tape of it, and here is how my conversation went with Major Bowes:

> **Bowes**: Round and round and round she goes, where she stops, nobody knows. First, Julius Gubenko, a xylophonist from Brooklyn and he plays "Czardas." How old are you, Julius?
> **Gubenko**: Twelve.
> **Bowes**: That's good.
> **Gubenko** (interrupting): My ambition is to get an interview with you for our school newspaper. I thought that if I got to play on your program, maybe you'd let me interview you afterwards.
> **Bowes**: I see. Well, that's not unreasonable.
> **Gubenko**: You don't have to answer any questions if you don't want to.
> **Bowes**: Don't be afraid. I'll give full particulars. Where does your talent lie: interviewing or xylophoning?
> **Gubenko**: I'm pretty good at both. All my friends and all my teachers are listening in. I'll give the telephone number: Murray Hill 8-9933. I expect to get a lot of votes!
> **Bowes**: (laughing): All right, Julius, you're a go-getter. Let's have Monti's "Czardas."

Of course this was all scripted. They gave me these dumb lines to say and to this day, I can't do lines. I can't act. I can ad-lib my fanny off, but I can't act. I'd never say things like that on my own. Even as a kid, it made me sick to say those dumb, corny lines.

After I won the contest, I went out on tour with Major Bowes. When we were playing the Stanley Theater in Pittsburgh, I looked out the window and saw these kids playing baseball and punchball in the streets. I sneaked out and went down the fire escape and joined them and came back all disheveled. They were bugged with me because I had gone out without their permission. They just wanted to make sure I didn't get in any trouble. I was bugged because I wanted to play sports and after that, they stopped letting me go out.

I remember getting a standing ovation on opening night. The next day, the reviews came out in *Variety*:

> As an extra attraction, youngster Julius Gubenko, who appeared on Bowes program in N.Y. only night before, is sent on for opening and kid just about steals the show with his crack stint on the xylophone. Literally had to beg off when caught, or rather the m.c. had to do it for him since the half-pint was too nervous to make the speech that would have taken him off.

A Real Go-Getter

I was so little that I had to stand on a box to play the xylophones. Once I started playing, I was never afraid and never got nervous. It's different playing light classical things like "Czardas" because, unlike jazz, where you're ad-libbing and what comes out comes out, you've got to play the right notes every time. You can't get away with making a mistake playing written music.

I went to school with a good friend of mine called Lenny Garment who later became a prominent lawyer. In fact, he was one of President Nixon's attorneys in the Watergate case. I worked the summer resorts with him. He was always the smartest kid in school and I was the dumbest. Actually, I wasn't the dumbest. I just wasn't interested in school and for some reason, I knew where I was going in life. I knew music was going to be my life. That or sports. I was good in sports but more so in music. I didn't care about history or anything. What do I care about Napoleon Bonaparte? What's he going to do for my E-flat chords or a C-minor seventh? So I never studied. But Lenny was great. He played clarinet and tenor saxophone and later worked with Woody Herman's band; he was a good jazz player. Lenny was also the student president. He'd come to my room and tell my teacher, "I have to have Julius Gubenko come down for a meeting" and he got me out of class and we'd go somewhere and jam. Just the two of us in some basement, wherever it was. He got me out of all the classes I hated.

When Lenny and I were about sixteen years old, we worked in the Catskill Mountains in a band headed by Abe Login, who is still one of my closest friends. Abe was a great piano player who changed his name to Alan Logan and has been playing exclusive private clubs in New York for a clientele that used to include Jackie Onassis and some other very rich people.

Lenny had a brilliant mind and a sick sense of humor. When we played at the Steirs Hotel in the Catskills, he used to get up early and swim. I'd always sleep late and so he'd come into our room that all five of us musicians lived in and jumped on me while I was in bed. He pinned my arms down with his knees and wrung his wet jockstrap out that he wore while swimming right in my face. They used to have these little garden snakes in the Catskills and I was deathly afraid of them. While I was sleeping, he hung a garden snake from the ceiling, about four or five inches from my face. He then screamed to scare me. Boy did I get scared. I almost had a heart attack, especially when I leaped right into the snake. Lenny had a warped sense of humor.

The summer I worked at Steirs wound up to be a strange job for me. The five of us in the band were Abe Login on piano, Lenny on tenor, Herbie Glabman on alto sax (who also went on to become a successful lawyer), Abe Cohen, (a great trumpet player even at the age of fifteen), and me playing drums and xylophones. We had what was called a social staff, which consisted of Al Murray, who was the social director, a male and female singer, and a comic. The band had to play a show every night besides playing dance music. We had other things that they made us do. The Catskills catered to a mostly Jewish clientele and in order to hold proper Jewish services on the Sabbath, there had to be a minimum of nine people present. This is called a *minyan*. On Friday nights when they had a minyan and they didn't have nine people, they would come and get as many people as they needed from the band. They would just drag us out of our rooms, whether we were dressed or not. The comedian got fired on the first night of the job for being drunk and Al Murray went to Alan and asked him if anybody in the band could help out and do some comedy. Al Murray was the straight man who would set up all the jokes for the comedian. Login said that he thought that I was pretty funny and being that I had experience performing, maybe I could do it. So, I wound up with the comedian's job. I had a funny, low, raspy voice that I used that sounded like Popeye. I used it later when I sang "Lemon Drop" with Woody Herman. So I spoke in my Popeye voice with a Jewish accent. I would have to rehearse every afternoon. I was never good at remembering lines so I used to ad-lib a lot. Al Murray, who was very proper, would get bugged with me because I would get a little blue and also say these far-out lines.

This is how the show went down. We'd start out with a band overture, with me playing drums. The moment the song ended, I'd run back stage, put on some dumb costume, and do a comedy bit with Al and one or two of the singers. Then I'd run back to the drums and play for the girl singer. Then back to the stage for another comedy bit. Then I'd play a xylophone solo with Abe accompanying me. Then back to the drums for the male singer. Then *another* comedy bit. Then back to the drums for the big finale with Al Murray and the two singers doing some ridiculous singing *schtick*. My salary was five dollars a week plus room and board. I did get a bonus of fifty dollars for the twelve weeks of running all over the place doing everything but washing the dishes.

By the time I was fifteen, I was playing on a radio show with my father. The music we played was all Jewish songs. The radio show went on Sunday afternoons at one o'clock on WLTH. Every Sunday morning was my time to meet the guys on the block and go play sports so what I would do is sneak out of my house by opening the window and throw my sneakers out. Then I would jump out and the guys would catch me.

We used to play baseball in a vacant lot with rocks and broken glass, or sometimes we'd fight another team. Now when I say fight, there were rules. Little guy always fought little guy, big guy fought big guy, and you couldn't fight dirty. If you fought dirty, your own guys would jump you. If you were a big guy, you had to fight a big guy, and if you didn't know how to fight, you could get beat up, for some big ox would be hitting you and that could really hurt.

One time I was fighting this little guy, and I had to do a radio show with my father at one o'clock that afternoon. I threw a right hand, he put his head down, and I hit him on top of his head. I could feel my pinkie going all the way back into my hand. I started screaming and crying, and all the fighting stopped. I showed everybody what had happened to my finger and we all got scared. We were all kids and didn't know what to do so somebody finally got a bright idea. "Anybody got a handkerchief?" Somebody said yeah. So they decided to put a handkerchief on my finger and on the count of three, everybody would pinch me all over my body: my arms, legs, face, anywhere there was a piece of flesh to grab on to. Then, on the count of three, somebody would pull on my finger and pull it out. There must have been twenty to twenty-five guys there. So on the count of three, they pulled my finger out. I never felt the pain of them pulling my finger out because they were pinching the heck out of me, especially the little guy that I had been fighting. He took advantage of the situation and gave me an extra pinch. I wanted to fight him all over again after that.

Now I had to go do the radio show with my father and all those old Jewish musicians with my broken finger. There was a man named Mr. Constantine who was a good trumpet player and was playing in the band. I didn't want to tell my father that I had a broken finger because he'd never let me go out and play and fight again. Unlike vibraphones, where you have a pedal to sustain the notes, on xylophones, you have to roll the note, which means that your hands are moving up and down, up and down, all over the place. Every time my hand moved, that pinkie was moving, and every time I moved it, I cried. It hurt so much that I actually had tears coming down my face. After the show was over, Mr. Constantine went over to my father and said, "Mr. Gubenko, I've got to tell you something. Not only is your son talented and has great technique, but he plays with so much feeling that when he plays, he cries!" What playing with feeling? I cried because I was in pain.

There was a percussionist who played with a New York symphony called Irving Torgman. He was a Russian Jew with a real thick Russian Jewish accent. He was also a very respected teacher. My brother once studied with him. He heard me play somewhere when I was about fifteen years old. He called my brother and told him that he thought I had a lot of talent and that he'd like to teach me for nothing. He lived close to my house in Brooklyn, so my brother arranged for me to go to his house for a lesson. When I first started talking with him, I almost broke up laughing because he sounded like the comedian on the Eddie Cantor show known as "The Mad Russian." First, he asked me to make rolls on a C-scale, which I did. He said, "No, not like dot!" and he started to make rolls and sing the notes *yam, dam, bam bam, yam, yam, dam-bee-am bam.* He said "You got to make everything music, even scales play louder and softer." I almost broke up when he started to sing. I don't know how I held back. Then we went over to a drum pad. He asked me if I could read drum music and I said yes. In fact, I was very good at reading drum figures. I played the first bar, which was in this rhythm:

If you said the figure I was reading, you would say "one-and-a-two-and a-flam-a-diddle four-and." After I played it, he got very emotional and said, *"No! Not like dot!"* and started to sing: *"Yam, didi-dam dam, tee-opp-a-deedle boom tzing! Yam, didi-dam dam, tee-opp-a-deedle boom tzing!"* That was it. I immediately broke up laughing. I couldn't hold it in any longer. He got bugged with me and threw me out of his house. He then called my brother and told him that I was a young wiseass snotnose and he wouldn't teach me for a million dollars. I didn't believe it. Yam, didi-dam dam, tee-opp-a-deedle boom tzing. If you were a comedy writer, you couldn't make that up.

Tiny Kahn was my best friend. From six years old until I was eighteen and went into the army, we were together every night. Our windows faced each other. Tiny was about six-foot-two and when he was fifteen he must have weighed about three hundred pounds. I was about five-foot-two and weighed about eighty-eight pounds. So to start with, we looked like a comedy team. By the way, I'm the only one who ever saw Tiny sitting on a toilet seat. Nobody else ever did. To tell you the truth, I didn't either because when Tiny sat on the toilet seat, you couldn't see the toilet seat.

Tiny and I would get thrown out of candy stores, which is what they called those places that sold ice cream and candies. They also had jukeboxes that had records by Count Basie, Artie Shaw, and all the big bands. That was the pop music those days. Tiny and I would put our nickels in the jukebox and order a two cents plain; that's what they called a glass of seltzer in Brooklyn. We'd play rhythm to the songs on the counters, on the tables, anywhere and get so carried away and play so loud that the owner would chase us out. We looked funny anyhow, one guy tall and fat and the other guy short and skinny.

A Real Go-Getter

Tiny was one of the funniest and most talented men who ever lived. His real name was Norman, and he died when he was only twenty-nine. I think he had a heart attack because he was always losing a hundred pounds and then gaining it back. It was too hard on his heart. When he was in his early twenties, he started a style of drumming that Mel Lewis picked up on and took to another level, but Tiny started that kind of drumming. If he had lived, he would have become a great composer. Johnny Mandel told me that he thought that Tiny could have written songs like "The Shadow of Your Smile" or better, if that's possible. Musically, he was far ahead of all of us. Tiny was, by far, the most naturally talented of all of us, and by this I mean all of the guys who hung out in Brooklyn like Frank Socolow, Manny Albam, Al Cohn, and Johnny Mandel.

Tiny and I used to go down to the basement of my house, put on big band records, and play drums along with the records. I was playing drums then too. We had similar styles except that I had a lot of Buddy Rich in my playing, which meant that I had much more technique than Tiny had. We both auditioned for bands in the neighborhood and I got every job because the most popular song those days was "Sing, Sing, Sing" that Benny Goodman made famous. It called for a long drum solo and that was my bag.

There was never any jealousy between Tiny and me. He would help me carry my drums when I played a job with the band that I won the audition with. There was one time when we auditioned with this band that had only Count Basie stock arrangements. No "Sing, Sing, Sing." Tiny ran away with that job. I felt good for him because he deserved it and probably some of the other auditions too, if it were not for having to play "Sing, Sing, Sing." We never looked at it as competition. In fact when we were kids, Tiny predicted that when we grew up, I would be the leader of a big band playing vibes and he would be playing drums in the band. When you're a kid, those dreams are very important to you.

Tiny also had a great comedy mind. He and I would walk down the street just saying silly things and breaking each other up. He would use a high Jewish voice and yell, "Gubenko!" And I used my "Lemon Drop" voice and say "Yeeeess!" and we'd ad-lib. I'll never forget this little piece of business that we did. It was all ad-libbed so fast.

Me: What do you do for a living?
Tiny: I'm a doctor.
Me: A doctor? Really? What are your hours?
Tiny: I work from three to six, six to nine, nine to twelve, twelve to three.
Me: When do you eat?
Tiny: Do I look like a man who eats?

Fifteen years old, three hundred pounds. Do I look like a man who eats.

He also could never get a date with a girl. A date back then was when you went out with a girl, and if you were lucky, you got to hold her hand. So I would tell Tiny, "Hey, I got a date Friday night," and he'd groan, "Ohhhh. What am I gonna do on Friday?" When you're young, girls aren't going to go out with a guy who weighs three hundred pounds. Not that I was good looking, but at least I was skinny. Tiny would moan and be so depressed that I'd say, "Okay, I won't go" and I'd just hang out with him.

After I got out of the army, I finally got Tiny a date. I was going with a girl named Peaches Federman and Shorty Rogers was going with a girl called Bubbles Epstein. Shorty and I would always laugh about that. Peaches and Bubbles. Two great names for two nice Jewish girls. Peaches' father was a doctor. Every time Tiny and I would walk by her house, he'd look at the sign with Dr. Federman's name on it and say, "There's no bet-ter man than Dr. Fed-er-man." Anyway, I got him a date with one of Peaches' friends. The Federmans were wealthy people. They lived in a big house, and instead of armchairs, they had these real big couches in their living room. Tiny didn't know what to do with a girl because he'd never been out with one before. We went upstairs to Peaches' house, and Peaches sat down on a couch and I lay down on the couch with my head on her lap. I was a little guy and there was no problem with that. Tiny's girl was sitting on another couch and when Tiny saw me do that, he tried to do the same thing. He put his head on his girl's lap, tried to put the rest of his body on the couch, and rolled right off the couch. He tried again and rolled off again. He couldn't make it.

There was another close friend of mine, Sid Roth, who studied saxophone but gave it up and made a lot of money as an accountant. We were in Sid's basement when Tiny and I got into an argument. Even though we were good friends, we were going to fight anyway. I think all kids have friendly fights. What was I going to do with this big ape? I weighed eighty-eight pounds and he weighed three hundred. We kept going around and around each other, so I backed up and got a running start, and made a flying tackle on him, knocking him off his feet. I got him in a headlock and he couldn't get out of it, but he kept rolling over me. I probably weighed sixty-four pounds by the time he got done rolling over me. He finally gave up. One more roll and that would have been the end of young Gubenko.

The orchestra leader at Tilden High School was Mr. Antonio Miranda. When something went wrong in the playing of the music, he would start cursing in Italian. The words he said sounded terrible. It wasn't until later on that I found out that what I thought he was saying had nothing to do with what he was really saying. He was actually saying things like "Those are beautiful flowers" or something else really pretty. But he sure sounded like he was cursing.

I had a wild thing going with Mr. Miranda. I was the timpanist in the school orchestra and I always thought that there was never enough music for the timpanist to play. Sometimes you'd have to count from fifty to a hundred bars of music, play four or five beats, then count again for awhile until it would be time to play the next passage. Every time the orchestra would get real exciting and play louder, I would add my own parts. I would make rolls on the timps to go along with the excitement of the orchestra. About every fifth day, Mr. Miranda would stop the orchestra and say, "What are you doing? There's no timps there!" I would say, "At bar 151," and he would say, "You idiot, we're at bar 90!" I would let about five days go by of just playing the music as it was written and then after being bored again just counting bars, I would do the same thing. I would add timps where I felt they should be and five days later, he'd catch me again and we'd go through the same routine, me telling him I'm at some bar number and him calling me an idiot and telling me I'm in the wrong place. He never really found out what I was doing.

I had another six months to go before I would graduate from high school and wasn't interested in my studies. Learning about Napoleon Bonaparte had nothing to do with what I wanted to do in my life so I sat there in class writing music and studying chords while the lessons were being taught. The teacher was having us memorize names and dates and I was memorizing the chord changes to "I Got Rhythm." My teacher, Mrs. Fleck, saw me writing and called on me. "Gubenko!" Without thinking, I looked up and said, "E-flat!" She said, "Get up and go get in the corner." She made me stand in the corner like a little kid. She'd walk by me standing there in the corner and every time she passed by me, she'd say, "Turn around, I can't stand your face." I started to get this burning feeling in my stomach. She came back the other way and said it again. After the third pass, she said it again. When I was boxing and got that burning feeling, I would try to knock you out. You could hit me twenty times and it wouldn't bother me. I would just have to try to knock you out. I think that's what they call the killer instinct. She said it again: "Turn around, I can't stand your face." This time I said, "Did you ever take a good look at your own?" and I threw a left to her stomach, and as she doubled over, I hit her right in the jaw. She must have been about six-foot-one and when she fell, she fell over five or six of the desks. Well, I got expelled for that. Unbeknownst to me, the band instructor, Mr. Satz, and Antonio Miranda, the orchestra leader, were going to give me a scholarship to Juilliard as a timpanist. They came to my house and told my mother and father that if I apologized to the class, the principal, and Mrs. Fleck, they'd let me finish school and get the scholarship. Back then, scholarships to Juilliard were almost impossible to get. I really didn't want to go back to school for I was too embarrassed, especially after hitting a lady teacher. My parents didn't make me go back because they knew I was very hyper and that I was going to play music anyway, scholarship or no scholarship. They were great because I could have resented them for the rest of my life if they had forced me to go back to school.

In my younger days, I wanted to be a boxer or a baseball player. There was a fighter in Brooklyn named Terry Young who I loved. When you emulate or imitate somebody, whether it's Babe Ruth or Mel Ott, your friends stick that person's name on you. So the name Terry stuck with me and I became Terry Gubenko to my friends. In my neighborhood, besides having a good punchball team, we had a fairly good baseball team, and I was the star of our team, which was called the Aztecs. The best team in the neighborhood was the Ravens, and everyone on the Ravens used to laugh at Tiny Kahn, who was our catcher. One time, Tiny hit a ball over the center fielder's head and got thrown out at first base. While he was running, his moccasin flew about fifty feet in the air.

Another time when Tiny was catching, there was a guy on third base getting ready to score and he kept yelling at Tiny, "Watch out Fatso, I'm coming home!" Calling Tiny "Fatso" was the worst thing that this guy ever did. Tiny's face got orange and red, and it became about eighteen feet wide, he was so mad. The next batter hit the ball to left field, the left fielder got it and threw it home, and the guy came in sliding. As the guy came in, Tiny tagged him on the head and said, "You're OUT!" And he sure was, for Tiny had knocked the guy half unconscious with the ball. Whacked him right in the head and knocked him halfway out. Nobody ever called Tiny "Fatso" again.

On *Yom Kippur*, religious Jews are supposed to fast for a day. Tiny and I would go to this synagogue on East Ninety-Fifth Street and take food with us. We brought mostly cake and we'd stand in front of the synagogue, and after the service, when everybody started to come out, we'd stuff our faces with the cake until our cheeks bulged out, right in front of those starving Jews. Boy, were we low.

I listened to the radio a lot back then. I listened to Benny Goodman and all the big bands. When I was sixteen, I'd be the first one in line at the Paramount Theater to see him, skipping school and everything. My mother didn't know I did this. All the theaters showed movies and also featured big bands: the Paramount, the Strand, and the Capitol. Benny Goodman, Tommy Dorsey, Count Basie, Artie Shaw, Duke Ellington, and all the bands would play there. The Paramount was the one I liked the best. The others had a stage where a curtain opened up, but at the Paramount, the stage would rise up out of the floor. You'd never want to sit in the front row because you couldn't see the rest of the band so we'd sit in the sixth or seventh row, and when you saw the stage come rising up, little by little, you'd start to hear Benny's theme song, "Let's Dance." Then we'd see the top of Benny's head and our hair would stand up on end. We were like bobby soxers, screaming for the big bands. Never in my wildest dreams did I think that I'd ever play with Benny Goodman.

Chapter 2
Dizzy, Bird, and a Bebop Breakdown

When you won a Major Bowes contest, the prize was going on tour with one of his many road shows. The one I went on was called the Collegiate Unit. Even though I got paid for the tour, I was too young to think about making a lot of money playing music. Back then, that was probably the last thing on my mind. I just wanted to play. Today, guys start a rock band thinking, "I'm gonna make a million dollars," and sometimes they do. To start with, when I was a kid, there wasn't any million dollars to make. I knew that Benny Goodman was famous and probably made a lot of money, and so did Artie Shaw, Count Basie, Duke Ellington, Tommy Dorsey, and others. But I didn't know what kind of money was involved nor did I care. I just wanted to play jazz. When we were kids and got a chance to play a job, we would get anything from ten cents to a quarter for the job. But we didn't care anyhow.

By the time I was sixteen, I started playing with some great young players who later became famous. One of the first musicians that I met was a guitarist named Chuck Wayne. Chuck came from a different part of Brooklyn than I did and he was big time to me. His name was getting out there to all the young teenagers who played jazz. He later went on to fame with the George Shearing Quintet.

Frankie Socolow, who I also grew up with, played saxophone with Boyd Raeburn when he was sixteen. I'll never forget the first time I saw Frankie smoke pot. He was about sixteen years old. I looked at him in shock and said to myself, "Oh, my god, Frank is a dope fiend!" We didn't really know anything about marijuana then except that it was called weed. There have been a lot of names for marijuana: pot, weed, boo, shit, grass, charge; every era had a different name for it. You had to keep up with the current name if you wanted to get high.

When I was seventeen, Tiny Kahn and I went to see Art Tatum at Café Society Downtown. New York clubs didn't allow anyone in under eighteen so we bought these wide-brimmed hats and painted on mustaches to make us look older and got in to see him play. They were pretty lax in those days. They never really checked to see how old you were, just so long as you could pay for your drink or cover charge; that's all they cared about.

Art Tatum played right on the floor instead of the stage and after the show, everyone gathered around him and watched and listened to him play all by himself. I was standing by the top register of the piano when Art was making one of his famous runs all the way up the keyboard. When he hit his last note, his right hand flew way out and hit me right in the crotch. It wasn't long before word got out all around Brooklyn that Art Tatum had hit Terry Gubenko in the crotch. For a while, that was my claim to fame: Art Tatum whacking me right in the crotch.

Not long after I got thrown out of high school, I got a job playing drums and xylophones with a pretty girl bandleader named Judy Kayne. I was already known as Terry to my friends because of the boxer Terry Young that I tried to emulate. When the flyer came out advertising Judy's band, it said, "featuring Terry Gibbs on drums and xylophone." I thought I had been fired. Who's Terry Gibbs? I called MCA (Music Corporation of America, who booked the band) and they said that Gubenko was too long a name. So that's how I became Terry Gibbs. MCA thought that I was very talented because I played both drums and xylophones and was only eighteen years old. There weren't many jazz players in those days that played the vibes or xylophones. Only Lionel Hampton and Red Norvo were famous on those instruments. There was another vibist called Adrian Rollini who was pretty well known. For years he played at a place called the Piccadilly Hotel in New York, playing cocktail music for dancing.

MCA really wanted to feature me. I actually feel that besides thinking that the name Gubenko was too long, they may have thought that it was too ethnic for those days. I went home and told my mother, and she was bugged. "What Terry Gibbs? Who's gonna know it's mine son?" Later on, when I went with Benny Goodman, she wanted the whole family to change their name to Gibbs.

For a while I was very uncomfortable with the name. The funniest part of the whole thing is that when I got drafted into the army, I got Tiny Kahn the job as the drummer with the Judy Kayne band, and since MCA wasn't about to change all of their flyers and all the publicity because it would have been too costly, Tiny became Terry Gibbs. I can imagine people's faces who saw me a few months before as a skinny little kid and then seeing this big blob on the drums who was also Terry Gibbs. They probably thought I had a glandular problem.

I turned eighteen in October 1942 and the following March, I went into the army. I was sent to Fort Dix, where thousands of new inductees first went. When I got there, the first thing they did was to show us a film on venereal diseases. I don't think that many of us knew or thought much about VD at all. The film started out kind of mild, but as it got into it a little more, it started to get very graphic. They didn't play games with you. They really showed you what could happen to you if you got syphilis. While I was sitting there watching the film with hundreds of other inductees, I started to sweat so much that I thought I was going to faint. It was so disgusting to watch that it made me sick. There were PFC's walking up and down the aisles checking to make sure that everyone was all right. At first I was too embarrassed to say anything to anybody, but when I started to feel like I was going to pass out, I had to find some excuse to get out of there. Finally, I said to one of the PFC's, "I've gotta go to the bathroom." He knew immediately what was happening. He said, "Come with me" and took me out to the lobby area. I think there were at least a hundred guys lying on the floor, each looking white as a sheet and probably ready to pass out also. He made me lie down with them. I was so relieved because I thought I was the only one that was going to pass out and cause a scene.

While waiting to be shipped to a designated camp, they gave us details like picking up cigarette butts. I was walking with about twelve other guys, one of whom was about thirty-nine years old, which was over the age limit for being drafted. He was about to be discharged any day. We had a PFC in charge of us who was a cocky little guy. He kept picking on this one older guy and was making him do most of the work. That really bugged me so I went over to the PFC and said, "Listen, what are you picking on him for? He's an old man." When I was eighteen years old, everybody over thirty was old to me. "Why don't you take it easy on him and let us do some of his work?" He said, "What's your name?" "Private Gubenko," I said. I thought the reason he asked me for my name was because I wasn't afraid to speak up and he would make me a sergeant immediately.

That night, about four o'clock in the morning, the PFC woke me up and said. "Gubenko, you're on K.P," which stands for Kitchen Patrol. I worked for twelve hours feeding hundreds of soldiers and cleaning and mopping up the floors. Then he dismissed everybody but me and another guy and made us clean these funky gigantic pots and pans that were the worst smelling things you ever smelled in your life; hundreds of them, because we were feeding a lot of people. I don't think he liked this other guy either, so he and I were picked to clean the pots and pans after hours. We didn't get to bed until twelve midnight.

The next morning at four o'clock, this little asshole woke me up again. "Gubenko, you're on K.P." It started to hit me that this guy didn't like me because of what I said to him. He kept me there again after hours to do the lowest, smelliest job in the world, cleaning those pots and pans.

The next morning he came to get me again. This time I said, "No, I'm not going. Why don't you and I go outside and settle this right now? I know what you're doing and I think it's a bunch of bullshit." He said, "No, soldier, you're in the army now. We're not going to settle this by fighting. You're on K.P." I said, "No, we're going to fight." He wouldn't fight me so I had go do my K.P. again.

The next day, he woke me up again at four A.M. and this time, I went after him. Somebody held me back, but I think I may have gotten a punch in. I could have been put in jail for that. But I still had to do K.P. The next morning when he woke me up at four A.M., I figured I'd better shut up and not say anything because I was only making it worse for myself. I hate to admit it, but it sure took a lot of the cockiness out of me. I found out that fighting wasn't the answer.

Thank God, the next day I got shipped out to the Eighth Armored Division in Leesville, Louisiana. I was glad because I wanted to go overseas and see some action. The army had other plans for me. Since they knew I was a musician, they wanted to put me in the Signal Corps. I had to take a test for that and purposely failed the test for Morse code, which really would have been simple for me to pass because of its sounds, its rhythms, and syncopations. It was like playing percussion instruments. I wanted to go overseas and fight, so I failed the test and did everything I could to screw it up so I wouldn't have to go into the Signal Corps. So they made me a tank driver.

The reason I wanted to see action wasn't because I was brave. It had to do with one of my close friends, Abe Cohen, who played trumpet in the Catskill Mountains with me when we were fifteen years old. Abe was drafted into the army, did thirteen weeks of basic training, got shipped to Germany, and got killed immediately. He was only eighteen when that happened. I had a lot of anger in me and really wanted to go overseas and fight. He was really a great trumpet player. He went to Music and Arts High School in New York with some great musicians: Shorty Rogers, and two guys who played lead trumpet on Woody Herman's "Four Brothers Band," Bernie Glow, and Stan Fishelson. At fifteen years old, Abe Cohen was the best of all of them. Who knows what he would have become if he had lived?

In the Eighth Armored Division, besides driving a tank, I had to learn all of the other things that went along with being in the tank, to start with, how to get in it. I think there were four of us and we had to go headfirst into the tank. One of the guys who was in my tank was really good and fast, and if he followed you, and you weren't fast enough, he'd push you in so he could get in. I got banged up a few times.

We also had to do guard duty and would do eight-hour shifts. This made us really tired, especially if our shift was from twelve midnight to eight in the morning. Somebody told me about Benzedrine inhalers, which were actually made for a stopped up nose. Benzedrine was legal back then but I think that later on, they took out the Benzedrine and substituted it with something else and called it Benzedrex. I'd get so tired when I had to do guard duty that I finally bought a Benzedrine inhaler. The first thing you did was break it open. Inside was a big strip of some kind of hard paper or cardboard that was coated with Benzedrine. I didn't know how much to take, so I cut the strip in half, which is probably like taking fifteen pounds of speed today, and put it in my cup of coffee. Benzedrine, together with the army coffee, which by itself could keep you awake for a week, got me so hyper that I was hearing sounds in Pittsburgh and I was in Louisiana. It was so dark at midnight that when anything at all moved, I would yell, "Halt! Who's there?" It could be weeds, armadillos, wind, anything, but I kept yelling, "Halt! Who's there?" When I finished my eight hours and was going to be relieved by another soldier, I told him that I would take his guard duty, because I was too up to go to sleep. I think I did everybody's guard duty for two days. That was the last time I ever used a Benzedrine inhaler.

Another time I was doing guard duty in the daytime, and the post I was given was way out in the woods somewhere. It wasn't too far from a little shack. I got to meet a young girl who was about seventeen years old who lived in that shack. I'd sneak over to the shack when she was alone and we'd just talk. She had that real southern twang of an accent and I sounded like I came from Brooklyn, which I did. I also had real dark, black hair in a sort of a pompadour. She was almost an illiterate and really didn't know much about anything. One time when we were talking, she said to me, "You French, ain'tcha?" I said, "No, I'm Jewish." She started to laugh and said, "You no Jew! Jews have horns!" I told her that some of us might have big bugles but no horns. That was the last time that I snuck over to her place.

After about a month or so, I was called into an office and was told that the Eighth Armored Division Band needed a marching drummer. They had probably looked up my records and found out that I played all the percussion instruments and so they transferred me to the band. They had two big bands. The better one was called the "Number One Band" and the other was the "Number Two Band." Either one would have been perfect for me, but unfortunately, both bands already had drummers who had been there for a while, so I went back to playing the vibes. I really was bugged because I was a better drummer than the two other guys who were playing drums with either band. All the musicians in the band really liked me. They thought that I was the best new vibes player they ever heard. Plus, I was the baby of the band.

Some funny things happened while I was with the army band. We had to march in a parade for a general, so for laughs, I decided to pray for rain so we wouldn't have to march. So I stripped down to my shorts and put on my steel helmet without wearing the regular helmet that normally goes under it. All you could see was my nose sticking out. Then I went outside the barracks into the street, and in my low Popeye voice, I chanted all kinds of dumb words in Jewish. Nobody knew what I was saying; I was just mumbling in Jewish. Believe it or not, it started to rain. This got to be very freaky because just about every time I did this, it rained! One of my sergeants was a guy named Harold Diner who was a great trombone player. Every time he found out we had to march, he'd come and get me, make me strip down and put my helmet on, and I had to go outside and say these stupid words in Jewish to make it rain. It rained just about every time. Pretty freaky.

I was only eighteen years old. All the other guys were a lot older, twenty-seven, twenty-eight years old. They were always talking about smoking pot and balling a million girls. I was still a virgin at the time, and I had never smoked pot in my life. I always thought it was like dope. A guy named Jack Schwartz, who years later wound up playing baritone saxophone in my big band, kept asking me if I smoked pot. I tried to be cool: "Yeah, I smoke pot." I didn't even know what it looked like. I saw Frank Socolow smoke pot that one time when we were sixteen years old but I never really got a chance to see what a joint looked like compared to a cigarette. I smoked a lot of cigarettes in those days, two or three packs a day. So Jack said, "C'mon outside with us."

We went outside, about five or six guys, and they started passing a joint around. I had never held a joint before in my life, but I wanted to be one of the guys, so I played it cool. Normally, if you're going to get high for the first time, there's always someone around to tell you what you're supposed to feel so you know you're not going to go crazy and jump off a roof or something. What actually happens is that you might get a little lethargic or a little hungry or you might laugh a lot. But nobody told me what to expect. I started smoking it like I would a cigarette and when I did this, Jack got hip to me immediately and knew I was full of shit. He knew I'd never tried pot in my life. He said, "No, no, do it like this; you'll get higher." He showed me and I did what he said. When we were finished, I didn't know what to expect so I went back to the barracks, got in my bunk, got under the covers, and forced myself to go to sleep. I wasn't sure what was going to happen. Would I be screaming, yelling, jumping off buildings, or what? Nobody told me what was supposed to happen. So I fell asleep. I never tried to smoke pot again until I got out of the service.

I think I was in the service about a year when they told us that we were going overseas. Even though the band wasn't a fighting unit, we still had to do everything that any soldier going overseas had to do. We had to get our shots and go through what they called the infiltration course, which is a replica of a battlefield. It was that real. The infiltration course had barbed wire about four feet high, and you had to crawl through mud on your belly for a hundred yards underneath it while they shot what seemed like real bullets over your head. We never found out if the bullets were real because we were too scared to stand up. They also had fake mines that would make all kinds of noise and release smoke if you stepped on them. I followed a guy who I think wanted to win the war all by himself. He was the first one through the infiltration course, and I was the second one out because I was following him. I think that this test is given so that if you get scared and stand up, they wouldn't let you go overseas. By standing up in real combat, you could show the enemy your position and get everybody killed.

If you passed the infiltration course, you were ready to go overseas. As I said before, the army never told you what was going on until the last minute, and the last minute for me was being shipped out to Dallas, Texas, along with the best bass player in the band, Irwin Manaday. When I got there, I had to audition for a big orchestra that had about twenty strings besides the regular brass, saxes, and rhythm section. The orchestra broadcast from WFAA's studios in Dallas and recorded music for Army training pictures. They needed a drummer, so I auditioned with about a hundred other guys and wound up with the job. I finally got a chance to play drums. I also played vibes and wrote a few arrangements for the band.

We lived in barracks right in town at Young and Austin streets in Dallas. The barracks were there just for the band. It was almost like we weren't in the army. No marching, no training, nothing. We just practiced, did broadcasts on WFAA, recorded music, and went out on bond drives. Out of the fifty guys in the band, there were eight of us who were jazz players. All of the other guys were what we called "legitimate" players. Some of them went on to play with symphony orchestras.

In the latter part of 1943, I went home on furlough. At this time, there was a record ban, which meant that musicians were not allowed to record because James C. Petrillo, the head of the musicians union, couldn't get the money he wanted for the musicians. So they went on strike, and there were no records made with musicians for more than two years. Vocal groups could record but they couldn't use union musicians.

When I got back to New York, Tiny Kahn was waiting for me. He couldn't go into the service because he weighed three hundred pounds and looked like a blimp. A lovable blimp. He could hardly wait for me to get home and tell me about a new music called "bebop." Now when he said "bebop," to me, that was like saying there was a new music called "RBBLGRPPRG," it sounded so strange. I didn't have the slightest idea what it meant or what it had to do with jazz.

Tiny took me to Fifty-Second Street to hear Charlie Parker and Dizzy Gillespie at the Three Deuces. I had never heard of them until Tiny told me about them. That was the first time I ever heard them play. When I heard them, I literally had a nervous breakdown. All my life, I had been looking for some form of jazz where I could utilize my technique, and these guys were playing double-time and triple-time figures. I didn't know what they were doing, but it was the most exciting thing I ever heard in my life. Every jazz chorus Charlie Parker played sounded like it was written by George Gershwin. Everything he played was like a song. You could have put lyrics to everything he played.

Dizzy was easier for me to get into because his double-time figures were like that of a percussionist. I could hear the articulation of the double-time figures he played and I knew that this was what I had been looking for all my life. I had all this technique but I didn't know what to do with it. I stayed on Fifty-Second Street until four o'clock in the morning. When they finished their job, Tiny went home, but I followed them everywhere they went. First they went to Minton's where they played until eight, nine, ten o'clock in the morning. Then they went to Small's for another few hours. Then they went to another place. They didn't stop until two o'clock in the afternoon and started in again that night.

I was so flipped out about the music that I never went home. I slept in doorways of stores in my uniform. I didn't bathe, I didn't change my clothes, and I hardly ate. I felt and looked like a street bum. When I'd wake up, I'd go back to Fifty-Second Street and wait for the clubs to open up again so I could hear Dizzy and Bird. For fifteen days, my entire furlough, I hung out around Fifty-Second Street. I didn't even call home. My folks actually called the police and had them looking for me.

I heard Oscar Pettiford in another club, and I think Thelonious Monk was there too along with guys like Max Roach, Kenny Clarke, Bud Powell, and on and on and on. These musicians were all new to me. It was getting to the point where I was really flipping out. I listened to all that music and absorbed whatever I could. When I went back to Dallas and told everybody what I had heard, they didn't know what I was talking about. They thought I was crazy. Because of the record ban, nobody had ever heard this music or knew who Charlie Parker and Dizzy Gillespie were.

After that, whenever we jammed, every four bars I played must have had a hundred notes in it. The first note was always right and the last note was always right, but in the middle, all wrong notes. But the time was always right, I had that down. And I brought bebop into our little army band.

Then I started writing. One of the first things that I wrote was a little riff on the changes of "Hot House," which was based on the chord changes to "What Is This Thing Called Love." That was the first song I got into. Then I wrote my own melody to "Groovin' High," which was based on the chords to "Whispering." Eventually, I figured out what the bebop musicians were doing. They were taking the great standard songs written by George Gershwin, Jerome Kern, and all the other great composers, and making their own melodies to their chord changes. Some of the songs I wrote back then were not too bad. They were beboppish and melodic but they were full of clichés that everybody played in those days.

The next time I went home on furlough, I immediately went back to Fifty-Second Street. There were still no recordings by any bebop players. Tiny Kahn took me down to Fifty-Second Street and tried to explain what bebop was all about. Tiny was way ahead of all my musician friends. I wouldn't call him a genius, but he was one of the most talented people that I ever met. I think only Charlie Parker could be called a genius. Dizzy Gillespie was one of the greatest musicians who ever lived, and so was Bud Powell, but Charlie Parker was the only one I could call a genius.

My definition of a genius in jazz music is when you can't find anything wrong with whatever they do. If there's a *maybe* somewhere, then they may be great, but not a genius. Even with Dizzy, you could have said that maybe his sound sometimes wasn't quite right. If there's a *maybe*, there's no genius. Art Tatum was so far ahead of everybody technically and harmonically in 1939 and 1940 that guys today can't even do what he did then. He substituted chord changes all over the place, but because he was so far ahead technically and harmonically, *maybe* he could sound a little cold. Just *maybe*. With Charlie Parker, there were no maybes.

In 1943, when I first heard Bird, my feeling was that there were only a few people who should have been allowed on stage with him. First there was, without a doubt, Dizzy Gillespie. Then there were two piano players: Bud Powell and Al Haig; and Oscar Pettiford the bass player. The other four were drummers: Kenny Clarke, Max Roach, Art Blakey, and Stan Levey. Those were the only guys who could play with Charlie Parker and make musical sense. Everybody else sounded like a child in comparison with Bird. He was that far ahead. Listen to the group Supersax, which voiced out his solos, and you can hear what a genius he was. What he came up with melodically was sometimes better than the original song he was playing.

There were some guys from the old school who tried to change their style to fit bebop. Don Byas, the tenor sax player, came close. Lester Young didn't have to change his style to play bebop; he fit right in. Prez's articulation was completely different from all the other tenor players, everyone from Don Byas to Coleman Hawkins to Herschel Evans to Ben Webster. In fact, the tenor players who later played bebop, people like Allen Eager, Al Cohn, Zoot Sims, and Stan Getz all came from the Lester Young school. When Prez was playing with Count Basie, he was way ahead of all the other tenor players. Tiny and I used to know all of his tenor solos by heart.

Benny Goodman was smart. For a while, he tried to change his style a little bit to play with bebop articulation, but he stopped just in time before he ruined himself. Benny didn't have to do anything but swing. Artie Shaw was foolish. He also tried to play with bebop articulation but he didn't have to because his chorus on "Stardust" was almost like a bebop chorus. If you listen to that chorus, he was playing double-time figures with great feeling. I never heard anybody play a better chorus on "Stardust" than Artie Shaw. But then he started to play triplets with the wrong feel, and it almost sounded like he was playing with a Jewish style of articulation. It wasn't necessary for Artie to change his style of playing.

Before I left the army, they shipped me out from Dallas to San Francisco's Presidio section to be discharged. While we were waiting for our discharge, we went to see Howard McGhee's band, which was playing at a place called the Back Street. I had a friend named Berrel who went with me to see them play. Berrel played trumpet in the army band with me and later became the road manager for my big band. Howard McGhee had Teddy Edwards and Tom Archer on saxes and Roy Porter on drums. It was the first bebop band I really got to hear on the West Coast. I got friendly with them, and they let me sit in with them and play two-finger piano.

Teddy and Tom wore their hair in pompadours, which made their hair look like it was six inches high. Their hair wasn't long; it was just that getting permanents made them look that way. That looked pretty hip to me. We had a warrant officer who didn't like jazz at all. He was one of those guys who lived by the book. He would be in the service whether there was a war on or not. My hair was starting to grow out, and I was just getting to feel comfortable again when from out of nowhere, this warrant officer said to me, "Go get your hair cut." I told him, "I'm getting discharged in a couple of weeks, what difference does it make?" He said, "Get yourself a crew cut now or you WON'T get discharged." He also told a friend of mine named Sherman the same thing, so we both went to get our hair cut.

We got to this one barbershop and there were three or four guys sitting under hair dryers. We were sort of casing out the shop to see who looked like a good barber. We finally asked one of the barbers why these guys were sitting under the hair dryers and he said that they were getting their hair "permed." What they would do is cut your hair down to about an inch from your head and perm it so it would stick up. That looked okay to us so we both got perms. When they were done with us, our one-inch hair looked like it was six inches high. When we got back to camp, the warrant officer flipped out. "I thought I told you guys to get haircuts!" We said, "We did. Go ahead and see for yourself." So this idiot warrant officer actually got a ruler and measured our hair, and it was just an inch long, with enough grease in it to last for a year-and-a-half. I had pitch-black hair then and you could see it shining a half-mile away.

After three years in the army, I was still only a PFC. I think they must have been too embarrassed to discharge me as a PFC, so just before I was discharged they made me a corporal. I couldn't wait to get back home and play music.

Chapter 3
Fifty-Second Street

After I got out of the service, I went back to New York and immediately went straight to Fifty-Second Street. I got together with Frank Socolow and we started jamming down in his basement. We considered Frank ultra-hip because when he was sixteen or seventeen, he was already playing with Boyd Raeburn's band.

Frank's basement was The Hangout. Everybody smoked pot down there. It reeked of smoke so much that it got upstairs to his mother's house. When that would happen, his mother would open the door to the basement and yell, "Frank, enough with the shit already!"

Frank's father, whose name was Izzy, always wanted to be one of the boys. He'd come down to the basement and without even knocking, just walk in and start fixing little things while we all were scrambling around, trying to hide the pot. It never occurred to him that the place reeked from smoke. He'd just do anything to hang out with us. He'd nail a picture on the wall and come up with whatever reason he could so long as he could hang out with us.

We had a girl in the basement that was known as "The Mole." She had a great figure but the ugliest face this side of Frankenstein. One night, everybody was naked including The Mole. There must have been about six guys there, when, without any warning, in came Izzy again. He walked downstairs and everyone tried to hide and cover their private parts. Izzy was just cool; whistling, walking around, and nailing pictures to the wall like nobody was even there. He just wanted to hang out with the guys.

When we weren't jamming, we used to play Monopoly. There was a trumpet player in our group named Normie Faye. Tiny Kahn was the only one who had a car, so we used to pick Normie up in the Bronx, drive him to Frank's house in Brooklyn, and we'd play Monopoly until four, five, six o'clock in the morning. Then we'd all get back into Tiny's car and drive Normie all the way back up to the Bronx. We were really getting into the game, and everybody had a monopoly except Tiny. Normie had the one property that Tiny needed to make a monopoly and Tiny wanted to buy it, but Normie said, "No, I don't want to sell it, I want to win the game." Tiny said, "Well, I'll be out of the game if you don't sell it to me. Everybody else is building hotels except me!" Normie wouldn't sell it to him so Tiny got knocked out of the game. Six o'clock in the morning came, the game ended, and we were all in the car driving Normie back to the Bronx. Tiny drove about four blocks to the subway station and made Normie get out and take the subway home. At six o'clock in the morning, the subway, which was called the local train, stopped at every station. Normally, with an express train, it might take an hour to get to the Bronx, but there weren't any express trains at that time of the day. The local would take about two-and-a-half hours. Normie got out and said, "Why are you making me take the local train? Why aren't you driving me home?" Tiny said, "Because you wouldn't sell me Atlantic Avenue. Take the subway home!" Poor Normie.

Coming back from Normie's house, we liked to stop at a place called Dave's Corner for egg creams. An egg cream had Fox's U-Bet chocolate, a little milk, and a shpritz of seltzer in it. The whole thing cost two or three cents. Dave's place was on Delancey Street and there used to be a lot of drunks who hung out there. As we were riding, we looked out the window and saw a drunk leaning into a garbage can, taking out food. Tiny got out of the car, saw the drunk eating some old spaghetti, and asked him if the spaghetti was *al dente*. The guy was juiced out of his bird and didn't know what Tiny was talking about.

There was a cocktail piano player around New York who wrote a famous song called "Miami Rhumba." His name wasn't familiar to most people, but amongst musicians, if you said Irving Fields, they would break up laughing. Tiny, who always had a great sense of humor, once wrote a song called, "Welcome Home, Irving, from Langley Field," and then wrote a sequel to that called "Welcome Home, Langley, from Irving Fields."

When Tiny and I were with people who we didn't know too well, I would always tell them that he and I grew up together. Then Tiny would say, "He grew up together." Tiny would always make up names for some of the famous musicians. He called Illinois Jacquet "Chicago Vestcoat" and Big Sid Catlett "Big Veal Cutlet."

After Tiny died, I couldn't go up to his house to visit his parents. They really didn't want to see me because for some reason, when they saw me, they saw Tiny, which was strange, because he weighed three hundred pounds and was over six feet tall and I weighed eighty-eight pounds and was five feet tall. But actually, I did understand it because every time his parents saw me, I would be with Tiny, and to see me alone, there was something missing.

I didn't have any vibes of my own yet but I did have a set of xylophones that I used for practicing. When we went to Frank's basement, some of the guys thought that they were ultra-hip. While we were playing, somebody turned all the lights out. I said to Marty Wisotski, a trumpet player who was sitting next to me, "What happened?" He said in his very hip way, "Man, when the lights are out and you don't see anything, you play better because nothing's in your way. You can visualize pictures in your mind." What pictures? Remember that I'm playing a xylophone, which has dark wooden bars. I can't even see my set. If I stand a half-inch one way or the other, I'll play the wrong notes. There I was, wanting to impress these guys, and when it came my time to play, I was feeling around for the sharps and flats. That was about the hardest thing I ever did because I was just getting to know these guys.

There was a guy called Pincus who was known as "The Mayor of Fifty-Second Street." That was the name laid on him because he was the doorman for just about every club on Fifty-Second Street. I don't think anybody ever knew his first name. He was just called Pincus by everybody. He was a little guy, about five-feet-two, had a big bugle, and wore a red coat that went all the way down to the floor. We were kids and couldn't afford to get into the clubs so we used to stand on Fifty-Second Street in front of one of the clubs that had the musicians who we wanted to hear play. There'd be ten or fifteen guys or more just trying to hear their favorite musicians, and Pincus would chase everybody away. It was like he owned Fifty-Second Street. He had that kind of power.

After I played the Three Deuces, the club owners started throwing my name around. In fact, Irving Alexander and Sammy Kay, the owners of the Three Deuces, wanted me to sign a lifetime contract making them my managers and put me in the Three Deuces. They would start out by giving me eighty-five dollars a week, which was leader scale, and give me a raise of five dollars every four months. That wasn't bad for 1946 but now, fifty-seven years later, I'd be making about $750 a week. They were both pretty sharp and were real hustlers, but were nice guys.

Pincus heard me play and even though he didn't know if I was good or bad, he went by the audience reaction when they left the club and by what he heard from the club owners on Fifty-Second Street. Then he started to treat me like an upcoming star and let me stand in front of any club I wanted to. It was great for me because I couldn't afford to go into a club and buy a drink.

I remember the first job I ever played on Fifty-Second Street. I was playing with Babs Gonzalez, the bebop singer; Roy Haynes on drums; Bobby Tucker on piano, who later worked with Billy Eckstine; and Gene Ramey on bass. That was the first bebop job I ever played.

In 1946, I did my first record date with Aaron Sachs, the clarinet player who was really good for that time. I had just gotten out of the service, and I think it was Tiny who introduced me to him. We rehearsed at my house, just Aaron and myself. Tiny wrote a song that was based on "Back Home in Indiana," but it was actually "Donna Lee," which had the same chord changes. When we recorded, Clyde Lombardi played bass, Tiny Kahn played drums, and Harvey Leonard was the piano player. I don't remember much about the date except that we did it for a company called Manor Records. I really wasn't too nervous on that date. I was playing with people I already knew. I had gotten to know Aaron because he would come over to my house to rehearse. I knew Clyde from Fifty-Second Street, and I had jammed a few times with Harvey. And of course, I grew up with Tiny. When we rehearsed at my house, Aaron and I would practice playing the melody together and we played it pretty good. He would then play some jazz and I'd go over to the piano and I'd comp for him. It didn't matter if you had a drummer or a piano player, you just played. It's amazing when I listen to the tapes that I have of us rehearsing. The time was really good, even without a drummer or a bass player.

Then a guy called Bill DeArango heard me play and hired me for a quintet that he had just started. Bill played electric guitar and was one of the first guitarists to play with Charlie Parker. Bill used to call me his "little man." He was really proud of me. Being that Bill was around a lot longer than me and had a little experience as a bandleader, I thought that if I ever started my own band, I could learn a lot from Bill of what to do. It turned out just the opposite. I learned from Bill what NOT to do. For example, I learned not to be as loose as Bill was as a businessman. We never showed up on time for a job. We never played forty-minute sets or whatever we were supposed to play. Everything he did had nothing to do with being a bandleader. In fact, I don't think Bill really wanted to be a bandleader, he just wanted to play. Also, the guitar wasn't really "in" those days. There was a time in the bebop era when guitar players couldn't get a job.

We played about two jobs in the whole time I was with Bill. We jammed a lot but only played a few jobs. We had a very subdued sound. Charlie Leeds was the bass player, Art Mardigan was the drummer, and was a great one, but unfortunately, he got screwed up on junk. Art was a very light and tasty drummer. He played beautiful brushes and Bill liked that sound. Harry Biss was the piano player.

Bill's quintet was the first group to feature the guitar-and-vibes sound that George Shearing made famous. The first job we played was at the Famous Door on Fifty-Second Street. We got a review in *Down Beat* whose headline read "Great Vibist Sparks The DeArango 5." It was the first review that I ever really got.

Terry Gibbs Astounds

Most exciting thing in the group, and the best young musician I have heard in many, many months is 22-year-old Terry Gibbs. Here is a bopper with flowing ideas, good taste, long phrases, developed solos, a swinging beat, and complete harmonic conception

This in short is a musician who excites everyone who hears him. Even more, he is one of these rare kids who is so chuck full of the stuff, he can't get it all out, plays solo after solo and still leaves listeners with the impression that there is yet a gang of stuff to come.

No Yipes Here

The *Beat* has yipped constantly lately about young musicians with ideas, but inadequate technique, or a too channelized approach. Here is one boy with whom no yips, save a minor beef that he needs better mallets and more attention to wrist lifts to get fuller tone.

A further caution: it is our impression that Terry is going to have a lot of people tell him how great he is in the next few months. It would be worth his while to remember that he is still a young man with much to learn about schooled music; no matter how fertile his native talent.

Down Beat, Chicago, June 18, 1947

I didn't know what wrist lifts were, but if I was as good as this guy said I was, why would I have to worry about anything? It was then that I realized that most critics don't know what the hell they're talking about. The ones I've met are ex-musicians who couldn't make it as musicians and became critics. After that review came out, I never believed any review that came after that. Then I knew that it was all full of shit. There are a few reviewers that I respect who don't really critique your playing. They look for the nice things that you played that they enjoyed. They never really give you a bad review. Only other musicians could know if I was playing good or bad, but never a reviewer. I still don't know what wrist lifts are.

We worked opposite Georgie Auld at a club called the Troubadour, which was also on Fifty-Second Street, but a block away from all the other clubs. Tiny was playing drums, Al Epstein was playing tenor, and Serge Chaloff was on baritone. After the last set, there must have been only eight people left in the club. Bill's group would finish the night from three-thirty to four o'clock in the morning and Tiny would wait for me so we could go home together. We were playing "I Can't Get Started" and Tiny asked me if he could play my vibes. He could pick up any instrument and make sense out of it. I said sure and went to the back of the club while Tiny played. Everything he played was beautiful. While he was playing, this little fat guy who ran the place and who probably had whacked out four people the day before, came over to me and said, "Hey! Get that fat idiot off the stage and get back up there and play!" I said, "Fat idiot? You're the fat idiot. Do you know how good he's playing?" I didn't give a shit if he was John Dillinger; he was way out of line. After I called him a fat idiot, I was lucky he didn't whack ME out.

Epstein, who was always ready to pull one of his practical jokes, once put a potato in Serge Chaloff's baritone bell. When the job started, Serge was having a little trouble with reeds and now when he started to play, it was getting worse and he couldn't get a sound out of it at all. Serge was changing reeds the whole night. He must have changed forty reeds until Epstein finally took the potato out of his bell and showed it to him. Serge was so stoned out on the last night of the job that he left his baritone stand there. Epstein found it and took it home. Three years later, they worked a job together and Serge saw the baritone stand. He said to Epstein, "Gee, that's a great stand. I used to have one just like that. Sure wish I could find another one." Epstein said, "I've got another one like this at home. I'll sell this one to you for five dollars." Epstein sold Serge his own stand back.

We had to play an audition at Billy Reed's Little Club, which was a swanky place on the East Side. Somebody told Billy about the kind of sound we had, so we went to audition for him. Harry Biss had the only car among us, so he drove. I didn't have any cases for my vibes at that time; the whole set came in pieces. So I loaded the parts in between the seats, people's legs, everywhere. Harry had a convertible and we had a two o'clock audition. Harry was a complete nervous idiot. He looked like a Virgil Partch cartoon. He had a girlfriend named Ruth, and they fought and screamed at each other all the time. It didn't matter who was around, every time he got in the car, she'd yell at him: "Watch out for that car, Harry! Watch out for this one! Make a left!"

Harry and Ruth sat in the front and Bill and I sat in the back with my vibes all over the place. We were driving on Fifth Avenue. New Yorkers are the rudest people in the world. Horns were honking, nobody was driving in their lane, and Ruth was screaming, "Watch out, Harry!" We stopped for a red light. Harry and Ruth were still fighting and without any warning, Harry opened his door, got out of the car, and ran away. Left the car in the middle of the street. None of us knew how to drive and everybody was honking their horns at us. I would have left, but my vibes were in the car in a million pieces. Finally, the police came and helped us push the car over to the side of the street. We never made it to the audition and Billy Reed never wanted to hear about us ever again.

Another job Bill DeArango's band played in New York was at the Three Deuces. We played there for a week and I made sixty-six dollars, which was big money in those days. This was 1946 or 1947 and I was just a twenty-two-year-old kid. Bill was three years older than me, which wasn't much, but it seemed like a lot to me.

The Three Deuces was about forty by forty feet. All the clubs on Fifty-Second Street were small. Sometimes we'd play one tune for a whole set. We would play a ballad for an hour. Bill would play twenty choruses and then I'd play twenty, then the piano would play, then we'd go back and play twenty more choruses each. The vibes were in front of the drums alongside of Bill and after Bill would play his choruses, he'd go stand behind the drummer while I took my solo. He didn't like to play rhythm guitar when someone else was soloing. After I played my choruses, I went behind the drums while the piano played and stood next to Bill. Suddenly, I smelled pot. A roach was what they called a joint that was real small, like a quarter of an inch or a half-inch long. If you got caught with a roach, you'd get sent to jail for six years. I looked over at Bill! and he handed me this roach. I whispered, "What are you doing?" I really got scared because I was always afraid of getting busted. He said, "It's cool. We're behind the drummer." I looked around. Who cared if we were behind the drummer? You could smell the pot four blocks away. I figured that Bill was older and wiser, so it was cool. When I think about that now, I realized how stupid we were.

We went to Chicago and played a place called Jump Town. We were an unusual band because we had that quiet bebop sound. There weren't any horns; it was just guitar and vibes plus the rhythm section. This time, we took along Tiny Kahn to play drums and Harvey Leonard to play piano with us. Even though none of us had any money, we checked into a hotel called the Alexandria. We weren't worried because Bill was responsible for that. We all had our own rooms, went to the club to play, and got fired after the first song. Bebop was very new and the club owner didn't know what we were playing. "What the hell is this music you're playing?" It was "out" to him. So after the first tune, he fired us. We only played one song.

We didn't know what to do. We didn't even have any money to buy some food so Bill checked us all out of our rooms and had the hotel switch us to one big room. Since Bill was the leader, it was up to him to try and get us out of this mess we were in. Charlie Leeds, the bass player, was a little guy and very thin. He must have been about five-foot-nine and weighed about seventeen pounds. He looked like he couldn't fight his way out of a paper bag. I could never figure out how he could get such a good sound out of his bass. Later, he became a beat poet and wrote a few books. He even went to jail for about fifteen years.

Charlie was always afraid of the dark, and I put him on one time. I put him in a closet and shut the door. "C'mon, Terry, let me out!" he yelled. When I went to open the door, it wouldn't open and Charlie started to panic. Then we all tried to open the door. We couldn't call downstairs to the manager because we hadn't paid our rent yet so we waited a half-hour for Bill to show up and get a key to get Charlie out.

While we were in Chicago, out of work, Bill tried to find some money to pay the hotel and get us back to New York. While he was doing that, the rest of us went to a club and heard a piano player named Lou Levy. Tiny Kahn and I fell in love with Lou's playing. Little did I know that in just a short time I would be sick as a dog, sharing a room on a boat with Lou on our way to Sweden.

Chapter 4
My Three Minutes with Tommy Dorsey

When I got back to New York after that ridiculous ordeal in Chicago with Bill DeArango, I got a call from Allen Eager, asking me if I would record with him. Teddy Reig, who was producing records for the Savoy label, thought that it would be a good sound with the tenor and vibes. Allen was becoming the hot new tenor player around New York and I was the new kid on the block starting to get some attention as a jazz vibist. I didn't know Allen too well then. At that time he was better known than Stan Getz, Zoot Sims, and Al Cohn. They all had similar styles. They were bebop players who came out of the Lester Young school of playing.

    I was scared as hell to do the date. Even though I recorded with Aaron Sachs, the musicians on this date were all famous beboppers. They all recorded a lot and this was only my second record date. Recording is very stressful. You really try your hardest to make sure that you play something that you really like. Once they say, "That's a take," that's what's coming out on the record. I don't think anybody is really satisfied with what they play when they record. You always think you could have played better.

    I wasn't sure how hard the music was and I really wasn't worried. I just wanted these musicians who I respected so much to like my playing. Max Roach was the drummer on the date. When I got out of the army, I saw Max play with Dizzy and Bird. He was the most respected drummer around, and sort of took Buddy Rich's place with the young players as the best drummer in jazz.

Duke Jordan was the piano player and Curley Russell was on bass. Curley also played with Charlie Parker. I knew them a little bit, but I didn't know them that well so that I could tell them to kiss my ass if I felt like it. I was in awe of all of them.

That was the most screwed up record date that I was ever on. First of all, I was leaving New York the next day to join Tommy Dorsey in California. I had to play on a strange set of vibes because my vibes were already being shipped out there. Allen wouldn't play until his connection showed up. Max wouldn't even set up his drums until he was paid for a date that he did for Teddy Reig a few weeks before. Teddy Reig was arguing with Max, and Allen was pacing around the studio, waiting for his connection.

I love Allen now, but as I said before, I didn't really know him too well then. He's a sweet guy and a very funny guy with a great Jewish sense of humor. I think his mother used to own a hotel in the Catskills. It was what they called a *cochalain,* where you bring your own food and cook for yourself.

Two of the songs we recorded I made up right at the date, and Allen put his name on them. One of them was called "Meeskite," which is Jewish for "ugly." Symphony Sid, the famous New York disc jockey, used to use that word all the time. The other song I wrote was called "Donald Jay." Allen came up with the title, but I don't even know why he named it that. Twenty years ago, Allen came to see me at a club in Florida and apologized for taking credit for writing those two songs. I think by that time, he had cleaned up his act and had been sober for years.

We were going to record a song Duke Jordan wrote called "Jordu." On the release, which is the bridge or the middle part, the chord changes were really different than what was being written those days. I walked over to Duke and because I really didn't know him too well, I quietly asked him what the chord changes were in the bridge. I knew the chord changes to the first sixteen bars and had learned the melody from Allen. Duke was out of it too, and he just said, "LISTEN, man." I said, "I AM listening, but I don't know what they are, because they go all over the place." He said, "Just LISTEN." He wouldn't tell me the chord changes. I went over to Allen and said, "Do you mind if I just play the melody with you, because I don't know the chord changes that well?" He said, "You don't have to play on it if you don't want to. Duke and I will play the solos, and you just play the melody with me." I said great.

Now we start recording. Allen played a chorus or two. Then Duke played about sixteen bars and we started back to the melody of the last chorus. When we went back to the last melody, Teddy Reig, who was producing the date, yelled in from the booth, "Hey! Wait a minute!" Teddy must have weighed four hundred pounds. I think it took him a half-hour to walk through the door. He came in and said, "Why isn't Terry playing on the song?" Allen said, "Terry doesn't want to play on this one." Teddy said, "What do you mean? I want Terry . . . !" Allen didn't even let him finish what he was going to say and yelled at him. "LISTEN, YOU FAT IDIOT! GET BACK IN THE BOOTH OR I'M GOING HOME! HE DOESN'T WANT TO PLAY ON THIS SONG!" I don't think we made another take on the song, plus it was never released anyhow. Teddy liked what I did and eventually wanted me to do a big band record date. I was new on the scene and he thought I had a lot of talent, enough to make a name for myself as a leader.

Teddy was one of the first guys I know who recorded bebop and took a chance recording music that most people didn't understand. I'm not sure what his background was in music, but he heard what Charlie Parker, Dizzy Gillespie, and Bud Powell were playing, and knew that they were great. The owner of Savoy Records was a guy called Herman Lubinsky who was in the booth with Teddy. They were both pretty good hustlers. I heard that they bought some songs from Charlie Parker for twenty-five dollars. Bird probably didn't care because that would be twenty-five dollars more that he could use to shoot up with.

When I listen to the records I played on with Allen Eager, I can hear what a big difference there is in how I play now compared to how I played then. I was just learning how to get around the chord changes to the bebop songs and how to articulate the notes and rhythms. I've grown a lot musically since then. If you don't learn something in fifty-five years, then you'd better go back to *shul*!

Allen was far ahead of all the tenor players and very much in demand. Unfortunately, he was screwed up on junk and I think that kept him from growing musically. It's easy to hear the blues and "I Got Rhythm" chord changes, but it's a different bag when you play a song like "All the Things You Are" or "Stella by Starlight," which harmonically go through completely different kinds of chord changes. Allen's articulation was beboppish but, as I said before, he played in the style of Lester Young. He was probably one of the first white musicians to get recognized in the bebop era. Everybody had a lot of respect for Allen Eager.

The next day, I got on a train to go to California to join Tommy Dorsey. This was a big-time job for me, which is one of the reasons I went with the band. They also offered me a hundred and fifty dollars a week, which didn't hurt either. Here I was, playing on Fifty-Second Street, making sixty-six dollars a week, working one week a year. That's about all I ever worked. Now, I was being offered a hundred and fifty dollars. I probably would have gone to work for Guy Lombardo for that kind of money.

A hundred and fifty dollars back then is like a thousand dollars today. I never thought about the money at all because I would have spent it all on clothes anyhow. The more money they gave me, the more clothes I would have bought. I was a clothes freak. On all the bands I played with, we'd always wear a band uniform, some dumb cockamamie suit. I always carried four or five suits with me, and they were tailor-made. The only time I would wear them was when I went back to my room, tried them on, and looked at myself in the mirror.

When I went to join Tommy Dorsey in California, my mother didn't want me to fly. She thought it was too dangerous. Those days, everybody listened to their mother. Today, kids don't respect their parents as much as we did then.

Tommy got me a compartment on the train and it took me five days to get to California. I was cooped up in a little compartment that had an upper and a lower berth. I got bugged sleeping in the lower all the time so every once in a while I'd sleep in the upper, just to change the scene.

When I got to California, they picked me up at the railroad station and whisked me out to a ballroom in Santa Monica called the Casino Gardens. I think Tommy was part owner of the ballroom. I set up my vibes and got a chance to play one song before the intermission. Some of the musicians in Dorsey's band at that time were Louie Bellson, Charlie Shavers, Ziggy Elman, Corky Corcoran, and Bill Miller. After I played that one song, I said to myself, "What am I doing here? They're playing 'Song of India' and I'm still trying to learn the release to 'Cherokee.'" I was really listening to Bird and Diz. I'm trying to learn how to play bebop, and they're playing things that sound eighty years old.

I went to Dave Klein, Tommy's manager, and said, "Mr. Klein, I've got to give you my notice." He said, "What notice? What are you talking about? You just got here about three minutes ago!" I tried to explain to him that I had been listening to a new music called bebop and was trying to learn it, and that the music they were playing had nothing to do with what I wanted to play. He didn't know what I was talking about or what the word *bebop* meant, nor did he care. But he went and told Tommy that I had given my notice.

In our business, if you quit a band, you have to give two weeks notice and pay your own way home. If Tommy fires you, then he would have to pay your way home. Nobody ever quit bands like Benny Goodman, Tommy Dorsey, or any of the good big bands. Musicians would stay in those bands as long as they could, or until they got fired.

You never quit, but I did, and after playing just one song. Dave Klein thought I was crazy.

At the intermission, I was talking with Louie Bellson and Charlie Shavers when, all of a sudden, somebody gave me a whack on my shoulder. I turned around and saw it was Tommy Dorsey. Tommy was about six-foot-two and as I looked up at him, he looked like he was nine feet tall because he was mad as heck. He looked down at me and said, "You little SHITHEAD! Did you just quit my band? NOBODY quits my band! You're FIRED!" I tried to explain, "Mister Dorsey, I'm trying to listen to a new music called bebop and . . ." "I DON'T CARE WHAT YOU'RE LISTENING TO! YOU'RE FIRED!" So I said, "Well, if you fire me, you've got to pay my way home." He said, "NO, YOU QUIT! PAY YOUR OWN WAY HOME!" and then walked away from me. He made me stay the whole two weeks, but he never let me play. I ended up turning pages for the bass player because I had nothing else to do.

Tommy was doing a movie with Danny Kaye called *A Song Is Born*. Tommy, Benny Goodman, Louis Armstrong, Lionel Hampton, Louie Bellson, and Mel Powell were all in the movie. Tommy would go home for the last set because he had to be up at six o'clock in the morning and we didn't get done until two. When he'd leave, Ziggy Elman would run the band and let me play. That's the only time I ever got to play. All I ever played every night were two original songs that were based on the chord changes to "I Got Rhythm" and the blues in A-flat and D-flat. It got to a point where, later on in my life, if you said, "Let's play the blues in D-flat" I'd go home. It was like a sickness. I couldn't stand playing the chord changes to "I Got Rhythm" or the blues in those two keys. I could play any song that had a lot of chord changes in those keys but it just became a mental block for me, playing the chord changes to those two tunes in A-flat or D-flat.

Louie Bellson couldn't understand why I was quitting the Dorsey band. He said, "Maybe you're just bugged staying in that funky Oban Hotel." My room in the hotel was about three-by-three and the hotel had to be about eighty thousand years old. It was really dirty and depressing looking. Louie said, "Why don't you move in with my brother Frank and me? Maybe you'll feel better." I said, "I don't want to hang you guys up." Louie said, "No problem. We've got a lot of room and two beds." I said, "How will we make it with just two beds?" He said, "Frank and I will sleep together in one bed and you'll sleep in the other bed." I said, "Really?" He said, "Yeah, no problem at all."

The next day he picked me up at the Oban Hotel and took me over to a little apartment that he and Frank were staying at. Actually, they were staying at a boarding house. When I walked into their room I didn't believe what I saw. The room was about seven by twenty feet and there were two army cots there. I said "Louie, you gotta be kidding. How the heck are we going to sleep?" He said, "You sleep in this bed and Frank and I will sleep in the other one." He didn't even call it a cot. You've got to know Louie Bellson, who is probably one of the nicest men who ever lived. I said, "You're putting me on." Louie said, "No, when Frank and I were kids, we always slept that way." All of the Bellsons are the same. Nice, beautiful people. They did everything possible to make me feel comfortable. The two of them actually slept in one cot while I slept in the other cot by myself.

Louie liked the way I played. I don't think he was even thinking about bebop those days because of the music he was playing with Tommy Dorsey's band. He thought that I would be perfect for Benny Goodman and he wanted Benny to hear me play, so he said, "Let's stay over after the job with Bill Miller and Ed the bass player. We'll make a recording, and I'll take it to the studio where we are recording the music for the movie. I want Benny Goodman to hear you play." That night after the job was over we recorded a few songs and Louie took it to the studio for Benny to hear.

The next day, the studio was starting a publicity campaign to plug *A Song Is Born*. They were going to have Benny Goodman, Tommy Dorsey, and Louis Armstrong riding on separate trucks with their respective groups, and jamming. They were going from Hollywood Boulevard all the way to Santa Monica and were going to ride caravan style with the movie actors on trucks in between the ones with the musicians so that each band wouldn't conflict with the other. Benny didn't have a drummer and Louie knew that I played drums, so he told that to the producer, and they hired me to play drums with Benny.

When they took a break from shooting the movie, Benny would always start playing some song on his clarinet. The moment he started to play, Lionel Hampton, who was always ready to play, jumped right in. Then Louie Bellson joined in and they started to jam. Tommy, who was tired and trying to get some rest, yelled at them, "Why don't you guys stop all that shit? I went to bed real late last night and hardly got any sleep. Stop playing! We've played enough music today." So Benny stopped playing.

About four minutes later, Benny, being in left field, started playing the clarinet again. Once again, Lionel jumped right in, Louie joined them too, and they started jamming again. After they were playing for about a minute, Tommy, who was really getting bugged, yelled out again, "HEY, C'MON, GUYS! I HAVEN'T SLEPT ALL NIGHT. CUT THAT SHIT OUT!" Benny stopped playing. It didn't take long for Benny to forget what Tommy asked him not to do, and he picked up his clarinet and started playing again. Sure enough, when they heard Benny, Lionel and Louie jumped in again and this time, Tommy was really bugged. He went over and hit Benny and knocked him down. Benny didn't fight back. He just got off the floor and went home.

The next day, when they had the publicity drive, Benny didn't show up, so they brought Charlie Barnet in to play for Benny on the truck. I knew who Charlie was but I had never met him. There we were, Charlie, Harry Babasin, the bass player, and myself on the truck: saxophone, bass, and drums.

It was twelve o'clock in the afternoon and the trucks were going about three miles an hour. We hadn't even played our first song when Charlie whipped a fifth of scotch out of his sax case, took a swig, and handed it to Harry. Before we had gone about a block-and-a-half, half the bottle was gone and both of them were juiced out of their bird.

We were in the middle of playing our first song when we saw a car on our right that had two girls in it. They were driving about three miles an hour also. What happened next, happened so fast, I couldn't believe it. Charlie started talking to the girls and if you've seen the old westerns where one guy on a horse would jump from his horse to another horse, that's what happened. Charlie, who was a bit out of it, put his tenor saxophone down, stepped on top of the railing of the truck, and jumped off the railing onto the top of the car that the two girls were in. They made a right turn into the next block and disappeared. That was the last we saw of Charlie. Now I was left alone on the truck with a drunken bass player who was trying to play time, but not the same time I was playing. I wasn't sure where he was at all. That was the last time that I saw Charlie Barnet until years later.

Louie Bellson took the recordings we had made for Benny Goodman to hear, but when Benny didn't show up, he played them for Lionel Hampton. Lionel liked what I sounded like, called me, and said, "Heeeeey, you play some good vibes, Gates! Louie said you play drums also. I'd like to have you play drums with my band. I'll feature you on ten vibes solos a night." About two days later, I got a call from Gladys Hampton, Lionel's wife and manager, who told me that Lionel wanted me to join his band. She said, "You'll play drums and we'll have to discuss the vibes situation." I wasn't any threat to Lionel Hampton, because he was so famous and would have wiped me out anyhow with all the schtick that he did. About an hour later Gladys called again and said, "We'd like to have you just play drums and NO vibes." I told Gladys that I wasn't interested in just playing drums because I was just getting back to playing vibes again, but I thanked her anyway. They were very nice about the whole thing because after my two weeks with Tommy were up, they paid my way home. I didn't even get a chance to meet Lionel. I just talked to him that one time on the phone. That was about the nicest thing Gladys ever did because from what I knew about Lionel's band, they never paid anybody in the band any kind of decent money. So she paid my way home, and I went back to New York.

Chapter 5
"Shooby Yockson" in Sweden

When I got back home, I got a call from Chubby Jackson. He was putting a new band together which had Gene DiNovi on piano, Frank Socolow on tenor, Conte Candoli on trumpet, and Tiny Kahn on drums. I knew Chubby's name because when I was in the army band, we used to listen to the Wild Root cream oil show with the Woody Herman band, and Chubby was one of the featured musicians.

In a way, Chubby was like Bill DeArango. He was both the greatest and the worst bandleader that I ever worked for. We never played the same place twice. We played a club called the Bengazzi in Washington, and we'd have to play forty minutes, take a twenty-minute break, and then play another set. Forty on, twenty off. We'd do about five or six sets like that every night. Instead of forty minutes on, we'd be having so much fun playing that the band would be on the bandstand for an hour-and-a-half. The club owner got bugged because there wasn't any time to sell liquor while we were playing because people would just watch and listen to us.

When we took our intermission, instead of being off for twenty minutes, we'd get lost for an hour. Chubby would take us out to his car, and we'd smoke some pot. When we got back on the bandstand, Chubby would say, "Okay, did everybody get high?" One of the guys that didn't go out with us would say, "No, I didn't get any." So we'd all go back out to the car. Another half-hour would go by before we got back on the bandstand. We got fired every place we played.

In December 1947, Chubby's band got booked to play in Sweden. We were the first bebop band to play there, even before Dizzy. For some reason, Tiny Kahn couldn't go, so Chubby hired Denzil Best to play drums. Gene DiNovi couldn't go either, so we recommended Lou Levy, and Chubby flew Lou in from Chicago. Chubby was great with all young musicians. If you were a friend of his and didn't have a place to stay, he'd take you to his house in Freeport, Long Island, and have you stay with him and his mother. I think she started to get tired of Chubby bringing all the out-of-work musicians home with him.

Chubby's mother used to be in show business. She used to play piano and sing in vaudeville. She sounded like a bad Sophie Tucker and played all the wrong chord changes on the piano, but we all loved her, and everybody called her Mom Jackson.

One of Chubby's good friends was the actor, José Ferrer. At about four o'clock one morning, Chubby bumped into José in New York. José had just come back from Europe where he was doing a movie and hadn't shaved. He looked filthy and said he was going to check into a hotel. Chubby said, "Forget it. Come home with me." So Chubby took him home and just as they got through the door, Mom Jackson walked in. She looked at José and said, "All right! No more bums in the house. Get that bum outta here!" Chubby had to explain that this was José Ferrer, the great actor, and that he wasn't a bum or was out of work.

When we went to Sweden, we spent ten days on a boat called the Drottingholm. Chubby flew over about ten days before us so he could set things up with the promoter. Mom Jackson came along on the boat with us. Lou Levy and I were roommates on the boat. Our room was about eight feet by ten and was next to the boiler room. The room had no porthole and we slept on bunk beds. I got seasick immediately and spent most of the ten days in bed while Lou spent about five days in bed. Because one of us was on the lower and the other was on the upper, we couldn't see each other, so we had somebody on the boat get us a mirror to put against the wall so we could lay in bed and see each other. It was like being in jail.

When we did get out of bed, which for me was about ten minutes, we'd find Mom Jackson playing piano and singing for all the old poor Swedish people who were in steerage, telling them how she had worked with Al Jolson. I remember Conte, Frank, Lou, and I peeking in through the door and watching Mom Jackson singing "The Man I Love." She kept repeating the first four bars without ever changing the chords or the words.

> Some day he'll come along, The Man I Love.
> Some day he'll come along, The Man I Love.

She'd break us up so much that we'd always try to catch her doing her act. But that was only when I could get out of bed. She used to make us steal oranges and then give them to these poor people. They loved her for that.

When we got to Sweden, Chubby met us at the dock with a musician named Simon Brehm, who was the best-known bass player in Sweden. Simon loved Chubby and had a five-string bass made just like Chubby's. He even tried to be just like Chubby. Chubby had a weird theme song called "The Happy Monster." He loved show business, so when the boat docked and we got off, there were about twenty Swedish musicians playing Chubby's theme song.

Before we left New York, we heard a George Wallington song called "Lemon Drop" that George had just written. About a year later, "Lemon Drop" would become a big hit for Woody Herman. We were flipping out about the song and wanted to play it for Chubby when we got to Sweden, so Conte, Frank Socolow, and I learned the melody. When we told him about it, Chubby said, "How does it go?" Our instruments were still on the boat and we couldn't play it for him, so we sang it to him in bebop scat singing. Chubby loved it immediately and said, "You guys gotta sing it like that on stage!" We said, "Wait a minute! Are you kidding? Us sing on stage? Forget about it!" But Chubby loved show business and talked us into singing it on stage anyway.

The first thing the promoter did when we arrived in Göteborg, Sweden, was to take us to this beautiful place called the Grand Hotel where they ordered all kinds of great Swedish food for us. They had the greatest pickled herring in the world, and Lou Levy and I, who were both very Jewish, couldn't stop eating the herring. When we got done with the food and they brought us some coffee, I saw Chubby pull out the fattest joint I ever saw in my life and light it up. He took a few pokes on the joint and then started to pass it around. We all got scared and said, "Chubby, what the heck are you doing?" He said that nobody in Sweden knew anything about marijuana and there wouldn't be any problem at all. So there we were, sitting in the Grand Hotel, smoking a joint in front of everybody in the restaurant, and nobody paid any attention to us. It was pretty scary.

Conte, who was always like a little boy, said a funny thing when we were sitting in the restaurant. He heard everybody speaking in Swedish and said, "I've never seen so many foreigners in all my life!"

When we first sang "Lemon Drop," we were as scared as could be because none of us ever sung before. Conte's bugle (nose) was kind of big and so were Frank's and mine, so when we sang, we had our noses close together with one facing the front and the other two facing sideways, never looking at the audience. We were too scared and embarrassed to look at anybody but ourselves because we didn't think of ourselves as singers. That was Babs Gonzalez but not us.

The only person I ever heard who could sing scat where it made any musical sense at all was Dizzy Gillespie. When Dizzy sang, it was just like he was playing his horn. Ella Fitzgerald was great, and even though she sang all the right notes, she sounded like a singer singing. Dizzy was really creating good music when he scatted. "Lemon Drop" became a hit in Sweden, and we even recorded it there for a Swedish label called Cupol.

Chubby was staying downtown, but he rented a house for the five of us to stay in. We didn't know the value of Swedish money. We were making a hundred and forty dollars a week. Seventy dollars was left for us as a deposit in the U.S., and then we got seventy dollars in Swedish money when we got there.

The Swedish money didn't look like real money; it looked like the coupons that came with Raleigh cigarettes. We took this cab ride to go to the house Chubby rented for us, and the fare might have come to fifty cents in American money. I think we must have given this guy a fifty-dollar tip. It didn't feel like we were giving him any money; it felt like we were giving away cigar store coupons.

When we finally got to the house, it was freezing cold in there. It must have been way below zero and it was so cold, we couldn't go to sleep. After looking for any way we could to get heat in the place and not having any luck, somebody got a bright idea. "Let's rip the wall-to-wall carpeting off the living room floor and wrap ourselves in it and keep warm." We never took our clothes off, and the five of us slept as close to each other as we could inside this heavy carpet. The next day, we got thrown out of the house, and Chubby had to put us up in a hotel.

Our first concert was pretty wild. Chubby had an amplified bass. I think he was the first guy to have one. He was standing off stage and had a microphone that was connected to his bass amp. His bass was on stage. We had somebody set up equipment with 84,000 wires going across the stage so we could record ourselves that first night.

They introduced us individually. Frank Socolow was the first one introduced. Frank was about five feet tall and very funny. Everything he said was a classic. He once went with a girl who was six-foot-two and said that every time he made love to her it looked like she was giving birth to him. In all the time I knew him, I never saw Frank run. He was so unathletic that when he walked, he had to watch where he was going or he would trip. He was the most uncoordinated person I ever met. They called his name: "Frank Socolow on saxophone!" and it took him about a half an hour to walk from the wings to the middle of the stage.

Then they introduced the rest of the band, one at a time. Now it was Chubby's turn. "Ladies and gentlemen, Shooby Yockson!" There was a round of applause and when it died down, Chubby took the microphone, put it by his fanny, and farted right into the mike. You never heard a louder sound in your life. We didn't know anything about show business, but we thought that was so funny that we fell on the floor, laughing like a bunch of idiots. People were staring at these weird Americans, wondering what was going on. We were just a bunch of kids having fun. When we finished the show, people came up to the stage and brought us flowers. We were surprised because we never saw anything like that in the United States.

Before we left New York, Chubby had his bass maker take his bass apart and put in about three or four bags of pot. He rigged it so we could take it out of the F-hole and Chubby rationed it out to Frank, Conte, Lou, and me. We were the only ones who smoked pot, along with Chubby. I don't think Denzil Best ever did. We would smoke it before we went on stage.

The stalls in the Swedish bathrooms had doors that went all the way down to the floor, so all four of us would go into one stall to smoke the joint that Chubby gave us. Even though Chubby was very open about his smoking pot, we were still kind of afraid of getting into trouble, so two of us would stand on the toilet seat and two would stand on the floor, and we'd smoke the joint. There was really only enough room for one person in that stall. By the time we finished smoking the joint and walked out into the bathroom, the place was full of Swedes. When they saw four guys walking out of one stall, they got the weirdest look on their faces. They couldn't figure out what four guys could do in one stall. We probably started a fad in Sweden of four people taking a dump at one time.

After we smoked all the pot that Chubby rationed out and had nothing left, we were kind of bugged. Somebody got a brainstorm and thought that maybe some of the pot might have trickled out into the bottom of Chubby's bass. So we put a bunch of newspapers on the floor and took turns shaking the bass. Conte and Lou would shake the bass, and then Frank and I would follow them. Frank wasn't too much help because he could hardly lift his side of the bass, so it was mostly the three of us. We smoked whatever came out; all the rotgut, dust, and funk. We smoked all that garbage and got sick. We smoked half of a Kaye bass, which wasn't a very good bass to start with.

The women in Sweden were so beautiful, we couldn't believe it. Lou Levy was my roommate while we were in Sweden, and he met a beautiful little blonde Swedish girl, but they couldn't communicate with each other. Lou was only about nineteen years old and the girl must have been seventeen. Lou was always very bashful; he didn't have very much experience with girls. One time I went to our room to find Lou and he wasn't there. I had to get something out of the closet and as I opened the door, there was Lou, kissing the girl. He was too bashful to sit in the room knowing that we might walk into the room and see him.

Conte went with a girl for two weeks until he found out she was six months' pregnant. He didn't even know it. I met a girl that Frank Socolow nicknamed "Mbulu" because he said half of her body was her head. I think he called her that because the name just sounded bigger than life. She was six feet tall and had the biggest head of any woman I have ever seen in my life. We were sitting in my room and neither of us had any clothes on. We were about ready to get into to it when she said, "You've got a *neger* in the band." I said, "What did you say?" She said it again, "You've got a *neger* in the band." I wasn't sure if I'd heard her right and me being against any racial prejudices, I threw her out of the room and then threw her clothes out after her. About ten minutes later, there was a knock on the door, and it was Denzil and he had the girl with him. Denzil told me that she was on her way out and was putting her clothes on, and he asked her what had happened. She was crying and told him, "You got crazy vibraphone player!" When Denzil asked why, she said, "All I said was you've got a *neger* in the band." Denzil, being the gentleman of all times, told her that that wasn't a nice thing to say. She told him, "You don't understand. In Swedish, *neger* means "Negro." It sounded like "nigger" to me, but I suppose there wasn't anything wrong with how she used it, even though it still bugged me. Denzil explained what she told him, and I apologized to her.

This was 1947, and there weren't many black people in Sweden at all. We were going somewhere in a train and noticed this little kid staring at Denzil. I don't think he had ever seen a black person before. So Denzil put out his hand to shake the kid's hand, and the kid shook it and then looked at his hand to see if the black came off. We all broke up, including Denzil.

While we were there, we did a radio show and a record date and that's where we first recorded "Lemon Drop." Conte Candoli wrote a song called "Crown Pilots" and there was another song called "Boomsie" and a ballad of Chubby's called "Crying Sands." My solo was on "Begin the Beguine."

Chubby was really funny onstage. He would do crazy things that only the band would understand. He'd say, "And now, we'd like to dedicate this song to Al Epstein." Nobody knew who Epstein was, especially in Sweden.

Then Chubby would say, "This next song was written by my rabbi" and we'd fall on the floor. Then, "Here, now, ladies and gentlemen, is 'Nate and Dave.'" That's what he called "Night and Day." He gave all the songs Jewish names. "It's a Long, Long While from Pesach to Purim" was his name for "September Song." "Begin the Beguine" became "Begin the Levine." "I'm in Love with You, Honey" became "I'm in Love with Lou Boudreau." Then there was "I Think of You with Every Shit I Take." "I Took a Shit on a Train and Thought about You." All these ridiculous titles. The audience didn't know what he was saying, but we just flipped out laughing. We had absolutely no stage presence whatsoever so we'd egg Chubby on to do more.

We used to go to this club and when Chubby walked in, when the people saw him, they would all scream, "Shooby Yockson! Shooby Yockson!" They treated him like he was a god.

Chubby had a little pipe that he smoked pot in, and one time he turned this little Swedish piano player on. The guy had never smoked pot before, but he loved it the moment he tried it. Every time we went down to this club, it could be in the middle of a song, if the piano player saw Chubby, he would leave the stage and run over to him with his pipe and ramble on in Swedish. It almost sounded like he was saying, "Ugh, ugh, ugh!" Even though Chubby didn't know what he was saying, Chubby knew that he wanted to smoke some pot. Chubby would always take him outside and turn him on.

One place we played had a set of timps, and they put them right next to Denzil so the two of us played a duet together, him playing drums and me playing timps. While we were playing, all the lights went out and they turned the two spotlights on Denzil and me. The rest of the stage was pitch black. On one of my eight-bar solos, I dropped a mallet, so I got on the floor and started looking for it. I must have been on the floor for about twenty minutes looking for my tympani mallet. The spotlight was on the timp heads but I'm crawling around on my hands and knees, looking for that *farcockteh* mallet on the floor. They finally had to put the house lights on because they couldn't see me and I couldn't find the mallet.

We learned a few Swedish words while we were there. We learned *hur mår du* because we had this driver who we were afraid was going to fall asleep, so we kept asking him, "Arnie, *hur mår du?*," which means "How are you?" You had to learn *jag älskar dig*, which means, "I love you," so we could say it to the girls. *Mer smör* meant "more butter." That's about as far as we got with the Swedish language.

Mom Jackson was a riot. She always had to have the floor and when she did, she was the queen of the ball. No matter where we went, she had to do all the talking. We went to the house of somebody who was Swedish royalty and were drinking what was called *schnapps* from these little demitasse cups that they gave us. It looked like gin but was twenty times stronger. We were talking about something that Mom

Jackson knew nothing about, and she couldn't find anything to say. Finally, there was a burst of silence that lasted about four seconds, and Mom said, "Oh yes, everything was very *berceuse!*" We didn't know what the hell *berceuse* meant and I don't think she did either, but we thought it was so funny that we broke up laughing. We kept saying "Berceuse? What the heck is berceuse?" And she just said, "Everything is just very *berceuse.*" So we left it at that.

The greatest part about that whole trip was that we were kids and were having the time of our lives. All the dumb things that happened, like the freezing house, the low class traveling, we didn't care. We just wanted to play music, and we were treated like royalty.

Chapter 6
Buddy Rich: Mr. Nice Guy

When we got back to the States, Chubby didn't have any work for us so he broke up the band. I then went to work for Buddy Rich. In Buddy's band, nobody made any more money than anybody else. We each got fifteen dollars a night when we worked, and we never worked more than four nights a week. The best job we had was when we came to California and played the Hollywood Palladium.

There were two sides to Buddy Rich. He could be nice, and he could also be an asshole. Buddy always played better when he was playing with somebody who could play up to his level, like when he played with Oscar Peterson and Ray Brown or with the Basie band. He had a lot of respect for my playing and featured me a lot.

He was real nice to me and gave me billing because he wanted to make me a star. Being that Lionel Hampton was called "The King of the Vibes" and I was much younger, he billed me as "The Prince of the Vibes." One place we played, they didn't know who I was and the billing read, "Buddy Rich and his Orchestra, featuring the Queen of the Vibes, Terry Gibbs." I was really bugged, but Buddy thought it was funny and wouldn't change the sign for me. So for a whole week I was Queen of the Vibes.

Buddy didn't know much about getting high on hard drugs. Unfortunately, Buddy's band had more junkies in it than even Woody Herman's band had. All of the trumpet players were hooked. One trombone player out of three was not. All five of the saxophone players were screwed up. The bass player was swallowing eighty-four bennies a day. Buddy never did anything those days, but he did start smoking pot later on in his life.

Once, while the band was playing, one of the saxophone players put his head down because he was so stoned out that he couldn't keep his head up. Buddy yelled at him, "Hey! Get up! We're onstage!" The guy said to Buddy, "I'm sorry. I just had a big meal before I got here." Buddy answered, "Well, eat a few hours before you get to work." He had no idea what was going on.

Tommy Allison, one of the trumpet players in the band, was a very good jazz player and a real nice guy. We were playing the Apollo Theater in New York, and I had just finished my two vibes solos and had gone upstairs to change into my street clothes. I was all through with my part of the show. The band was still playing onstage when Tommy walked into the dressing room. I didn't know what he was doing there because the show was still going on. I saw him take his belt off, go over to his trumpet case, and take a spoon out and what looked like dope. I watched him try to tie his belt around his arm and while he was doing it, he was shaking and having trouble holding it. Because I thought that junkies were criminals, I felt like going over and hitting him. After struggling with the belt, trying to put it around his arm, he said, "Terry, could you hold this belt for me, please?" I don't know what made me do it but I went over to him and held the belt. I couldn't stand to watch him and looked the other way while he shot up. When he went back downstairs, I was still in my underwear and was sweating. I felt sick and had to lie down on one of the dressing room tables, which were only about eighteen inches wide. I felt so faint that I thought I was going to pass out.

In the summertime, when the band played at the Paramount Theatre in New York, Buddy challenged the stagehands to a baseball game. We had to get up early and play the game before the first show. We beat them in the first game so they asked us for a rematch, which we also won. Now we had to play them a third time. Buddy told us if we won that game, he would take us out to this Italian restaurant downtown on Mulberry Street in an area called Little Italy. When we played the third game, Buddy fell and broke his left arm. They rushed him to a hospital, and we played without him. He came back to the theater with a cast on his left arm. We won the game and Buddy, who didn't have much money, treated the whole band to a great Italian dinner.

Buddy never thought about money. Whatever he wanted to buy, he bought. He always owed money to somebody. In fact, he owed the government a lot of money, and they withheld his salary. But he really didn't care, and the next day, he went out and bought a new Lincoln Continental.

After we closed the Paramount Theater, we opened at the Apollo Theater in Harlem. Buddy was a big attraction in the black theaters; the black audiences really loved him. Buddy could only use his right hand because his left arm was in a cast. When he played his drum solos, he used his right foot as his right hand and his right hand as his left hand. What he was doing with his foot and his hand was unbelievable. You never heard anything like that in your life. It was the most amazing thing I have ever seen or heard a drummer do and some of the greatest drum solos I ever heard Buddy play.

His arm was in a cast for about three months. If you know anything about having a cast, you have to have the doctor take it off when he thinks it should be taken off. If you take it off at the wrong time, it could break again. Three or four months later, we were playing at the Regal Theater in Chicago. I happened to be in Buddy's dressing room with one of the guys in the band when Buddy said, "I'm getting tired of this shit on my arm. I can't take it anymore. I'm gonna take it off." We said, "You're crazy! You can't take it off. You'll break your hand again!" He said, "Get out of my room!" and he chased us out. The other guy and I were talking outside the room and we said to each other, "He's crazy." Then we heard him playing with drumsticks on a chair. He had cut the cast off and was practicing. When he went downstairs to play the next show, he played his drum solo using his left hand for the first time in months. Now, if I don't play or practice for four days, I sound like a child trying to learn a scale, like a real klutz. He played a drum solo on that show that I have never heard anybody play, including him. He did that just to show us that he's Buddy Rich and no matter what, even with his left hand being in a cast for four months, nothing was going to stop him. One of the greatest drum solos I ever heard. I couldn't believe it; taking the cast off after having it cooped up for months. There was only one Buddy Rich.

There was a recording of a song called "Queer Street" by Count Basie that had a two-bar drum solo by Shadow Wilson that became famous. Every drummer flipped out over it. Buddy had Jimmy Mundy, who did the arrangement for Basie, make a copy for him. Every time we played it, Buddy tried to play a better solo than Shadow Wilson's. As great as he was, he couldn't do it any better. It was just a freaky two-bar drum solo that Shadow played so when Buddy tried to top that and couldn't, he changed it to a four-bar drum solo.

Buddy was late for a rehearsal so we started without him and Stanley Kay played the drums. We rehearsed a few songs and when it came time to play "Queer Street," I asked Stanley if he'd let me play it since I knew Shadow Wilson's drum solo backwards and forwards. He said go ahead. About sixteen bars before the two-bar drum solo, Buddy walked in. When he heard me play Shadow's drum solo exactly like the record, he came over to me and said, "Get off my drums." He was bugged because I had played Shadow Wilson's drum solo just like Shadow had played it on the record.

I also found out one way to make Buddy play a great drum solo. In the old days, Gene Krupa was the most famous drummer in the world, and Buddy was the new kid on the block. Now Buddy was the famous drummer, and Max Roach was the new kid on the block. God forbid you should ever mention Max Roach's name to Buddy. No matter how good Max played, Buddy always thought HE was the greatest drummer ever, and he probably was. But if you mentioned Max Roach's name, you could see horns coming out of Buddy's head, and he'd look at you and sneer. When my friends came to see us play and I wanted Buddy to play a great drum solo, I'd wait until just before we went onstage and I'd say to Buddy, "The other night I heard Max play a solo that you wouldn't believe." When Buddy heard this, he wouldn't even let me finish talking. When we got onstage, he'd play his drum solo, sneer at me and say, "Max Roach?" and play the most unbelievable drum solo you ever heard in your life. It worked every time. The funny thing about Max and all the other drummers was that they all loved Buddy and looked up to him as The Man.

We used to argue a lot about which one of us could play faster. When we played a theater date, I used to play an arrangement of "You Go to My Head" that Tiny Kahn wrote for me. Then I'd play "Crazy Rhythm" at a medium-fast tempo. We were playing at a theater in Baltimore, and my spot on the show was about five minutes long. Stanley Kay played the show and all the slow songs, and played for me on "You Go to My Head." Then Buddy ran up to the drums and played a four-bar high hat solo, which led me into "Crazy Rhythm." I played the melody, two jazz choruses, and an ending. We finished the first song, and Buddy ran up to the drums and started playing ten times faster than we ever played it before. I played the melody and then got into my jazz choruses. After I played my two choruses, I was getting ready to go into the ending when I heard Buddy yell, "One more!" So I played another chorus. Then Buddy yelled out again, "One more!" He kept yelling "One more!" for about thirty-four choruses until my arms were starting to cramp up. Then I realized what he was doing. He wanted me to screw up so I would drop out. In the middle of the thirty-fourth chorus I realized that he wanted me to stop playing, so I said to myself, "I'll stay onstage all night if I have to." I must have played for twenty minutes. After the show was over, I went up to Buddy's room to tell him off. We were ready to get into a fight when the manager of the theater walked in and said to Buddy, "What are you doing? We have a time schedule here! What do you mean, featuring this kid for twenty minutes? Nobody knows him, and you're screwing up the schedule. The movie should have started fifteen minutes ago!" Buddy looked at the manager and yelled, "GET OUTTA MY ROOM!" He threw him out and closed the door.

After we cooled down and were getting ready for the next show, I told Buddy that I had some friends in the audience who came to see us play. What I didn't know was that if you told Buddy that you had friends in the audience, when he'd play his drum solo, he'd purposely screw around. He'd hit the bass drum with his drum stick and do everything to make sure he sounded like a little kid on the drums. I'd be embarrassed because my friends were out in the audience, and I had been telling them what a great drummer Buddy Rich was.

When it came to my spot in the show, Buddy introduced me, and I came out on the stage and started to play "You Go to My Head." Once again, Stanley Kay played for me. On my next song, Buddy ran up to the drums and played his four-bar intro, but this time he played it at HALF the original tempo. Ding, ding-duh-ding, ding. Now, my spot was taking twenty minutes again because he was playing the song real slow. The show ended and I went up to his dressing room, ready to really have a fight with him. We were yelling and screaming at each other and the manager walked in again and said, "What are you doing? You're giving this kid twenty minutes AGAIN? This is the last time you'll ever play THIS theater!" Buddy threw him out of his dressing room and shut the door in his face. It was like a comedy scene.

While we were in Baltimore, Buddy found a water gun. During the show, he felt cute and started squirting a few of the guys onstage. He thought it was funny. After the show, everybody in the band went out and bought water guns too. I had mine in my pocket while I was playing my solos. We were playing my solo piece, "You Go to My Head" when Buddy turned around and zinged me with his water gun. Right in the middle of the show. I stopped playing, took out my gun, and started squirting right back at him. Then all the guys in the band started squirting their water guns, all onstage. It looked like Milt Britton's band.

For anybody who has never seen Milt Britton's band, it was all violins with a rhythm section. They were all good players. When they played, you'd notice one of the violin players quietly start to argue with another violin player. "Hey, what are you doing? That's the wrong note." The other one would say, "Mind your own business." Eight bars later, they're getting louder and all of a sudden one of them would stand up and whack the other guy in the head with his violin. Boom, and the violin would break. Then the other guy would whack him and break HIS violin. Then the whole band would get into it and whack each other over the head. They all had these breakaway violins. Tiny Kahn was playing drums with the band when I went to see them play.

My friend, Normie Faye, was also in the band playing trumpet, and while the whole violin section was whacking each other, Tiny would take his bass drum and put it through Normie's head. Well, that's what Buddy's band looked like with the water guns and the whole band running around the stage squirting them all over the place.

We were playing in Philadelphia at a place called the Click Club. The only bands that played there were the big name bands like Glenn Miller, Artie Shaw, Count Basie, Benny Goodman, and Duke Ellington; all the class bands. The owner of the club, Frank Palumbo, ran Philadelphia. This guy loved Buddy so much that he had us play his club. It was a Saturday afternoon and we were getting ready to play a matinee. I was standing next to Buddy when Frank came over, and like a real gentleman said, "Listen, Buddy. We're having a private party at the club with about three hundred old ladies. Have the guys play with mutes." That was the worst thing he could ever say. You may ASK Buddy to do something, but nobody ever TELLS Buddy what to do. When Buddy heard that you could see the horns coming out of his head. He said, "Look, you run your saloon and I'll run my band." Then, I knew we were in trouble. I don't think ten minutes went by before three goons walked over to us, flipped their jackets open and we saw that each one of them was carrying a gun. Very nicely, they said, "Mr. Rich, Mr. Palumbo would like to have you and your band out of town in a half-hour." I didn't even wait for the band boy. I packed up my own vibes myself. I think we were out of town in about twenty-six minutes.

Buddy drove a Cadillac, while the band went in a bus that traveled about fifteen miles an hour. It took us something like eighty hours to go two hundred miles to get to the next job. Buddy treated me like a star because he didn't want me to leave his band so he invited me to ride in his Cadillac with him. While we were riding, we started talking about music and the band and I said, "Buddy, have you ever smoked pot?" "No, I never did that," he said. I asked him if he'd like to try it. I think he must have tried it at one time but had not gotten into smoking it regularly. So I whipped out a joint and he took a few pokes. After a while, when he got into a good mood and was mellow, I said to him, "You know what? The guys in the band think that we're as good as Woody's band, and you're always yelling at them. Why don't you talk nice to them and let them know that we have a good band?" That night, Buddy got onstage and said, "Okay, gentlemen, let's have some fun. Let's play." Everybody was surprised, and the band swung that night.

The next night, we got back in the car, and by now, he was starting to like the feeling of getting high, so we smoked some pot again. He got really relaxed and once again, we started to talk about the band.

This time I said, "You know, everybody likes Johnny Mandel but you never let him play." Johnny didn't have good chops and he'd flub a lot of notes on the bass trumpet, but everything he played sounded like "The Shadow of Your Smile." Every chorus he played was an "Emily," it was all so beautiful; every note was a gem. That night, sure enough, Buddy pointed to Johnny and he played a solo.

The next night in the car, I told Buddy about Nick Sands, who was a favorite of the band and who played very good alto sax. Once again, that night, he let Nick Sands play.

On the fourth night, we were going through the Arizona desert. It was about four o'clock in the morning, and it was pitch black outside. Buddy was driving ninety miles an hour in his Cadillac. So here we go again, I got him high, and I started telling him, "You know, Buddy, the guys . . ." And he interrupted me, "Wait a minute!" And he stopped the car. "Listen! I don't want to hear your bullshit anymore! I'm getting tired of hearing all this from you. GET OUTTA THE CAR!" I think he realized that I was telling him what an asshole he was being. I said, "Whaddya mean, get out of the car? We're in the middle of the desert!" Buddy screamed, "I DON'T CARE! GET OUTTA THE CAR!" Now, normally, I'm afraid of a cockroach and I knew the desert was full of snakes, so now I was really scared. But I thought he was putting me on so I got out. Vroom! He drove away at ninety miles an hour.

For the next ten minutes, which seemed like an hour to me, I stood there on the road, waiting for him to come back and pick me up. By this time, I was hearing noises and jumping in the air. I must have jumped in the air thirty times in ten minutes. The wind was blowing the brush around and every time it hit me, I thought it was a snake. I didn't know if the bus was taking the same route that Buddy took. He never came back. I waited about an hour and a half and luckily, the bus finally showed up. By that time, I was a complete nervous idiot, jumping in the air at least seven hundred times because I kept hearing noises in the dark. The noises were probably all the tumbleweeds that were flying all over the place. But Buddy just left me there. The next time I saw him, I wanted to punch him out.

Buddy used to pick on all the guys in the band. Johnny Mandel played bass trumpet, and everything he played sounded like a very pretty melody. We thought our band was almost as good as Woody Herman's band, but Buddy treated the guys badly. He'd say things like, "You'd better not make a mistake or you're fired!" and scream at everybody, so the morale of the band was pretty low.

We were doing one-nighters at theaters where we would play six or seven shows a day. Buddy had been picking on some of the guys in the band and I was defending them, so Buddy and I went through a scene where he had me barred from the theater. This made no sense at all to me. I was wondering what he was going to do with my spot. I snuck in and heard Johnny Mandel play my solo on "You Go to My Head." Even though Johnny kept missing notes, whatever he played was just as good a song in itself as "You Go to My Head." In my opinion, Johnny was as melodic as anybody I'd heard other than Charlie Parker and Al Cohn.

In between shows, Stanley Kay and I were shooting pool at a poolroom next to the theater when Buddy walked in and started needling me. This was the first time in my life that I really lost my cool. I don't know what brought it to the boiling point, but all I know is that I got that burning feeling in my stomach. Normally, I would have thrown a punch, but I turned my cue stick around and swung the fat side of it at his head. Luckily, Stanley grabbed it before it hit Buddy's head. I'm sure part of Stanley's hand flew across the poolroom, I swung so hard. I was sick after doing that.

Because we only made fifteen dollars a night, what we did to save money was, two of us would check into one room in the hotel and then four of us would sneak up into the room. We would take the mattresses off the box spring and spread them out, and then the six of us would sleep on them.

Unfortunately, most of the guys in Buddy's band were hooked on hard drugs, mostly heroin and morphine. I'll never forget this one scene. We were on the road at some hotel, and I happened to be in the room with three of the guys who were strung out. They were all out of dope and had some connection fly in and bring them twenty caps of morphine and heroin. That's how they were sold those days, in capsules. After they scored, they stole about twenty more caps of dope from the connection. All of a sudden, the door opened and the connection ran in. He shut the door and pulled out a gun. Pointing to the right side of the room, he said, "You three get over there!" Then he pointed at me and told me to stand on the left side of the room. This all went down very fast. He called them all kinds of dirty names, "You dirty, so-and-so" and used every M-F word in the book. "I flew in and brought you all this shit, and then you STEAL my shit? Where is it?" All the time he was yelling, he was waving and pointing the gun in their faces. They said, "We don't have it." The connection, who had the look of a madman, said to the first guy, "Okay, I'm not going to kill you but on the count of three, if you don't tell me where it is, I'll shoot you in the leg." Then he pointed to the other guys, "Then I'll shoot YOU in the leg, and then I'll shoot you."

Now, normally, if it was just a guy who was going to beat them up, I might have jumped him. But a gun or a knife, forget it. I just stood there. After he said to the first guy, "Where's my shit?" and he counted, "ONE, TWO . . .!" He said it that fast. He didn't wait. There was no pause in that one sentence. Before he could get to three, the guys all said, "Wait a minute! Wait a minute!" They panicked. They all got in a little huddle. While the guy was waving his gun up and down, one of them went into the closet and took out the twenty caps they had stolen and gave them to him. The guy said, "Okay, get back over there against the wall." Then he went over to each one and whacked them in the head with the butt of his gun and left.

I didn't believe it. It was like a movie scene; everything went down so fast. After it was over, I think I was shaking more than the other guys. Luckily, we were off that night because I don't think any of us could have played. We were all too shook up to do anything that night.

When we worked at the Hollywood Palladium, Mel Tormé, who was a good friend of Buddy's, came in to hear the band. Mel loved to play the drums and he idolized Buddy. He tried to act like Buddy and would probably have given up all of his talent just to be able play drums like Buddy. Buddy used to have a habit of hitting me on the top of my arm, but he made sure that his knuckles weren't sticking out and hit me with the flat part of his hand. I always knew when it was him and got very bugged. I would turn around, ready to swing at him and say, "Buddy, don't do that" and we'd almost get into a fight. When I first met Mel, he saw Buddy do that to me. The next day, while waiting to go onstage at the Palladium, somebody hit me on my arm. I didn't know who it was but I knew it wasn't Buddy because whoever hit me did it with their knuckles sticking out. Now, coming from Brooklyn, which was a pretty rough place to grow up, if somebody hit me that way, I'd immediately turn around and without looking, throw a punch. That's just what I did. I turned around and swung. By the time I saw who it was, it was too late. Luckily, I recognized him as I swung. It was Mel Tormé. I couldn't stop my follow-through, but I was able to open my hand up so my fist didn't hit him, but I still slapped him halfway across the Hollywood Palladium floor. Needless to say, Mel never did that again.

I did two fifteen-minute movie shorts for Paramount, one with Buddy, and one later on with Woody Herman. What we would do is record all the music in a studio beforehand and then lip-synch (or in my case, vibe-synch) your solo to the movie. There was always a dancer, singer, or vocal group; fifteen minutes of music that would be shown in between the movie pictures. Will Cowan was the producer. We made the recording and they gave me an acetate of it. I went home and had to try and memorize my solo, which those days was impossible because I tried to play different solos every time. I could sing it, but I couldn't play it. What I did was memorize the time figures. I was playing all the wrong notes in the studio but nobody would be able to hear that. When Buddy's band played "Not So Quiet Please," he'd drum-synch the band part, but when it came time for his drum solo, he refused to do it on the movie part. He said he wanted to do it live on film. They told him he couldn't do it live because they didn't have recording equipment in the studio so Buddy and the producer had a big argument. Buddy kept insisting on doing it live and the producer told him that this wasn't a recording studio. Buddy got real nasty, and when he had to drum synch to the film, if the film showed him hitting a cymbal, he would hit a bass drum with his stick. And every time you saw him hitting the bass drum, he stood up and hit his cymbal. We were there for four hours making four hundred thousand takes and finally, believe it or not, they had to bring all kinds of equipment in so they could record him live. You might be thinking, "What an asshole Buddy was," but because of the way Buddy played, there was no way that he could have synched an eight or ten minute drum solo. He was all over the drums and it would never have looked right. If you ever get to see that movie short, you can tell the difference in the drum sound when Buddy plays with the band compared to the drum solo. For once, Buddy was right.

In 1970, I was going through a terrible divorce with my ex-wife Carol, and I wasn't getting to see my kids. My daughter Jerra was two years old and my son Gerry was six. Gerry was sort of a child prodigy on the drums. He'd listen to records of Buddy, who was his favorite drummer at that time. Later on, when he was seven or eight years old, he started buying and listening to Elvin Jones records. He was that talented.

Gerry was a little blonde-haired kid with blue eyes and I always wanted Buddy to hear him play the drums. Whenever Buddy came into town, I would try to get Buddy to meet Gerry. By court order, I had my kids for the weekend every other week. When Carol found out about my plan to have Gerry meet Buddy, she did everything to stop it. I'd go to wherever she was living to pick up Gerry and Jerra, and she'd always make up some story so that I couldn't take them. She'd say, "They can't go, they're sick" and shut the door right in my face. This happened two or three times.

A few weeks later, Buddy called me. He was working at Disneyland and said, "Terry, they had a cancellation on *The Tonight Show* Friday, and I'm going to be at NBC taping the show. Try and bring Gerry to the rehearsal." By coincidence, that was my weekend to see my kids. I didn't tell Carol where we were going, but once again, she made up some phony story. This time it was that Jerra was sick. There was nothing I could do about it without getting a marshal, so I picked up Gerry and we went to *The Tonight Show*.

When we got there, we found out that Buddy wasn't going to play the drums; he was going to sing a song called "Green" which he had recorded a while back. Eddie Shaughnessy, the drummer with *The Tonight Show* band, gave Gerry a pair of sticks and we went into Buddy's dressing room. Buddy had this real hip way of talking and said to Gerry, "Heyyy, your father tells me that you play the drums." All the time Buddy was talking to him, Gerry was staring at him; he was so in awe of him. He finally was getting a chance to meet his idol. Buddy put a chair in front of Gerry and said, "Play something for me." Having Gerry play on a chair was not going to show how he actually played the drums, but a chair it was. Gerry had great chops and if he tried to play something real fast to impress Buddy, that would have been the end of that meeting. But Gerry sat down and played a very simple "ding-ding-uh-ding ding-uh-ding ding-uh-ding" on the chair, just keeping time. That knocked Buddy out because kids didn't play that way. Especially in the sixties. Back then, rock and roll was the "in" thing and every young kid was trying to be the next great rock and roll drummer. Gerry played that figure like a grown up jazz drummer.

Buddy listened and then said, "Heyyy, that's pretty good. Do you know what four bars are?" Gerry was still staring at him with love, and Buddy was starting to get nervous. He never got that kind of love from anybody. Gerry said, "I think so" and Buddy said, "Can you play four bars of time and then four bars of a drum solo?" Once again Gerry said, "I think so." So he played "ding-ding-uh-ding-ding-uh-ding-ding-uh-ding" and then went into his four-bar drum solo. If he would have played four million flashy things, which had nothing to do with playing time, Buddy would have said, "Nice, kid," patted him on his head, and sent him home. But Gerry played four bars of "splank-a-dank, splank-a-dank, splank-a-dank, splank-a-dank." He played like a dancer danced.

That knocked Buddy out. He called his band boy over, a guy called The Whale. "Hey Whale, get me some sticks!" He went and got them and now Buddy and Gerry were sitting opposite each other, playing four bars each. All this time, Gerry was staring him right in the eye. Buddy was trying to play all these syncopated figures to hang Gerry up, and Gerry was just going straight ahead, looking him in the eye and playing sensible four-bar solos. Buddy was now falling in love with Gerry.

When they finished playing, Buddy said, "That was very good, kid. Listen, Christmastime is coming, and I want to buy you something. What can I get you?" Gerry stared at him and said, "I'd like to have your drums." All of a sudden, the horns came out of Buddy's head. He forgot he was talking to a six-year-old kid and yelled, "WHAT? MY DRUMS? I CAN GET A MILLION DOLLARS FOR THOSE DRUMS, ARE YOU KIDDING?"

Then he realized that he was talking to a six-year-old kid and once again asked Gerry, "What can I get you for Christmas?" Gerry said it again: "I'd like to have your drums." What was strange to me was that I owned a music store called the Music Stop and had all kinds of drums in the store. I guess he just wanted Buddy's drums. Buddy looked at Gerry, looked at me, and said, "We close tomorrow night, come pick up the drums."

The next night my friend Berrel and I went to Disneyland to hear Buddy play. When the last show was over, the Whale and Berrel packed up the drums and put them in my station wagon and I took them home. I'll never forget what Buddy did by giving Gerry his drums.

Years later, I conducted a telethon in New York that Steve Allen was hosting. Those days, telethons weren't produced like the Jerry Lewis telethon where you rehearsed all week for that one show. We'd have about a four-hour rehearsal for the twenty-four-hour show, and if any new acts were brought in while we were doing the show, the librarian would collect the music, and just hand it out to the band while Steve would be talking to a guest. You'd have to sight-read the music right onstage. Now they have people who take donations on phones in completely different buildings, but then, there were people onstage taking pledges. The calls came right to the stage and they would show that on television. They thought that looked kind of good, people onstage getting phone calls and picking up pledges.

It was always very noisy onstage. Conducting a telethon in New York was much harder than the ones I conducted in California. Most of the talent came from Broadway shows. They never would bring any of the famous songs from the show; they'd bring the most obscure tune that nobody ever heard before. The music would be all marked up and you wouldn't know where you were half the time.

I had Paul Smith playing piano for me on the telethon. He's the best accompanist I ever worked with. If I was conducting a piece of music that was so marked up and it confused the band, I would cue everybody out and point to Paul. He would take over and accompany whoever was performing. Then I'd look for a letter or bar number and cue the band back in so that we'd always have a big ending.

Buddy was a guest on the telethon. After he played his first song with the band, I was ready to tap off the next one, when Steve went over to the mike and started to tell the story about Buddy giving Gerry his drums. He knew that story because I was working for Steve at the time that I was going through that whole mess with Carol. Steve started to tell the story and then he said, "Why am I telling this story? Terry, come here, you tell it." There was so much noise on the stage that Buddy couldn't hear Steve start to tell the story. There were no monitors onstage for anybody to hear anything except the piano, bass, and the regular drummer, who all wore headsets. I knew that if Buddy heard me tell the story, he'd walk off the stage and go home. I don't think that he cared if anybody thought that he was a nice guy or not.

I started to tell the story, but I still wasn't sure if he could hear me, so I turned around to him and said, "Hey, Buddy!" He was way back at the drums. I said, "Come on down here." Buddy said, "Whaddya want?" I said, "I want to ask you a question. Come on down here! This is a telethon, we're trying to collect some money." He came down, looked at me, and in his wiseass style of talking he said, "What do you want?" I waited a second and then I grabbed him by the head and got him in a headlock. He thought I was crazy. He didn't know what I was doing. This was all happening while the camera was on us. I started to tell the story. When he heard this, he tried to wiggle out of the headlock. By the time I got about a minute into the story, he stopped fighting me so much. I held him in the headlock the whole time we were on camera while I told the story about him giving Gerry his drums.

When the Dream Band sessions first came out, I had copies of them on reel-to-reel tapes. I used to go to Las Vegas with my friend Berrel. We'd leave my house at ten o'clock at night and get to Las Vegas by two or three in the morning and hang out with Peggy Lee, Bobby Darin, and any other celebrities that I knew. We'd hang out with everybody all night and then check in at seven in the morning so we could get a room for the whole day for nothing.

One night I was hanging out with Buddy and I played my reel-to-reel tape for him in his room. He flipped out over it. He was so knocked out by it that after I took the reel off of the machine, he grabbed it out my hands. I said, "What are you doing? Give me back my tape!" He said, "Make another one for yourself." I said, "Forget it, give me back my tape!" Like two idiots, we started wrestling on the floor with my tape in Buddy's hand. He got on top of me and because of his knowledge of karate, he had me pinned down. He said, "I'll give it back if you promise to make me another tape." I didn't believe what was going on. I told him I would make him another tape, and he let me up. I ended up making him an acetate of the tape. It knocked me out he thought that much of the band.

Buddy wasn't the greatest when it came to complimenting other drummers. That just wasn't his bag. Buddy had a heart attack and was recuperating in Palm Springs. This was before the Dream Band records ever came out. Buddy and Shorty Rogers used to come over to my house and try to get me to release the Dream Band tapes. They'd say, "Let the world hear that band. That's the greatest band in the world." Buddy called me from Palm Springs and said, "I've got nothing to do down here. Why don't you make me a cassette of those tapes so I could have something to listen to." I did and gave the tape to Freddie Gruber and Freddie took it down to Palm Springs to Buddy. I wasn't working much but Buddy's band was hot at the time.

After about a week he called me and said, "I've got an idea. Those arrangements are great, and I'd like to record them. You put a band together, and I'll play drums. I don't care what you pick, but I want to play 'Don't Be That Way.' Make sure that's in there, and you can pick the other ten or eleven arrangements." I felt great about that whole thing.

Another week went by and Buddy called me again. "Listen, forget about doing that album. What the hell am I going to do that would be any better than what Mel Lewis did? Forget it." That was a left-handed compliment.

After the Dream Band albums came out, Buddy called me from Pittsburgh and said, "Terry, I want a copy of 'Day In, Day Out.'" I said, "Buddy, I don't give my arrangements to anybody." He said, "Yeah, but I have to have it, please send it to me. I'll make a copy immediately and send it back to you by FedEx." I never gave my arrangements to anybody, but he was so helpful by encouraging me to get the records out that I figured that I'd send him that one arrangement. I sent it FedEx and about four days later I got it back FedEx. He had it copied and sent me back my music. When I got it back, I checked the parts and saw that there was no vibes or drum part. I called Buddy in Pittsburgh and said, "Hey! I got the arrangement. Where's my vibes part?" He said, "Do I play the vibes?" I said, "No, but where's the drum part?" He said, "You know I can't read music!" and hung up on me. That was the end of that. I never got my parts back, and I had to memorize my vibes part by listening to the Dream Band record and rewrite the whole drum part from looking at the lead trumpet part.

Before he died, I came to him with an idea that I thought would really be great for him. I wanted to produce an album with him just playing snare drum and bass drum. Buddy was the greatest snare drummer that ever lived. That's all he really needed. On this album, he would have a guitar player and a bass player and play songs like "Cute" which had open spaces, and he'd play with brushes and sticks. He really thought it was a good idea and really wanted to do it. I think that every drummer, whether it's a rock and roll drummer or a polka drummer would have bought that record. It would have shown him off doing something nobody else could that do that good. He was one-of-a-kind, musically and personally.

In 1987, I was working in New York, and I got a call from Freddie Gruber in California who told me that Buddy had just been taken to the hospital in New York with a brain tumor. I immediately called Buddy to find out if I could do anything to help him. He told me that the doctors wanted to operate on him, but he wanted to go back to California and have the operation there. The doctors told him that he should be operated on now, but Buddy always called his own shots and wanted to go back to Los Angeles. I think he waited too long. I spent a lot of time visiting him in the hospital when I got back home. Freddie deserves a medal for what he did. Buddy and his wife were not getting along. She'd visit him at three o'clock in the afternoon and then wouldn't come back at all until the next day. At eight o'clock at night, nursing care wasn't very good. Buddy had a private room, and I think Frank Sinatra picked up the tab for it. Freddie would sleep on a small love seat in Buddy's room and made sure he got what he needed.

The first time I saw Buddy, I felt sick, for Buddy's left arm and left foot were like pieces of rubber. He couldn't move them. There was no way he could ever play again and he knew it. He used to make jokes about himself. He'd call himself "the crip." Buddy had a sister-in-law and a niece who were both very big in the business. One of them, Barbara Corday, had a very important position at Columbia Studios and the other one, Elaine Rich, was the producer of the *Dynasty* show. They knew that Buddy would never play the drums again and wanted to open a club for him. He used to say, "The crip is going to retire and have his own club." And every time he'd say something wiseass like that, he'd always cry.

He went through some really hard times in the hospital, but through all of this, his sense of humor was always there. They were going to give him some anesthesia and they asked him if he was allergic to anything. Buddy said, "Yeah, country and western music."

Buddy had a big ego. He knew he was the greatest drummer in the world. I was in the room the day after they operated on him. He had bandages all over his head. Eileen Barton, the singer who sang "If I Knew You Were Coming, I'd Have Baked a Cake" was in the room with me. It was about ten o'clock at night. The nurse came in to give him some pills. She said, "Mr. Rich, you have to take these pills." And she put the pills in his mouth, and he said, "Bleh! What the hell is this?" She said, "Mr. Rich, this is to make the swelling in your head go down." He opened his eyes and said, "What? Buddy Rich with a swelled head?" and then he started to cry.

Ray Brown and I were with Buddy the night before he died. The custom in the Jewish religion is that you have the funeral a day or so after you die. Buddy's was held at the same cemetery where Marilyn Monroe is buried. It was a closed funeral, not open to the public. I got a call from Mel Tormé saying that it was Buddy's wish that Ray Brown, Sweets Edison, and I play at his funeral. Ray was out of town and we couldn't find Sweets anywhere, so Mel said, "You have to play, Terry." I told him I couldn't play at Buddy's funeral. "That's going to be the hardest thing in the world for me to do." He said, "Terry, you HAVE to play."

I called Al Viola, the guitarist, and Tom Warrington, who once played bass in Buddy's band, and we played the funeral. It was one of the most emotional things I ever went through in my life. To start with, the three of us were right near the casket. Jackie Cooper, who is a good friend of mine, was standing next to me, and both of us were crying like babies. Seated in the front row were Mel Tormé, Johnny Carson, Frank Sinatra, Artie Shaw, and Jerry Lewis. Each one of them said something about Buddy at the funeral.

Mel said a few things about his relationship with Buddy and then Johnny Carson, who loved to play drums, had everybody in tears because he really loved Buddy. Then Frank Sinatra got up and talked about how he and Buddy were always fighting when they were with Tommy Dorsey's band but that he loved Buddy no matter what. He said that after he joined the Dorsey band, Tommy said, "Now I've got TWO assholes in the band."

Then Artie Shaw spoke. Artie had a way of saying things that sounded like he was putting everybody else in the world down. Buddy's lying there in the casket, and Artie Shaw said, "I went to see Buddy's band some years ago and I told him, 'You know, you played loud bass drum when you played for me, and you play louder bass drum now.'" Then Robert Blake read a poem that Jack Jones wrote and just like a television cue, after his last line, I came in and played "My Buddy." I was shaking so much, that I had to hold my right hand with my left hand to keep it steady, just to play the first two notes.

After it was all over and everyone left, I stayed and played for about fifteen minutes. I figured that if there was any such thing as the supernatural, that I would be the last thing that Buddy Rich ever heard.

Chapter 7
Woody Herman and the Four Brothers Band

I quit Buddy's band in San Francisco. Four of us quit at the same time: trombonist Jackie Carmen, lead trumpet player Frank LaPinto, and Johnny Mandel. Johnny went to Los Angeles to work out his union card. The union rule was that you had to live in a city for six months before you were allowed to work there. So Jackie, Frank, and I went back to New York.

Jackie was the only one who had a car. I'm not sure what kind of a car it was, but none of us knew how to drive except Jackie, so we had to make that long trip from California back to New York with only one driver. We only had about eighty-four dollars among the three of us. Gasoline was pretty cheap in 1948, about nineteen or twenty-three cents a gallon. We drove a few hundred miles, and by the time we got to Elko, Nevada, we were already running out of money. So somebody got a bright idea and said, "You know what? We're in Nevada. Let's gamble, win some money, and make the trip back in comfort." Sure enough, like anybody else, we lost all our money in about twelve minutes.

Frank LaPinto called home and got his mother to wire him a hundred dollars. Neither Jackie nor I could get any money so we had to make it with the hundred. We went out and bought about twenty dollars worth of cheese and salamis. We figured we'd ration it out and it would last for about five days. Being that Jackie was the only driver, he'd drive and sleep a little bit, then get up and drive some more. By the time we got to Pittsburgh, the car stunk real bad, and we still had to get to New York. After not sleeping for about six or seven days, we finally got to New York with our car really stinking from salami and that funky cheese. We got about one-quarter of the way through the Holland Tunnel when the radiator blew up. There we were, stuck in the tunnel. New Yorkers, who happen to be the rudest people in the world, were honking their horns, screaming and yelling at us and calling us all kinds of names. The three of us got out and pushed the car the rest of the way through the tunnel. When we finally got out, Frank went his way, and Jackie took his car to get it repaired. I took my suitcases, got on the subway, and got to my house about eleven o'clock in the morning, filthy and smelly, swearing that I would never go on the road again.

About a half-hour after I got home, the phone rang. It was Woody Herman. He asked me if I wanted to join his band in Chicago. I didn't believe it, for that was the band that every young musician would give anything to play with. I completely forgot about the tunnel, the salamis, the car, that dumb trip, everything. All I could think of were the musicians in that band: Stan Getz, Zoot Sims, Al Cohn, Serge Chaloff, Shorty Rogers, Earl Swope, Ernie Royal, Don Lamond, Chubby Jackson, and Ralph Burns and the great arrangements that he wrote. I almost had a heart attack at the prospect of joining that band. It was such a high for me to be offered that job because I looked up to every one of those guys. Here I was, scuffling with Buddy's band and before that with Chubby and Bill DeArango and now, here I was, being asked to play with what was considered to be the greatest band in the world. I didn't even ask how much the job paid. I was only making fifteen dollars a night playing with Buddy Rich's band working four nights a week, so how much less could Woody give me? And I would have taken it anyhow.

As soon as I hung up with Woody, I jumped in the shower, changed my clothes, and said hello and good-bye to my mother at the same time. She really didn't have the slightest idea what was going on, but I told her that I'd call her and explain later. "What?" she said, "Just hello and good-bye?" Then I went to the airport, got on the next plane to Chicago, and took off.

I joined the band at the Blue Note. It wasn't until later that I found out that it was Chubby Jackson who got me in the band. He had told Woody about me and without even hearing me, Woody hired me. About a week after I joined, Chubby also got Lou Levy in the band.

Woody Herman was without a doubt the greatest bandleader I ever worked for. He may not have been the greatest clarinet or alto player in the world but he sure knew what a band should sound like. I also think that he should have gotten a lot more recognition as a singer. He had his own unique style and sound.

Woody was so proud of that band that we hardly ever did one-nighters; we always played clubs. On one-nighters, they paid Woody about $1,500 for the whole band. In clubs, he got about $4,000 for the week, so you knew that he was losing a lot of money playing clubs. He was so proud of that band that he wanted people to hear it in major cities. We played the Blue Note in Chicago for a month, the Empire Room in Los Angeles for a month, and the Royal Roost in New York for a month. Everywhere the band played, every hip musician and celebrity would show up. They all thought that Woody had the greatest band in the world. When we went to New York, that was really big for me because that was my hometown.

I learned a lot from Woody. For example, Woody never started the first set with an opening song. He'd start with a closing song. By that I mean he'd start with something so fast, that swung so hard, that he'd win the audience over immediately. I loved that because I like excitement. We used to open up practically every night with "That's Right," a song written by Shorty Rogers. The version we played on the job was about six times faster than the record and it was all written around the vibes. The last bunch of notes was an F-scale going down two octaves, which I ad-libbed on the record date. It felt and sounded so right that I made it part of the arrangement and played it all the time. The hardest thing to play on the vibes is a C-scale because all the notes are straight in line and there's nothing to aim for. The next hardest are F and G because they have only one note to aim for: B-flat for the F-scale and F-sharp for the G-scale. I had a two-octave run to do on the F-scale. After ten hours of riding in a bus, trying to sleep crouched in a small seat, mostly resting on my arms, we'd have to run into the club and open up with "That's Right." It was like opening with "The Flight of the Bumble Bee."

I did my first recording session with Woody's band in December 1948. One of the songs we recorded was "Lemon Drop," which we had brought over from Chubby's little band. I don't think we had ever played it in a club before we recorded it. At the record date, just for laughs, I sang the scat chorus in my low Popeye voice and Woody said, "I've got an idea. Why don't we use that on the record? You sing eight bars of it at the end by yourself and then we'll repeat those eight bars with Chubby singing the high voice and Shorty the regular voice."

That song was such a hit that I got two raises from Woody. I was making 150 dollars a week, which was probably the lowest salary of anybody because I was the newest guy in the band. Most of the other guys were getting about 175 dollars. The highest paid was probably Ernie Royal, and later on, Bill Harris, who got between 250 dollars and 300 dollars a week. I knew a little bit about the business because of working with my father. One thing that I learned was that if you ask for a raise and you don't get it, you have to quit the band. Otherwise, you'll never get it. Unfortunately, it's almost like a game, but that's the gamble you take.

After "Lemon Drop" came out, we were getting requests to do it three and four times a night. It became a hit because my low voice was important to the song. So I went to Woody and asked him for a twenty-five dollar raise. I told him, "Woody, I'm starting to get popular because of the record. Charlie Ventura offered me 175 dollars a week." He said, "I'm sorry, I can't give it you, Terry." So I said, "Well, then, I gotta quit" and I gave him two weeks notice. Those were the hardest seven words I ever had to say in my life "I gotta give you two weeks notice," because that band was my life. I couldn't believe I was in the Woody Herman band and really didn't want to leave.

About five days went by and I really suffered for those five days. On the fifth day, Woody came to me and said, "Terry, I'm going to give you that twenty-five-dollar raise." I was never happier in my life, for the last thing I wanted to do was leave that band. About a month-and-a-half later, we were doing "Lemon Drop" seventeen times a night because people were running up to Woody and requesting it. Singing that song was hard on me because doing the low voice was a strain on my vocal chords. I was singing my fanny off doing "Lemon Drop." So I went to Woody again and said, "Listen, Woody, Charlie Ventura's office called me again and offered me 200 dollars a week to join his band [which really wasn't true]. I gotta have another twenty-five-dollar raise." The same thing happened. Woody said, "I can't give it to you, Terry" and I gave him my two weeks notice again. This time, I really was nervous about the game I was playing, for I really didn't want to leave the band. He waited until about three days before the two weeks were up. Finally, he asked me if I could get out of that job with Charlie Ventura. I said, "I don't know. Let me check." Woody said, "Well, if you can, I'd like you to stay." I told him I would talk to Charlie's manager and give him an answer that night. If I had said yes right then, he would have known that I was full of crap so I waited until that night. I could hardly wait to tell him. So I told him I would stay and got my second twenty-five-dollar raise. The big drag was that I didn't get the raise because of my solos on "Early Autumn" or "That's Right" or anything else that I played. I got it because of the dumb eight bars I sang on "Lemon Drop."

A few years after I left Woody's band, Capitol Records had about four unreleased sides left from that session but they didn't know who was in the band. So they found the withholding slips from the record date and put all those names on the back cover of the album. When it came out, one trumpet player was listed as Milton Rojonsky. That was Shorty Rogers' real name. Then there was Robert Chudnick, who was Red Rodney, Burton Swartz, who was Buddy Savitt, and Julius Gubenko, who was me. When the record came out, it was reviewed by a critic in San Francisco, who loved the album and said, "The vibes player, Julius Gubenko is great, but he copies Terry Gibbs." I wrote him a letter and told him that he was wrong, Terry Gibbs copied Julius Gubenko.

The most amazing thing about Woody's band was that even though Woody had all those great soloists, it was still an ensemble band. If you listen to all the records, you'll hear this. It was such a great ensemble band that a lot of the soloists really didn't get enough time to show how great they could play. I got to play more than a lot of the guys in the band. I played two or three choruses on a lot of songs, and was always featured on a solo piece, but usually it was sixteen bars here, eight bars there.

Nobody in a big band gets a chance to show how good he or she can really play. You play the same tunes every night and if you get two choruses, you're lucky. Woody used to let a guy stretch out and play two, three, or four choruses sometimes, but that was about it. We'd play "Apple Honey," "Northwest Passage," and "Caldonia," which all have the same chord changes as "I Got Rhythm." Each might have been in a different key but they all had the same chord changes, so you're really playing the same song all the time. You couldn't judge what a guy could really do unless you could catch him jamming in some club.

I think Woody gave me a lot of solos because I didn't have to play in a section like the brass or the saxophone players. Plus, I was probably the most commercial looking player in the band because of the instrument I played. It was very visual, sort of like watching a drummer because when I played, I was always moving. Most people don't really understand what a jazz soloist is playing, but they see me moving around and playing fast, and I suppose it's very entertaining to them.

Another reason was the other guys' personalities were not the greatest. They were half-zonked most of the time. They were either juiced or stoned out. Chubby and I were the two liveliest looking guys on the bandstand. We were always laughing and having fun.

I think another reason why Woody let me play more than anybody else is that I was one of the few sober guys in the band who could stand up. The unfortunate thing about Woody's band was that there were a lot of guys fooling with narcotics and some of the ones who weren't were drinking a lot. I can talk about that now because most everybody is gone. As I write this there are only three of us left: Chubby Jackson, Don Lamond, and myself. A lot of guys in that band were very sick.

Woody's saxophone section was something else. He put up with guys who were hard core junkies. All of the "Four Brothers" were on junk. That's what the saxophone section was called, because of the song that Jimmy Giuffre wrote. Most of the arrangements were written around three tenors and baritone, rather than the usual two altos, two tenors, and baritone. Woody's Second Herd became known as The Four Brothers Band. The saxophone section had Stan Getz, Zoot Sims, and Al Cohn on tenors, Serge Chaloff on baritone, and Sam Marowitz on alto. We mostly used the five saxes when we played ensemble shout choruses, because it would fill up the sound of the band. When the band played "Four Brothers," after the melody, every saxophone player got to play sixteen bars each. So what you saw would be one head up while he was soloing and three heads down, nodding. Then the one head that was up went down and the one that was soloing went up. Up and down, up and down, up and down. It was terrible to see that. You'd look at that section and you'd see Sam Marowitz, smiling in the middle, and the other four guys looking like they were ready to go to sleep. It must have looked strange to the audience to see that without knowing what was happening. Unfortunately Stan, Zoot, Al, and Serge were all stoned out.

Lou Levy and I were roommates and were very close. In fact, after ten months of rooming together, I married my first wife, Donna, and Lou felt lost and had nowhere to go. So he moved in with Donna and me. What was funny about that situation was that when we had double beds, everything was cool. But when we had one bed, I'd have to sleep in the middle. You can only do those things when you're young.

When I first met Donna, I was working with Buddy Rich. Donna wasn't Jewish and when you came from a religious Jewish family like I did, if you married out of the religion, it was like you were dead to them. That was the old-fashioned style of thinking. Donna was really great because she said that she would go through a *mikvah*, which would make her Jewish.

Woody's band was working in San Francisco, and I went to Los Angeles to get married. I didn't know anybody in town so we hired a strange rabbi and now had to get nine witnesses, which is called a *minyan*. We hired nine strange old Jews who came because of the wine and the cake. The only people we knew in town were two hookers and a pimp. The two hookers were putting the old Jews on and they thought that not only were they getting wine and cake, but maybe they would get lucky too.

Donna and I had a cat, but you couldn't bring cats or any animals into hotels. It was wintertime and back then, the hotels all had elevator operators who would drive the elevator manually by turning a wheel.

Since there were no buttons to press, the wheel made the elevator go up and down. After we checked in, as many of us as could fit got on the elevator, maybe about nine or ten guys. Donna was hiding the cat under her coat. The guys, all stoned out, had their heads down waiting for the elevator to move. The elevator went so slow that it seemed like it went about an eighth of a mile every four hours. All of a sudden, the cat went "meow." The moment it did that everybody woke up and made all kinds of wild animal sounds. "Woof-woof! Bow-wow! Woo-woo!" just so the elevator operator wouldn't know that we had a cat. You never saw a more confused looking person in your life. He probably thought we were a bunch of nuts. Then when the doors opened and we got out, the guys probably lowered their heads again. I would have loved to see the look on the poor elevator operator's face. He was completely confused over this whole scene.

Not everybody in the band was out of it all the time. In the trumpet section, Ernie Royal was straight. Bernie Glow fooled with junk for about two years, but later straightened himself out and became one of the greatest lead trumpet players in New York. Stan Fishelson was straight. I don't remember much about Marky Markowitz because he wasn't there long and then Red Rodney came in, and Red was also screwed up. Shorty Rogers, unfortunately at that time was chipping. Chipping means that he wouldn't do it all the time, maybe once or twice a week, which was bad enough, but later on, Shorty stopped altogether also. Shorty was such a beautiful guy that if he was in the room and somebody offered him some dope, he couldn't say no. But I don't think anyone offered anything to him or anybody else. All the guys who were junkies bought their own dope and would hide it from the rest of the band. They didn't want to split it with anybody.

In the trombone section, Bill Harris never fooled with junk, but unfortunately, he drank a lot. Earl Swope was a junkie. I don't remember much about Ollie Wilson and Bob Swift but I do remember that Ollie was a great lead trombone player and that Bob Swift was a good jazz player. Sam Marowitz just smiled a lot. He didn't even drink.

In the rhythm section, Don Lamond was an alcoholic, and he still belongs to AA now, but he's been straight for years. Lou Levy was a junkie then. Chubby Jackson, nothing. If he smoked some pot, it was a big deal. He never got into any hard drugs at all. Chubby was really needed in that band because of the spirit that he added. Most of the guys were stoned out of their bird and didn't want to hear him cheer them on. I got the feeling that they thought you were being commercial when you looked like you were having fun. I think that inside they were thrilled when Chubby would yell, "Go get 'em!" or whatever. It made everybody feel good.

Chapter 7

After about four months, Chubby quit the band because he said he was fed up with the music business and all the screwed-up musicians in it. It wasn't just Woody's band that was fooling with hard drugs. That seemed to be the fad those days; get stoned and play jazz. Chubby swore that he'd never play music again, and if he did play, he'd either start a Lawrence Welk-style band or play with that kind of band because the musicians in those bands probably never got stoned and took care of business.

Two months after Chubby left, we were still on the road. When we finally got back to New York, everybody we bumped into asked us, "Have you heard Chubby's band?" I didn't know what they were talking about because Chubby said that he would never play music again. Somebody told me that he was at the Royal Roost so I went down there and got the shock of my life. Chubby had one of the swingingest bands I ever heard. Tiny Kahn was playing drums and writing for the band and the soloists and ensemble work were great. The weirdest thing was that Chubby said that he was tired of the music business and all the screwed-up musicians and half of the guys in his band were junkies. You figure that one out. Unfortunately, they only recorded four arrangements, which are collectors' items today.

From what I've seen about people getting on dope, there's the physical thing, which they can't handle because of the pain, and then there's the mental thing. When you're stoned, you start to believe that you can play better. The reason you think you're playing better is because you're physically okay and that's because you just shot up and there's no pain. When Red Rodney worked for Charlie Parker, Bird threatened to fire Red about twenty times because he was going to try junk. He didn't want anybody else getting on it. In other words, "I can do it, but you can't." Indirectly, I think that Bird screwed up more musicians because he played so great, that they thought that dope would make them play like him. Forget it. There was only one Charlie Parker.

I remember when I actually thought that these guys were criminals. I was really hard on them. I didn't realize that they were sick people until I worked with them and lived with them. I had just come from the Buddy Rich band, which was nine-tenths full of junkies, and when I got to Woody's band, I could tell who was stoned and who wasn't. I could tell by their eyes and the way that they talked to me. Some of the guys would get stoned before the job and some would wait until the job was over and then get stoned. These were really sick guys and I really felt bad for them.

I think the band's reputation preceded them enough so that in any town we went to, they knew somebody who knew somebody who could get them something. Back then, if you got caught with half a joint of marijuana, you went to jail for six years. Can you imagine what they'd do to you if they found hard drugs on you? Our country has always been screwed up that way. I remember years ago that in England, a guy hooked on junk could go up to a policeman and say, "Look, I'm really screwed up, I'm on dope and I can't get any, and I'm really sick." The policeman would take him right to the hospital. In our country, if you told a policeman you were sick because you were on dope, he'd beat the crap out of you and take you right to jail. I always thought that was terrible because these were sick people. These weren't criminals, they were just sick.

People used to think that smoking marijuana led to other things like cocaine and heroin. The reason I think people thought that was because you might not get the high from marijuana that you thought you'd get, so you'd try another drug that would make you higher. I really never thought that smoking pot was ever a big deal. Pot really didn't affect me in any bad way. I suppose there were certain people who couldn't handle it. It probably made them a little schizo. I'll bet there are people you respect, whether it is in politics or anywhere who have all smoked pot in their day. When you first start smoking pot, you get what they call "virgin kicks." That means laughing a lot, sometimes not even at funny things, always wanting to *nosh* (eat), and getting tired. You also get the feeling that it makes you more creative in whatever you're doing, especially when you're improvising jazz. I never thought that you should go to jail for years for using pot, but without a doubt, you should go to jail for selling pot or any other narcotic to minors. You'll hardly ever see two guys on pot get into a fight. But you can walk into a bar and see two guys drinking, and if they are heavy into some discussion, out of the clear blue sky, they are liable to get up and want to fight and try to beat the heck out of each other. Liquor can do that to you but I don't think that pot does.

I'll tell you what I think happens when people get on drugs. When you've been on it long enough, you don't get high anymore. You take it to feel normal. There are reasons why I never got into hard drugs of any kind. First of all, I like to laugh. When I saw these guys get stoned, they never laughed. Secondly, if I ever caught a cold and had to go to my doctor to get a shot of penicillin, he had to catch me first. I'm deathly afraid of needles. I'm not afraid of a guy six-foot-ten; I'll fight him if I have to. But I am afraid of a gun, a knife, and a needle. I have no use for a gun or a knife, but once in a while, if I have to get a shot, the doctor has to catch me first. Actually, when I saw guys shooting up, it really made me kind of nauseous, so I tried not to be around when they did it.

Drugs never hurt the performance of the Woody Herman band. These guys were such great players that it didn't make them play any better when they were stoned, because they'd play the same way if they were sober. It would have hurt them more if they couldn't get drugs when they needed it, especially when they were feeling physically sick, but not when they were stoned. When they were stoned, they were normal, but it didn't make them play any better.

Woody knew exactly what was going on. Woody was a big drinker, not onstage, but after the job was over. He put up with the drug thing because if you took one guy out of that band and replaced him with somebody else, that band would have sounded completely different. They were made for each other and Woody knew that. Later on, when Zoot got fired, that's what happened. We brought in a great player, Jimmy Giuffre. Then when Stan Getz quit, we got Gene Ammons, also a great player, but the whole sound had changed.

Before Lou Levy joined the band, Ralph Burns was our piano player and arranger. Ralph wrote "Early Autumn," which came out of a suite called "Summer Sequence." After that, Shorty Rogers became the chief arranger. We still did the great old Neal Hefti arrangements of "Caldonia" and "Apple Honey" that the First Herd did, but Woody tried to do all new things with this band because this was more of a bebop band than the First Herd was. The First Herd was more of a Count Basie style band, but they started getting into bebop a little because of Neal Hefti and Pete Candoli. Neal and Pete were both bebop players and they tried to get everybody to fall in with that style of playing. A lot of the head arrangements they played were based on chord changes of songs like "I Got Rhythm" and the blues. Neal wrote a few things later on for Woody, but Shorty and Ralph were the main arrangers when I was there.

When we recorded "Early Autumn," we must have done about eight takes. Stan Getz and I both thought that we played pretty good solos on take four but after the eighth take, Woody said, "That's a wrap. We'll use take two." Stan and I weren't too happy with that because we liked take four better. We went to Woody's room later that night and told him, "Woody, you know what? We liked take four better because we played better solos." Woody said, "Yeah, but the whole band sounded better on take two." We said, "Yeah, but we played the solos and we liked how we sounded on take four." By this time, Woody had had enough of us and said, "Get out of here, we're using take two" and he threw us out of his room. Stan and I were bugged. We didn't talk to Woody for two or three days after that. The record came out and became a hit. The next year, Stan and I both won the *Down Beat* poll. If

Woody had listened to us, I probably would still be looking for a job. Woody knew what he was doing.

When the *Down Beat* poll came out the next year, both Stan and I were already out of the band. One thing about that award and others that I won; I knew they were just popularity polls. God gave me the greatest gift in the world; to know when I was playing good or when I was playing bad. A good player never sounds bad to an audience but sometimes you feel like you're not really playing anything that you never heard yourself play before. I knew that when I won the *Down Beat* award that I would have to be an ego idiot to think that I was better than Lionel Hampton, Milt Jackson, Red Norvo, or whoever else was behind me on the list. All you had to do was buy the magazine, clip out the ballot, and vote for whoever you liked. My butcher could have bought five magazines and voted for me five times.

Teddy Charles, the great vibes player in the fifties, once bought five *Down Beat* magazines and voted for himself in every category: best vibes player, best trumpet player, best female vocalist, best vocal group, and best on every other instrument. He got five votes in every category.

I was the most popular vibes player in the early fifties. I won all the polls for about five or six years, but then the Modern Jazz Quartet got hot and Milt Jackson became the most popular vibist. Then after him, Gary Burton. It was only a popularity poll and I realized it. The good thing about it was that it got me more work because *Down Beat* and *Metronome* were very big jazz magazines. The nice thing about the *Down Beat* award is that you got a plaque when you won. With *Metronome*, no plaque. All the winners got to make a record together. When you got to the date, everyone would look at the other winners and think, "Why did HE win?" Everyone wanted somebody else to win, so before anything ever got started, it was already a drag, really strained up.

Mary Ann McCall was the band's singer, and she was about as bad as any of the guys and a bit of a juicie. I'll never forget the time when we were leaving town one night. It had to be just about the time of day when it was getting dark and all the stores were closed. I was standing in the front of the bus, looking out the front window, and standing in front of Woody's car were Woody, Mary Ann, and Walt Yoder. In Woody's early years, Walt played bass, but now he was the manager of the band. In fact, he played in the Four Brothers band when it first got started. Anyhow, the three of them were really juiced and having an argument about who was going to drive Woody's car. None of them should have been driving anyhow because they were really out of it, but finally they let Mary Ann drive. If you have ever seen an accident in the making, that was it. The car was parked against the curb when I heard it start up. All of a sudden I saw it turn right instead of left. Right over the curb and through a barbershop window. I don't remember how we got out of that but I do remember sitting in the bus for hours before we left town. Need I tell you that Mary Ann never drove Woody's car again, juiced, or sober.

As bad as Mary Ann's driving was, that's how good her singing was. Mary was known as a singer's singer, and by that I mean that all the young and old singers, famous and non-famous, were Mary's biggest fans. She came from the Billie Holiday school of singing. She was really a great singer but she had to perform what the music in the band called for and really couldn't be herself until she went out on her own. She did record a song called "Detour Ahead" with Woody's band that became a bit of a hit for her.

Most of the time I got along with everybody in the band. I once saved Red Rodney from getting beat up. Red had gotten into an argument with me and one of the guys in the band, a real strong guy (I can't remember who it was), but it got to the point where the argument was going to turn into a fistfight right in the bus. Somebody said, "Stop the bus!" and Red and the other guy were going to get out and fight out by the side of the road. Everybody said "Red, don't go, you'll get hurt." Finally I said, "I'll go out and fight Red." Red was a little guy and didn't know how to fight. In fact, he was more afraid of me than anybody else in the band. So I took Red out, and because I knew he didn't know how to fight, I faked a left hook and he didn't know what to do. He tried to block it, took a swing, and swung so hard that he fell down. I picked him up and we got back on the bus. Red Rodney wasn't a fighter; that wasn't his bag. Because I knew how to box, I just took the guy's place that was going to beat him up and didn't do anything. We just got our tempers cooled down.

I learned a lot from Woody. He knew what he wanted to hear when we got a new arrangement to play. Sometimes he would take the last chorus and make it the first chorus, then maybe add an interlude for jazz choruses. He would change things around. He knew what to do with an arrangement and knew what a band should sound like. Throughout his whole career, there has never been a bad Woody Herman band. I think that the first and second Herds were the greatest bands he ever had. I liked the Second Herd better and not just because I was in that band. I just think we had more good soloists than the First Herd had. The First Herd, which was also a great ensemble band, had great soloists like Flip Phillips and Bill Harris. Bill was in both bands. In the trumpets they had Pete Candoli, Sonny Berman, and a few other good soloists. But we had Stan, Al, Zoot, Earl Swope, Lou Levy, Red

Rodney, Shorty Rogers, and Bill Harris. We were loaded with great soloists.

Also, the band was powerful. Chubby called it the "charge-through-the-brick-wall" kind of jazz. We were playing for Woody and what Woody wanted was excitement.

I'll tell you how important Woody was to the band. Sometimes he'd go home before the last two tunes were played, and after that, we didn't sound the same. Even when he took off the whole last set, we'd call our own tunes and it just wouldn't be the same. He knew pacing and knew exactly who to choose for the solos. He knew when Zoot should play and when Stan should play. Stan got a lot more saxophone solos than anybody did because he was young, handsome, and thin. Not that Al Cohn and Zoot were ugly; it's just that Stan looked like a matinee idol. Also, Stan was the most commercial looking of all of them. But Zoot and Al were monsters on the saxophone also. Al really got better as time went on and he started writing some great charts for the band, including a solo piece he arranged for me on "Out of Nowhere." It's a shame we never recorded it, though you can probably find it on bootleg records of Woody's band.

We not only played clubs but we also played dances. We were playing in Maryville, Kansas, in this big barn, and it was raining outside. At that time we had two black guys in the band, Ernie Royal and Oscar Pettiford. There was this one big guy standing in front of the bandstand. He must have been around six-foot-five. As he stood there, drinking and staring at the band, suddenly he yelled out real loud, "All they got in this band is Jews, wops, niggers, and faggots!" And he kept saying it louder: "Jews, wops, niggers, and faggots!" When he said "faggots" he kept pointing to Serge Chaloff. Serge always looked so neat with his hair always combed nice. His underwear was ripped but his hair was always nice and combed and he was very far away from being a faggot.

Finally, the job ended, and we were waiting for the band boy to pack up. Nobody went outside because it was raining and all the guys were going into the different toilets, shooting up, or whatever they were doing. Somebody was playing the piano when all of a sudden we saw this bigot walk out of one of the bathrooms, this big six-foot-five ape, who probably had gotten so drunk that he had passed out. We saw him and he saw us and everything stopped. The talking, the packing, the piano playing. When he saw that there was nobody there but us and him, he looked like he was ready to panic. Then somebody yelled, "LET'S GET HIM!" We ran after him and chased him outside. We stopped at the door but he kept running. He ran outside into the fields in the rain. There were bushes that must have been eighteen feet high out there, and he ran right through them. He's probably still running today, he was so scared. Little did he know that even if we had caught up to him, we wouldn't have done anything to him anyhow.

Now a little about the guys in the band. I'll start with the trumpet section. Ernie Royal was a beautiful guy, and was one of the great high-note trumpet players who knew how to play in a section. As good a trumpet player as Maynard Ferguson was, and still is, Maynard could maybe stick out a little when he played. That's why when Shorty Rogers would write for a high-note trumpet player, Ernie played the part and blended in with the section. If we were playing a medley of ballads or if there were any requests from the audience, Woody would point to Ernie. Ernie knew every song in the world.

Ernie was the only black guy in the band for a time and although there weren't any racial problems in the band, there were plenty of problems in the world. Ernie had an advantage because he was very light-skinned and maybe a lot of people didn't realize he was black. When Oscar Pettiford and Gene Ammons joined the band, it was a little different for the black guys.

I'll never forget when we played this little town somewhere in the Midwest, and they didn't have a black hotel for Oscar and Gene to check into, and they had to sleep on the bus. That was one of the most degrading things that I've ever seen in my life. There was nothing we could do about it. The white musicians I knew never held any prejudices against black musicians, and that was a great feeling. We just wanted to play and play with the best players. In fact, I don't think I ever knew a white jazz musician who was ever prejudiced. I don't think any of us thought about black and white. If we were ever good enough and could afford to hire either Charlie Parker or Dizzy Gillespie, without a doubt, any one of us would have been honored to do so.

When we played the Royal Roost in New York City, which was a wide-open town, I don't think that the people who came to hear us play cared about race either. Same thing at the Blue Note in Chicago and the Empire Room in Los Angeles. They just wanted to hear some good music. The musicians in the band didn't think about it. The audience may have, but we didn't. We went straight ahead; screw them.

Some people have asked why there weren't more black musicians in Woody's band. Well you know the cliché: if it's not broke, don't fix it. You don't just change a winner by hiring Jews or Italians or blacks just to intermingle the ethnic groups. You hire the best players, and as I said before, all the guys in the Four Brothers band were meant for each other.

I've always been against any kind of prejudice. In fact, in my younger days, if I was facing one way and somebody in back of me said the word *wop* or *nigger* or *kike*, I would just turn around, hit him as hard as I could, and then run. Those things made me sick. All of the little groups I had after I left the Woody Herman band were integrated groups.

Red Rodney and I got along well because we got a chance to jam together a few times before we were with Woody. In Woody's band, if you had an arrangement that called for a real good bebop soloist, you'd give the solos to Red. Red was a monster. I did a terrible thing to him one time by accident. We were recording the song "That's Right," and as I said before, sometimes we'd record eight or ten takes before we got one that Woody liked. We kept playing it at different tempos until we got the right one. We were playing "fours," which means Red played four bars, then I would play four bars, and then Ernie Royal played four bars. Red kept playing the same thing on all eight takes. This stayed in my mind, so on one of the takes, I played his lick. Woody picked that take and Red got really bugged with me. He said, "You stole my lick!" I apologized and told him that those four bars that he kept playing over and over sounded so good and stayed in my head and it just came out by itself on that take.

Red was a very bright guy, although he was screwed up then, too. He was also the greatest liar in the world. When Red and Phil Urso, an ex-Hermanite who played very good tenor saxophone were in my band, both of them were fooling with junk. I didn't allow that in my band. If we were playing in Yugoslavia, it didn't matter where we were, if I caught you with junk or you were stoned on hard drugs, you were fired and you had to pay your own way home. Phil wasn't the brightest guy in the world. When Red couldn't score enough dope for him, he would rip him off and mix whatever dope he had with sugar, put it into little bags, and sell it to him. Phil could never understand why he didn't get high enough. My friend Epstein later said, "When Phil gets a good case of diabetes, he'll wonder where he got it from; he got it from Red Rodney selling him sugar."

Bernie Glow was one of the most unheralded lead trumpet players I ever knew. He played lead on "Early Autumn." He was also a funny guy to be around. I'm not sure how much junk he was into, but he wasn't into it as much as the saxophone players were. I knew he was chipping a lot, but then later on in his life he quit. I used to do a silly thing where I'd put my two fingers up on my forehead and wiggle them. It was my way of saying "god forbid" or "knock wood" to myself. Bernie would see me do that and it took him a long time to figure out why. So every time something would happen where you might say "God forbid" or "knock wood," he'd mimic me and put his two fingers up on his forehead and I'd say, "Not now, Bernie. It's the wrong time." He eventually did catch on to that dumb thing that I did.

Shorty Rogers and I were very close. We wrote a lot of songs together. I would usually write the song and then Shorty would write the arrangement. I always figured that the arranger was just as important as the songwriter was because after you play the melody, the arrangement becomes the most important thing. We wrote "T&S" and "Lollypop" together. Sometimes at about three or four o'clock in the morning, I would get an idea, call Shorty's room, and sing my melody to him over the phone while he wrote it down on paper. Then he'd write a release and we'd put both our names on it. We did that with "Lollypop" and "Last But Not Least," which Nat Cole recorded. Shorty loved the way I played and gave me a lot of solos on all the arrangements that he wrote.

Shorty talked so slow that it would take a half-hour for him to get a sentence in, and I talked so fast that whatever Shorty would take a half-hour to say, I could say in two minutes. There was a rumor going around that to save money, when Shorty would call his wife, after he talked to her for a few minutes, he'd give me a written copy of what else he wanted to say to her, which would usually take him fifteen minutes to say. I would then tell her that whole thing in two minutes.

The word *kvetch* fit Stan Fishelson. You didn't ask Stan "Is everything okay?" You'd ask "Is ANYTHING okay?" That's how you'd start out with Stan. He'd *kvetch* about anything, the room, the restaurant, the hotel. But Stan was a beautiful guy. He just liked to *kvetch*. Stan also was a lead trumpet player in the band and every time Woody picked out what Stan thought was a hard chart, he'd complain and then play the heck out of it. He was one of those guys that would never lie down on anything.

We had three trombone players when I joined the band: Earl Swope, Ollie Wilson, and Bob Swift. Earl was an unheralded trombone player who the whole band loved. He was such a great player and very lyrical.

After I arrived, a rumor started that Bill Harris was going to join the band. We were kind of bugged because we didn't know him too well. Bill had been in the First Herd and was an established jazz star. The only ones who knew Bill were Don Lamond and Chubby Jackson, who worked with him in the First Herd. We figured, uh-oh, Woody's starting to bring back some of the old guys and this would hurt the feeling that we had for each other. We were beboppers, and now Bill Harris would try to take over the trombone section. Bill was about six-foot-one and looked like a college professor. Little did we know that he was a complete idiot and that he fit right into the band. Not only did he never take a trombone solo away from Earl Swope; he would compliment Earl after they played fours with each other. They played real well together.

Bill always called me "The Kid." He used to do something that I really loved and he'd do it all the time, but mostly for me. If he was standing near a pole and I walked over to him and said, "Bill, what time does the next set start?" Bill would turn to the pole and start talking to it like it was a person: "Do you believe this kid? He's been with the band all this time and he doesn't know when the next set starts . . ." Then he'd pause like he was listening to the pole answer him and say, "Now, wait a minute, don't tell ME about that," and start having an argument with the pole. He'd even start wrestling with the pole. You had to see it to believe it; this big guy who looks like a professor, wrestling with a pole. A complete idiot.

We were playing at the Empire Room and some young kid came over to Bill and asked him for an autograph. Just as he was about to sign it, I went over to him and seriously asked, "Hey, Bill, what time does the next set start?" He stopped, turned to a chair that was near him and screamed, "How many times do I have to tell this guy . . ." and all the while, the kid was standing there with a pencil, waiting for an autograph. Bill kept arguing with the chair and suddenly grabbed the chair and fell on the floor, wrestling the chair. This poor kid was watching all of this, looking at Bill on the floor with the chair like he's some kind of lunatic. He looked like he was in shock. Bill finally gave the kid an autograph and the kid walked away looking stupefied. Bill would do that for me all the time.

Unfortunately, Bill Harris was a big drinker and at times he'd get a little too juiced. Woody was afraid he'd louse up the whole trombone section and the band too, so he purposely wouldn't give him any solos when he drank. After awhile, Bill started to catch on to this. I was featured on "What's New" which started with me playing the first two notes of the song after which the trombones would come in with a nice soft chord. Right at that moment, Bill stood up in front of the whole section and played his harmony part as loud as he could: "WHOOOOOOOW!" Bill could play louder than any trombonist alive; he could play louder than an entire section if he wanted to, and he did that on that one note. It scared me to death because I was facing the front and Bill was standing behind me. He did that to let Woody know that he knew what Woody was doing.

Earl Swope was a real nice guy and a real gentleman. Of all the guys in the band, if you looked at them and tried to figure out who was a junkie and who wasn't, you'd look at Earl and say, "Nah, not him, not him at all." He was just a clean-cut all-American looking guy. He once had a chance to play professional baseball with the Washington Senators. Strong, athletic type, and handsome; a really sweet guy.

Now, about the saxophone players. What a group they were. Sam Marowitz looked like a basset hound, with the sagging cheeks and eyes. He had that kind of face. Sam was the assistant conductor and straw boss for the band, but he didn't tell anybody how to play or anything. This was such a great band; they didn't need to be told anything. Shorty would write an arrangement and they'd play it through once and were ready to record. Sam was the only guy in the saxophone section who wasn't on junk. During some of the shows, Woody would let Sam conduct some of the acts.

We were working at a theater and after I finished playing my two solos, I went backstage. I was standing next to a young guy who started talking to me. Back then people didn't call homosexuals "gay," they called them "fags" or "faggots." Well, it sounded like he was hitting on me, so I went over to this girl named Lou who was a friend of some of the guys in the band and said, "Say, who is he?" She said, "Oh, he's a friend of mine, a big faggot. I think he probably wants to make it with you." I thought she was putting me on. When he finally did hit on me, I said, "Hey, I got no eyes. That's not my bag." For laughs, I said, "Listen, is there anybody else in the band that you want to make it with?" The guy thought a minute, and then said "I'll make it with Woody." So when Woody finished conducting and while somebody was being featured on a solo, which didn't require him being onstage, I called him over and said, "Hey, Woody. Come over here a second!" I leaned over to him and said, "Listen, Woody, this guy wants to make it with you." Woody just gave me a dumb look and said, "What are you talking about? Get outta here!" and went back onstage. Now I wanted to have some fun so I said to the gay guy, "Anybody else in the band you want to make it with?" He thought again, pointed to Sam Marowitz and seriously said, "I'll make it with anybody but him." Poor Sam. After the show, I told this to him and he said he felt terrible. Sam said, "I never would have made it with him, but I feel bad that he didn't want me."

Sam was also our instant fart artist. We'd tap him on his shoulder and say, "Sam?" and he'd let one go, just like that. Instantly. We were riding on the bus and noticed that there was this really foul smell in the bus. Somebody yelled, "SAM!" and Sam said, "What are you looking at me for? That wasn't me, I swear! I only fart when somebody taps me on my shoulder." We didn't believe him. "C'mon, Sam, it had to be you!" So we stopped the bus and we all got out. We waited until they aired out the bus and we all got back on again. We were all really bugged with Sam because we knew it had to be him. About a year later, Al Cohn told me that it was Mary Ann who had farted in the bus. He didn't want to say anything because he was going with her. And we had blamed Sam the whole time.

Stan Getz, Zoot Sims, and Al Cohn were three of the best tenor players that ever lived. I knew Al from my Brooklyn days. There really wasn't that much excitement with Al that I remember except that he always had some dumb jokes to tell you. Even when he was stoned he'd tell you something funny. Al always had an up attitude, even when he was out of it.

Zoot Sims got fired because he and Woody got into an argument, and Zoot spit on Woody. Woody didn't really want to fire him. He was hoping that he would apologize. So everyone went to Zoot and said, "Zoot, you don't want to break up this band. You're going to ruin everything. Please go to Woody and apologize," but Zoot just wouldn't do it.

Zoot did a funny thing when anyone would fall asleep on the bus. He'd walk over to whoever was sleeping, and put their light on. He always had a newspaper with him, so he'd tap the guy on the shoulder and wake him up. Whoever it was would say, "Wh...Wh...Whaddya want?" Zoot would show him a part of the newspaper and point to a word like "and" or "is" somewhere in the story, and then leave the newspaper with the guy and walk away. For ten minutes the guy would go nuts trying to figure out what he was supposed to be reading.

Stan Getz was only twenty-one when I joined the band. He was a handsome kid and he could play. He knew that horn inside and out. Woody featured him more than any of the other saxophone players. If he played with a quartet, he'd play songs in different keys. For instance, he'd play "Cherokee" in B instead of B-flat or he'd play "Pennies from Heaven" in the key of D instead of C. Plus, he memorized all of his parts in the Woody Herman library. Never opened up his book at all.

I always thought there was a little bit of coldness between Al and Zoot towards Stan. First of all, Stan got most of the solos, especially when it was on a ballad. I think that Al thought that Zoot played better than Stan did, and Zoot thought that Al could play better than Stan could. I think that in 1948, maybe both of them might have been right. But Stan kept progressing and eventually became the monster tenor player that he was. More than that, he became a virtuoso saxophone player. Not only did he become better technically, he got better harmonically. Once you put those two things together, where every note is a song, then you've really got it down. Stan Getz was a giant.

Stan once said that the perfect tenor saxophone player would have Al Cohn's notes, Zoot Sims' time, and his own sound and technique. He wasn't far off. Al was the most lyrical tenor player I ever heard. He was the George Gershwin of the tenor saxophone. Everything he ever played was a melody. Even though he KNEW chord changes, he never sounded like he was THINKING chord changes when he played. He played the blue notes, like in George Gershwin songs.

But when it came to fooling with junk, these guys were really screwed up. We had a week off before we opened at the Empire Room in Los Angeles, so Lou Levy and I rented a little house with a garage. Lou and I actually took Stan Getz into the garage and tied him to a cot and fed him every day because he was really trying to kick his habit. We kept him there for a whole week. By then he started to feel a lot better. When we opened at the Empire Room, he went back to making junk again.

Right after this happened, Ava Gardner came to see Woody's band at the Empire Room and instantly fell in love with Stan. She'd have Howard Duff, another movie actor, bring her in every night to see him. She was beautiful and famous and wanted him real bad, and Stan felt good about that. After we'd get done with a set, Stan would walk towards Ava and get to within five feet of her table. Then, out of the corner of his eye, he'd see his connection and like a flash, boom; he'd make a left turn, and then split. This went on for about five or six days where he did this. After being fluffed off every night, Ava finally called me over and asked me, "Terry, am I pretty?" I stammered and stuttered because she was the most gorgeous thing I ever saw in my life, and I said, "Y . . . Y . . . Yeah, of course!" And she said, "Well then, why does Stan Getz keep running away from me?" I couldn't tell her that his dope connection was more important than she was, so I made up some dumb story. But he would look out of the corner of his eye, see his connection and make a left turn, leaving Ava Gardner, the most beautiful woman in the world sitting there, trying to figure out why Stan kept fluffing her off. That's what dope will do to you.

Serge Chaloff, unfortunately, was the sickest of all of them. He was as big a junkie as Charlie Parker was. He would make what they called speedballs, which had one or two caps of heroin, one or two caps of morphine, and one or two caps of cocaine. He'd mix it all together and then shoot it. After Shelly Manne joined the band, we were playing Balboa Beach, and Shelly and I were walking along the beach after the job at about three or four o'clock in the morning, when we bumped into Serge. Serge had cut his finger and it was bleeding so badly that we rushed him to a hospital. There was a young intern on duty that apparently couldn't recognize a junkie when he saw one. The intern examined Serge and doctored up the cut as good as he could, but Serge was still very much in pain and told the doctor that he was hurting badly. The intern said, "All I can do is give you a little morphine to kill the pain." Serge heard the word morphine and tried not to look too anxious. He acted very hesitant and said, "I'm not sure about a needle going into my arm. It's probably going to hurt." He hemmed and hawed for a short while and then said, "Wellll, maybe you'd better." He acted like he'd never heard of morphine before in his life. So he got his morphine. The bad thing about all this was that any time we played in little towns and Serge got sick and couldn't score, he'd cut his finger and go to a hospital and get them to give him whatever narcotic they had to stop the pain. He was that sick.

I remember doing a theatre date where I was playing "You Go to My Head," the arrangement that Tiny Kahn wrote for me. I had played that arrangement with Buddy Rich and brought it into Woody's band. While I was playing my solo, I heard a weird sound behind me: "WOOOOOOAHHHH." I didn't know what had happened, but I had to keep playing so I finished the song. When I left the band and collected the parts, I discovered that there was no baritone part. Then I remembered that strange sound and put two and two together. Serge Chaloff had thrown up all over the music and then threw it away.

Serge was way ahead of all the other baritone players. He was one of the first baritone players to play bebop. Pepper Adams was probably the closest to his way of playing because he was also a hard player. Everything Serge did was hard; he shot speedballs, he stayed up late, carried on, and played hard too.

Lou Levy, Serge, and I were invited to an after-hours party. The three of us were sitting around a piano with a bunch of people. It was real late and Serge couldn't keep his head up. He kept nodding. Lou was wiped out too, but he was trying his best to stay awake. At the same time that Lou put his head down, Serge woke up. He looked around, saw Lou nodding and said, "Lou, wake up, they'll know!" Wake up, they'll know. He was stoned out for ten minutes and he's telling Lou "wake up, they'll know."

Serge was really out there. He was always stoned out. Outwardly, he always looked neat and clean. He dressed real nice, had his hair combed back, and spoke with that nice Boston accent. We were traveling to a job, and it was so hot in the bus that Serge, who was all strung out, started pacing up and down the aisle. Finally, he took all his clothes off except for his underwear, which was all torn up. With his shorts and undershirt all ripped up he looked like he was wearing a Tarzan outfit.

Serge was also a pretty intelligent guy. His mother had been a concert pianist and a famous teacher in Boston, so Serge was a well-schooled musician. He also played the piano fairly well. It was just a shame to see somebody that talented be that screwed up.

Chapter 7

We were doing a series of one-nighters in theaters where the band was the only attraction. We would do seven or eight shows a day, so we never could really check into a hotel. In between shows, we slept in the dressing rooms on the floor. Whoever got to the dressing room first got to sleep on the dressing room table they had in there. We couldn't even change our clothes, so we wore the same clothes all the time. This went on for a whole week where we couldn't change our underwear or socks; we couldn't even take a shower. Nothing. Finally, we checked into a hotel and Lou Levy and I were getting ready to go to whatever job we were playing, when there was a knock on the door. It was Serge. "Hey man, does anybody have a pair of socks they can lend me?" I said, "I don't have any," even though I did. I knew how funky he was and I didn't want to give him any of my clean socks. "Hey, Lou, do you have anything?" Lou said, "No, I don't have any either." Serge looked on the floor and saw a pair of socks that Lou had worn every day for a whole week. They were so beat up that they were standing up by themselves. Serge asked, "Whose socks are those?" Lou said that they were his. Then Serge said, "Can I wear them?" Lou said, "Serge, I've been wearing those for the whole week." Serge grabbed them and said, "Well, they're better than the ones I've been wearing." Serge had probably worn his own socks for three weeks.

When you checked into a hotel with Woody's band, the first thing you would do would be to make sure that if Serge was on the twelfth floor, you checked into a room on the third floor. You did that because Serge would always fall asleep with a cigarette in his hand and you had to make sure that if he started a fire, you could get out of the hotel as fast as possible. Sometimes he'd burn a hole in the mattress.

Serge had a very elegant way of speaking and was one of the best liars in the world. There were many times that I walked by his room and heard somebody telling him, "Listen, you burned a hole in the mattress, you're gonna have to pay for it." And Serge would always say "How DARE you, sir! I'm the winner of the *Down Beat* and *Metronome* polls. How DARE you sir . . ." And he'd how-DARE-you-sir until the guy wound up apologizing to HIM.

One time we got on an air pistol kick. We all bought air pistols and at night, everyone would open the windows of the bus and shoot at trees. We probably killed seventy-four cows because we didn't know what the hell we were doing. Nine-tenths of the time, Serge was asleep. When he checked into his room, he put a telephone book against the door, and with his air pistol, tried to hit the book. I think that out of twenty-four shots he probably hit the telephone book once. The other twenty-three shots ended up in the door and made a bunch of holes in it. Because I was a clothes freak, I always carried two suitcases with me. I remember going to Woody's tailor and spending a hundred dollars a suit. I could have bought a suit for sixteen dollars but I would buy five suits at a hundred dollars each. I saved all my money to buy clothes. I was getting ready to check out and was walking out the door with my two suitcases full of clothes, when I passed Serge's room. He saw me and said, "Terry, wait a second" and went back to "How DARE you, sir! I'm the winner of the *Down Beat* and *Metronome* poll . . ." Then the manager said, "I don't care who you are. You shot the door full of holes. You're going to have to pay for it. It's going to cost you twenty-four dollars!" Serge tried again: "How DARE you, sir!" The guy wouldn't go for it. "You give me twenty-four dollars or I'm calling the police right now!" Serge stopped how-DARING-you and said, "Okay, if I'm going to have to pay twenty-four dollars for the door, I want the door." Serge paid the twenty-four dollars, the guy unhinged the door and Serge and I walked out of the hotel carrying my two suitcases and a screwed-up door.

Serge hated the cat we had, and one time, he even tried to hide it from us. I used to say, "All right, Serge, what'd you do with the cat?" Serge said, "Man, don't be ridiculous, leave me alone." He'd say that all the time. "Man, don't be ridiculous." In fact, Shorty Rogers once wrote a solo piece for Serge called "Man, Don't Be Ridiculous." Donna, Serge, and I were all standing outside in front of the hotel, waiting for the bus, and it was raining. The cat suddenly jumped out of Donna's arms, ran across the street, and went under a parked car. Serge ran across the street in the rain, dodging cars, crawled underneath the car, and got the cat out. We didn't believe that he would do that. He went from hiding the cat and "Man, don't be ridiculous" to saving the cat's life.

We had a great rhythm section. Lou Levy joined the band about a week after I did. Lou was probably one of the best big band piano players ever. He knew how to play in a rhythm section with a big band and how to place little fill-ins when Don Lamond was just playing time. He knew how to comp for you, too, especially when you were playing a solo. Lou was really one of the giant bebop piano players. Of the other bebop piano players, Bud Powell was in a class of his own. The others were guys like Al Haig, Walter Bishop, Jr., and Hank Jones. Lou was in the same class as those guys.

Every big band is built around its drummer. Benny Goodman had Gene Krupa, Tommy Dorsey had Buddy Rich, and so on. The drummer is almost like the bandleader because he is really the most important musician in the band. Don Lamond was the perfect drummer for Woody's band. After he left, we had some great drummers follow him, but Don Lamond's style of drumming added to the success of the Four

Brothers band. Drummers usually made all the band figures, but Don Lamond had his own style of playing. Sometimes he wouldn't make the figures, he'd play the in-betweens of the figures, and when he dropped those bombs, it sounded like Fibber McGee and Molly's closet, with everything falling out.

After Don Lamond left to go with Harry James, we went through some great drummers: Tiny Kahn, Shadow Wilson, and J.C. Heard, but nobody sounded right with the band until Shelly Manne came in and kept time. Since we were beboppers, everybody thought that you had to play bebop drums with the band. You don't play that kind of drums with a big band. You keep time and you make the figures. You had to make sure that the band knows exactly where they are at all times so that they can all come in together. All sixteen guys have got to know where they are. Some of the drummers who auditioned for the band thought they could play little band style, but that didn't work. When Shelly Manne came in, he played the time and kept the band together.

A big band drummer has to what I call "sit on it." He can't play on top and he can't play behind, he just has to sit on it. In a little band, a drummer can give you that edge or fire to make up for not having all the brass and saxophones behind you. There weren't many guys who could play great in both settings.

Chubby Jackson was the cheerleader of the band. Every time the band was ready to play the last chorus, Chubby would be yelling and screaming, "WHOAAA, WHOOPEEE, YIPPEE! LET'S GET IT!" Believe it or not, even in that band, that would give us that extra little burst of energy to play even a little harder.

Chubby was always writing books or stories. It was always something as dumb as you can think of, but he made sense. Don Lamond, Serge, and I were driving to a job in Chubby's car. We sat in the front and Chubby was lying down in the back seat, smoking pot and writing these dumb things. He once wrote a book called "Free the Fart." He thought everybody should be able to fart any time they wanted to. We were in this little town and couldn't find where the job was. Serge, who was sober for a minute and was driving, asked, "How do we get there? Do I go left or right?" Chubby was lying down in the back of the car and he pointed and said, "Make a left turn." Serge said, "It says 'no left turn.'" Chubby said, "Make it anyhow." So we made a left turn. Sure enough, a cop pulled us over, looked inside the car and said, "Say, fella, did you know you just made an illegal left turn?" Serge said, "Yeah, I know." The cop said, "You do? Who told you to make a left turn?" Chubby was lying in the back and said, "I did." The cop looked in the back. "What do you mean, you did? Who the hell are you?" Chubby said, "I'm Chubby Jackson, the bass player with the Woody

Herman Band." The cop was impressed. "Oh, you guys are with the Woody Herman Band?" Woody Herman was big time in this little town. He didn't even detect the smell of pot in the car. Not only didn't he give us a ticket, he escorted us to the job.

When Oscar Pettiford was in the band, he always played a bass solo in the one-day theaters the band would play. One time he played about four or five bars of his solo, put his bass down, and ran off the stage. We didn't know what was going on. We thought that he had flipped out. When he came back, he had a cello, and played the rest of the solo on it. He could play the heck out of it, too. He played it so good he amazed all of us. He picked it just like he did the bass.

I loved listening to Oscar and Gene Ammons talk to each other when they were on the bus. They were beautiful. Oscar thought that Lucky Thompson was the greatest tenor player living. Lucky played in the Coleman Hawkins-Don Byas school of tenor playing but Gene was a Lester Young fan and thought that although Lucky was a good tenor player, he couldn't swing. Their conversations would always go something like this. Oscar would say, "Lucky Thompson is the best tenor player living!" And Gene would say, "But Doo-E Swing?" No matter what Oscar would say after that, Gene would always answer, "But Doo-E Swing?"

Woody also hired a few different arrangers. Johnny Mandel was not only a very good bass trumpet player, but I think he also started a different style of writing jazz arrangements; he didn't write riff after riff. His arrangement of "Not Really the Blues" went on like a suite. It just went on and on and hardly ever repeated any phrases. That was a style that Johnny started and later people like Bobby Brookmeyer and Bill Holman picked up on. Shorty Rogers' style of arranging made Woody's band sound the way it did, just like Neal Hefti's writing made the First Herd sound like they did. "That's Right," "Lemon Drop," and "Lollypop" were all big ones that Shorty arranged.

We did a movie short, and since black and white musicians couldn't be on camera together, after Ernie Royal recorded his trumpet solo, Al Porcino stood up and lip-synched Ernie's solo for the visual part. When it came time for Gene Ammons' solo, they brought in some white ringer tenor player to synch for him. Ernie and Gene weren't even allowed to sit in the band when we did the shoot. The dumbest thing of all was, the producer didn't like what Mary Ann McCall looked like, so when it came time for her to sing "Jamaica Rhumba," they brought in this pretty movie actress to lip-synch Mary's solo. We all got real bugged and Mary was really insulted when they brought her on the set. Actually, it wasn't bad for me because I wound up with the pretty actress for a while.

Chapter 7

We did a tour with Nat Cole. He was working with his trio at the time and after the job, we'd all sit around until everybody got packed up. This one night, I was sitting at the piano, noodling around, playing a few of my songs, when Nat came over and stood behind me looking over my shoulder. Finally he said, "What's that?" I said, "It's a new song I wrote called 'Peaches.'" He said, "That sounds good, let me hear it again." He sat down next to me, and I showed it to him. He picked it up immediately and then said, "I'd like to record that." I said great and then he said, "You got anything else?" I said, "Yeah, there's one more tune that Shorty Rogers and I just wrote called 'Last But Not Least.'" So I played that one for him too and he liked it and recorded both of the songs. Nat's trio records stopped getting airplay when he became a full-time singer. Years later, when Nat's daughter Natalie came out with that duet record of her and Nat singing "Unforgettable," they started re-releasing Nat Cole records. Suddenly, out of left field, I started getting royalty checks for those two songs. About a year later, George Shearing did a tribute album to Nat and recorded "Peaches" too.

I made Nat Cole an honorary Jew by calling him Nat Cohen. He loved it. He was such a gentleman and I was so proud of him because after 1948, he became an even bigger star because he started singing a lot more. Every time I played in a town where he was appearing, he'd come into the club where I was playing and sit in with me and play piano, which really made me feel good because I don't think he did that too often.

When we were on tour with Nat, we would close the show with "How High the Moon." Gene Ammons and the other tenor player, Buddy Savitt, would play four bars each, then the trombones would play four bars each, and then Nat and Lou Levy would play fours. One time, Lionel Hampton was in the audience. Nat brought him on stage to play with him. Lionel played one song with Nat and tore up the place. On "How High the Moon," Lionel and I had to play four bars each but I really didn't know Lionel that well. I was just a young kid and wanted to "cut him." That's what we'd say when we wanted to outdo somebody.

There are some musicians you should never try to cut and Lionel Hampton was, without a doubt, the champ of them all. If it meant wiping you out, Lionel would leap over four tom-toms and land on an A-flat. When Lionel and I had to play four bars each, I played first. I had all the technique in the world so in my first four bars, I must have played a million notes. All he did when it came time for his four bars was grunt, "Aaaaaaaaaayyyyyy" and hit one note. That made the audience start to scream which made me nervous, so on my next four bars I played TWO million notes. I was going to do him in. Once again

Lionel grunted, "Aaaaaaaayyyy," slobbering all over the vibes, hit that one note again, and got everybody screaming even louder. I got more nervous and went back to one million notes. Then I went down to one-hundred-eighty. Then fourteen notes. Finally, I looked at Woody. "GET ME OUTTA HERE!" Lionel was wiping me out. Lionel Hampton was the champ of cutting anybody.

There are some other musicians you never fooled with. Dizzy Gillespie was another one you never tried to cut. If you tried, he'd make some funny announcement and just keep fooling around until the audience would forget you were on the same bill with him. Plus, he could play better than anybody living anyhow and just wipe you out with his playing.

Oscar Peterson was another one. He had more technique than anybody did and if you fooled with him, he'd play everything he ever knew in two bars. If you played fast, he'd play slow. The moment you played something slow, forget it; he'd play something so fast in octaves that you had nowhere to go after that but outside to cry.

Of course without a doubt, you didn't ever fool with Buddy Rich because no drummer could do what he did. If you tried to do him in, he'd play everything you played with both hands and then play it with one hand and still wipe you out.

But the champ of all of them was still Lionel Hampton.

Years later, I was playing in Las Vegas at the Sands Hotel. It must have been around 1960 and Lionel was playing at the Flamingo. I went over to see him. When he saw me he said, "Heyyyyy, there's my man, Terry Gibbs!" He loved me; he really loved me. He thought I should have been recognized a lot more than I was. In fact, in one of the *Down Beat* magazine Blindfold Tests, he gave one of my records five stars and said that I should be given way more credit than I was being given. Anyway, he asked me to come up on the stage and sit in with him. I remembered when he had wiped me out back in 1948, and this time, when I got on stage, if he played one note, I would play one note. If he played two notes, I wouldn't play three notes, I would play two. I was not going to do anything to upset him and make him do that to me again.

Billie Holiday, who Lester Young named "Lady Day," was working at Billy Berg's, which was just down the street from the Empire Room where Woody's band was playing. She did two shows every night and after she was done, she'd always come out for our last set to hear Woody's band. One time she pointed at me and said, "Hey, Woody! Let that boy play something for me! Play 'Can't Get Started with You.'" Woody said okay and I played the song with just the rhythm section. After we finished, she pointed at me again and said,

"Hey boy, c'mere!" When I got over to her table, before I knew what was happening, she grabbed me, bent me over and gave me a big kiss, right on my lips and right in front of the whole audience. I was really embarrassed, but at the same time I was happy because she was so famous and so beautiful. I don't think that I washed my lips for three weeks.

I was very fortunate to work with Billie Holiday at the end of her career. I did a tour with her on the East Coast, about six one-nighters. Of course, I went on first and then she'd close the show. Just before she would go on, as they were introducing her, she would drink an entire pint of gin before she walked out on stage. Her voice wasn't all there, but she still had that little sad crackle in her voice and that was good enough for me. She didn't look good at all. She was sick. It was a shame to see her that way because I loved her so much.

The Woody Herman band had a baseball team, and Earl Swope and I were its two best players. Earl played third base and I played shortstop. We had the left side so well covered that you couldn't get a ball past us. I was also one of the best hitters on the team. Shelly Manne's wife, Flip, has a home movie of me hitting a triple in a ball game. When I joined the band, it was September, which was still baseball season. I was a shortstop and a very good one, but when Zoot Sims found out, he said, "Hey, wait! I'm the shortstop!" Chubby Jackson was the captain, so he held a tryout and said that whoever was better would get to be the regular shortstop. Well, to be perfectly honest, I wasn't just better than Zoot; I was twenty times better. I won the tryout and wound up playing shortstop. Zoot didn't talk to me for a while but later on we got along great.

Harry James' band also had a baseball team and they were very serious about it. Harry was a real baseball nut and when his team came out to play, they had uniforms, cleats on their shoes, baseball caps, the whole nine yards. We came out looking funky; we'd wear anything, even our band uniforms, because some of the guys slept in them half the time anyhow. We beat them in the first game, and they beat us in the second game. So before the rubber game, Harry told us that if we beat them in the third game, he and Betty Grable, his wife at the time, would throw a party for us at the Empire Room where we were playing. We got together the day before the game and Chubby got up and gave us a pep talk. He said, "Okay, fellas, listen. Let's all stay sober for the game tomorrow so we can beat them and have that party Harry and Betty promised to throw for us." Everyone said, "Yeah, great."

Stan Getz was the pitcher. When he pitched, and I'm not exaggerating about this, the ball would take a half-hour to get to the catcher. It went so slow that the batter would either knock it four miles away or he'd miss it entirely because he was so overanxious to hit the ball. Serge Chaloff was the catcher. Now they're warming up and Serge crouched down like a catcher does. Stan threw the ball and it took about a half-hour to get to Serge. When it finally hit his glove, Serge fell backwards. Fell completely over, stoned out of his bird. We were so bugged and this was only the warm-up. What would happen by the third inning? Well, we beat Harry James in that game and he and Betty Grable made a big party for the band at the Empire Room. Later on, Harry stole Don Lamond off of our band because he needed a drummer and a center fielder. You had to be a good baseball player in order to play in Harry James's band.

After Chubby left the band, Oscar Pettiford played left field for us. I saw Oscar break his arm in three places. What happened was that somebody on the other team got a base hit to left field. I was the shortstop, and when that happens, it's the shortstop's job to go out into shallow left field and get the relay from the left fielder. So I yelled to Oscar, "Throw it to me!" Shelly Manne was playing second base and also yelled to Oscar, "Throw it to me!" Earl Swope was playing third base and HE yelled "Throw it to me!" All three of us were yelling at the same time. Oscar tried to throw it to all three of us at the same time, twisted his arm, and broke it.

We played Les Brown's band and beat them two games in a row. When we got ready for the third game, we saw a guy warming up who we had never seen before so we went to Les and said, "Les, have you got a ringer on the team?" He said, "No, this guy's with the band, he's one of the copyists." First time at bat, this guy hit a home run over the left field fence. Second time at bat he went over the center field fence. Third time, the right field fence. I didn't find out until later from Irv Cottler, the drummer, who was with Les, that this guy was not only a ringer, he was a semi-pro baseball player. He hit four home runs off of us that day.

When Zoot got fired, he was the first one to go and Jimmy Giuffre came in and took his place. Then Stan Getz quit and to this day I don't know why. Gene Ammons came in to replace Stan. Then Al Cohn quit and Buddy Savitt came in. Then a bunch of us quit. Ernie Royal and I quit because of the new manager who came in named Abe Turchen. Abe was the guy that screwed Woody and stole all his money. Woody eventually went broke.

Abe was a jeweler and knew everybody on every narcotics squad in America. We were playing some ballroom in the Midwest and had just finished playing our first song when Abe called Woody over to the side and whispered to him, "The men are out there." That's all that Woody needed to hear. He came out front and told the guys, "Listen, fellas, the fuzz are out there in the audience somewhere. Whatever you have, go get rid of it." So we played a few more songs and then he called an intermission. The guys went out back to the bus to get rid of their junk and this is how they did it. They took it from the tops of their suitcases and put it in the bottoms of their suitcases. Who was going to look in the bottoms of their suitcases? That was their way of thinking.

Abe wanted to save Woody money by chopping everybody's salary, and that's what started everybody leaving the band. He cut me back to a hundred and fifty dollars a week and when he did that, I gave my notice and quit. I had been on the band for a year, but was married and the band just wasn't the same anymore. It wasn't much of a life being married and going on the road rooming with my wife and Lou Levy, so I quit the band and went back to New York City.

For most musicians, playing music is our crutch. If you have nothing else happening in your life, at least you know you can play music. If things are bad, for whatever reason; your wife left you, you're not making any money, you can't pay the mortgage, you can always pick up your horn and play and boy, it gives you something that you can't buy. All those guys in the band, with all their troubles and problems still had that. They could all play.

My favorite Woody Herman story involves an arrangement Johnny Mandel wrote for me on "What's New." I would start out and play the first two notes of the song and then take off like a blur. I had so much energy that my first chorus would start out like it was my eighteenth chorus. I was all over the vibes. After I played the song the same way for about a week, Woody came over to me and talked to me like a father would to a son. He put his hand on my shoulder and said, "Terry, listen. Next time, why don't you just play the first eight bars of the melody and then . . . " I wouldn't let him go any further. "Who are you telling how to play?" I yelled at him so much that I think he really felt like crying. Years later, I was playing in Toronto at the Royal York Hotel and Woody came in to see me. This was not long before he died, maybe six months before. It was great to see him because it was the first time I had seen him in many years. He didn't look too bad for what he was going through at that time. The IRS was taking his house away from him and they were giving him a salary to live on after the band was paid off. He told me that he had to account for everything he spent. If he wanted to buy a pair of pants while he was in Toronto, he had to have a receipt for that. I really felt bad for him because I remember what he had done for my career and everybody else that ever had worked for him. I always felt like he was a talent scout for finding young jazz players and helping them find themselves. I really loved him. When I got up on the bandstand, I told the audience my "What's

New" story and then said, "Woody, this is for you," and I played two full choruses of the melody to "What's New." Not one note of jazz. Just the melody. I owed him that.

Chapter 8
Bellson, Shavers, and Dorsey (Again?)

When Donna and I got back to New York, we moved into a basement apartment in my parents' house. It was nice and comfortable. My sister Sherry and her husband at the time had it built for them. They lived there for the first few years of their marriage. I was a little burnt out after my year with Woody Herman and wasn't that anxious to go back to work. Plus, nobody was breaking my door down asking me to work. I was only married a short time and wanted my family and friends to get to know Donna.

The first band I ever had after I left Woody, the front line was Stan Getz, Kai Winding, and me, with Stan Levey on drums, Curly Russell on bass, and George Wallington on piano. We played a place called Soldier Meyers' in Brooklyn. We worked there for two weeks and after that, we couldn't get a job. We followed Miles Davis, who couldn't get a job after that either. We were all young. This was 1949, and we weren't that well known.

A few weeks later, I bumped into Louie Bellson, who told me that he and Charlie Shavers had quit Tommy Dorsey's band because they wanted to play little band jazz. After talking for a while, we both thought that we should talk to Charlie about starting an all-star band with the three of us being the leaders. We had a meeting with Joe Glaser, president of Associated Booking Corporation, the biggest jazz agency in the world. We started a band called "The All Stars" with Lou Levy on piano, Oscar Pettiford on bass, and a clarinet player called Jerry Winter. We were together for about six months. Even though

Louie, Charlie, and I were coleaders, Charlie ran the show. He would announce the songs, introduce the musicians, and did practically all the talking.

When we played in Minneapolis, Oscar would play a cello solo about the third song of the set. Oscar had played cello a few times in the Woody Herman band. After we played about two or three songs, Charlie said, "And now, we'd like to feature Lou Levy on the piano." As soon as Oscar heard Lou's name, he put his bass down and started to walk off the stage. Charlie asked him, "Where are you going?" Oscar yelled, "Hey, motherfucker, I'm supposed to play a cello solo now!" Charlie yelled back, "Hey motherfucker, I'm running the show." Oscar said, "Motherfucker, I'm supposed to play a solo now!" There they were, motherfuckering each other on stage, arguing like two idiots in front of a few hundred people in the audience. It wound up with Oscar playing his cello solo, or he would have walked off the stage and we wouldn't have had a bass player the rest of the night.

About a month later, Oscar left the sextet because he didn't want to travel. We hired Nelson Boyd to replace Oscar on bass. He worked with Charlie Parker and a lot of the great beboppers who were on the scene those days. Nelson was a funny little guy. We were playing at some club during the Christmas holidays and every once in a while, we would play a jazz version of one of the Christmas songs. We were about to play one of these songs when Nelson said to Charlie, "Let me sing a Christmas song." That threw us all a curve because we never knew that Nelson could sing. Charlie asked Nelson what he wanted to sing, and Nelson said, "How about 'Santa Claus Is Coming to Town'?" Everybody said great. This is how he sang the words to the melody.

Ji bop en-du-ee- Ai duben blah
Ji bop en-du-ee- Shi-bil ya Dil-ya Du wah
Santa Claus is coming to town

We didn't believe it. I don't think that the audience knew what he was talking about, though all the phonetics fit the real lyrics to the song. He really broke the band up. In fact, for the whole week of Christmas, we had Nelson ji-bop-en-du-ing every night.

Louie Bellson was such a sweet guy, I don't think he knew the meaning of the word "no." It's not in his vocabulary. We'd close every set with Louie playing a drum solo. Sometimes he'd play for about ten to fifteen minutes. When he finished, he'd walk off the stage sweating profusely. One time when he finished playing and came off the stage soaking wet, some drunk stopped him. He put his arm around Louie like he was his best friend and started talking to him. He was babbling for about five minutes, and Louie was standing there like a *nebbish*, not even saying, "pardon me" or anything to get away from this drunk. I was watching this whole scene and finally, I couldn't take it anymore. I went over there and said, "Hey, Louie, you got a phone call," and pulled him away from the drunk. If I hadn't done that, he'd still be standing there today. He just didn't know how to say no.

We couldn't afford to fly so I bought a brand new 1949 Chevy. Donna and I didn't know how to drive, so Charlie Shavers drove our car. In the front was a bench seat so three people could sit comfortably. We all sat in the front while Charlie was driving. Donna sat in the middle between Charlie and me. After a while, I noticed that Charlie was putting his right hand down by his right leg, which was right next to Donna's left leg. I didn't want to say anything to Charlie, but he kept doing that all the time. He also kept hitting his right foot with his hand. I was kind of bugged and told Louie about it. I said, "Louie, I think Charlie's getting fresh with my wife. He keeps putting his hand near Donna's leg." Louie said, "Terry, you've got to understand something about Charlie. He's got low blood pressure, and to keep himself awake when he's driving, he whacks his right foot so he wouldn't fall asleep." I then remembered when I was on Tommy Dorsey's band that he used to whack himself on the foot to stay awake onstage too. Sometimes when he wouldn't whack himself, he'd fall asleep, and Tommy would go over and play the loudest and highest note on the trombone right in Charlie's ear and wake him up.

I had that Chevy for about three or four months when we met this car dealer in Minneapolis. This dealer was a very hip guy who used to come in and see us play at the club. He told us that there was a new car called a Hudson. He had two convertibles available and said that we had to see them and he could get us a good deal on them. There was something new on these cars where you could either use the shift or you could drive on automatic. This was a new thing they were experimenting with. But he couldn't get us a good deal unless we bought both cars. He said he would give me a good trade for my Chevy. In fact, he said that he would give me back all the money I paid for the Chevy. Lou Levy and I went to see the cars and flipped out. They had different kinds of lines, and being a convertible, they really looked hip. Lou and I each bought one. Mine was a yellow convertible and Lou's was black. They lasted about six months. The cars were lemons.

Somebody once did a terrible thing when we were playing in Louie's hometown of Moline, Illinois. It was New Year's Eve and while we were playing, they turned the lights out just before twelve o'clock. Some idiot yelled out, "Charlie, open your mouth so we can see your teeth!" and we got so bugged, we refused to continue playing until they threw that idiot out.

Charlie had some of the greatest sayings. When business was slow, he'd say, "It's so quiet in here, you can hear a mouse pissing on cotton."

We were together for six months when Tommy Dorsey called us and asked us if we would join him as a group. He really wanted Charlie and Louie back with his band because they were very important to him. He promised that he'd take the whole group as a sextet. Nelson Boyd had left, so it was just Jerry Winter, Lou Levy, Charlie, Louie, and me. Five of us. Tommy said that if we joined him at the Strand Theatre in New York, he'd take us to Europe and feature the sextet, which would give us much more exposure than we were getting playing little clubs. We said great. After two weeks, he fired Jerry Winter. Two weeks after that, he fired Lou Levy. He couldn't understand what Lou was playing. He couldn't fire me because I had a contract with Louie and Charlie. He was also afraid that if he did fire me, then Louie and Charlie would leave. So just like before, I hardly played at all. I think that Tommy didn't know how to feature the vibes.

Once again, Tommy's music was a drag because he was still playing the same arrangements that he was playing when I was with the band the first time. We were playing at the Astor Hotel in New York City when I finally got up enough nerve to go to Tommy and say, "Mr. Dorsey, let me ask you a question. It's already 1950 and we're still playing the same music you played when I was with the band in 1947. Even Benny Goodman is playing more modern music. How come you're not?" He looked at me and said, "Terry, come with me." Said it very nice. Didn't get mad at me at all, which surprised the heck out of me because Tommy was known for his bad temper. He took me over to the box office. The Astor Hotel Ballroom was packed and you couldn't get in. At the box office, I saw a line of people waiting to get in. When I saw that, I realized what a young idiot I was. I was telling him to change his style of music and you couldn't even get into the hotel. I humbly apologized and said, "Mr. Dorsey, forget what I said. I apologize." This man was probably the most successful bandleader around, and I was telling him to change the style of his band.

Frank Sinatra and Ava Gardner came up to the Astor Hotel to see Tommy's band. Frank was drinking a lot, and he and Ava were always fighting. Tommy knew that Frank wasn't in any shape to sing, and being Mr. Evil, he made a big announcement that Frank Sinatra was there and said, "Let's get him up to sing." Frank didn't want to sing and said, "Tommy, I'd love to, but I'm having trouble with my throat." Tommy kept insisting and riled up the audience to where everybody was screaming so Frank was forced to get onstage and sing. It was the only time in my life that I ever heard Frank sing badly. He had no chops. He couldn't hold a note, his pitch was off, and he was out of tune. Everybody in the band felt terrible except Tommy. I think he liked it because I think he was jealous that Frank had become more famous than he was.

In the Astor Hotel band room, there's a spot marked on the wall with a circle. That's where Frank Sinatra threw a pitcher at Buddy Rich. It missed Buddy's head and hit the wall. Buddy and Frank were always getting into it when they both worked with Tommy's band. Buddy was the star until Frank joined and had all the young girls screaming for him. They called those girls "bobby-soxers."

We were there for about a month and were going out on the road up towards Pennsylvania. We were playing this one-nighter at a ballroom in the mountains. I had my car on the road with me, and Louie and I did all the driving. We had Danny Banks, the baritone player, sitting in the front next to whoever was driving. Danny couldn't drive, for unfortunately, he was born with a clubfoot. Louie and I would take turns sleeping or resting in the back seat. When I was sleeping in the back seat and Louie was driving, the car stopped and I woke up and said, "Where are we?" Louie said, "I don't know." I took a look at a sign and saw that we were going in the wrong direction and were about 150 miles out of our way. I asked Louie, "How come you didn't make a left turn when we got to Route 17?" He quietly said, "Danny told me to make a right turn." I said, "Didn't you know it was left?" He said, "Yes, but I didn't want to make Danny feel bad." Once again, Louie, being such a nice guy, couldn't say no to Danny and tell him he was wrong. We headed back the other way and got there fifteen minutes before the job started.

I once played this ballroom when I was with Woody Herman's band and a lot of people remembered me. They kept coming over to me and asking me when I was going to sing "Lemon Drop." I told them that Tommy's band didn't do "Lemon Drop" but I'd probably play the vibes a little later.

We had a singer called Johnny Amarosa. On one of his songs, there was a four-bar band introduction. Then I'd go over to the vibes, play three or four chords: bong, bong, bong, bong, and then I'd sit down. I had been sitting down for an hour-and-a-half and hadn't played at all. I was getting more and more bugged, because, once again, Tommy never let me play. Tommy called a song for Johnny Amarosa to sing, and I went over to the vibes. When the audience saw me go over to the vibes for Johnny's song, about thirty people ran over to the front of the vibes to hear me play. I hit my four chords and sat down. When it came time for intermission, I flipped out. The band went out for about ten or fifteen minutes and I got so bugged that I packed up my vibes, put them in the back of my car, and took off. I didn't tell anybody, I just left. I must have been going eighty or ninety miles an hour through the mountains, I was so bugged. I drove straight home. I didn't even give him my notice. Tommy was probably happy that I went home. He didn't want me in his band; he just wanted Louie and Charlie back. I don't think I ever saw Tommy Dorsey after that.

Chapter 9
Benny Goodman: El Foggo

After I left the Tommy Dorsey band, I was out of work for about six months. I couldn't buy a job. I was being labeled a "bebopper," and because of all the notoriety that Charlie Parker got as a junkie, it didn't help being called that. I was really running out of money. Donna and I rented an apartment at 121st Street and Pleasant Avenue in Manhattan. It was a terrible neighborhood. We actually couldn't afford to pay the rent they asked for, so they made us a proposition. If we would be the janitors of the building, they would let us have the ground floor apartment that faced the street, with all the outside noise, for fifty dollars a month. The job of being the janitor entailed showing the empty apartments to people who were looking for one. We didn't have to do any kind of repairs or any kind of manual labor, which wouldn't have been my bag anyhow because I'm a complete klutz. Work was really slow for me. I would play an occasional Monday night at Birdland and a few small-paying jobs here and there.

Then I got a call from Benny Goodman's office offering me seventy-five dollars a week to do a TV show with Benny for the Dumont Network called *Star Time*. I really thought I should be making more money, but when you've been out of work for as long as I was, you didn't have any bargaining power, so seventy-five dollars it was. Eight weeks later I wound up making five hundred dollars. Nobody knew how much money I was earning, but when you work for Benny Goodman, everybody thinks you're making a million dollars.

I used to get phone calls to do record dates from Mitch Miller and all these big producers just because I was with Benny Goodman. I would show up at the record date, look at the music, and all they'd have were three notes for me to play. My grandmother could have played them. But because I was with Benny Goodman, I'd get those calls.

Whatever I say about Benny Goodman in this chapter is true. I'm not putting him down. That's not my purpose. I know that a lot of musicians have said some terrible things about Benny and I've seen him be mean to some people. But my stories are said with love because growing up as a kid in Brooklyn, and going to the New York Paramount Theatre to see him in person, he was my idol. I was so in awe of him. But Benny was two different people. When he was playing the clarinet, he was something else, but when he wasn't playing the clarinet, he was out in left field, as foggy as you can get.

I used to hear these far-out stories about Benny Goodman from other people. They always sounded so farfetched. For example, if somebody told a story about a green sweater and the story was passed around to other people, by the time it got to the eighteenth person, the green sweater would become a pair of black shoes. That's how farfetched these stories sounded to me. Nobody could be that far out.

After I started to work for him, I realized that every story I ever heard about him was true. Mel Powell and I spent a lot of time on a cruise just talking about Benny Goodman. He told me some of the funniest stories. Before I ever worked for Benny, I never would have believed any of them. Nobody could be that out of it. But unfortunately, Benny Goodman was completely out there.

One rumor about Benny was that he had a way of looking at musicians that got to be called "the ray." This scared them because he would stare at you and you didn't know why. I'd heard about that ray, and one time while I was playing for him, I felt this icy stare on my back. Those were my young cocky days; so I stopped playing, turned around, and said, "What the hell are YOU looking at?" He looked at me, shook his head and said, "Oh, was I looking at you, Pops?" I actually think that he was so completely out there, that he was not staring at me or anybody else. His mind was always a million miles away.

Benny was odd in many ways. He could memorize "The Flight of the Bumble Bee" overnight, pick up the clarinet the next day, and play it perfectly. He could memorize anything except your name. He called everybody in the world "Pops"; women, children, dogs, fire hydrants, you name it. Everybody was Pops. One time we were rehearsing up at his house in Connecticut and his wife Alice came in and said, "Benny, shall I bring the guys some Cokes?" Benny said, "Not now, Pops." He couldn't remember his own wife's name. Called HER "Pops."

Birdland was the hot club those days. I worked at the Royal Roost when I was with the Woody Herman band. Then Birdland opened; the same people owned it. When I played with Woody at the Royal Roost, I was treated like a king. At Birdland, you had to pay a ninety-nine cents door charge to get in the club. PeeWee Marquette did everything for the club. He was the maitre d'; he announced the acts, ran the lights, worked the door, and was the club greeter. PeeWee would see me walk in and he'd say, "Ninety-nine cents, Terry!" and make me pay to get in. After I joined Benny Goodman, PeeWee saw me on television, and not knowing that I was only making seventy-five dollars a week, treated me like I was the biggest star in New York. I'd go down to Birdland and walk down, ready to pay my ninety-nine cents, and PeeWee said, "Terry Gibbs? You're with Benny Goodman, you don't pay! You're a big TV star," and he would let me in for nothing. Thank God he never knew how much money I was making.

Benny used to rehearse three or four times a week, and the rehearsals were fun and very informal. We'd talk a little, have a few laughs, and then Benny would tell us what song we were going to play on the show. At the first rehearsal, I asked where the music was. He said "There's no music, I'll play the melody and you just noodle around what I play." We'd make it up right there. He liked what I did.

A few weeks later, when I came to rehearsal and asked Benny "What are we playing this week?" He said, "Temptation Rag." "Temptation Rag?" I told him that I didn't know that song. I never heard it before. So he started playing it for me. Usually, when we played something, he would play the melody and then say, "Find a part, Pops," so I'd always find something to play. "Temptation Rag" never stopped and had four million notes. But all Benny could say was, "Find a harmony part, Pops." What harmony part? I couldn't even find the melody! Luckily, I had good ears and found one. What did he care? He played the same thing all the time anyhow.

When we played, it was our regular routine: piano intro with drums and bass, then Benny would play the melody, and I would noodle behind him. The piano would always play his jazz choruses first, then Benny would play, and then it would either be the guitar or me following Benny.

Benny used to bug me every time I would start to play my jazz choruses. He would let me play for about eight bars, and if I started swinging, he'd immediately pick up his clarinet and join me in playing. But first, he'd put his cigarette down on the edge of my vibes and then start playing with me. The first time I saw him do that, I stopped him and said, "Hey, Benny, this is no toy. These are my own vibes. Please take your cigarette off of there." He said, "Oh, I'm sorry, Pops." It came time for me to play again, and when it started to swing, he put his cigarette back on my vibes so he could join me again. This time I pushed it off and it fell on the floor. He must have done that about twenty times. When he stopped playing, he always looked for the cigarette on the vibes, saw that it wasn't there, and lit another cigarette, never realizing that the first one was on the floor. By the end of the rehearsal, there must have been two hundred cigarettes on the floor. He kept putting them on and I kept pushing them off.

The biggest drag about him joining me was that I never got a chance to play a full chorus. Every time I started to swing, he would jump right in and start playing with me. It got to the point where I tried not to swing so I could play a chorus or two by myself. It's hard to purposely try not to swing, especially if you know how to.

Benny was the worst dresser in the world. He'd pick out any jacket and any pair of pants and just put them on. Nothing matched. Once he walked out on stage with his fly open and his shirt sticking out through his zipper. I don't think he ever got high on anything. I think that every time he took a deep breath he got high. He was stoned on air.

Benny liked my sick sense of humor and loved when I would tell him jokes. He'd break up all the time. One time, I was telling him this joke and was really getting into it. He's looking right at me. I've got my hands up in the air above my shoulders, ready to hit him with the punchline, when all of a sudden, he turned around and walked away from me, leaving me standing in the street looking like a complete idiot with my hands up in the air. He didn't even know I was telling him a joke.

On one of our days off from the show, I had Art Blakey, Teddy Kotick, and Billy Triglia over to my funky apartment for a jam session. While we were jamming, the phone rang. It was Benny. "Hey, Gubenko, what's happening?" Benny loved my last name Gubenko. He called everybody else Pops, but called me Gubenko. "Hey, Gubenko, what are you doing?" I said, "I'm having a jam session." He said, "Where?" He's calling me at my house and he asks me where. "Where? At my house!" He said, " I'll come over, sit in, and jam with you." I said great, gave him the address, and hung up. I thought, he's not going to come over to my house and jam with us. Not Benny Goodman.

About an hour-and-a-half later, we saw a cab pull up in front of the apartment house and Benny stepped out. He came in and I introduced him to everybody. We talked for a little while. Everyone was in awe of him. I think they were all calling him Mr. Goodman, and even though I introduced them by their names, he still called everybody "Pops."

While we were jamming, I could see that he didn't like Art Blakey at all. Art was too hard of a swinger, too savage a drummer for him. Benny loved the Louie Bellson kind of a drummer. Louie had a very clean style of playing. Everything Art did was raw and roaring. Art

Blakey could swing you right off the stage, but he wasn't Benny's type of a drummer.

After they all left, Benny said to me, "Say, Gubenko, that drummer. Do you really like that drummer?" I said, "Yeah, he plays very good." Then he looked around my funky apartment with that foggy look, saw all the holes in the wall, and said, "Say, Gubenko, you ought to get yourself a new apartment." I said, "You know, I'm looking for one, Benny." He said, "I may have something for you." I didn't pay any attention to what he said. We did about two or three more shows, and two weeks went by. I was back home one day, sitting around, and I got a call. It was Benny. "Hey, Gubenko, I think I have an apartment for you." I said, "Really?" I wasn't really looking for one. I said, "What does it look like?" He said, "It's five rooms." Here I was, living in a place where I wasn't sure I even had a bathroom. "Five rooms? What's it going to cost me?" He said, "Oh, only five hundred dollars a month." I said, "You idiot, you're only paying me seventy-five dollars a week!" Benny said, "I am?" and he hung up on me.

I called him an idiot all the time because he used to do all these dumb things. We got in the cab for a short ride. He was sitting behind the driver and I was sitting behind the meter. We were just going a short distance, so after we stopped, he said, "Gubenko, what's the meter say?" I said, "Forty cents." He said, "Gimme twenty cents." I said, "What for?" He said, "We'll chip in." I said, "You idiot! Are you kidding? Either you pay it or let me pay it!" I think I called him an idiot about two thousand times the whole time I worked for him because he kept doing all these stupid things, not remembering people's names and doing every stupid thing you could think of.

Alfonso D'artega had a large orchestra on the show and they were doing a New York kind of a scene, and needed somebody to play the xylophone part. Benny told D'artega, "Terry Gibbs will play the part." I wasn't even getting paid for this. I had to stay there all afternoon because when I got the part and looked at the music, there were four billion notes. I never stopped playing for three minutes at a time; I just kept playing. Thank God I was good at memorizing music. Reading that part on sight would have been hard, even for a xylophonist with a symphony orchestra. When we played the New York scene on the show, I played the part pretty good. I stayed there all afternoon, all for seventy-five dollars a week.

Everybody was in awe of Benny Goodman and was afraid to tell him when he did something wrong. We were doing this record date and Mitch Miller was the producer of the session. While we were recording, Benny's nose was running and he had snot hanging down from his nose to his lip. It was disgusting. Everybody knew it, but nobody said anything to him. Finally, Terry Snyder, who didn't give a shit about Benny Goodman at all because he was so busy at CBS, finally said to Benny, "Hey, Benny! Wipe your nose, you've got snot hanging out!" Benny took his sleeve, wiped his nose, and then wiped the sleeve on the back of his jacket. He looked like he was doing a juggling act with snot.

Terry Snyder got too busy at CBS and had to leave, so I got Benny to hire Charlie Smith, a drummer who had been working with me at the Down Beat Club. Benny usually never hired anybody without hearing them first, but he trusted my judgment and hired Charlie. We went to our first rehearsal and Charlie knocked Benny out. He loved Charlie's playing. He was one of the best brush players I've ever played with. Charlie was a very aggressive little guy. When we finished the rehearsal, Charlie went over to Benny, put his arm around him like they had been friends for four hundred years and said, "Hey, man, let's go get something to eat." Benny got this bewildered look on his face, took Charlie's arm off of him, came over to me, and said, "Hey, Gubenko, what the hell is with the drummer? Tell him to call me Mr. Goodman or at least Benny. Where does he get that 'man' shit?" I had to go over to Charlie and tell him that you can't get that friendly with Benny.

Because of the TV show, I started to get calls to do record dates that my grandmother could have done. I told Teddy Wilson I was going to leave and he asked me why. I said it was because I was making only seventy-five dollars a week. He didn't know what I was making, but I think he knew that I should be getting a lot more than that. So Teddy asked me, "What do you think you have to have?" I said, "At least a hundred and fifty dollars." He said, "Go ask Benny for three hundred dollars a week." He knew Benny pretty well.

When you talk to Benny Goodman about money, you never look him in the eye. Benny had that ray going and would just stare right through you while you're talking and before you know it, you've talked yourself out of a raise. I went to Benny and looked halfway on the floor and said, "Benny, I've got to leave. I'm starting to get a lot of phone calls for jobs and I can't make it on seventy-five dollars a week." He said, "What do you have to have, Pops?" All of a sudden it became business, and the friendliness of calling me Gubenko went out the door.

I said — and it was hard to say — "Uhhh, I've gotta have three hundred dollars a week." Benny said, "Oh, Pops, you couldn't get more than a hundred and fifty dollars a week for a show like this." Teddy hit it right on the head. So he gave me the hundred and fifty dollars.

Now another three or four weeks went by, and I was really starting to get busy, making more money recording with other people. So once again I told Teddy I was going to have to leave, and he said, "What do you think you want to make?" I said, "Three hundred dollars." He said,

"Go ask him for five hundred dollars." I said, "That's hard. Six weeks ago I was making seventy-five dollars." Teddy interrupted me, "You know, I've worked for Benny Goodman for a lot of years. Go ask him for five hundred dollars." Teddy was a very soft-spoken guy. So I went to Benny again and said, "Benny, I gotta give you my notice." "What happened now, Pops?" "Well, I'm really getting very busy. I'm getting calls for all kinds of dates that pay very good and can't take them because they would interfere with the TV show." He said, "What do you have to have?" Now I'm really looking on the floor. God forbid I should really look him in the eye. I hemmed and hawed, looking at the floor, then got a little bit stronger and said, "I have to have five hundred dollars." Once again Benny said, "Pops, you couldn't get more than three hundred dollars for this job. Any vibes player would do this for three hundred dollars." Right on the head. Everything Teddy said was right on the money. I got my three hundred dollars.

Now another four weeks went by and I was REALLY getting busy. But I was getting valuable to Benny Goodman because the producers really liked me. The sextet was one of the highlights of the show and I was a big part of the sextet so I went to Teddy Wilson again and told him that I was leaving. Teddy said, "What do you have to have?" I said, "five hundred dollars." He said, "Go ask him for eight hundred dollars." I said, "Teddy, that's hard." He said, "Terry, listen to what I tell you. Go ask him for eight hundred dollars." I went to Benny and once again asked for my raise and he said, "What do you have to have now, Pops?" I tried to say eight hundred dollars but it wouldn't come out so I said, "Seven hundred and fifty dollars." I couldn't say eight hundred dollars. I just couldn't get it out. "Pops, I won't give you any more than five hundred dollars," and went through that whole thing again and gave me the five hundred dollars.

I learned something from all this. Whoever is important to the bandleader will make the most money. Not everyone makes the same amount of money in a band. I don't know what Teddy was making, probably a lot more than me, and deservedly so.

Teddy once told me a great story. One time Benny called him to come to his house in Levittown on Long Island for an afternoon party. He told Teddy it was a black tie affair. Teddy was happy that Benny had invited him to his house for a party. He showed up in his tuxedo and saw everybody wearing white shorts like they were going to play tennis. This was in the summertime. The only ones he saw wearing tuxedos were a drummer, a bass player, and the great violinist Isaac Stern. Teddy knew immediately why Benny had invited him to the party and wear a tuxedo. He wanted him to play. Teddy asked Benny if he could talk to him. They went into a bedroom and Benny said,

"What's happening, Pops?" Teddy said, "Benny, let me tell you something. I'm so happy you invited me to your party, but if I play one note on the piano, it's going to cost you a thousand dollars." Benny had to pay him a thousand dollars because he invited all these people to hear the quartet and there wouldn't have been any piano player. El Cheapo.

Chapter 10
Finally, a Full-Time Bandleader

After the Star Time TV show ended Benny Goodman broke up the sextet. But by then, I had started to get a little popular. In 1950, I came in first in both the *Down Beat* and *Metronome* magazine jazz polls. I signed a contract with Joe Glaser, who had his two best agents, Bert Block and Larry Bennett, show up at every club I played so they could watch me work. This way, when they talked to a club owner, they'd know how to sell me.

Joe booked me into Café Society downtown, one of the classiest clubs in New York City. We played opposite the Weavers, who had a big Jewish following. At Café Society, most people came in to see the main attraction, so when we played, they would walk around, talk to each other, and nobody paid any attention to us at all. Joe Glaser was trying to sell me to a club and brought the owner in to hear me play

On a job like this, the bandleader usually emceed the show. Sid Bulkin, my drummer, said to me, "You know something, Terry? You're doing good, emceeing the show. Why don't you talk more to the audience and maybe even tell a joke?" A few days before, we had heard some sick jokes that we both thought were funny, so I asked Sid which joke he thought would make it with this type of an audience. He said, "Tell one of the jokes we heard the other day." One joke had something to do with a show business agent and being that Joe Glaser was there, I thought that I would give it a try. People were still walking around talking to each other, trying to get seated, and there were people still coming in. Nobody was listening to us.

Chapter 10

I played my first song and told the audience the name of the song and then said that my agent was in the club sitting right in front of me. I thought that I would use Joe Glaser as a set-up for the joke. I started out by saying, "My agent called the Paramount Theatre in New York City and told the manager, 'Get rid of whoever you got because I've got an act that's so hot, you'll have lines going around the corner.' The guy said, 'Are you kidding? I have Frank Sinatra, Bing Crosby, and Benny Goodman, and we're packed now.' My agent said, 'I'm telling you, get rid of them, you'll have lines going around the corner.'" Nobody's even listening to me except Joe Glaser and the club owner that he brought in to hear me play. There was a puzzled look on Joe's face because he didn't know where I was going with this joke.

I said, "So the guy finally said, 'All right, who do you have?' My agent said, 'I've got ADOLF HITLER, alive!'"

The moment I said Adolf Hitler, the whole place got quiet. Now this was 1951 and you still couldn't even mention the name Adolph Hitler or even make jokes about Hitler. The club was full of Jews who were there to see the Weavers, and even the people who weren't Jewish stopped doing whatever they were doing and were now looking at me. I never told a joke in front of an audience before in all my life. Now I got scared and lost all my energy to finish the joke and was starting to whisper, but I had to finish the joke. "'You've got Adolf Hitler alive? Really? Wonderful! Wait a minute. People hate that guy.' My agent said, 'Look, the guy made a mistake.'"

Nobody laughed. They looked like they were in shock. I was holding the mike so tight that it felt like it was bending, the way Uri Geller would bend a spoon. It felt like I stood there for fourteen hours. Finally, some drunk at the bar yelled out, "Why don't you shut up and play some music?" If it weren't for that drunk, I'd still be standing there today. To make it even worse, Joe Glaser came down to my dressing room after the show was over and called me every four-letter word in the book and told me to just play music and leave the jokes to the comedians.

Instead of starting a regular group, Joe had me go out on the road by myself, doing a single. Every club I played had a house rhythm section to back me up. The first job he booked for me was at the Blue Note in Philadelphia making five hundred dollars a week. That was the most money I had ever made playing bebop. I really loved Joe Glaser. He was sort of like my second father. He was great to all his clients, but if you screwed him out of five cents, you would never work anywhere ever again. He also would never take any commission for any job that I played in New York before I signed a contract with his agency. That's what I call a *mensch*.

Finally, a Full-Time Bandleader

I did so well at the Blue Note in Philadelphia that I signed a contract to play there two weeks at a time six times a year. I'd go there myself and play with different rhythm sections. The guy who owned the club, Jackie Fields, was an ex-trumpet player and he loved me. One night he said, "Terry, I'm going to take you to hear something you've never heard in your life." It was his club; he could do what he wanted. He told me we were going to hear a rhythm-and-blues group that played in the Louis Jordan style. When we got to the concert, the group played a few songs and sounded good. Then the bandleader said, "Ladies and gentleman, we'd like to present a new trumpet sensation, Clifford Brown!" and this young kid walked out. I had never heard of Clifford Brown before. Nobody I knew ever heard him of before, either. Clifford used to get into this little crouch when he played and I swear to you, next to Dizzy Gillespie, I never heard any trumpet player play that good. He was twenty years old at the time. A few years later, as we all know, he became a giant. I think that even though Dizzy was my favorite trumpet player, if Clifford had lived, he might have become the greatest of them all. His sound was warmer than Dizzy's, he had as much technique as anybody, and he had a beautiful, harmonic approach to music.

When I wasn't on the road doing a single, I'd put a quartet together of the best musicians I could find and get an occasional Monday night at Birdland. We always did well with the audiences. I was a crowd-pleaser, so every once in while, they would give me a two-week engagement playing opposite some famous people.

I worked with Georgie Auld at the Apollo Theatre in Harlem for one week. Red Rodney and Al Epstein were in the band. It was Georgie's band and I just came out and played a few featured vibes solos.

Epstein, who was playing baritone saxophone in the band, bought about twenty gross of condoms. What he did was to put a pin in a condom and try to pin it on the back of Georgie's jacket or catch anybody when they weren't looking and pin it on them. He got Georgie on the back of his jacket just before he went out to play. Sometimes Epstein would put a little water in the condom so it would hang down and look like it had just been used. Georgie didn't know there was a condom on the back of his jacket until the show was over. He played the whole show with the condom hanging from the back of his jacket. Red Rodney, who was sitting on the top riser with the other trumpet players, had a few choruses to play. He got down from the riser and had to walk past Epstein in order to get to the stage where the main microphone was. As Red walked by the saxophone section, Epstein, who sat on the end, caught him on his left elbow. When Red put his left hand up to play his trumpet, his elbow had a condom hanging down from his sleeve. He never knew that he played his two choruses with the condom hanging down from his elbow. Before we went on stage to play our next show, everybody in the band was checking their clothes to see if Epstein had caught them.

When I went out on stage to play my solos, I checked myself out and I was cool. After they introduced me, I went over to my vibes, picked up my mallets, and was about ready to play, when I saw two condoms on the balls of my mallets. Luckily, there was a band introduction to my first song, which gave me a little time to grab another pair of mallets. I always had two extra pair between the bars on the low end of the vibes, just in case I dropped or broke a mallet while I was playing. In the middle of my solo, I saw something hanging from the front of my vibes. I didn't know what it was until I got to my next song. I turned around to the band to count off the tempo and looked at Epstein. He was sitting there with just one shoe on and one bare foot. I then realized that what was hanging on the front of the vibes was Epstein's other sock. Epstein looked so funny sitting there with one shoe on and one bare foot. There's only one Epstein.

Charlie Parker had a way of conning people out of money. He'd see you walk out of a club with your horn, then walk over to you and ask you for some money. If you told him that you didn't have any, he would ask you, "Where are you working tomorrow night?" When you told him, he would say, "I'll come sit in with you" and you would wind up giving him whatever money he asked for because you felt honored that Bird was going to play with you.

Word would get around when Charlie Parker said he was going to show up at your job and sit in with you, and the club would be packed. Of course, he would never show up. One time, I was walking out of Birdland when Bird hit on me for a dollar. I've always been very vocal about things that bugged me, and that really bugged me. I got on him and said, "Bird, you're the greatest musician living and you're going around begging for money. You should be ashamed of yourself." He did his usual routine. "Where are you playing tomorrow night?" I told him that I was playing at Georgie Auld's place called Tin Pan Alley. Bird said, "I'll come sit in with you." I told him off, but his routine must have worked, because like an idiot, I gave him a dollar.

Word got around that Charlie Parker was going to sit in with Terry Gibbs at Tin Pan Alley. It was a small place and it was packed; you couldn't get in. It looked like people were sitting on top of each other. We just finished playing our first song and I was starting to play the melody to "Out of Nowhere" when Bird walked in with his plastic alto around his neck. He walked through the crowd right to the bandstand, played the last eight bars of "Out of Nowhere" with me, and jumped right into his first jazz chorus. I didn't know how many choruses he was going to play, but just the thought of having to follow him was scaring the heck out of me. If you asked me if I would rather fight Mike Tyson in his prime or follow Bird, without a doubt, I'd fight Mike Tyson. At least it would be one punch and I'd be out of there.

"Out of Nowhere" was a thirty-two bar song. I waited until the thirtieth bar of the first chorus that Bird played, and then I bent down on the floor and untied my shoe and didn't get up until he was into the next chorus. On the thirtieth bar of the next chorus, I bent down, tied my shoe, and loosened a screw on my vibes. On the thirtieth bar of every chorus Bird played, which was about twenty choruses, I was on the floor. I must have looked like a nervous idiot, getting on the floor, standing up, and then back on the floor again for twenty choruses. When he finished playing, I wanted to make sure that I was on the floor and not standing in front of my vibes. On about the sixteenth chorus, my piano player Harry Biss looked at me on the floor and said, "I know what you're doing and I'm not gonna follow him either!" Harry was really flipping out. We were like a bunch of scared kids. The only one who had enough nerve to follow Charlie Parker was Tony Scott who was sitting in the audience. He had his clarinet out ready to play. Tony wasn't all there.

Teddy Wilson and I once went down to Birdland on a Monday night, which was jam session night. Bud Powell, Red Rodney, and Zoot Sims were playing there. On the first song of the set, they started out by playing the melody. Then Zoot played a bunch of choruses, Red played some, and finally Bud Powell played. And he kept playing. Teddy and I must have counted about thirty-five choruses that he played. When he finished, he got very little applause. The music continued and then all of a sudden Bud got up and walked over to the microphone. Bud had never said anything over a microphone in his life. When all the guys in the band saw that, they stopped playing. Morris Levy, the owner of Birdland, happened to be standing at the bar at that time. This is what Bud said: "Ladies and gentlemen, I just played thirty-five choruses, and you didn't give me so much as a pat-pat-pat. I make scale, eighty-four dollars a week. George Shearing comes to this country, makes out like he's blind, and gets fifteen hundred dollars a week. You're all a bunch of simple motherfuckers." And he walked off the stage. It was the first time I ever heard Bud Powell talk. Morris Levy ran towards the stage, ready to beat the crap out of Bud.

Bud Powell never believed that George Shearing was blind. Every once in a while, when George was playing, he'd walk onstage, take his hand, and wave it in front of George's face. When George wouldn't move, Bud would slap him on the head. George immediately knew it was him, and he'd say, "Bud? Bud?" Bud also gave him a hotfoot. He put a match in his shoe, lit it, and when it burned his foot, George would say, "Bud? Bud?" Bud never believed George was blind.

George Shearing and I shared the same bill at Birdland. Don Elliott was playing vibes with George and he was one of the most talented people I ever met. He had perfect pitch. If you played something he liked, he could play it right back at you. I knew Don was good as a mellophone player, but I didn't know how good he was on the vibes. A mellophone looks like a French horn but it sounds like a bass trumpet. Don never got to play much with George. He would only get to play sixteen bars here or eight bars there. One night after he got done playing his last show with George, I had him sit in and play some vibes with me. There must have been about twenty or thirty people there at the time because it was three-thirty in the morning and it was the last set of the night. We both had our own sets of vibes on the stage. We started out playing a few choruses each on our own vibes and then we played some fours. Then, just to have some fun, we started playing together on one set of vibes. We both knew a little about show business, so we made it fun.

When two vibes players play on one set of vibes, you don't have enough room to get to the note you're trying to hit, so you wind up pushing each other and running around each other to get to the notes. We tore the audience up; I mean they were screaming. The twenty or thirty people that were there applauded so loud that it sounded like a few hundred people were there. Afterward, I told Don that if he ever left George Shearing and didn't have a job, he'd be welcome to join my band and play mellophone and then we would play vibes together at the end. Don was a giant mellophone player. He won the *Down Beat* award four or five years in a row on mellophone under "miscellaneous instrument."

Morris Levy opened a new club called the Embers and hired me to play there. I had Marian McPartland on piano, Bill Goodall on bass, and Don Lamond on drums. Being that this was the opening, Morris wanted me to have an all-star band, so he hired Coleman Hawkins on tenor saxophone and Roy Eldridge on trumpet as sidemen for me. When bebop came in, if you weren't a bebopper, you had a lot of trouble getting a job. Musicians like Coleman Hawkins and Roy Eldridge couldn't find any work. I felt strange because I was the youngest one there, and now I was leading this group with musicians who were my idols. The Embers bandstand was very small and the vibes were up in front, so there wasn't any room for anyone to stand beside me. Hawk and Roy had to stand in back of me. I felt very insecure being the leader because I was so in awe of them. Before we played any song, I would turn around and ask them what they wanted to play. It got to a point where Roy took me on the side and said, "Terry, please don't turn around and ask us what we want to play. They'll think we're trying to take over your band, and we'll be out of a job." I felt terrible when he said that to me because these were musicians that I idolized all my life and now I was telling them what to do.

I started to get a lot of calls to work. Monte Kay, who actually was the brains behind the success of Birdland, offered me a job working at a new club that he and Irving Levy, Morris' brother, were opening in New York called the Downbeat. The house trio at the club was Billy Taylor on piano, George Duvivier on bass, and Charlie Smith on drums. Monte paid me a hundred dollars to play three nights: Friday, Saturday, and Sunday, which was decent money for those days. He knew that I was getting calls to travel because of my television exposure with Benny Goodman, plus winning the *Down Beat* and *Metronome* polls. If I couldn't be there, that was okay with Monte. My vibes stayed at the club. If I had to leave town, when I'd return, I could always show up at the club on the weekend and play there.

It was a great job. The Downbeat was a small, very intimate club. It was so small that there was no bandstand. When you walked in, there was about two feet between my vibes and the wall and you had to walk by my vibes to get into the main part of the club, which was longer than it was wide. The club also had a balcony, which gave it a completely different look.

There was a guy called Johnny Roberts who could be pretty rough, if necessary, but he had a lot of respect for me and always treated me like a star. One night he came into the club, walked by my vibes while I was playing, and slapped them with his hand. He thought he was being cute. He had a ring on his finger and could have scratched the bars and gotten them out of tune. That bugged me and I yelled at him in front of everybody in the club. "YOU DUMB FAT IDIOT, NEVER DO THAT AGAIN!" After the set was over, I walked to the back of the club where my dressing room was. Johnny was waiting there for me. He grabbed me by my arms and picked me up. He was like a little bull and was built like Tony Galento, the prizefighter. He looked like he was frothing from his mouth and was gritting his teeth like a madman. He said, "Don't ever do that again. If I didn't love you, I'd kill you," He was serious but I really wasn't afraid of him because I knew that he respected me. I told him that it was his fault and that he showed no class when he touched my vibes. He really could have put my whole set of bars out of tune and me also. I lucked out on that incident.

I saw Johnny get into a fight once with Irving Levy. Irving wanted to be like his brother Morris but Irving was a *zhlubbo*, which is something like an idiot. He really didn't have the business sense that Morris had and he was always picking a fight with somebody. I think he must have had eleven fights in the club and lost every one of them. Johnny and Irving were good friends. One time I saw them get into a fight and it was disgusting to see. For some reason, Irving pushed Johnny out of the club. Even though they were friends, this fight wasn't too friendly. Johnny got Irving in a headlock and ran him headfirst right into the side of a car. Then he went back for another taste and rammed his head back into the car again, knocking him out cold.

I had a friend of mine come in the club, a black guy named Nat, who was about Irving's size, maybe a little shorter. A nice quiet guy. He sat down at the bar next to some white girls and like a gentleman, he asked them if they would like to have a drink. Irving, who was behind the bar, came over and said, "They don't want a drink!" Nat said, "I wasn't talking to you." That made Irving mad and he got belligerent, jumped over the bar with a baseball bat in his hand, and went after Nat. Once again, Irving got wiped out. Nat knocked him to the floor and poor Irving got beat up again. Nat left Irving bleeding on the floor and called me later to apologize. Years later, Irving was killed at Birdland. He once again got in over his head and this time he got stabbed to death.

While I was working at the Downbeat Club, I got a call from somebody at *The Mel Tormé Show*. Mel's show was one of the first color television shows and some great talent came on with Mel. Kaye Ballard, a very talented singer and comedienne, was on the show and also Peggy King, another good singer. Mel had a vocal group called the Mellowlarks and the Red Norvo Trio, with Tal Farlow and Charlie Mingus. They called me because Red got sick and they wanted me to come in and play for him. Mel kept his drum set on the stage because he used to play drums with the trio and his pianist, Al Pellegrini.

I came in and played the vibes with the trio. Mel was singing something and when I saw his drums, I went over there and sat in and played the drums behind him. Mel heard this and said, "Hey, you play drums?" I said, "Yeah." So he had me play drums when he sang on the two or three shows that I did. About a week went by, and I got a call from the producer telling me that they had fired the Red Norvo Trio and asked me if I wanted the job permanently. Because I was the leader of my own group, they made me co-leader with Al Pellegrini and we put a different band together. Red and the trio had a contract for thirteen weeks. He put a claim into the musicians union, and in order to get their money, they had to show up for every show for the next eight weeks, even though they never played. I felt terrible because indirectly, I knocked Red out of a job. Mel wanted me there for two reasons. One is that he could play drums when I played vibes, and when he sang, which was most of the time, I could play the drums. I also played drums for Peggy King, Kaye Ballard, and the Mellowlarks. Eventually, Al and I put a great little band together with Neal Hefti on trumpet, Bill Harris on trombone, Chubby Jackson on bass, Hal McKusick and George Berg on saxophones, Al on piano, and me doubling on drums and vibes. It was pretty strained up between Red and myself because he had to be there all the time we rehearsed and played the show. I didn't know Red Norvo very well then. Later on in life we became good friends and would laugh about that whole scene.

Sal Salvador, a guitarist who once worked for me, told me about a drummer from his hometown who was really good and said that I ought to hear him play. I was always interested in hearing a good new drummer so I told Sal to have his friend come to the club before we played our last set and play a few songs with us. The next night, he showed up at the club and told me that Sal said that I wanted to hear him play. His name was Joe Morello. Joe wore glasses that looked like they were four inches thick and he looked weird to me. I don't think that he knew how to dress because his top button was buttoned to the second buttonhole from the top. Everything about him looked strange. He didn't have the look of a musician.

The first thing that came to my mind was that I couldn't let him sit in and play with my band. I made up some cockamamie story about my agent being in the audience and that he had brought somebody in to hear my band play. Joe came back the next night and looked even weirder to me than the night before. Once again, I made up some dumb excuse not to let him sit in with the band. He kept coming in every night and my excuses got so out that by the fifth night, I think I told him that the attendant in the men's room wanted to hear one of our arrangements. I kept fluffing him off and wouldn't let him play and he finally stopped coming in the club.

A few months later, I went on the road. When I got back, Donna and I went to the Hickory House to eat and also because we wanted to hear Marian McPartland, who was playing there. As we walked in, I saw Joe Morello sitting at the bar. I said to Donna, "Oh, no, there's that weird looking drummer friend of Sal Salvador. Let's go sit in the corner." I thought that Joe was there to bug Marian to let him sit in and play with her. I watched Marian walk up to the stage and Joe Morello followed her. He walked over to a drum set that had his initials on the bass drum head and adjusted a few parts of the drum set. When they started to play, I didn't believe what I heard. Great sound, great time; he had it all. What an idiot I was. This guy was a monster and I never gave him a chance to play for me. He later went on to become one of the most famous drummers in jazz because of his great playing with Dave Brubeck.

A lot of musicians used to come into the Downbeat Club and want to sit in with us. I would let some of them sit in, but never in the rhythm section. If you get a bad drummer or a bad bass player, then you're screwed for the whole set. If it's a horn player, he could play a few choruses, and you could say, "Thank you very much" and he'd go home.

One night this guy walked into the club and he was almost like another Joe Morello. His shirt was sticking out of his pants, his jacket was buttoned with the buttons in the wrong place, and his hair was completely screwed up. He wore thick glasses and had a little mustache, almost like an Adolf Hitler mustache. When we got off the stage, he came over to me and said, "I'd like to sit in and play a song with you." I said, "What do you play?" He said, "Harmonica." I said, "Harmonica?" There was a musician called Eddie Shu, a tenor saxophone player who also played a little harmonica. He played fairly decent but the only guy around who could play harmonica really well was Larry Adler. I never knew him to play much jazz, but Larry was a great harmonica player.

I said to the guy, "What's your name?" He said, "Toots Thielemans." That was strange to begin with. A name like Toots Thielemans with his big thick glasses and buttons all in the wrong place and hair all screwed up. I said, "Well, maybe the last tune." So at about ten-to-four in the morning when the club was empty, I let him play our last tune with us. Nobody ever played the harmonica like Toots Thielemans. He played bebop, he played all the right changes, and he played as good as any of us onstage played.

The Downbeat Club became my stomping grounds. I played there most of the time I was in town. I had the freedom of going anywhere, knowing that I could always come back there to play.

While I was playing there, Benny Goodman called me to do a record date and play a job in Hull, Quebec. We rehearsed at Nola's Studios, and although they had tuned the piano, I don't think they ever cleaned it. They flew Paul Smith in from California to play piano. At the first rehearsal, Morty Corb subbed on bass for Sid Weiss, who had another commitment. Sid Bulkin played drums. We did our usual routine with Benny playing the melody and me finding a part. When Paul started to play his jazz chorus, Morty started playing in four: ding-ding-ding-ding. Benny waited for about three or four bars and stood there biting his tongue, looking like he was out in left field. Then he said to Morty, "No, no, no, play in two." So Morty started playing in two. Paul waited a few bars and then said to Morty, "No, play in four." Benny was not used to hearing somebody tell any musician in his band what to do, especially after he had just told Morty to play in two. He waited another three bars and again he said, "No, no, no, play in two." Morty was getting more and more confused so he went back to playing in two. By this time, Paul was getting irritated and he said, "No, play in FOUR!" Benny looked at Paul and now HE was getting bugged and said, "Teddy Wilson can swing in two." As soon as he said that, Paul stood up, all six-foot-four of him, and slammed the piano lid down. All the dust that probably had been in the piano for twenty years flew up in the air. He looked down at Benny and said, "Then go get Teddy Wilson, but until you do, on MY chorus, he's gonna play in FOUR!" Benny looked up at him with a frightened look on his face and said, "Oh . . . Okay, Pops."

After a few months of just playing weekends, Monte Kay asked me to bring a group in for six nights a week. I heard that Don Elliott had left George Shearing, so I called and asked him if he would like to join my band. He said "Heck, yes!" I already had Sid Bulkin on drums, George Duvivier on bass, and Billy Taylor on piano. A few months later, I added Phil Urso on saxophone to make it a sextet.

The band I had was like a little jazz show band. We were pretty well rehearsed, but at the same time, we were loose. Actually, the rehearsing was done while we were performing on stage. If I wrote a new original song, we would play it on the job. We'd make up background riffs for the soloists. When we played the same song the next night, we would try to remember the same riffs. Most of the time we ad-libbed different riffs. We played the Downbeat Club on and off for about two or three years

While I was working there, Teddy Reig called me to do a record date with a new singer called Crying Jimmy Scott. Louie Bellson played drums on the date. As I mentioned before, Teddy Reig weighed about four hundred pounds and you could hear him breathe a mile away. He usually sat in the booth and called the shots. He felt like sitting with us in the studio for one of the takes. Everything Jimmy Scott sang was twice as slow as anybody who ever sang it. When he sang, "I Understand" it would sound like "Iiiiiiiiii Unnnn-durrr-stannnnd." Teddy Reig was sitting there, breathing so hard that when you heard the playback, first you'd hear the intro, then a break, and just before Jimmy started singing, you'd hear Teddy breathing. This is what it sounded like: Break. "Ehh-Uhh-Ehh-Uhh-Ehh-Uhh-Ehh-Uhh, Iiiiiiiii Unnnnn-durrrr-stannnnd." Every time there was an empty spot, you'd hear Teddy panting. After we heard the playback we threw Teddy out of the recording studio and sent him back to the booth.

Chapter 10

Oscar Pettiford could drink more than anybody and when he drank, he got nasty. When I was working at the Downbeat Club, I lived on Tenth Avenue in New York and I had a one-room apartment that was as big as a football field. After the job ended at four o'clock in the morning, for anybody working in any of the clubs close to where I lived, it was always, "Okay! Everybody over to Terry Gibbs' apartment!" and there'd be twenty guys over at my place, hanging out. Percy Heath named me "Waterglass" because I'd buy all these big bottles of liquor and have them at the house, but I never had any shot glasses. So I served the liquor in all these big water glasses.

Oscar Pettiford was at my apartment, and it was now eight o'clock in the morning. Everybody left, and now I had to get Oscar out of my house. He didn't want to leave and I didn't want to have a fight with him because, as I said, he got nasty when he drank. Finally, I got an idea. I said, "You know, Oscar? I'm going over to the newspaper stand by the subway station and get my paper." That was his subway station and I figured I'd get him to come with me, get him there, and say, "Oscar, it's been a lot of fun, we'll have to do this again sometime," and he'd go home. Oscar walked me to the subway station, I got my paper, and he walked me back home. He stayed at my apartment another three hours. I couldn't get rid of him.

One time, I played the Monday night jam session at Birdland and Paul Chambers, who was just a young kid at that time out of Detroit, was playing bass that night. I knew Paul from when I played in Detroit. He was in an after-hours group there. This was before Paul went with Miles Davis. We did our set and had to walk through these saloon doors to get back to the dressing room. We got through the doors and there was Oscar Pettiford, juiced out of his bird. Paul was carrying his bass to put in the back room and Oscar said, "Hey, motherfucker, play 'Body and Soul.'" Paul looked scared. Paul didn't want to play because first of all, he was in awe of Oscar Pettiford. Oscar was the greatest bass player in the world at that time. Paul said he didn't feel like playing but Oscar insisted and it got to the point where he started getting nasty about it. "Play 'Body and Soul!" So Paul started to play "Body and Soul." Oscar didn't even wait for Paul to play eight bars before he grabbed the bass out of Paul's hands and said, "No! Not like that!" Then Oscar played the melody to "Body and Soul" and he made the bass sing. He really embarrassed Paul and made him look like a little kid. Oscar played the eight bars as beautiful as you ever heard, handed the bass back to Paul, and walked out.

While we were at the Downbeat Club, a new place called the Band Box opened up right next to Birdland. Billy Eckstine was the hot singer in those days and he headlined the bill. Everybody that knew him would call him "B." Just "B." When they introduced him on stage, they would call him "Mr. B." He deserved that recognition because he paid his dues in the beginning of the bebop era. He had one of the greatest big bands around. Musicians like Dizzy, Bird, Art Blakey, and many more greats worked in his band. They also named a shirt for him. It had a very high collar and was called "The Mr. B."

Monte Kay, who was now part owner of the Band Box, asked me if I would work opposite Billy Eckstine for two weeks with a quartet. That worked out good in a way, because Don Elliott, Billy Taylor, and George Duvivier had other commitments. I told Irving Levy, who had bought Monte Kay out and now was the sole owner of the Downbeat Club, that I had a chance to play opposite Billy Eckstine at the Band Box and that we'd be there for two weeks. Then we'd come back to the Downbeat. With the exposure of playing opposite "B" and the publicity of a new club opening, we'd have even bigger crowds than before.

Actually, the Downbeat club was very small and we were packing it every night anyhow. Irving said that he didn't want me to leave. He was like an old-style hood and said, "No, you can't go." In the Capone days, if you played a club and the owner wanted you to work there for the rest of your life, you stayed there unless you wanted to walk around with a few broken legs. I said, "What do you mean, I can't go? I can go if I want to, as long as I give you two weeks' notice." Once again I tried to explain to him what it would do for my career, plus what it would do for his club. He didn't care and he didn't like that I had given him two weeks' notice. When I went up to his office to get paid for the last night of the two weeks, he had my money all laid out in rolls of nickels and dimes. The scale for sidemen was 85 dollars and leader's scale was 115 dollars. He said, "Here's your money." There was 540 dollars in nickels and dimes lying there. I was so bugged that I made him take every one of those rolls apart so that we could count it. It must have taken a few hours to do it. If you ever tried to carry eighty-five dollars in change forget it, you'd get a hernia. We put the nickels and dimes back in the original rolls they came in and I had to pay all the musicians with these rolls. I really felt sorry for them, having to carry the money along with their instruments when they left the club. The only one who lucked out was George Duvivier, who owned a Cadillac, which he had parked in front of the club. I told that story to Leonard Feather, the jazz critic, and he printed it in *Down Beat* magazine. I asked Leonard if he would say that Irving paid me two cents more by accident.

Milt Buckner, the organ player, was on that same bill. It was a great two weeks. I even got a chance to do a broadcast with Milt's group, which was released on a Brunswick LP. When they changed the bill after a few weeks and brought Harry James' band in along with Buddy Rich's little group, they asked me to stay for two more weeks. I told Monte that I would do the two weeks and that I was putting my sextet back together again after the two weeks were over. A few days later, Monte came to me and said, "Terry, Charlie Parker is coming out of the hospital and he's going to play the club this weekend. He'd like to play with you." I said great, I'd love to play with him.

By this time, I wasn't afraid to play with Bird, even though I still wouldn't follow him when he finished playing his choruses. It had been three or four years since that first time that I tried making any sense playing with him. I also had learned a heck of a lot more about getting around chord changes than I knew then.

Those days, all sidemen dressed up; they wore dark suits and ties. That was the uniform for everybody. Bandleaders usually wore whatever they wanted to. Came time for the show and I gave Bird a big introduction: "Ladies and gentlemen, the greatest musician of our time" and used all the accolades I could think of. Finally, I said, "Charlie PARKER!" Bird came up onstage dressed in a shirt and tie, but his shirt was made of terrycloth, which for those days didn't make any sense at all. I don't think he owned another shirt.

The audience gave him a big hand. When he got close to me I said, "Bird, what do you want to play?" He looked at me, put his horn in his mouth and started to play "Fifty-Second Street Theme." He played it so fast that when the rest of the guys came in, none of them played in time with each other. Some were on one and three, others were on two and four; they were all in different places. Charlie Parker played so straight ahead, his time was so perfect, that if you were sitting in the audience, you'd think that was the greatest rhythm section you ever heard. Then I remembered that I had heard some musicians who had played in Charlie Parker's rhythm section and hired one or two of the guys for my band. When they played with me, they were terrible; wrong notes, bad time. It was then that I realized that Bird played so straight ahead, that he made everybody sound good, everybody except some of the soloists that had to follow him.

I learned something later on in life. In the 1990s, I took a group to Europe called Terry Gibbs and the Woody Herman All-Stars with Nat Adderley, Urbie Green, Don Lamond, Ernie Wilkins, Nat Pierce, Bucky Pizzarelli, and Red Callender. Nat Adderley told me a funny story. When Nat came to New York with Cannonball in the early fifties, he was just a kid, and they were playing in a place called Café Bohemia. Nat was a little younger than Cannonball and he came to him and said, "Cannon, I heard that Dizzy's coming in tonight. What if he comes up and plays? I don't know what I'm going to do! I'm going to pass out." Cannonball said, "I'll tell you what to do. After we finish playing the melody, you come in playing right away, even if he starts playing. You keep playing until he stops. Don't follow Dizzy. Let him follow you because you won't know what to play at all. He would have played everything you know."

That's what happens when you get around someone who's that much of a heavyweight like Charlie Parker. I wasn't afraid to follow him, but it took a good sixteen or thirty-two bar chorus before I forgot who I was following.

I don't think many audiences know how great a jazz player is. The jazz player may get to them emotionally or make them tap their foot, but I don't think they can get the whole story that a musician gets. A musician who really knows what Bird is playing gets a different feeling when he hears Bird. Jazz is instant composing. Bird plays one chorus after another and every chorus is a new melody. He could take thirty-two choruses and every one would sound like a completely different song. He started the so-called "clichés," where he would quote other songs in what he was playing. He was the first guy I ever heard do that.

After we played the Band Box, we started to play at Birdland a lot and that's when I really started getting hot. They would always have me on the same bill with all the famous stars that packed the club and I started to get a lot of exposure. I was sort of like the new kid on the block. I worked there so often that I felt like the house bandleader. I didn't mind being the third attraction on the bill. How much better could it be for me when I would look at the marquee and see "Duke Ellington, Dinah Washington, and Terry Gibbs" or "Count Basie, Sarah Vaughan, and Terry Gibbs"? You couldn't get any better bookings than that. I played there any time I wasn't traveling.

Duke Ellington was the loosest bandleader I ever saw. I worked opposite him a few times. Usually, the bandleader would be the last one onstage. The band would be seated, then the bandleader would make his entrance, and usually everybody would applaud. But not with Duke. He was the first guy onstage and he'd start playing piano by himself while the rest of his band was at the bar, having a drink. Three minutes later, a trombone player would go up onstage and sit down, so now there was a trombone player and Duke. Then a trumpet player would sit down and then, little by little, after eight or ten minutes, ninety-nine percent of the band would be sitting there except for Johnny Hodges. Johnny wouldn't go onstage until everybody sat down first. He had to be the last one onstage.

Some of the regulars that showed up at Birdland were some of the greatest boxers who ever lived. They were coming to see Duke, Basie, Dinah, or Sarah, but I was there too, and got to know them pretty good.

Chapter 10

Sugar Ray Robinson, Joe Louis, Ezzard Charles, and Willie Pep were some of the greatest fighters that ever lived.

Sugar Ray was one of my idols. He could knock you out while moving backwards, counterpunching. I think the title they laid on him was exactly how I felt. "Pound for pound, the greatest fighter that ever lived."

Don Budge, who was one of the top five or ten best tennis players ever, used to come down to Birdland all the time. Tennis wasn't a big sport then and I didn't know much about who Don Budge was. I also didn't know that Don used to play the drums. Every time he'd come over to talk to me, as I was talking to him, out of the corner of my eye, I'd see one of the great fighters in the club, excuse myself to Don, and run over to talk to the fighter. This must have happened about five to ten times. As I look back now, I felt like I must have been a complete idiot fluffing him off like that. I've always looked to see if I could find Don Budge, but unfortunately he died a few years ago and I never got a chance to apologize to him.

Once again, Benny Goodman called me and asked me if I would do a TV show with him. The sextet was booked on *The Ken Murray Show*, which was one of the most popular variety shows at that time. Teddy Wilson, Benny's regular piano player, could not make it because he had another commitment. Teddy was very famous and everybody in the world knew that he was black. Benny's manager hired a piano player to replace him named Bernie Leighton, who was as white as could be, had light hair, and was fairly light-skinned.

We were there a whole week, rehearsing a song called "The World Is Waiting for the Sunrise." We'd rehearse the song about eight times a day. In all that time, seven days, Benny never said hello to Bernie, didn't know his name, and didn't talk to him. He would have called him Pops anyhow. We practiced the song and then Benny would walk off, going to the right of the stage.

Now it was show time. We finished "The World Is Waiting for the Sunrise," and while the applause was going on, Ken Murray got the sign to stretch, which meant that they needed more time because the show was running too fast. So Ken Murray had to do a little ad-libbing. We were ready to go off to our right when Ken Murray said, "Hey, Benny. Come over here for a second." Benny had never heard that at rehearsal and it threw him a curve so he turned around and said, "Yah?" Murray said, "Come here, Benny!" Now Benny had to walk to the left, which threw him another curve. He didn't have the slightest idea why he was walking over to Ken Murray because we had never rehearsed that. And also, Ken Murray didn't have the slightest idea what he was going to say to him.

Finally, a Full-Time Bandleader

Finally, Ken Murray said, "Uh, Benny, uh, uh, uh, who's in the band?" That REALLY threw Benny a curve. Benny looked at me first, tried to say "Terry Gibbs," hemmed and hawed, couldn't think of my name, and said, "On vibes, uh, uh, on vibes, GUBENKO." Great. My mother loved it. All my Jewish relatives who saw the show loved it.

He got Terry Snyder, the drummer's name right and also Eddie Safranski, who was on bass. Then he looked at Bernie Leighton, who he had never said hello to, but had rehearsed with for eight hours every day for a whole week. He looked at Bernie and said to Ken Murray, "And on piano . . ." He hemmed and hawed a little and finally said, "Uh, uh, TEDDY WILSON!" The whole band turned around to see who was playing piano. We had to look and see if Teddy was really there. We couldn't believe it. Make up a name, Irving Schwartz, call him Pops, anything but not Teddy Wilson. The whole world knew Teddy Wilson was black and here was this white guy, as white as could be, and Benny called him Teddy Wilson. Benny was REALLY out there.

We were really doing great. Don Elliott and I would break it up playing vibes duets. Not only did we play the Downbeat and Birdland, we played all the other good jazz clubs in New York. We were the hottest little attraction in town.

We played opposite a nine-piece band led by Herbie Fields at Birdland. He was a good tenor player but not in the bebop style. He was more of a "honker" and played what they called rhythm and blues. He did that very well but he wasn't a Birdland-style attraction. Morris Levy didn't like Herbie Fields. Morris wasn't one of my greatest fans either because he was a control freak and I wouldn't let him control me. He never would tell me what to do or what to play; it's just that our personalities clashed. He was a very good businessman and had a lot of street smarts. He came to me and said, "What can you do to really cut Herbie?" We were doing great on our own but I think he wanted something louder. I said, "Let me hire a few more musicians. He's got nine; we've got six. Give me three more guys." At that time I had Sid Bulkin playing drums, plus Billy Taylor, George Duvivier, Don Elliott, and Phil Urso. I hired Allen Eager on saxophone, Fats Ford on trumpet, and Mundell Lowe on guitar. Count Basie was the "in" band in those days so we were going to Basie it up by playing all the Basie riffs. By having the guitar, we could fatten up the bottom since Mundell could play five notes at one time. Then Don Elliott and I would end the set with the vibes duet with the horns backing us up. We'd always end with "Flying Home" and really go out swinging with the whole band.

We were doing great with our regular six men anyhow, but now we were really shouting. We had much better soloists than Herbie and this made Morris Levy feel good because now not only were we outswinging Herbie Fields, but we were really outdoing him.

Slim Gaillard worked opposite us at Birdland. He was a lot more talented than I thought he was. When Don Elliott and I did our vibes duet, Slim, who had real long arms, would come on stage, stand behind us, and put his arms around BOTH of us and play the vibes with us.

On my day off, I always took my mallets home with me after my job. When I came back to work after my day off and took the cover off my vibes, they were all scratched up. Slim was having fun on stage and couldn't find my mallets, so he took a pair of knives and played my vibes with them. When you hit the vibes with anything metal, it can chip them, which puts them out of tune. Luckily, I had another set of bars because I had to send the scratched-up ones back to Deagan to get re-tuned.

Working with Slim was always a lot of fun. He said so many out things. Everything was "McVouty" or "Orooni." He'd make up all these drinks like "bourbon and garbage juice." There was a bit that he did that always knocked me out. All I had to do was hand Slim any old piece of paper; it didn't matter what was on it. In fact, most of the time, it was a blank piece of paper. He'd look at it, look at me, and say, "Ohhhh, Terry, we have a married couple spending their honeymoon here at Birdland! Draggy-rini, they should be out in Regooneyville, lock the vouty and throw the reeny away!"

When Horace Silver left Stan Getz he joined my band and started working with me. He also went on the road with me. We did a record date for Bob Thiele, who was putting together a jazz show called *Jazztime USA*, which was supposed to be on the order of Norman Granz' *Jazz at the Philharmonic*. Just a big jam session. We recorded a song called "T&S," which stands for Terry and Shorty. Shorty Rogers and I wrote it. Horace played an eight-bar intro on the piano and it was so good, that after he left my band, I had every piano player play that eight-bar intro.

We got called to play a concert for a disc jockey in Buffalo called Joe Rico. The concert also had people like Lester Young, Sonny Stitt, and Kai Winding, who subbed for Don Elliott on trombone for me in my band. "T&S" had become a hit in that area. The audience at this concert was completely nuts, just like at *Jazz at the Philharmonic*, where people would be screaming after solos. Every time we got hot, they were ready to throw each other off of the balcony. They got so out that the police were going to stop the show. One time they actually did stop the show and came backstage and told us to tone it down and not get the audience that excited. When we went back on stage, I played my ballad and then tapped off the introduction to "T&S." As soon as

Horace played the introduction that he played on the record, the audience started screaming and looked like they were ready to jump out of the balcony. The police came out on stage, stopped the concert, and took us backstage again. Joe Rico said, "Terry, I'm going to have to give the people their money back if this doesn't stop. Play ballads." I asked him how he expected me to play ballads for the rest of the show and he said, "What else can we do? They're going to stop the concert again if you get too hot." So I asked Kai Winding, "Can you play a ballad, Kai?" He said, "I can do a thing on 'The Boy Next Door,' just with me and the piano." I said great, that would do it. We went back on stage and Kai played the melody rubato. After he finished the rubato part, he went into a tempo and started swinging. The moment the bass, drums, and piano came in, WHOOOOOO! The audience started screaming again and went nuts. They stopped the concert. That was it.

We were booked in Toronto, Canada. Curley Russell played bass and we still had Horace Silver, Sid Bulkin, Don Elliott, Phil Urso, and myself. I didn't care if the guys smoked pot but if I thought somebody was fooling with hard drugs like heroin or morphine, they'd be fired immediately.

We were driving to Toronto, and Phil Urso, unbeknownst to me, was screwing around with junk. I knew that he used to fool with it but I didn't think that he would do it while working with me. Phil wasn't the brightest guy in the world but he could play. We stopped at a Howard Johnson's on the turnpike and we went into the bathroom. Phil went into one of the stalls and left the door open. I walked in and was going to where the urinals were when I saw Phil in the stall with the door open, opening a bag full of dope. He was going to shoot up. When I saw what he was doing, I grabbed him by the throat and was ready to hit him. I wanted to fire him right there but we were about to open up in Toronto. This was a real big job for us. So I took everything away from him: the heroin, the needles, everything that he had, and put it in a little bag.

I had a big van that we used to travel in. I was driving and Phil was sitting near me. I was really fuming. I couldn't believe that this idiot would do that. Finally, I got so bugged that I turned around and said, "Phil, if we were anywhere else, I'd beat the shit out of you. Then I'd throw you out of the car," and I started to throw all the dope out the window. Phil yelled, "Terry! What are you doing? Don't waste it! At least YOU shoot it up!" At least you shoot it up. Isn't that wonderful? That's when I really wanted to kill him.

I was playing a club in Detroit when I got a call from Joe Glaser. He said he had to take me off the job Saturday and fly me to Philadelphia to play a wedding for Blinky Palermo's daughter. Blinky Palermo and Frankie Carbo ran the fight game in Philadelphia. They were the Don King and Bob Arum of their time, except that you won or lost when they TOLD you to win or lose. These guys were bad, but Joe said that Blinky's daughter was a big fan of mine and Buddy Greco's. He worked it out with the club owner where I could take off and the rest of the group would stay there. Then I could fly to Philadelphia and play the wedding and come back for the second week.

I figured that I'd better call Buddy Greco and ask him what to play at an Italian wedding. He said he didn't know. I said, "You're putting me on! You're the Italian! What do we do?" He said, "I don't know." I figured that if they hired me, then they wanted to hear some jazz. I also thought that we would have to play some Italian music so I went out and bought some Italian song books, just in case some of the older Italian people wanted to dance. I took Don Elliott and Sid Bulkin with me and hired my friend Epstein, the practical joker, to play the tenor saxophone. Epstein was the guy who once decided it would be funny to put a bomb in Buddy Rich's car. Buddy Greco played piano and we had a good jazz group.

We got to the job and were playing some jazz and swinging for about twenty minutes when all of a sudden, I saw what looked like the grandmothers walking in. When we finished the song we were playing, I said to the guys, "Take out number thirty-four in the Italian books." As soon as we started playing the Italian song, Blinky Palermo ran over to the stage like a madman, growling, and said, "What the hell are you doing? I wanted JAZZ!" If you've ever seen those guys who can rip a telephone book in half, that's what Blinky did to my Italian songbook. It had to be a good inch-and-a-half thick and he ripped it right in half. "I want JAZZ! Just JAZZ!" He called a waiter over and said, "Hey, you! Come over here. You're the band's waiter. You only serve the band. Give them whatever they want." We had our own waiter and we're playing jazz. I don't care if you're John Dillinger or the Pope; everybody wants to be in show business. Everybody. At the end of the job, while we were packing up the instruments, these five goons came up on stage, gathered around each other like a barbershop quartet, went over to the microphone, and starting singing "Down by the Old Mill Stream." They were all half-juiced and having fun. Epstein saw this and went over to them and started to conduct them. "Down by the OOOOlllld . . ." All of a sudden, Epstein went over to one of the goons and slapped him in the face. The guy was startled and like a little boy, said, "I'm sorry." Every time one of these guys got off-key, which was every four notes, Epstein would interrupt them and slap one of them in the face. These guys were like little kids and would say, "I'm sorry! We're TRYING!" I was watching all of this and being that their jackets

Me (Julius Gubenko) at 6 months, 1925. I've got the same body today. Thank God I'm taller.

The Gubenko Family, Brooklyn, New York, c. 1936. Standing L-R: older brother Sol, mother Lizzie, father Abe; Seated L-R: sisters Shirley (Sherry) and Sonia, Julius. This is about the time I won the Major Bowes contest.

My father's business card.

Me at 16 playing the drums. Would you believe I'm playing a ballad?

Private Gubenko reporting for K.P., sir!

How do you win the war by playing "I Got Rhythm"?

My friend, Tiny Kahn (all three hundred pounds of him).

Bird. Genius (no maybes).

Tommy Dorsey: six-feet-two; me: five-feet-seven; my hair: three-feet-four.

Chubby Jackson and his Fifth Dimensional Jazz Group performing in Sweden, c. December 1947. L-R: Chubby Jackson, Frank Socolow, Conte Candoli, me. Hidden behind me is Denzil Best. Missing from photo: Lou Levy. Frank and Conte are trying to copy my licks.

Chubby Jackson and his Fifth Dimensional Jazz Group, the first bebop band to play in Sweden, December 1947 or January 1948. L-R: Me playing drums, Chubby Jackson, Denzil Best, Frank Socolow, Conte Candoli, Lou Levy.

My son Gerry playing Buddy Rich's drums, which Buddy gave to him. Whatever Gerry wants, Gerry gets.

Woody Herman's Second Herd, at a Capitol Records session, probably December 1948. Guess who the sober one is.

Where's Lou Levy? This is the band that Louie Bellson, Charlie Shavers, and I started called the All-Stars. L-R: Jerry Winter, Nelson Boyd, Louie Bellson, Charlie Shavers (who's checking me out), and me.

The Benny Goodman Quintet on *Startime* (DuMont Television Network), 1950. L-R: me, Benny Goodman, Bob Carter, Teddy Wilson, and Terry Snyder.

Vibes Summit I, hanging out after hours at Birdland in the early 1950s. L-R: Don Elliott, Red Norvo, me, and Teddy Charles (Cohen). The inscription on the back is from Teddy: "There's only one Gubenko. Jewish or not, you're the Prez. Cohen."

The Benny Goodman Quintet, 1952. L-R: Sid "Pops" Bulkin, "Pops" Gubenko, "El Foggo," Nancy "Pops" Reed, Paul "Pops" Smith, and Sid "Pops" Weiss.

Publicity photo for my first record date for Mercury Records, 1955.

T 'n T, getting ready to battle, 1956.

The Dream Band, Hollywood, 1959. Trumpets: Conte Candoli, Al Porcino, Lee Katzman, Stu Williamson. Trombones: Bob Enevoldsen, Joe Cadena, Kenny Shroyer. Saxophones: Med Flory, Charlie Kennedy, Joe Maini, Bill Holman, Jack Schwartz, and me up front. Not pictured are Mel Lewis, Max Bennett, and Pete Jolly.

Ad for my big band's appearance at the Dunes Hotel in Las Vegas, 1959. I wonder what Benny had to say about my title, "The New King of Swing!"

The Dream Band. This was the last group to play the Avalon Ballroom on Catalina Island, California. Back row, L-R: Herbie Harper, Berrel Saunders (doing his Salvador Dali impression), Al Porcino, Buddy Clark, Joe Burnett, Med Flory, Frank Huggins, Dick Zubak, Kenny Shroyer, Conte Candoli, Hub Houtz. Front row, L-R: Mel Lewis, Frank Strazzeri, Jimmy Witherspoon, me, Jack Nimitz, Bill Perkins, Charlie Kennedy.

Montage of my appearance with my big band at the Apollo Theatre in New York City, the week of September 11-17, 1959.

THAT'S a Regis Philbin!

The Terry Gibbs Sextet on *The Regis Philbin Show,* 1964. L-R: Carrington Visor, Colin Bailey, Mike Melvoin, Monte Budwig, guest star Dizzy Gillespie, boom operator Ray Johnson, Herb Ellis, me.

Operation: Entertainment on location with guest star Ray Charles. Now that the show is over, we both can laugh.

Steve Allen is playing with ten fingers, and I'm only using two. This picture was used as the cover for our Signature LP in 1960.

This is the first time Buddy DeFranco and I played together in the U.S. on a television program for KCET, Los Angeles, 1980. Milt Hinton is on bass.

Vibes Summit II. L-R: Me, Lionel Hampton, Gary Burton, and Red Norvo. I don't know what Gary and Red are looking at, but Lionel is showing me the one note he played to wipe me out when I was with Woody's band.

Dizzy and me, marching to the same drummer while in France in the 1980s.

Me with Milt Jackson. The first two bebop vibes players.

Beauty and the Beast. Rebekah doesn't look too bad for a Beast.

Terry Gibbs and the Woody Herman All-Stars at the Jazz and Blues Festival, Germany, 1989. Back row, L-R: Don Lamond, Ernie Wilkins, Urbie Green, me, unidentified non-musician, Nat Pierce. Front row: Bucky Pizzarelli, Nat Adderley, Red Callender.

were unbuttoned, I could see their holsters with their guns sticking out. They may or may not have had gun permits, but when I saw this, I went over to Epstein and said, "You'd better cool it. One more slap and that may be the end of us." Epstein had these five goons acting like a bunch of choirboys. Each one of them probably killed forty-eight people that week, but onstage, they were meek little boys

When I got home after the tour ended, I got another call from Benny Goodman.

Chapter 11
El Foggo Rides Again

Benny called me to ask if I wanted to go on a month-long tour with him. I also got a call from my agent, Joe Glaser, who was booking this tour. I told Joe that I didn't want to break up my sextet because I didn't want to lose Don Elliott so I told Joe that if Benny hired Don and Sid Bulkin, I would go. He said, "Talk to Benny about Don and Sid." Joe also told me that if I went on the tour with Benny, he would book my sextet in every place we played. Benny came to the club, heard us play, and said that he didn't know what to do with the mellophone. I told him that Don also played the trumpet and he said, "Okay, I'll hire him to play trumpet." He liked the way Sid played, so he hired Don, Sid, and me. He also hired Jimmy Lyons on piano and Sid Weiss, the bass player that had played with Benny in his old band.

We played a one nighter in New Brunswick, Canada. It was the first time in years that Benny had played up there since he gave up his big band. There must have been 10,000 people squashed against the stage. Somebody put a microphone under my vibes and really turned it up loud. We played our first song and people were screaming and applauding. Benny was just standing there, looking foggy, and biting his tongue. He looked like he was completely out there. The moment the applause died down, he looked at me, and said, "GODDAMMIT, GUBENKO, SHUT THAT MIKE OFF!" Real loud. That embarrassed the hell out of me. I figured that I'd better get off the stage before I lost my cool. I started to walk off and Benny said, "Hey, where are you going, Gubenko?" I said, "I've got to talk to you," smiling as I'm walking off. I was smiling, but I had that burning feeling and was afraid that I was liable to hit Benny right onstage. He started to follow me off the stage but stopped by the microphone and told the audience, "There will be a short intermission." We've only played one song and this idiot's calling an intermission.

When we got off, I called him every four-letter word in the book. You name it; I said it to him. "IF YOU EVER DO THAT TO ME AGAIN, I'LL KICK YOUR ASS!" I was ready to hit him as soon as we got backstage. He looked at me and said, "There's nobody out there." Ten thousand people out there, squashed up against the stage, and he says nobody's out there. After telling him off and getting it out of my system, we went back onstage.

The song that the beboppers all played then was "How High the Moon." I don't think Benny had ever played it in his life. We got on stage and he said, "What do you want to play, Gubenko?" At this point, I didn't care. I was okay and just wanted to get back to playing. He looked over at Jimmy Lyons and said, "How High the Moon." I knew that he was playing that for me.

Benny always kept tunes short; we'd each play sixteen bars and that was it. Most of the time was spent on the jamming at the end when we were playing the last bunch of choruses. Now he had picked "How High the Moon." I had already gotten it out of my system when I screamed at him and I didn't really want him catering to me. I idolized this man and was just thrilled to be playing with him. This time, he let me play two choruses and didn't join me, even though we were swinging. That was his way of apologizing to me.

Benny was hard on a lot of people, but he wasn't with me. I think it was because I stood up to him. In fact, Sid Weiss told me that in all the years he worked for Benny, he never heard anybody talk to him like I did. If you let Benny step all over you without sticking up for yourself, he'd take advantage of you, and bug you.

We played the one-nighters and Benny kept picking on Sid Bulkin. Benny can bug anybody but he really got on Sid. First he said, "Hey, Pops, your pedal's squeaking." Sid was nervous to start with just playing with Benny Goodman; now he's trying to fix the pedal and play at the same time. Then Benny turned around and said, "Your high hat's a little too loud." By the end of the night, Sid was turning screws, fixing his high hat, tightening up the drum, and trying to play time all at once. Sid got so nervous that he was getting sick. If that wasn't bad enough, after we played the one-nighters, Sid got into an automobile accident and had to leave the group. We had to go back to New York for one night and Benny hired Morey Feld on drums to finish the tour.

He wanted to add a guitar player also so I recommended Don Roberts, who I had played with before. Benny had a short rehearsal so that he could hear Don play. He liked the way he played and I heard him tell Joe Glaser to offer Don 125 dollars a week. I went over to Joe and said, "Is Benny kidding? You have to give him at least 150 dollars," which was decent for those days. He did and we went to Chicago and opened at the Blue Note.

Benny was from Chicago and he hadn't played there in years. Now he was making his comeback in his hometown. On opening night, you couldn't get into the Blue Note. The club seated about four hundred people and it was mobbed. Benny was so thrilled when he saw this that after the job, he took us all out for breakfast. We went to this breakfast hangout called the Corner House and ordered our food. After we ate, the waitress brought the check to the table and Benny grabbed it and paid it. I couldn't believe it because Benny wasn't too generous with money. I wouldn't call him thrifty or frugal; actually he was cheap, but he picked up the tab.

The next night, the club was even more packed. Twenty times more people than the first night. Once again he said, "Hey guys, let's go out to breakfast." So we went, we ate, and once again, he asked the waitress for the check. He looked at it and said, "Okay, Gubenko, that's a dollar-and-a-quarter for the hamburger steak, Pops, that's a dollar eighteen for you, ninety-five cents for you, Pops . . ." He collected money from all of us. I didn't believe it. That was the REAL Benny Goodman.

Business was so good that they added an extra show. One night at the extra show, there couldn't have been more than forty or fifty people left in the club. Frank Holtzfield, who was the owner of the Blue Note, was one of the greatest club owners I ever worked for. When I played there with Woody Herman, he treated me like a star. He even treated Woody's band boy like he was a star. Before we went to start the show, he went to Benny's dressing room and told Benny that since there were only forty or fifty people out there, he didn't have to play the last show. Frank was so nice, that he thought he would be insulting Benny by having him play for only forty or fifty people after we had been playing for four hundred-plus. But Benny was on percentage, which meant that after a certain amount of money was taken in, he would get a percentage of that money in addition to what the contract called for. Benny being Benny said, "No, that's all right, we'll play it." Of course he was going to play it. That would be another eighty-four dollars in his pocket to go with the eighty-four million he already had. So we played the show for forty people.

Although the way I played was more bebop oriented, it fit in with Benny's playing because he swung. It was very easy playing with him. I just played my normal way, but I didn't play as much double-time. The rhythm section dictated the feel. They would play just straight four-four and I would still play bebop, and it swung.

As great as Benny played, it almost seemed like he was jealous of us. I always felt that if the audience liked what you played, and showed it by applauding for you, he wouldn't let you play much on the next song. When Don and I played our vibes duet and did our hand schtick, the audience really reacted to it. But Benny would start playing, which had nothing to do with what Don and I were doing. It just seemed like he was trying to get the attention on him. I could never understand why he would do that, for every time he played, he broke it up.

I loved hanging out with him. I'd get a chance to ask him questions about the band he had with Gene Krupa and all the musicians that I knew from records and seeing them in person at the Paramount Theater. Here's one of our conversations:

> **Me**: Benny, who are your all-time favorite lead trumpet players?
> **Benny**: Bunny Berigan and Doug Mettome.
> **Me**: What did you think of Harry James?
> **Benny**: Harry James? I don't remember Harry James.
> **Me**: Harry James. The trumpet player. "Sing, Sing, Sing." "Ciribiribin." What do you mean, you don't remember Harry James?
> **Benny**: I don't remember him.

And he walked away from me.

I didn't understand why he said that until later on when Sid Weiss told me a few stories about Benny. He said that in the old days, Benny never hung out with the guys in the band and when he did, he called everybody Pops because he didn't know who was who.

Sometimes Benny would practice the clarinet all day. But for some ridiculous reason, he would always practice naked. Don Elliott needed some money and wanted to make a draw so I said, "Let's go to Benny's room." Don had met this young girl who was about eighteen years old and she was with him at the time. I said, "Come on, we'll all go up to Benny's room and because you don't know him too well, I'll ask him for some money for you." As we were walking toward Benny's room you could hear him practicing a mile away. I knew he was naked. We got to the door and I knocked real loud. The playing stopped and we heard, "Yeah? Who's there?" I said, real loud, "Benny, it's Gubenko and Don Elliott. Don wants to draw some money. We also have a Y-O-U-N-G G-I-R-L W-I-T-H U-S!" I said it as slow as possible, and loud so he could hear me. I said it again. "W-E H-A-V-E A Y-O-U-N-G G-I-R-L W-I-T-H U-S!" He said, "Come on in, Pops!" We opened the door and, sure enough, there he was, standing there naked. Completely naked. I figured it would make more sense if I went in alone, so I left Don and the young girl in the hall, went into the room myself, and Benny gave me some money for Don. Have you ever gotten any money from a world-famous naked man? Forget it. I didn't know where to look I was so embarrassed. When we left, he went right back to playing the clarinet. Completely out there.

About a year-and-a half after I left Benny, I was on the road with my quartet with Terry Pollard on piano, Herman Wright on bass, and Frank DeVito on drums. We were playing in Chicago and by coincidence, Benny was coming back to Chicago with another group to play the Blue Note. The owner of the club I was playing at was great. I told him that I'd love to see Benny's first show and he let us off so we could go down and see Benny. Frank Holtzfield, who owned the Blue Note, loved me. He gave us a table right in front of the bandstand. In fact, it was so close, the spotlight that hit the stage also hit the table we were sitting at. I was always bragging my fanny off to everybody in my quartet about how Benny loved me and had told them all these stories about us playing together and about how close we were. Now came the announcement. "Ladies and gentlemen, Benny Goodman!" Benny came out, walked towards the stage, and when he got as close to us as he could get, I stood up and put my hand out to shake his hand. He looked at me, walked right past me, and went over to somebody else and said hello to them. I didn't believe it. I'm standing there with the spotlight on me with my right hand sticking out, looking like an idiot. He walked right by me. Didn't know who I was.

Some years later, Joe Glaser was putting together a tour with Benny Goodman and Louis Armstrong. Benny wanted to get as many of the guys from the old bands as he could. He told Joe, "Make sure to get me Ziggy Elman." I was with Benny and Joe that day and went with them to rehearsal. We walked in and Benny looked over the band. Georgie Auld was there and a few of the guys from the old band. He looked at the trumpet section and said to Joe Glaser, "I told you to get me Ziggy Elman." Joe, who used the "F" word as though everybody used it, said, "What the fuck are you talking about? There's Ziggy up there!" Benny says, "That's not Ziggy Elman." Joe was getting bugged now. "What are you talking about, you fucking idiot, that's Ziggy Elman up there! I flew him in." "That's not Ziggy," said Benny, and walked out. I honestly think that he didn't know the difference between Chris Griffin, Harry James, and Ziggy Elman. It's like what Sid Weiss told me. Those days, Benny was a little mightier than thou. He never hung out with anybody in the band, ever. When he did hang out, everybody was Pops.

In 1970, I was going through a sick divorce where I lost a million dollars. I had built a fourteen-room house that I had to move out of while my ex-wife was living there until we sold it. The courts took all our money and gave me five hundred dollars a month to live on. I moved into an apartment and still had to make the payments on that house until everything was settled. In the meantime, I had an idea for a television show for Benny Goodman. I was learning a little about producing from working for Steve Allen. I put my idea on paper and wanted to present it to Benny. Most of the show was going to be done like *Candid Camera*. We would tape all the rehearsals *Candid Camera*-style and nobody would know about this but Benny, the producer, the director, and me. We would purposely put wrong notes in the music so that the musicians who were unaware of all this would ask questions to whoever was rehearsing the band. This way, the viewing audience would get to see a legitimate rehearsal, probably for the first time. We would get Georgie Auld, Ziggy Elman, Gene Krupa, Peggy Lee, and as many of the musicians that were still alive from the old bands. The only segment that wouldn't be done *Candid Camera*-style would be re-creating Benny's famous 1938 Carnegie Hall concert. That was the idea of the show.

I didn't have much money to call Benny. I also had to call him in the afternoon person-to-person, and that cost more money because there is a three-hour difference between Los Angeles, where I was, and New York. His office was on the sixty-sixth floor of the Sixty-Six Building. I had about seventeen dollars left for the week with which to eat. I made out a schedule just like a rundown on a TV show. Benny loved baseball and loved the Giants and the Dodgers. I didn't want to jump into the story about the television show so I figured we'd talk two minutes on baseball, a minute of this, two minutes of that, then ease into the show. I knew what it cost to call New York from California so I figured the whole thing would cost about four dollars and ninety-five cents. That would leave me with twelve dollars to eat for the rest of the week. I had a stopwatch with me to time every segment of my schedule.

I called person-to-person, Benny got on and I said, "Benny, it's Terry Gibbs." "Heyyyy, Gubenko! How ya feeling?" "Great, great, how are the Giants and the Dodgers doing?" We talked for about a minute, and I was actually a little ahead of schedule when all of a sudden, Benny said, "Gubenko, someone wants to say hello to you." Muriel, his secretary got on the phone. I didn't have her on my rundown. Muriel ran everything. You had to go through her if you wanted anything from Benny. She happened to like me, but if you weren't nice to her, you wouldn't get to talk to Benny.

So now I was talking to Muriel and looking at my stopwatch the whole time. Five minutes went by and now I'm behind my schedule and hadn't even gotten to talk to Benny about anything. Finally I said, "Listen, I've got to go to a record date," which I didn't have to go to at all. "Let me talk to Benny." She said, "Wait a minute, I think he left." And she put the phone down.

I was holding the phone and I swear to God, I must have held that phone for about eighteen or twenty minutes. Now I was into NEXT month's chopped liver. He completely forgot I was on the phone and went downstairs. Sixty-six floors.

Muriel found him in the lobby, brought him back up, and I finally told him about the show. Then he said, "Who's going to sponsor it?" I said, "Benny, I have to have your permission to use your name so I can go after a sponsor." He said, "Show me the sponsor and then we'll talk about it." I said, "Benny, it doesn't work that way. You've got to tell me you're going to do it first to get a sponsor." We kept repeating the same thing. Show me the sponsor. It doesn't work that way. It finally wound up with him asking me to send him a script. P.S. We never did the show.

One time while I was working with Steve Allen, Steve was in Boston and got snowed in. I had to meet him there but because I couldn't fly into Boston, I met Steve in Philadelphia so that I could go on to the next engagement with him. I didn't have to work with Steve in Philly, for all he had to do on this show was introduce Benny Goodman and his Sextet. Before I left for Philadelphia that morning, my wife heard on the radio that Benny's wife had died. I figured that with his wife dying and with Steve snowed in, and since I couldn't get ahold of Steve, Benny wouldn't show up. I thought I'd better go to Steve's office and get some more of Steve's music just in case he was going to sub for Benny. I wanted to verify the story so I called his brother Irving Goodman first. Irving hadn't heard anything about Benny's wife dying. She actually had died about three days before this happened. His own brother didn't know anything about it. Benny never told him. To make sure that Benny's wife had really died, I figured I'd make one more call, so I called Muriel, his secretary. I got her on the phone and said, "Muriel, I just heard a rumor that Benny's wife died. Is that true?" She said, "Yes, three days ago." You would have thought that he would have told his brother.

I flew to Philadelphia, took Steve's music with me, and was surprised to see Benny there. The show was being held in a gym in a high school and they built a stage in the middle of the gym. Before the actual show started, Steve, who wasn't being paid to perform, went up onstage and played a song on the piano to warm up the audience. Steve then introduced Benny, and as they applauded, he walked off the stage. That's all he had to do, just introduce Benny. At the end of the show when Benny got done, people were really applauding for him. So Steve thought he'd walk onstage and bring Benny off to get a little more applause. As Steve was walking up the steps, Benny pushed Steve down as if he was some flunky. Steve really was hurt because he loved Benny, but Benny acted like he didn't know Steve at all.

Benny loved Naftule Brandwein, the greatest *klezmer* clarinet player that ever lived. We talked about him many times. A while back, I had heard that Benny was coming out to California to play a concert. At that time I was working with Steve Allen and had my own big band. I wrote Benny and told him that when he came out to California, I would like to play with him again. He wrote back, saying that he was coming out, but had already hired Peter Appleyard. He said it sure would be fun to play together again and signed it, "Naftule."

With all that I have said about Benny, most of it sounding negative, it's not really that way, because that's how he was. Try talking with some other musicians who worked with Benny and they'll tell you some nasty stories about him.

The most important thing for me about working for Benny was that I respected his playing. He was without a doubt one of the greatest clarinet players that ever lived, and could he swing!

Working with him was one of the highlights of my career. I loved playing with him, although once again, I must admit that when he wasn't playing the clarinet, he was out in left field. Mr. El Foggo.

Chapter 12
Terry G. and Terry P.

After I got off the road with Benny, Joe Glaser kept his word and booked some class jobs for me. I was really starting to get some recognition. I won the *Down Beat* and *Metronome* polls in 1950 and won them every year through 1955. In 1953, I started a group that had Chick Keeny on drums, Kenny O'Brien on bass, and Teddy Corabi on piano. Chick Keeny's real name was Louis Ciccone, but he changed his name by just using his last name. He always wanted to be a gangster and was strong as an ox. In the sixties, they found Chick's body in the trunk of a car somewhere in Florida. He was done in by the bad boys.

Our first job was in Detroit. A year before we played there, Dizzy Gillespie told me that if I ever got to Detroit, I should go hear a trumpet player named Thad Jones, who was then completely unknown. On our day off, a friend of mine named Pete Flory, who was in the army with me, took me to a place called the Beehive to hear some jazz. I asked him, "Who was playing there?" Pete said, "They've got a sensational trumpet player called Thad Jones." That name rang a bell and then I remembered Dizzy telling me about him. We went down to the club and had a few drinks at the bar. They had a bunch of musicians that I never heard of before, including Thad Jones on trumpet, Elvin Jones on drums, Beans Richardson on bass, Billy Mitchell, a great tenor player who went on to play with Basie, and a young girl on piano named Terry Pollard. They were all unknowns to anybody outside of Detroit.

Thad Jones knocked me out because, just like Dizzy told me, he was great. Everybody in the band sounded great. Then I heard this girl Terry Pollard who played piano completely different than any girl I had ever heard play. She played bebop and she could swing. I thought that maybe because I had a few drinks, this was the reason she sounded that good. There weren't many female jazz players, and the few that were around mostly played the piano: ladies like Marian McPartland and Barbara Carroll, who played good but as the old cliché goes, they were "good for a girl." They didn't have that hard bebop articulation that Terry played with. She sounded like a man. Terry was the first female I ever heard swing that hard.

Teddy Corabi was screwing around with junk so I fired him, and now I needed another piano player. After her show, I asked Terry if she would come to the club I was working at and play for me. The next afternoon she came out to the club where we were playing.

When I audition somebody, I don't pick a song with a million chord changes; I try to pick something like "I Got Rhythm" or the blues to make them feel comfortable. Everybody usually knows the changes to those songs. In four bars I can tell how good they are. I was also sober and wanted to see if she sounded as good as she did the night before. We played the blues and "I Got Rhythm" and I couldn't believe how good she was.

Then, I wanted to see how she'd accompany me on a ballad. One of the ballads I played was a song called "You Don't Know What Love Is." I asked her if she knew the song and she said that she didn't, so I said, "Hit an E-minor seventh, flatted five," and turned around to the vibes. She hit some dumb chord and I turned back around, thinking she didn't hear what I said. Once again, I said, "E-minor seventh, flatted five" and turned around back to my vibes. Again she played some cockeyed chord. This time I really started to get bugged and said, "E-MINOR SEVENTH, FLATTED FIVE!" She said, "I don't know any chord changes." I said, "How are we going to play this song?" She said, "Why don't you just turn around and play the melody." I didn't know what to say to her, so I turned around and started playing.

I didn't believe it. She played every chord that belonged and a few substitute chords that sounded just beautiful. You'd never know that she didn't know one chord from another. Then she told me that she played a little vibes too. I said, "Really?" I went over to the piano and played some chord changes for her while she played the vibes and we played some blues. She played the heck out of the vibes; as good as any vibes player playing those days. In fact, I don't think there are many vibes players today that could swing as hard as Terry Pollard could in 1953.

I wanted to hire her, but she had never been on the road with a white band before. In fact, I don't think that she had ever even been out on the road with ANY band. She was pretty and only twenty-two years old. She didn't know many of the standard songs; all she knew were the bebop songs. I wanted her to go on the road with me and didn't know what to do.

I had a friend called Bill Matney, who was writing for the local Detroit paper and who later on became an NBC correspondent. I called Bill and said, "Bill, you've got to help me get this girl in my band. She'll tear up New York. She'll tear it up anyplace." I knew what we could do because of what Don Elliott and I did. This was going to be even better. Not only would she knock everybody out with her piano playing, but when we would do the vibes duet, and people would see a black girl and a white guy battling it out on the vibes, I knew that we'd break it up everyplace we played. We met with Bill, Terry, her pastor, her mother, and her father. I told them that Donna and I would take care of her and that she could stay with us. They all agreed and Terry Pollard joined my band.

We had one job to play before we opened in New York at Birdland. Kenny O'Brien had other commitments and went back to New York, so Terry recommended Ernie Farrow, who was Terry's boyfriend at the time. Ernie could only stay for a few weeks so I hired another Detroit bass player, Herman Wright, who stayed with my quartet for about three years.

Our first job was in East St. Louis, which at that time was an all-white town. We were lucky in that they had an apartment above the club that we all lived in. I don't think there was a hotel close by that black people could stay in.

On opening night, there were about four hundred people packed in this place. The people went nuts every time Terry played a piano solo. To close the show, Terry and I did our vibes duet for the first time. We were pushing and shoving each other, trying to get around the vibes and we tore up the place. The audience was screaming and cheering and gave us a standing ovation. The vibes duet ended and while the people were standing and applauding, Terry and I faced each other and gave each other a little peck on the lips. Suddenly, everything stopped. It was like somebody gave four hundred people a "cut-off." It got so quiet; it scared the hell out of me.

Our dressing room was straight across from the bandstand in the back of the club. I knew that we had to go through the audience to get to the dressing room. A lot of people who ran the casinos in Las Vegas were from East St. Louis. All the bad guys who wanted to be like them lived there. As we walked through the crowd, I didn't care if they called me a dirty kike or called her a nigger, so long as they didn't touch me. If they touched me, I probably would have pushed their hands off of me and before you knew it, eighty-four guys would hit me right in the mouth. It took a lot of restraint and shutting my ears to get past them to our dressing room and luckily, nobody touched me, or I might have been killed.

I don't remember hearing anybody calling us names, but they must have, because afterward, Terry told me that she wanted to go home. I had to sit and talk with her like a psychologist and I told her, "Screw them, they were applauding for you, YOU'RE the star." I told her that she'd probably encounter this in a lot of places we'd play. But I didn't think it would ever be as bad as it was in East St. Louis. We had a good long talk and worked it out, and we went to New York and opened up at Birdland.

Opening night, we tore Birdland up. Charlie Parker was there. He heard us play and offered Terry a job. In fact, he came in every night and kept offering her a job. She turned him down and to make a long story short, she stayed in my band for four years. That was one of the winningest groups I ever had and it became a highlight of my life.

PeeWee Marquette, Birdland's emcee, always used to go around asking everybody for a dollar. When I asked him why, he'd say that he was going to announce my name real big so I made the mistake of giving him two dollars. George Shearing was the headliner and his record of "September in the Rain" had just been released and was getting a lot of airplay. I was on the same bill with George and wasn't as well known as he was. When PeeWee Marquette announced the acts, he said, "Ladies and gentlemen, sit back and relax because we've got George Shearing and his quintet tonight and ON VIBES WITH HIS OWN QUARTET, THE FABULOUS TERRY GIBBS!" He must have gone on like this for a half-hour, which embarrassed the heck out of me, all because I gave him two dollars.

When I worked there with Terry Pollard and my quartet, I knew PeeWee's schtick about asking everybody in the band for a dollar. This time, I went to him and said, "PeeWee, here's five dollars for my quartet, a dollar for each person and two dollars for me." After about three nights I noticed that he was really talking a lot about Terry Pollard. I went to Terry and said, "Boy, PeeWee must really love you." She said, "He made me give him two dollars." I went to PeeWee and said, "PeeWee, I already gave you five dollars for my band. Why did you hit on Terry for another two dollars?" He looked up at me and said, "Terry, business is business."

PeeWee had a way of ruining everybody's name. I played the jam session on Monday night with Eddie Shaughnessy on drums and Teddy Kotick on bass. This is how PeeWee announced them: "And on drums, we've got Eddie Shaw-genessey, and on bass, Teddy Kotex!"

I was working at Birdland one of the years that I won the *Down Beat* magazine award. *Down Beat* was going to present me with a plaque on *The Steve Allen Show* so I had to miss a set at Birdland. Here's what PeeWee told the audience: "Terry Gibbs is going to be a little late because he's getting the PLAGUE on TV. *The Steve Allen Show* is giving him the *Down Beat* PLAGUE!"

The dressing room at Birdland was very small, about six feet by twelve feet. When we were on the same bill as Count Basie, that meant the sixteen musicians in Basie's band plus my quartet all had to use that dressing room. When I got done with my set, I went to the dressing room because I sweated so much that I usually had to change all my clothes. I had just taken my shirt off when Basie's manager ran in and said, "Terry, Gus Johnson is late. Want to play some drums?" I was hurrying to put on my shirt so I could play with Basie's band when Frank DeVito, who was with me in the dressing room and was so skinny that he couldn't even fight a fly, threw me against a wall and ran out to play the drums. I never did get a chance to play drums with Count Basie but it was a really big thrill for Frank.

A few months later, as I was coming out of Birdland at the end of the job, I ran into Charlie Parker. I had just bought a brand new 1953 Oldsmobile, which had the first soft, padded dashboard. Bird, who was stoned out, said, "Terry, take me up to 125th Street." Donna was with me and I said, "No, we're going home." We lived on Sixty-First Street in the Prescott Hotel. Bird, who wasn't in his best mood, then said, "Then take me home." I think he was looking to score and was a little shaky and belligerent. I asked him where he lived and he said Thirty-Fifth Street. I figured that it would be easier to get him to Thirty-Fifth Street than to go uptown to 125th Street. We got in the car, and I drove while Donna sat between Bird and me.

When you drive in New York, you have to stop every forty seconds because the traffic is the worst. While we were driving, Bird was nodding off, and every time I stopped, he leaned forward. When he did this, his cigarette got closer to my new padded dashboard. That bugged me, so I said, "BIRD! WAKE UP! YOU'RE GOING TO BURN MY DASHBOARD!" He said, "Don't worry. I know what I'm doing." Once again, as we were driving, he leaned forward. I must have woken him up about twenty times. Finally, we got to Thirty-Fifth Street and I said, "Bird, you're home." He said, "Take me to 125th Street." I shut off the motor to the car, got out, walked around to his side, opened the door, and said, "Bird, when you're playing onstage, I'll kiss your ass because you're the greatest musician living. But right now, you're not playing, SO GET OUT OF MY CAR!" and I threw him out of the car. I felt terrible doing that, but this wasn't the Charlie Parker I respected.

We were booked in places that didn't play jazz attractions. I learned that if you play something in the beginning that they recognized and the same thing at the end, then you could do whatever you wanted in the middle. When we played those show houses that were not jazz clubs, I used to open up with one of our closing songs. Sometimes I would play ten choruses and sweat so much that I couldn't miss getting their attention, and they loved it. Then, for the next three or four songs, they wouldn't know what the heck we were playing.

My ballads always got to them because at the end of the song I would always play some kind of technical cadenza that would impress them. Then I'd do two-finger piano, and Terry and I would close with the vibes duet and tear them up.

Everybody has his own *michigasses*. Every once in a while, when Terry would catch a cold, I'd find her in her dressing room rubbing her stomach. It would look like she was trying to push something out of her, and she would say, "Get out, Devil! Get out Devil!" I figured if it worked, wonderful.

Terry was always helping me meet the ladies. If there was a girl in the audience that I thought was pretty, she'd follow her into the ladies room and tell her I thought she was pretty and that we were having a party and would she like to come. Terry was great and I never had to pay her a finder's fee.

After working together for about three months, we got very loose with each other. Even though we knew that anybody who used words like "kike" or "nigger" must be a bigoted asshole, we used them all the time. When we worked at Birdland and did the vibes duet, we'd push each other to get to the note we wanted to hit and run around each other. Terry could never whisper, so when we ran around each other, I'd run past her and whisper, "nigger!" and she'd run by me and yell, "KIKE!" Real loud. In Birdland, at least half the people there were Jewish and the other half were black. They really couldn't hear me say "nigger," especially the black waiters. But she said the word "KIKE" so loud, you could have heard it in Yugoslavia.

I used to brag about Terry Pollard to everybody I talked to. We were playing at the Rouge Lounge in Detroit when, during the intermission, Mel Tormé came in. Mel had never heard Terry play and I was bragging about her to him. I asked Mel if he wanted to sit in and sing a song with us, and he said, "I'd love to." So I made a big announcement that Mel Tormé was in the club and was going to sing a few songs with us. When Mel came up onstage, I asked him what he wanted to sing. He said, "How about 'Violets for Your Furs?'" That's a song that not many people know. I asked Terry if she knew "Violets for Your Furs" and she said she didn't. Knowing Mel like I did, I felt that he was going out of his way to make it hard for Terry. Most of the songs she knew were the bebop songs and the songs that I wrote that we played with the quartet, but she said she'd try it. Then I asked Mel what key he wanted to sing it in and he said E. Jazz musicians hardly ever played in the key of E, which has four sharps. Most jazz musicians didn't even play in sharp keys. I think most of the standards were written in flat keys. I don't think that we got into playing in sharp keys until rock and roll became very big. All the rockers played everything in sharp keys.

I was really bugged with Mel because with his type of voice, he could have sung it in E-flat or F and it would have been the same to him. I think Mel just wanted to try to hang Terry up because I had been bragging about her. Terry didn't know "Violets for Your Furs" from "Stardust" or "The Star Spangled Banner." Herman Wright, the bass player, didn't know the song either, so he had to watch her left hand to see what chords she was playing. That was the worst thing he could have done because Terry, not knowing chords, voiced them her own way. She was liable to play a G-sharp on the bottom of the E chord and Herman could have thought that was a G-sharp chord, which would throw him off even more.

Somehow, Terry played every chord change perfectly. She had what we called "big ears," and heard every chord that belonged in that song. Mel was amazed. The only one that really got hung up was me, because I didn't know that song either and the only time I played in sharp keys is when I played classical music when I was a kid

Detroit was always big for us, mostly because of Terry Pollard. I always stayed at the Wolverine Hotel. A few of the baseball players on the Detroit Tigers stayed there. I met Al Kaline in the lobby when he was twenty years old. Al would eventually become a Hall-of-Famer.

I got to know Bobby Layne of the Detroit Lions, but not from the hotel. We got very friendly and he was a frequent visitor to any club I played in Detroit. Bobby was one of the greatest quarterbacks who ever lived and he was a big fan of mine. Everywhere he went, people would mob him for his autograph. He was a millionaire but also an alcoholic. He didn't have any inhibitions at all. Sometimes, if he was really drinking, he'd come up on stage, take a handkerchief, make it look like it was a saxophone, and make believe he was playing jazz while we were playing. When he'd come to the club where we were playing, he'd bring half the team in with him, people like Joe Schmidt, Dorne Dibble, and Hunchy Hoernschemeyer, and they'd make a great audience for us. They were always ready to party.

One night, Bobby and I partied until about four o'clock in the morning. The newspapers were saying that Bobby's arm was bad and that he was out of shape. The Lions had a practice the next morning in Ypsilanti, which was ninety miles away. Bobby, who was juiced out of his bird, asked me to go with him to his practice. I said, "Forget it,

Bobby, I've got to go to bed." He kept asking me and I finally gave in. Money didn't mean anything to him, so we took a taxicab ninety miles to Ypsilanti. The fare had to be three or four hundred dollars. When we got there, he made me sit on the bench with these big apes. These guys looked like King Kong next to me. Joe Schmidt, who used to be a lineman with the team, was now the coach. He used to let Bobby run the team. I knew that Bobby was half-juiced when they practiced. The next day, when the papers came out, the headline on the sports page said, "Bobby Layne's in better shape than he's ever been." He sure was. He was juiced out.

Another hero in Detroit who I got to hang out with was Soupy Sales. He's still one of my close friends. When I go to New York, if my job starts at nine o'clock, he's there at eight o'clock waiting for me. Soupy had two television shows in Detroit; one was a kid's show in the daytime, and at night, he had a hip show for adults. I wrote a song for him called "Soupy's On."

Soupy is one of the biggest jazz fans in the world. He would show up at all the jazz clubs, and like Bobby Layne, he'd be mobbed by fans. Whatever jazz attraction was working in Detroit would appear on his daytime show, but not to play music. While he was doing his kiddie show, and when he was in the middle of talking with one of his puppets like White Fang or Black Tooth, he'd have some famous jazz musician slowly walk across the stage. This had nothing to do with the show and it wouldn't even be a close-up of the musician. It would almost look like somebody bungled and forgot there was a show going on. He had Thelonious Monk walk across the set, really relaxed. Then, two minutes later, Monk would walk back the other way. Nobody performing on the show would pay any attention to him. The show would go straight ahead like that never happened. Soupy just had a wild sense of humor.

Soupy also loved my low "Lemon Drop" voice, especially when I did it with a Jewish accent. When I'd come on the show, he'd make me ad-lib with him, but he'd make me talk with the Jewish accent. His producer/director, Pete Strand, didn't like when I did that and asked me not to. On one of the nighttime shows I did with Soupy, they wrote a bit for me to do with him. It was a take-off on the Lone Ranger called "The Lone Stranger." It was only a five-minute bit, and when we rehearsed it, I did it in my low voice, but speaking without the Jewish accent. When it came time to do the actual show, which was always done live, Soupy told me to say my lines with my low voice in the Jewish accent. Pete Strand was in the booth, flipping out, but he couldn't do anything about it because it was live. Soupy didn't care.

We just loved each other's sense of humor and would talk on the phone to each other once in a while. I could be sitting in my house when out of the clear blue sky, the phone would ring, and Soupy would call me with a dumb joke. When I worked Detroit, after the job was over, Soupy, his ex-wife Barbara, my ex-wife Donna, and I would sit around and laugh at each other's jokes until five o'clock in the morning.

We played at a club in Cleveland called the Loop Lounge. It looked like a big barn with a high ceiling. Every time the drummer hit a rim shot, the sound bounced all over the place. Sometimes it would throw me off to where I would get lost and lose meter. When that happened, I'd go back to the hotel feeling sick. This one night that it happened and after the job was over, I was sitting at a White Castle hamburger joint right across the street from where we were staying. It was about four o'clock in the morning. I was still bugged about losing meter and screwing up. While sitting there eating a hamburger, I noticed some young guy in his twenties staring at me. Finally, he came over to me and said, "Can I please have your autograph?" That got me into a good mood and I started feeling a little better. I gave him my autograph and signed it, "Best wishes, Terry Gibbs." He looked at it and said, "Ohhh, I thought you were Buddy Greco." That brought me back into the toilet again.

We opened at a new jazz club in Montreal that had another club upstairs that had female impersonators. On opening night, I was into my third or fourth song when somebody yelled out, "When is Terry Gibbs coming on?" I thought the guy was putting me on, so I went over to the mike and said, "I AM Terry Gibbs!" He said, "YOU'RE Terry Gibbs? WHERE'S TERRY GIBBS THE STRIPPER?" I told him the strip joint was upstairs.

When I came to work the second night, the club was empty except for a few people who were at the bar. I couldn't understand why the club was packed on the first night and now there was nobody there. We were supposed to start at nine o'clock. I waited awhile and finally we went on the bandstand and started playing. As soon as we started, the bartender yelled over at me, "Hey! Shut up! Stop playing!" I said, "What's going on?" It turned out that everybody at the bar was watching the Stanley Cup playoffs on television between Montreal and Toronto. They're nuts about hockey in Canada, especially in those two cities. The playoffs were on the whole week we were there and I think we played twenty minutes a night. When Montreal won, they loved us. On the night Toronto won, it wasn't a fun night to play jazz. If there ever was a Terry Gibbs, the Stripper, that night we could have used her.

Max Roach and I used to follow each other playing the same clubs. He'd play Toronto when I was in Detroit, and when he finished Toronto, I'd go there, and he'd go to Detroit. There was a disc jockey in Windsor, Ontario, which is right above Detroit, called Phil McKeller. I wrote a theme song for him called "That Feller McKeller." His show covered most of the East Coast. When I finished an engagement and was driving to my next job, I'd call Phil and tell him that I was at the Howard Johnson's number seventeen on the turnpike. He would say that on the radio and within a couple of hours, Max and his quintet would show up. We usually took the same roads because he was coming from the club that I was going to and vice versa.

Max and I used to make 1250 dollars a week for our groups. We always made the same amount of money. I used to go up to Joe Glaser's office and sneak in where the contracts were. God forbid if I found out that Max was getting more money than I was getting. If I saw him getting fifty dollars more than me, I would have pitched a bitch.

Frank DeVito played drums in my quartet for about two years. We went back to East St. Louis and on that job, we had to play until four o'clock in the morning. Plus, on Sunday, we would do an afternoon matinee. There was a disc jockey that used to come to the club a lot. One night he came to me and said, "Terry, I know that you don't get off until four o'clock in the morning but I'd love to have you appear on my radio show. The only drag is that it starts at seven in the morning." I asked Frank if he wanted to stay up and do the show with me and he said sure.

When we got to the station, the disc jockey took me aside and said, "Terry, I want you to do me a favor. I know that you have this crazy Jewish sense of humor and say these out things on stage, but nobody here knows I'm Jewish, so please try to stay away from your Jewish clichés." Well, that rubbed me wrong. He actually was ashamed to tell anybody he was Jewish. I almost didn't do the show. But finally, I did go, and after he introduced us, the first question he asked me I answered in Jewish. He looked at me, got flustered, and then asked me another question and I answered that question in Jewish, too.

Now he was really confused and he turned to Frank and asked HIM a question. Frank, who also had an out sense of humor, answered in ITALIAN. After that he went to a commercial and threw us out.

In 1955, we played at the Blackhawk in San Francisco opposite Dave Brubeck. Dave was the hottest attraction in the country and the place was packed. We were making fun of Dave because people were saying funny things about him. They actually were praising him by saying that when he played, he threw in a little bit of Beethoven, Bach, and boogie-woogie. We thought that was pretty stupid and we said some really unkind things about him. When I look back at what we said about Dave, I kind of feel ashamed of myself because Dave Brubeck is one of the nicest people I ever met.

When that job was over, we had to go down south to Los Angeles to play a club for two weeks and then go on to Las Vegas from there. I drove my car and Frank DeVito always followed me in his car. When you drive caravan-style on the road, and if you're driving on a four-lane highway and want to pass a car, if you're the lead car, you don't pass the front car first and let the other guy try and catch up to you. You put your blinkers on and let the back car know that you're going to pass. Then when everything is clear, the car behind me moves over to the left and then I move in ahead of him. It stops you from having an accident.

I had a cold and we were right around King City, California, and still had quite a ways to go, so I let Herman Wright drive my car. It was the first time I ever let anybody do that. Herman wasn't an experienced driver so Frank took over as the lead driver. Frank forgot about the caravan-style that we were doing and passed another car on a two-lane road. Now Herman had to try and pass that car to catch up with Frank. We were up in the mountains where if you made one wrong turn, you could go off a cliff but Herman decided to try and pass. Thank God we were on a road where we were surrounded by mountains.

As he pulled out into the other lane, another car came at us. Herman stepped on the brake too hard; we turned sideways, and got hit on the right side where I was sitting. The car rolled over a couple of times. Herman didn't get hurt, he just fell out of the car. I was on the other side of the car and got hurt real bad. What saved my life was that my vibes had a steel bar that held the two ends of the instrument together. That bar was sitting on the floor in the back seat and that stopped the other car from crashing through our car. While I was lying there on the ground, bleeding, cars were stopping and people were getting out to see what had happened. A lot of people were gathered around and staring at me. Frank DeVito told me that the first thing I said when the people were staring at me was, "And now for an encore, I'd like to break my leg." I was pretty delirious.

They couldn't stop the bleeding so I was taken to a private hospital in King City where they put twenty stitches in my head. I was there for about three or four weeks. I really lucked out, for the doctor who started the hospital handpicked everyone who worked there: the surgeon, the internist, the gastroenterologist, a psychiatrist; about ten doctors in all. Luckily, the surgeon who operated on me was good. He told me that the cut on my head was about a thirty-second of an inch from a vein. Any closer and I could have bled to death. I still have a plate in my head from that accident.

While I was in the hospital, I wrote a song dedicated to where the accident happened, and called it "King City Stomp." I recorded it on my first album for EmArcy.

When I got out of the hospital, we rented a place in Hollywood called the Elaine Apartments, right across from the Hollywood Ranch Market. The place looks like a toilet now. My right arm was paralyzed and I didn't think I'd ever be able to play again. I was thirty-one when that happened and was at the height of my career. I kept thinking that I'd never play music again. Mentally, I almost went nuts. They gave me all kinds of diathermy treatments and it took about nine weeks before I was able to play again.

My agent canceled all of my jobs and he was able to push Las Vegas back until I got well. By that time, Frank wanted to stay in California and left the band. Then I hired a drummer from Sweden who called himself Bert Dale, whose real name was Nils-Bertil Dahlander. He was the number one drummer in Sweden; six-foot-four, and completely nuts. Completely out there. I mean OUT THERE. Sometimes he would forget he was in America, look me straight in the eye, and talk to me in Swedish. I'd say, "Nils, what are you talking about? You're talking Swedish!" And he'd say, "Oh" and would never realize it.

We finally opened in Las Vegas at a new hotel called the Royal Nevada. For some reason, the hotel didn't last long. They said it kept losing money. The main act in the showroom was the great comedian Jimmy Durante and opera singer Helen Traubel. We played in the lounge. A few years later, when the hotel closed, the Stardust Hotel bought the property and changed the Royal Nevada into the Stardust Convention Center.

In 1955, Las Vegas hotels didn't have separate little clubs; the whole casino was open. The gambling tables were maybe forty yards away from the bandstand and the last row of where the people sat would be about twenty yards from the gambling tables. If you had a good crap game going on and someone was winning a lot of money, they'd shut the mikes off on the bandstand because the music would get in the way of the gambling. They hardly ever had jazz in Las Vegas because it wasn't conducive to people just sitting around, listening to music. Because this was one big open room, if they weren't gambling, they'd sit down at a table and listen to whatever music was going on; it could be country-western or anything.

The place was packed because the hotel had just opened, so I figured I would try to hit a home run and open with one of my closing tunes. I played "T&S," which had a big flashy ending. There must have been two or three hundred people sitting there. When I got done playing, maybe ten or twelve people applauded. That made me nervous. I'd never had only ten or twelve out of three hundred people applaud before. We always had all three hundred screaming.

Then I played a ballad. I always played a cadenza on the end that was flashy and very technical and it always got to them. This time, maybe twelve people applauded. Now I really got nervous, so I thought I'd better go into our closing vibes duet, which always tore them up. When we finished with that, maybe seventeen people applauded.

I figured that they just didn't like us in Las Vegas and I thought I'd better go talk to the entertainment director. I went over to this real nice guy, whose name was Dave Wilkinson, and I said, "Dave, if you want us to leave after the week is over, I'll let you out of the contract." Dave said, "What happened?" I said, "Weren't you out there when we played our show?" He said, "No, what happened?" I said, "We played our closing tune, which really tears everybody up and seventeen people applauded." He said, "Seventeen? Great! That's wonderful! NOBODY ever applauds! They don't ever listen to anybody. Seventeen? You deserve a raise!" We went through six weeks playing like that, with no more than twenty people applauding at a time.

Nils didn't know much about the race situation in the U.S. In 1955, there were stars like Harry Belafonte, Lena Horne, and Sammy Davis, Jr., who couldn't stay at the hotel where they were performing. They'd have a trailer outside the hotel for them to dress in, and they would stay at a place called the Moulin Rouge, which was in the black part of town. That's where Terry Pollard and Herman Wright had to stay when we worked there. What bugged me was that after we played each set, Terry and Herman had to go sit in the back dining room, which was empty. Just the two of them, sitting there. It was a drag.

We were there for six weeks and when option time came up, they wanted to pick the option up and hold us over for six more weeks. I didn't want to stay because we couldn't hang out together. We had such a great family feel. Just seeing Terry and Herman sitting in the back room made me sick. I felt bad because I could do and they couldn't do.

Our usual salary was 1250 dollars a week for the group, but in Las Vegas we made 1750 dollars. A five hundred-dollar raise back then is like 5,000 dollars today, because back then, you could get a room for nineteen dollars a week. Today that room will cost you 180 dollars a day. The weird thing was that Terry and Herman wanted to stay because I was paying them more money.

After working there for a few weeks, I hired a black girl called Cardella DiMilo, who was a great blues singer. She was only in the band for a day or two when I heard Nils ask her out on a date. I went over to him and said, "Nils, you can't take Cardella out. They don't allow black people in restaurants or hotels." He said, "Nay, yes!" I told him again, "Nils, they won't let you in anywhere." Then I went to Cardella and told her that Nils was going to ask her out and she was great about the whole thing. She understood what was happening in Las Vegas. If you were a black entertainer, it was a known fact that after you got done with your show, you couldn't go out into the audience and mingle with the people. In 1975, Cardella was running Monday night concerts at a club in Los Angeles called the Parisian Room and presented me with an award that said, "Thanks for your contributions to the music world."

Liberace came into the lounge to hear us play. He was the hero of Las Vegas; the biggest attraction they had there at that time. He came in, heard Terry Pollard, and loved her playing. He came to me after the show and said, "I really liked your piano player. Could you ask her to come over and have a drink with me?" I said, "I don't think they'll let her come out here." He called one of the guys over who ran the place and was told that Terry couldn't come out. Liberace really pitched a bitch and caused a big scene. He said that if she wasn't allowed to come out and have a drink with him that he would leave and never come back to that hotel again. They didn't want Liberace to leave so they said okay. I went back to Terry and told her that Liberace wanted her to come out and have a drink with him. At first she didn't want to come out. She said, "If they don't want me out there, I'm not going out." I said, "Terry, Liberace just went through a whole scene because he wants you to have a drink with him. Screw the rest of those people." Finally, she did come out. Liberace was great because he went through a scene that you wouldn't believe. That was really nice of him to do that.

The biggest drag was we couldn't hang out together after the job was over. I didn't want to hang out with Nils because he was out there. He used to do a funny thing for us. He used to wear one of those beanie caps with a little brim. He would go down to the busiest part of town, stand on the corner, put his hat on the floor, and start singing Swedish songs. Nobody knew what he was singing about. He looked like he was begging for money. Believe it or not, people came by and dropped money into his hat. Of course, he didn't do it for the money, he did it just to break us up. Sometimes he'd get two or three dollars.

Bobby Shad, vice president of Mercury Records, wanted me to sign a contract with Mercury and record my group. I said, "Bobby, the only way I'll record for you is if you'll let me record as if we were doing a live date. I want to have some fun; maybe bring a few bottles of juice in, drink a little, and have some fun just like we were playing on stage." Those days, when you recorded, if you accidentally dropped a stick and it made a noise, they'd have to stop the take and start over. I told him that if there was a noise that really wasn't too loud to keep recording. I just wanted to go straight ahead and not stop for anything. He said, "You got it."

Bobby Shad was one of the best producers I ever worked with, even though I produced practically every date I ever did. I didn't care who got producing credit as long as they let me do things my way. Bobby was smart. I had a rehearsed, tight quartet, and he would have been dumb to try and change anything. He would just sit in the booth and laugh with us, drink with us, and have fun.

We went and did our first date and recorded all day. We were drinking and carrying on and were on our sixth tune, when all of a sudden, I heard a loud thud. BOOM! I turned around to see what had happened. Nils was so juiced, he fell backwards off of the riser and passed out on the floor. Six-foot-four, two hundred pounds. We tried to wake him and couldn't. We tried to lift him up and couldn't even do that. He was dead weight and stoned out. So we left him there and went home. When we came back the next morning, he was still out, lying there on the floor. We woke him up and finished our record date. After a while, because he couldn't understand the racial problems in this country, Nils had a slight breakdown and went back to Sweden. He just couldn't understand how people could think the way they did.

Ever since Charlie Parker recorded with strings, everybody tried to copy the same idea. When Bobby Shad came to me and wanted me to do an album with strings, I said, "Bobby, I don't want to do the same thing as Bird, but I know what you're looking for. Why don't we do the same kind of a thing, only we use five saxophones instead of strings?" I had Manny Albam write the arrangements and that album became the biggest hit I ever had. They called it "Vibes on Velvet." Even today, you can go into elevators or department stores and hear it. After I moved to California, it was selling so well, that I did another album that was called "More Vibes on Velvet." I used the Dream Band saxophone section for that.

The first few years we were together, we worked about fifty weeks a year. We were going from one job to another. We played in East St. Louis at the Terrace Lounge, did a matinee from four until seven, and then went back on stage from ten until four in the morning. When the job was over, we packed up and drove five hundred miles to Oberlin College in Cleveland. We got there about an hour before the show started, set up, did our show, then had to leave immediately to drive to New York, where we opened up at Birdland. Once again, we got there about an hour or two before we set up to play. Nobody went home, nobody even checked in anywhere. We had to play our job first.

Chapter 12

For some reason, as much fun as I tried to have onstage, I couldn't smile or laugh. Terry Pollard was the same way. Neither of us could laugh, we were so wiped out. The next day, we went to a doctor who told us we were suffering from nervous exhaustion and if we didn't take a few weeks off, we were going to have a nervous breakdown. I told the people who ran Birdland about our situation and they said that they understood and to come back when we were feeling better.

The doctor gave us a prescription, and we went to the drugstore to fill it. Now, there we were, a black girl and a white guy, both of us looking zonked out, walking into a pharmacy and looking half dead. I was walking up to the guy behind the counter to get the prescription filled when I heard a noise. I turned around and saw Terry lying on the floor. She had passed out. Now we REALLY looked like two junkies, without a doubt. We were off for about four days when the adrenaline started to kick in. When you're young, four days of a nervous breakdown is enough so I called Birdland and we went back to work.

When we played the vibes duet, "Flying Home" was our closing tune. We were working opposite Illinois Jacquet. Illinois was a cocky little guy and in my opinion, one of the best tenor players I ever heard. He had more of a rhythm-and-blues band than a bebop band. He always thought that he made Lionel Hampton famous because of the chorus that he played on "Flying Home." We closed our set playing it and had the people screaming for us. This was the first time that Illinois had played Birdland. He had never seen our act before. The moment we got off the bandstand, he had to follow us. His ego got the best of him and he said, "Now, ladies and gentlemen, the ORIGINAL 'Flying Home!'" Then he went into his famous chorus. That was our closing song but his ego wouldn't let it go and he had to open his set with the same song.

Lionel Hampton was going to do a Jewish album and Joe Glaser wanted me to teach him how to play "Eli, Eli." I was still working at Birdland and he was ending his engagement at the Capitol Theatre. Lionel was going to open at a club about three or four blocks from there called Basin Street. I went up to the Capitol Theatre to spend some time with Lionel, teaching him to play "Eli, Eli" on two-finger piano. Lionel had no inhibitions at all. The first time I went up there, I had to wait because he had just gotten done with the show and was going to change his clothes. I was sitting there waiting, and someone said, "Terry, Lionel said for you to come in." I walked in and he was standing with his hands up in the air, completely naked, and his valet was wiping him all over with a towel. He was wiping him everywhere, even his crotch and I didn't know where to look. I spent a few hours with Lionel showing him some Jewish phrases on "Eli, Eli."

Three days later, Lionel opened at Basin Street. On Saturday nights, Basin Street closed at three-thirty. At three-twenty, all of the tables were cleared and the waiters had their jackets on and were ready to go home. Most of the waiters at Basin Street were either Jewish or black. I finished at three o'clock, and by the time I changed my clothes and got over to Basin Street, it was three-twenty. Basin Street must have held about 300 people, but by this time of night, there were maybe only fifty there. Lionel started to play "Flying Home." It's three-twenty and these waiters were ready to kill him because not only was he playing "Flying Home," he was marching through the audience with the band. He got back on stage and by now it was three-thirty-five and the waiters were looking at him like they really wanted to kill him. The fifty people were applauding, and Lionel looked over, saw me, and said, "Heyyyyy, ladies and gentlemen, now a very special arrangement for my friend Terry Gibbs, 'Eli, Eli.'" If he had said "Stardust" or any other song except "Eli, Eli," those Jewish waiters would have shot him right there. But the moment they said "Eli, Eli," they had to listen. He got done at three-forty-five. Lionel was beautiful.

Morris Levy and his partners opened up a Birdland in Miami, Florida. As bad as Morris could be, he was very liberal in certain areas. Miami didn't have any clubs where black and white people could mingle until Morris opened up the club. People were picketing the club because of the interracial policy. We played there opposite Erroll Garner. Terry Pollard and Herman Wright couldn't stay on the beach, so they had to stay in downtown Miami. That wasn't that big a deal because we had two cars and Miami wasn't too expensive. The beach had all the resort hotels, and rooms cost something like 300 dollars a night. Luckily, I had a room connection, Cy Coleman, the famous writer of Broadway shows. Cy was playing cocktail piano in the resort hotels and lived there. When he found out that I was going to be appearing at Birdland, he called me and told me that he would find me a room in somebody's house and it wouldn't be too expensive.

More than anything else, I think that Cy would have liked to have made it as a jazz piano player. His jazz playing was good, but not in the class of the heavyweight piano players. When he wrote "Witchcraft," we were all surprised because we didn't know that he had that kind of talent as a songwriter. He went on to become one of the most successful songwriters around, and I lost my room connection.

I just finished a set and was in the dressing room, when someone came in and told me that there was a gentleman named Lenny Garment who wanted to see me. I hadn't seen Lenny since I was a kid. I knew that he had become a very prosperous lawyer but we'd been out of touch for a good twenty years. So I told them to send him back to my dressing room. Lenny came in wearing a pair of white pants and a white shirt, but he looked like he had slept in them all night. He was all disheveled and dirty and probably hadn't shaved in a year. He looked terrible. I heard that he'd been drinking a lot so naturally, I thought that he was scuffling, because he looked like a bum.

I didn't want to embarrass him by giving him some money, so I figured I'd ask him where he was staying. Maybe I'd ask him to stay with me if he had no place to go. I said, "Lenny, you okay?" He said, "Yeah. Could I sit in and play a song with you?" I noticed that he had a clarinet case in his hand. "Great," I said. "Where are you staying?" He said, "I've got a suite at the Tropicana Hotel." I said, "Tropicana Hotel? What are you doing in town?" He said, "We're suing the state of Utah."

I thought Lenny had become a drunken bum and here he was on what was probably an eighty-four million dollar case and I was going to give him two dollars.

While I was working in Miami, my father took a train there to visit us. Donna and I put him up in a kosher hotel for a week. When we finished the engagement, we drove back in my car. Somewhere along the way, we were going through a town and stopped to get something to eat. There was a sign on the restaurant that said, "no colored allowed." My father looked at that sign and asked me what it meant. I told him that they didn't allow colored people in to eat at the restaurant. That was what everybody called black people back then. He said, "That's a *shandir*," which means, "that's a shame." We walked into the restaurant, sat down, and my father saw a black man behind the counter cooking and a black waiter. He asked me about it and I said, "Yeah, Pa, they can work here but they don't allow them to eat here." He started to cause a scene. "What do you mean, colored people can't eat here? They're allowed to work here but they shouldn't be allowed to eat here?" We never finished our food because we could have been killed, so we got out of there and left.

I had to do a big band record date and I wanted to use my regular quartet rhythm section. I had the copyist send me all the piano parts while we were on the road so that I could show Terry what and where to play. When we got to the record date, she would always put the wrong song on the piano when she played. All twelve charts were put on the piano. Terry never bothered to put the right piece of music in front of her. We could be playing 'Happiness Is Just a Thing Called Joe" and the music in front of her would be "Bewitched, Bothered, and Bewildered."

Besides memorizing the charts, she had big ears, and after we rehearsed the arrangement once, she had it down. She didn't even think about ever turning the pages of the music. It stayed the same way through the whole arrangement.

The biggest show that Terry and I ever played in was called the Birdland All-Stars of 1957. Billy Eckstine, Sarah Vaughan, and Count Basie's big band with Joe Williams were the headliners. Basie's band was loaded with some of the best players around, including Frank Foster, Frank Wess, Sonny Payne, Joe Newman, and Thad Jones. Also on the bill were Chet Baker and his group, Jeri Southern, Lester Young, Zoot Sims, the Phineas Newborn Trio, and Bud Powell's Trio; all on one show. Sonny Payne the drummer and Eddie Jones the bass player, who were both with Basie's band, played with Terry Pollard and me.

Unfortunately, on the third day out, when we were in Philadelphia, Chet Baker got busted. Billy Eckstine wanted to quit the tour after that happened. He was the most popular singer at that time and making a lot of money and didn't want the narcotics squad coming around. Everybody was smoking pot. The bus would reek from the smoke and he didn't want to get busted.

We had to make five hundred-mile trips and had nothing to do, so we played a game called Kangaroo Court. Here's how the game was played. Billy Eckstine was the judge. If you had some kind of grievance, you might say something like, "When Sonny Payne was playing behind me, he was rushing." I had to go to the kangaroo court with B as the judge, pick someone to be my attorney and Sonny would do the same. Whoever lost the case, the loser and their attorney would each have to buy a bottle of whiskey for the show. We had a case of every kind of alcohol on the bus: Scotch, vodka, gin, rum, cognac, etc. Sarah's valet, Johnny Gary, had to make sure that before we left town, all of the bottles in each case were full.

Terry Pollard had an affair with Eddie Jones, the bass player. Afterward, they had a little scene on the bus. They were arguing and finally Terry said, "And you ain't shit in bed!" This is it! Court time! Pick a lawyer. Kangaroo court was in session.

Terry lost the case, but her fine wasn't a bottle of whiskey, it was the silent treatment for a week. Nobody in the show, including the bus driver, could talk to her. Because she was in my quartet, all I was allowed to say to her was "Go, baby!" "Yeah!" and "You got the next chorus." That's all I could say to her on stage for the whole week. Nobody could talk to her; that was her punishment.

After three days of the silent treatment, Terry walked to the front of the bus, crying. She said she wanted to apologize and that she was wrong and went through this whole scene. Billy Eckstine was nice and let her off of her punishment for the rest of the week. It was harder on me because we were so close.

Prez, who had trouble getting to sleep, would get up and accuse somebody of one of the most ridiculous things you ever heard of so that we could start kangaroo court. He once said that he saw Phineas Newborn touch Lady Pollard's leg and so they both had to get attorneys to defend themselves. The weirdest thing about it was that Phineas sat seven rows away from Terry, but Prez couldn't sleep and we all had to wake up and stay awake with him.

When we'd get to the job and get to the dressing room, Prez would always start a crap game. We usually played for dimes and quarters. After about ten or fifteen minutes of playing craps, Billy Eckstine and Morris Levy or Count Basie would walk in to where we were playing, and all of a sudden, the quarter became five dollars, then up to a hundred dollars. Prez would be bugged because that would throw him out of the game immediately. Every once in a while, we would have a crap game, but Prez would only invite about four of us, and we'd go down to the basement instead of the dressing room and try to get our game in for the fifteen or twenty-five cents we normally played for.

Zoot Sims knew every chorus Lester Young ever played. He and Prez and I would go to the same dressing room and while Zoot was warming up, he'd play all of Prez's solos from all of the old Count Basie records, like "Taxi War Dance" and "Lester Leaps In." He knew every one of them. While he was playing them, Prez would sit back in his chair with a smile on his face, nod his head and say, "That's right, Lady Sims. That's right, Miss Zoot." He called everybody "Lady" or "Miss."

He also had his own way of saying things. Until you were around him for a while, you weren't sure what he was talking about. When Prez, Sweets Edison, and Papa Jo Jones got together, NOBODY would know what they were talking about. I was on stage playing a ballad and Prez was on the side of the stage listening to me. While I was playing, he yelled out to me, "Lady Gibbs, take another helping!" meaning that he wanted me to play another chorus. It made sense to me.

Prez was drinking about a fifth of cognac a day. I asked him what it did for him and he said it gave him a little bit of a lift, which cognac actually does, if you don't drink it excessively. I think they gave people with heart problems a little cognac every once in a while. Because he was drinking so much, he didn't always sound like the Lester Young of yesteryear when he played with Basie. When he was on, we'd all go down to the stage to hear him.

I found out that black people living down South could be just as bad as white people towards other blacks. When we were down south and we had to check into a hotel, there were no reservations at the hotel for anybody including the superstars like Sarah Vaughan, Billy Eckstine, or Count Basie. Whoever got to the desk first, got their room first. Prez, being such a sweet and laid back guy, was always the last one out of the bus. I'd check Prez into the hotel so that he'd have a decent room. One day he said to me, "Lady Gibbs, you're my new manager."

When we played down South, we used to have to eat in the bus because they wouldn't let black people eat in restaurants. By this time, I was the only white person left in the show because Chet Baker had gotten busted, Jeri Southern was fired for being drunk, and Zoot had left for other commitments. Some of the guys said, "Terry, why don't you go out and eat? We understand the situation. There's no reason for you to have to suffer." But I said "Forget it," and we used to go into supermarkets and buy canned tuna fish and sardines and eat them in the bus.

PeeWee Marquette traveled with us and emceed the show. When we weren't on stage, he wore the same red shirt every day for about six weeks. It probably was so funky that it could have walked around by itself. Sarah Vaughan got bugged and took the shirt and burned it. Then she bought him six brand new shirts, but she didn't tell him about it. We were about to leave town, and PeeWee couldn't find his red shirt.

We were all sitting around backstage and Basie was relaxing in this comfortable chair. PeeWee thought that Basie had hidden his shirt and said, "Basie! Give me back my shirt! I know you took it!" Basie said, "Motherfucker, leave me alone." PeeWee said, "Basie! I said give me back my shirt!" Basie said, "YOU LITTLE MIDGET, I'LL KICK YOUR ASS IF YOU DON'T LEAVE ME ALONE!" Finally PeeWee said, "Basie, I'm getting mad!" and he whipped out a switchblade knife and pushed the button that released the blade.

Now, if you've ever seen a switchblade knife, when the blade comes out, it's usually about six to eight inches long. Well, when PeeWee's blade came out, it couldn't have been any longer than an inch-and-a-half. This time, when he pointed the knife at Basie, and once again said, "Basie, give me back my shirt!" everybody just broke up. Then Sarah Vaughan gave him his six shirts and PeeWee broke up also.

I really got bugged with Sarah. I felt like she was carrying a chip on her shoulder. I knew that the South wasn't the most pleasant place to be for black people because of how a lot of white people felt towards blacks so I said, "Sassy, a lot of people here are prejudiced, but you're treating all white people just like they're treating you. Every time somebody asks you for an autograph, you just walk right past them and fluff them off. A few days ago, some white doctor invited Joe Williams, Joe Newman, and me to his house after the show for some food and a few drinks. There were three white girls there who were friends of the doctor's and all we did was laugh and dance with them. When the townspeople found out that these girls had danced with black musicians, they all got fired from their jobs. Not everybody in the South is bad."

Billy Eckstine had a white millionaire doctor friend. On Saturday night, after the job was over, we were all starving and were going to go to the bus and eat our canned food. Billy said, "Listen, nobody eat in the bus tonight." The bus went about three or four blocks and parked in front of a nightclub. We didn't know why we had parked there. About a half-hour later, we saw about a 150 or 200 people coming out of the nightclub. A lady came over to us in the bus and told us to come inside. Billy Eckstine's friend had paid everybody's tab in the club, bought the club for the night, and we were wined and dined.

We used to follow Jeri Southern in the show. Unfortunately, she was drinking too much, and it showed when she was on stage. She'd perform while being drunk. In Montreal, when people didn't like you and wanted you to get off the stage, they didn't boo you, they'd stomp their feet on the floor, and wouldn't stop until you left the stage. Even when they didn't boo her off the stage, she'd bomb because she was half drunk. Terry and I used to follow her in the show and really break it up. I thought that Jeri's bombing was the reason we were breaking it up.

That's when I found out something I never knew about show business. Billy Eckstine, who closed the show, insisted that we go on just before him. I didn't realize why he did that until Jeri Southern got fired. They fired her on the spot and had to rearrange the show, so they had us follow Joe Williams and the Basie band. I figured we were really going to bomb following Joe because he used to tear up the place. He closed his part of the show with "Everyday I Have the Blues," with Basie's band roaring behind him. Who would want to hear a quartet after that? I was wrong, for when he left the stage, he had everybody in the audience in an up mood. That's how I found out why B wanted us to follow him. When Terry and I got done playing the vibes duet, we had the crowd all worked up so that when B was introduced and walked out on stage, the crowd gave him a standing ovation even before he sang his first note.

Bud Powell never should have been on the Birdland tour, but unfortunately, the people who owned Birdland had power of attorney for Bud and had taken him out of a mental hospital. I think they were his legal guardians and took him out of the hospital just to do that tour. In the two months we were on the tour, he may have played good about four or five times. We would hear him playing while we were in the dressing rooms because of the monitors in the rooms. When he was playing good, everybody in the show would run down to the wings to listen to him.

Besides Bud, we were loaded with other great piano players like Count Basie, Bobby Tucker, who played for Billy Eckstine, Jimmy Jones, who played for Sarah Vaughan, Phineas Newborn, and Terry Pollard. When Bud played good, all of them ran down to hear him, but that didn't happen very often. He never should have been there. He wasn't well.

We traveled by bus everywhere we went, except for one night when we had to charter an airplane. We weren't sure this airplane could get off the ground, it looked so raggedy. Terry had never been in an airplane before and was really scared. When everybody in the show found out how scared she was, we all put her on. "It's nothing at all! You get up there and the plane goes down, it goes up, it goes to the side, it shakes, but don't worry, it's all normal." We took off, got up in the air, and were flying for about a half-hour when suddenly, we hit an air pocket, and the airplane dropped about 100 feet. Everybody on the plane really panicked except Terry Pollard. She was the only one who didn't get scared because we had told her that the airplane would do this. She was cool and we were a bunch of nervous idiots.

Donna and I got divorced in 1956. It wasn't a bitter divorce. I was on the road all the time and the marriage was going nowhere, so we split up. We were married for about five years but we were really living two different lives. I was on the road six to eight months out of the year. After being divorced about seven months, we started calling each other. I was getting burnt out being on the road and Terry Pollard had a little boy that her mother was helping her raise. Terry and I both thought that the four years we had together were a winner and a lot of fun, but now it was time for us both to try and settle down. We had about three more weeks of contracts to fulfill, and after that, I broke up the quartet. We each went our own way but always managed to keep in touch with each other, for we were as close as two people could be without being lovers.

Terry had a stroke in the 1980s and they had a big benefit for her at the Cadillac Hotel in Detroit. Every musician who ever worked Detroit, the Tommy Flanagans, the Kenny Burrells, and the Barry Harrises all showed up. I asked Steve Allen if he would do me a favor and go to Detroit with me and play an afternoon concert at Cobo Hall so that we could raise some extra money for Terry. Steve was the type of person who would go anywhere to help anybody in need, and he immediately said yes. He even paid his own airfare to get to Detroit.

I was told that Terry was in a wheelchair and every five minutes or so she'd fall asleep, and then wake up. She's a lot better now but back then, it was right after the stroke and her brain wasn't functioning right. When Steve and I finished our afternoon concert, I immediately changed my clothes and went down to the Cadillac Hotel to see Terry. When I got there, every newspaper and television photographer was following me around because they knew about the relationship I had with Terry. As I was walking through the audience, people were taking pictures of me all over the place. I finally got to about five feet from Terry, and saw that she had fallen asleep. Her head was down, but I walked over to her anyway and gave her a big hug. The flashes on the cameras were all going off now, and as I was bending down and hugging her, she woke up and said, "Terry, they're taking our picture. Don't show your profile." I cried and laughed at the same time.

Chapter 13
California, Here I Come!

Donna and I thought that if we moved to California and got away from the hectic life we were living in New York, that maybe we could make the marriage work again. Being that I played all the percussion instruments, I figured that if I got some studio work and didn't have to travel, it would make things a lot easier for both of us.

When we got to California, we rented a small place about three blocks from Cahuenga Blvd. There was a place called Duffy's Tavern nearby that had a comedian working there that somebody had told me about called Lenny Bruce. They told me that he was funny, but worked very dirty.

We were in that apartment for about three weeks, and one day, we decided to take a walk around the neighborhood and check it out. We didn't realize that Duffy's Tavern was real close to where we lived. Then I remembered about the comedian who worked there, so we went in. It was just a bar that was once a strip joint. When we walked in, Lenny Bruce was on stage. He was telling all these far out stories and did about ten minutes of bits and we didn't hear one dirty word. We had forgotten that somebody told us that he worked dirty.

While he was doing one of his bits, he stopped, looked over to his left, and said, "Ladies and gentlemen, you'll never believe who's here. Anybody remember when this was a strip club? Well, Dixie Dunbar's backstage! Dixie, come on out and take a bow!" He kept repeating it and made everybody applaud like a bunch of idiots. Nobody came out so Lenny said, "Let me go get her." He had a mike off stage and we heard him say, "Hey, Dixie, just come on out and take a bow. They'll remember you." He did this for about two minutes and finally, we heard, "All right, she's coming out!" Lenny walked out onstage all alone, completely naked, with just a pair of shoes on. He looked at the audience, turned around, bent over, showed his *tuchis*, straightened up, and walked off the stage. We didn't believe it.

After we got settled, I called Al Lapin, who was the most powerful contractor in the business. He contracted all of the shows at NBC: *The Dean Martin Show, The Dinah Shore Show, The Tonight Show,* and all the variety shows. I called him and asked him if there was a chance to get on staff and he said, "Let me think about it." He knew who I was, plus I knew that he would check with the other musicians who were on staff at NBC. When he called me back, he said he would put me on staff.

By this time I started to feel a little better and was ready to go out and play some jazz again. But I found out that if you had a staff job, you couldn't work at night. They had what they called a quota, which meant that if you were on staff, you couldn't work nightclub jobs, because they wanted to pass the work around. I didn't know what to do because I didn't want to give up playing jazz, so I had to find an excuse for not wanting the job. When he called me back and offered me the staff job, I said, "I'd have to have a double check." He said, "You little *cocker*, what double check?" He got mad at me. "THE ONLY GUYS WHO ARE GETTING DOUBLE CHECKS ARE CONRAD GOZZO AND IRV COTTLER!" Then he hung up on me. Conrad was one of the greatest lead trumpet players in California, and years later, Irv became Frank Sinatra's regular drummer. I figured, "Good, now I can go back to playing jazz."

About a week later he called me again and said, "You little *cocker*, I'm gonna give you a double check." Later, I realized why he did that. If he put me on staff, he could use me as a guest star on all of the variety shows without NBC having to pay me any more money. I finally wound up telling him why I didn't want to go on staff. Surprisingly, he understood.

I always hated names given to jazz. I couldn't tell the difference between the so-called East Coast sound and the West Coast sound because most of the guys who played on the West Coast came from the East Coast. But they called music that was being played on the West Coast "cool jazz." Chet Baker and I could have played together, and Shorty Rogers and I did play together. When Shorty had a big band, it wasn't cool; it was a hard swinging big band. Those ridiculous names given to jazz are just commercial names made up by people trying to sell records. Shorty made a lot of noise out here with what they called a cool sound and so did Gerry Mulligan. The Lighthouse All-Stars wasn't even close to what was considered to be cool jazz. With drummers like Shelly Manne, Max Roach, and Stan Levey, who all came from the East Coast and were beboppers, it wasn't cool, it was hot. They could swing you off the stage. Some of the soloists like Frank Rosolino, who came from Detroit, and Conte Candoli, who came from Michigan, were also beboppers

When I left New York, I owned about 10,000 dollars worth of stock. That was like a million dollars to me. I had investments in Phillips Petroleum, General Motors, and General Dynamics, which were Class A blue chip stocks. The stock market was taking a little beating and I was down about a thousand dollars. I had been with Bache & Company in New York and didn't know anybody in California, so I went to their office and talked to some young guy who worked there. He told me that the only way I could get my money back was to sell everything and buy these five-dollar stocks. I didn't know anything about the stock market so I took his advice. The first day I made about five hundred dollars. The second day I made about six hundred and then five hundred the next day. Then all of a sudden, I started to lose: four hundred, then three hundred, then four hundred again, and before I knew it, the ten thousand was down to six thousand. I panicked and sold everything. I thought this guy gave me the wrong advice and I was going to lose it all.

Then I bumped into Georgie Auld and he mentioned that he owned a delicatessen on Victory Blvd. in Van Nuys. We went over there to have a hot dog and I told him that I had just gone through a scene with Bache where I'd lost all this money buying these *farcockteh* stocks. Georgie said, "I've got an idea for you. Tony Martin is investing in these big apartment houses and he wants me to go in with him." He introduced me to a guy named Irv who he said was his partner and then said to me, "I want to get out of this delicatessen. I get 115 dollars a week out of it every week. That's 5,980 dollars a year. I'll sell you my half of the restaurant for 6,000 dollars and you can make your money back in a year and then have a steady income after that."

I talked it over with Donna. That was all the money we had and finally, I went back to Georgie and told him that I couldn't do it. Two weeks later, the delicatessen went down the toilet. The delicatessen was bombing and Georgie was going to get out of it by stealing my money. My good friend Georgie Auld.

Back in 1949, when Woody Herman's band was playing at the Royal Roost, Georgie was there with one of his hooker girlfriends whose name was Evelyn. Georgie was a very handsome guy and all the hookers in New York loved him. His brother Barney, who I really liked, was supposedly connected with the bad boys in Toronto, Canada. Every time I read about an eighty-four-million-dollar heist in Canada, I'd think of Barney.

Georgie could be bad in a different way. There was a guy from Minneapolis called Nate Supack who was very wealthy and loved Georgie. It was four o'clock in the morning and Georgie was a little juiced out. I was sitting with him when some guy came over and asked him for an autograph. Georgie signed it and then the guy went over to Evelyn and said, "You've got to be somebody too. Can I have your autograph also?" Evelyn said, "I'm nobody. Leave me alone." Real nasty. The guy didn't believe her and asked for her autograph again. After he said it again, Georgie yelled, "GET OUTTA HERE!" picked up a glass ashtray and whacked the guy right in the face. As the guy was falling down, Nate Supack, who was sitting there too, hit him and knocked him up in the air. Georgie would fight anybody in two seconds, but only if he had somebody to back him up.

That same night, Serge Chaloff, Lou Levy, and I were in a cab with Georgie and three hookers, one of whom was Jewish. We were going up town to some after-hours club. Georgie was smoking a joint and Serge and Lou were stoned out. I couldn't believe that Georgie would light up a joint in the cab. We all could have gotten busted if the cab was stopped for any reason at all.

These were high-class hookers. In 1948, these girls were getting $200 a trick, which is like $2,000 today. Georgie was Jewish and we used to talk to each other in Jewish. When I spoke Jewish, I sounded like what the comedian Phil Foster would sound like if he spoke Jewish. Georgie sounded like Noel Coward. He had a great command of the Jewish language. While we were riding in the cab, Georgie was needling this Jewish hooker named Shawn, who was Serge's date. He called her Jew Baby, which she didn't like at all. He kept saying it over and over. "Hey, Jew baby? What's the matter, Jew baby?" We stopped for a traffic light, and Shawn got so bugged with Georgie that she spit on him. He smiled at her and then from out of nowhere hit her right in the mouth, her head hitting the car door.

Being that the cab wasn't moving, Shawn opened the door and got out. The light turned green and the cab went about thirty yards when Georgie said to the driver, "Stop the cab!" got out and ran back to where Shawn was. Lou and Serge were nodding off and didn't know what was happening. I didn't know what to do so I got out of the cab and ran after Georgie. When I found them, Georgie was kicking Shawn while she was lying in the street. He was beating the heck out of her. I grabbed him around his middle. I didn't want to fight Georgie but if he was going to try and fight me, I was going to hit him in the solar plexus, which could have knocked him out. I didn't want to fight him because he was my friend. He almost looked like he was having an orgasm and stopped kicking her. I helped Shawn get a cab and went back to my hotel. Poor girl, she was hurt pretty bad.

Georgie was my friend. A strange friend, but a friend just the same. Years later when Georgie died, Barney invited me to his funeral. I was sitting with Neal Hefti, Chubby Jackson, and Pete Candoli, and we were listening to the rabbi say all these nice things about Georgie. We looked at each other and said, "Are we at the right funeral?" That wasn't the Georgie Auld WE knew. As good as Georgie could play — and he could play — that's how bad he could be.

After I passed on the delicatessen deal with Georgie, I put together a quartet with Lou Levy, Max Bennett, and Gary Frommer, and we played all the little clubs around town. Donna and I started looking for a house. We wanted to live in Hollywood, for most of what was happening in music was in that area. Jack Schwartz, who was in the army with me and later played baritone in my big band, was working for a company selling houses and took us around the Hollywood area. Everything we saw that we liked, we couldn't afford, and it was getting to the point where Donna and I were so bugged that we started arguing. We couldn't find anything, so Jack invited us out to his house in Woodland Hills to relax and forget about the dumb day we went through.

Back then, the Ventura Freeway stopped at Laurel Canyon Blvd. We didn't want to live that far out from Hollywood. We drove all the way out to Jack's house and when we saw it, it was so beautiful that we bought one of the houses that was in the same tract that Jack lived in. Those houses sold for 25,000 dollars then. Now, they're around 600,000 dollars.

Before we could buy the house, I had to go to the bank to get my credit application. The guy at the bank said to me, "Do you have a car?" I said yes. I was a little cocky with the guy at the bank because I had a Cadillac and a little van for the instruments that I owned outright. He said, "Who do you make your payments to?" I said, "Nobody. I paid cash for them." He said, "Okay, do you have any credit cards?" I said, "No, I pay everything by cash." He said, "You can't get a house. You have no credit." He then told me to deposit 5,000 dollars in the bank and then borrow 5,000 dollars, make about three payments and then pay it off. And that's what I did. It took an hour to go from Hollywood to get out to Woodland Hills, but it was worth it. It was the first house I ever owned.

We didn't have much money to buy furniture so to start with, we bought a few necessary things, like a bed and a television set. We filled the living room up with musical instruments. We had a piano, a drum set, and two sets of vibes. We eventually bought a couch for the living room and two comfortable chairs for the den so that we could watch TV.

The living room turned out to be our rehearsal hall. I rehearsed my saxophone section there for the album "More Vibes on Velvet" plus the quartets I put together for the jobs I played around town. Little by little, the house became a hangout just like the apartment I had in New York.

There was a talk show on television called *The Larry Finley Show*. Dick Grove was the musical director and he had a trio on the show. Later on, he opened the Dick Grove Music School. Larry used to come into some of the clubs I played and he liked my playing and my dumb sense of humor. He gave me a standing invitation to appear on his show anytime I felt like it. When I had something to plug, like a club that I was going to play at, or the release of a new record, I'd call Larry and he would make room on the show for me."

The scale for playing on the show was only nineteen dollars, but one of Larry's sponsors was a wine company, so when I played on the show, besides the nineteen dollars, Larry would also give me a case of magnums of champagne. There had to be twelve to sixteen magnums in each case. At one time, I had about thirty cases in my house. I had one of my parties and everybody who came got a magnum of champagne. You couldn't finish a magnum without throwing up or passing out.

In January 1958, I went back on the road again, but just for two weeks, to Denver, Colorado. I took Claude Williamson on piano, Frank Severino, who replaced Gary Frommer just for the two weeks, and a young bass player, Gary Peacock, who has since gone on to fame playing with Keith Jarrett and Jack DeJohnette.

When I got back to California, I worked practically every weekend for about four months, but I wasn't making any money playing locally. Then, the Associated Booking Corporation Agency called me and asked me if I wanted to do a three-month tour back east for some decent money. Donna and I talked it over and we figured that she felt comfortable and secure in our new house, and since we could always use the money, I accepted the tour.

Gary Frommer joined the quartet again, and Claude and the two Garys and I drove back to New York City. We played all of the same clubs I played when I was living in New York. The tour started with a few one-nighters in upstate New York and then we went to my old stomping grounds, Birdland in New York City.

When we were at Birdland, Steve Allen came in to see me and asked me if I would like to appear on his television show and play with him at a new jazz club that was opening called the Roundtable. At first, I thought it might be a problem because we were booked solid for three months, but since the people who owned the Roundtable also owned Birdland, there wasn't any problem at all.

About a month later we had to play Birdland again, so they switched the booking around so I could play with Steve at the Roundtable. On that job, besides the two Garys, we added Mundell Lowe on guitar and Gus Bivona on clarinet. Claude Williamson had it real easy. He was paid his full salary just to play piano when Steve and I played vibes together.

Everybody who came into that club was a celebrity: Milton Berle, Phil Silvers, Marlon Brando, Wally Cox, you name it. Everybody was either a comedian or a very famous actor. Most of the same people were in the club every night. It became a hangout for people in show business.

Steve and I were doing our vibes duet and Phil Silvers was sitting right in front of us, which may have been about eight or ten feet away from the bandstand. As we were doing some crosshanded schtick, suddenly a mallet flew out of Steve's hand and flew right by Phil Silvers' head, missing him by about a quarter of an inch. It happened so fast that nobody even knew it. If it had hit Phil, it probably would have broken his glasses and a lot more because the ball of the mallet was made with a hard piece of rubber. Luckily, I kept extra sets of mallets on the vibes, so Steve picked one up and went straight ahead and we finished the vibes duet and got a standing ovation, even from Phil.

It was a long tour. We went right from one place to another without a break. After the Roundtable, we went to a place called Cappy's in Buffalo, New York. Then we played the Westdale Hotel in Hamilton, Ontario, the Fairmont Grill in Jamestown, the Ridgecrest in Rochester, the Modern Jazz Room in Cleveland, the Town Tavern in Toronto, Baker's Keyboard in Detroit, and Crawford's Grill in Pittsburgh.

Before going to work I'd always lie down and rest for an hour before getting dressed for the job. When we were at the Carleton Hotel in Pittsburgh, I was resting when I got a call from someone who told me that the San Francisco Giants were in the lobby. They were in town playing the Pirates. I was a big Giants fan going way back to when Mel Ott was my idol, so I ran downstairs thinking that maybe I'd get to see what Willie Mays or Orlando Cepeda looked like in person. I felt like a kid again. When I got to the lobby, I saw Orlando Cepeda. I knew that he and Cal Tjader knew each other because Cal once wrote a song called "Viva Cepeda" for Orlando. I started to walk over to Orlando and wanted to introduce myself to him. He started to walk towards me and now we were walking towards each other. I was about to say something when he said, "I know who you are! I a big fan of yours! Vibraphone! Terry Gibbs!" We stood in the lobby talking to each other for about fifteen minutes. If anybody would have heard us, we had to sound like two idiots. I was talking baseball and home runs, and he was talking about how many flats were in the key of F. Two completely different conversations going on at the same time.

Sometimes we'd get into town just in time to get on stage without checking into a hotel first. I was hot in those days and did good business for everybody. The quartet had a lot of fun and we ended our tour by playing in Las Vegas for a week.

It felt good to get back to California because I missed the laid-back life I was living before we went on tour. Three weeks later, we started working again at a club called the Slate Brothers. Scotty Lafaro, an up-and-coming young bass player, replaced Gary Peacock. That was one of my better paying jobs and we played there for four weeks. Then I went back to playing my small paying local jobs for about three months.

Associated Booking called me again to play a three-week engagement in Denver as a single. The club supplied me with a rhythm section.

When I got back to California, my career took a completely different direction. I went from being a small bandleader to a big bandleader.

Chapter 14
The Dream Band

The Dream Band was the biggest fluke of my life. I never wanted to form a working band; I just wanted to record an album with a big band. I recorded one in New York, which I didn't like at all. It was actually my fault because I wanted to use the rhythm section with the quartet that I was traveling with. The big drag was that my drummer, Jerry Siegel, didn't have the experience of playing with a big band. I was so disgusted and bugged because that was my first big shot at recording a big band album. I had a great contract with Mercury Records. Bobby Shad loved my playing and would let me record anytime I came up with a good idea for an album.

When I first moved out to California, I heard Med Flory and Bill Holman rehearsing what was called a "kicks" band at the musicians union. Playing for kicks meant just playing for fun. Med and Bill were both great big band arrangers and wanted to hear their arrangements played by a big band.

Mel Lewis was the drummer with both bands and his drumming reminded me of the way Tiny Kahn played. I first met Mel in New York when he was working with Tex Beneke's band and all he wanted to talk about was Tiny Kahn. I never really got a chance to hear Mel play with a big band but I did hear him play with small groups in the local clubs. His style wasn't what I wanted for my quartet; it was too laid back and I wanted that little edge in the time. Bill and Med's bands were great and Mel played the heck out of the arrangements. He was, without a doubt, a giant big band drummer. His playing reminded me so much of Tiny, but I think that he even took that style of drumming to another level and it became a Mel Lewis style of drumming.

Chapter 14

In listening to both groups, I got that feeling of wanting to record a big band again, but I had to come up with an idea, and finally, I did. I called Bobby Shad in New York and told him what I wanted to do and he liked my idea. Once again Bobby came through for me. He got Pete Rugolo, who was the West Coast recording director for Mercury Records, to sit in the booth and supervise the date.

The premise of the album was to take six different bandleaders: Duke Ellington, Lionel Hampton, Count Basie, Benny Goodman, Artie Shaw, and Tommy Dorsey. Then I would take two tunes that they each made famous, take sixteen bars from each of those tunes, and put them into the new arrangements that I was going to have written. We used sixteen bars of Artie Shaw's chorus from "Star Dust," sixteen bars of Ben Webster's chorus from "Cotton Tail" by Duke, sixteen bars of Illinois Jacquet's chorus from "Flying Home" by Lionel, and so on.

I hired six different arrangers for the album. Al Cohn for the Ellington charts, Med Flory for the Hampton charts, Marty Paich for the Dorsey charts, Bill Holman for the Shaw charts, Bobby Brookmeyer for the Goodman charts, and Manny Albam for the Basie charts. Any of the arrangers could have written any of the arrangements for any of the songs, and they would have sounded great. I just guessed who to give the assignments to and they all did a great job for me.

After getting all the arrangements copied, I wanted to rehearse the band before we recorded, but I found out that the union fined a very famous musician a thousand dollars one time for rehearsing for a record date. The union had good intentions and wanted you to rehearse in the studio so that if it went into overtime, you would get paid extra money for rehearsing. I was bugged because I had all this music written and couldn't rehearse the band.

At the same time this was happening, I was still playing little clubs around town. A movie columnist called Eve Starr heard me play and liked what I did. We became friendly and every once in a while she'd mention my name in her column. She told me about these friends of hers, Harry and Alice Schiller, who owned the Seville nightclub on Santa Monica Boulevard in Hollywood. The club was doing bad and was about to close. They tried Latin music and country-western, but nothing worked. Eve told Harry Schiller about me and suggested that they put some jazz in the club, so I agreed to play there with a quintet on a Tuesday night, and if it went good, we would do it again the next Tuesday.

The quintet I put together had Conte Candoli on trumpet, Russ Freeman on piano, Charlie Haden on bass, and Stan Levey on drums. We played that one Tuesday night and it went good. We drew enough people for the club to make some money, so we did it again the next Tuesday.

In the meantime, I found out that although you couldn't rehearse for a record date, you could rehearse for a nightclub job, which made no sense to me at all. I still had all this big band music, so I went to Harry Schiller and said, "Harry, how would you like to have a big band for the same amount of money you're paying me for five musicians?" I was getting way over scale, which at that time was fifteen dollars a man, so I could afford to pay everybody union scale. The band would have played for nothing because they wanted to record this album as much as I did. Harry said, "I don't care how many musicians you have, as long as it doesn't cost me any more money."

Big bands were not "in." It wasn't feasible to form a big band, because musicians like Dave Brubeck made as much money for a quartet as Count Basie made for his whole band. In the old days, a guy would leave a band to start his own band, but in 1959, because of the money situation, there was no reason to start a big band.

We had to sign a new contract with Harry Schiller for sixteen musicians instead of five. This was my big shot to not only record the band, but to play in the club with the band. I used Jack Schwartz, my baritone player, as my contractor, and Berrel as my band boy and road manager. Larry Finley was a good friend of the Schillers and was going to publicize the show, so he met Jack, Berrel, Harry, and me at the club.

We were sitting at the bar having a few drinks and talking about where we were going to put the bandstand and other things, when all of a sudden, Jack Schwartz fell over backwards off the barstool. BANG! His head hit the floor. The most selfish things went through my head when that happened. "My God, Jack Schwartz just dropped dead! He just had a heart attack. That asshole just dropped dead and I haven't even signed the contracts yet. I won't even get to open up at the club!"

As Jack was lying on the floor, Berrel bent down to see how he was. He looked up at me and said, "He's snoring." Jack had one too many drinks, passed out, and was on the floor, sleeping. We got him up and now I wanted to sign my name on the contract as fast as possible. I didn't even get to my last name, Gibbs, before Jack fell back off the barstool again. We just let him lay on the floor until I signed the contract.

I told Steve Allen that I was putting a big band together to play at a club for one night. He gave me a plug on his show on NBC and we told a bunch of musicians around town about it. We didn't expect to draw more than twenty or thirty people in the club.

The personnel of the band that did the record date had Al Porcino, Ray Triscari, Conte Candoli, and Stu Williamson on trumpets, Vern

Friley, Frank Rosolino, and Bob Enevoldsen on trombones, Joe Maini, Charlie Kennedy. Med Flory, Bill Holman, and Jack Schwartz on saxophones, Pete Jolly on piano, Max Bennett on bass, and Mel Lewis on drums. We were very fortunate in that band. We hardly had any subs. Even though Pete Jolly recorded the first album, Russ Freeman played the first job with the big band. Pete had other commitments on the first Tuesday we played at the Seville. He did come back the next week for a few Tuesdays. When Pete started to get real busy, Lou Levy joined the band. The rest of the band stayed practically the same.

We rehearsed at the club on Monday, the day before we were to open with the big band. Then on Tuesday, we went in the studio and recorded all day. We got to the club at nine-thirty that night to get ready to play at ten. When we got there, sure enough, there were only about twenty or thirty people there. That's all we expected. I only had thirteen pieces of music and we were going to have to do three or four shows. They were all short tunes, because those days, you recorded three or four-minute songs so that you could get airplay on radio.

I figured I had about forty-eight minutes of music to play for four sets, so we went in the back room and I said to the guys, "Conte, at letter A, you've got a thousand choruses. At letter B, Frank Rosolino, you've got two million choruses." I needed to stretch each tune out to be about ten or twelve minutes long and had to make an arrangement on top of an arrangement so we could open it up in order to kill time.

When we came out of the band room to play, the place was packed. There were three hundred people in the club. Sitting there were Louella Parsons, Fred MacMurray and June Haver, Johnny Mercer, Steve Allen, Jerry Lewis, Steve McQueen, Soupy Sales, all these famous actors plus every musician in town. When I saw this, I said, "Okay, guys, back to the band room!" We got back there and I said, "Gentlemen, we're starting a band tonight. The first rule is there's no drinking off the bandstand. If you want to drink, you've got to drink on stage. It's a party. So hurry up and relax."

After the first tune, "Just Plain Meyer," we got a standing ovation. That first song was our good luck charm. It was an arrangement that Bobby Brookmeyer wrote for the album I did in New York. We played that first and tore up the place. That one we didn't open up; we played it as a three-minute arrangement and hit them in the head with it.

I was about ready to tap off the second song when Med Flory stood up and said, "I need a beer, Terry! WAITRESS! A BEER!" Al Porcino then stood up. "I DON'T HAVE ONE EITHER!" The five waitresses at the club were now on the bandstand serving the band, not the people in the audience. Everybody was screaming for a drink, but the band knew the rule: no drinking off the bandstand. Everybody made fifteen dollars for playing the job but their bar tabs were twenty-three dollars. You've got to either love music that much or be a complete idiot to go to work and lose eight dollars every time you played.

That night was such a success that the Schillers and I agreed to do it again the next week. By that time, Bill Holman and Med Flory each lent me three or four of their arrangements. We rehearsed at the union and got a chance to open up the arrangements so that more guys could blow some jazz.

On the next Tuesday, when we got to the club at nine-thirty, once again, twenty or thirty people were there. We figured it was one of those flukes. It was nice for that one day and we had a ball. We went into the band room to talk things over about what we were going to do. When we walked back out, once again there were 300 people packed in the club. You couldn't get any more people in the place if you tried. In fact, there was a line of people outside waiting to get in.

We did this for five or six Tuesdays in a row and then Harry Schiller said, "Why don't we do this five days a week?" We figured, okay, why not? We'll give it a shot. When we signed the contract to do the five days a week, we didn't realize that Count Basie was opening up at the Crescendo, which was about five blocks away, the same day that we were going to start doing the five days. Not only did we out-draw Count Basie's band, but between sets, Basie's band was at OUR club listening to OUR band. They didn't believe how great the band was. Nobody believed it.

One reason why that band was so great is that we all felt the same way about how the music should be played. If you talked to all the guys individually and asked them, "Who are your favorite musicians?" they'd all say Charlie Parker and Dizzy Gillespie. We were all bebop freaks and articulated the music the same way. There was something I was looking for in the playing of the music. I like over-exaggeration. If it's supposed to be played loud, play it louder, and if the music says soft, play it softer. When I used to conduct television shows, I would tell the guys, "Everybody follow me and even if I'm wrong, you still follow me, because if we're all wrong together, we will sound right."

After that first rehearsal, they knew exactly what I was looking for. When we got some new arrangements and rehearsed them, I never had to do anything except say, "One, two, three, four." Everybody knew exactly how I wanted the music played. No matter what tempo we played, the band knew the difference between an eighth note and a quarter note. It was like one person playing all the parts.

If you talk to four trumpet players today and ask them who their favorite trumpet player is, they might say Miles Davis or Freddie Hubbard or Wynton Marsalis or Art Farmer. You'll hear four different styles of playing. Even though they came from the same school, you'll hear four different ways of articulating the same piece of music.

A very important plus is that we all loved each other. The camaraderie in the band was something else. We used to break each other up on stage. Guys in the band would applaud for each other. Conte would play a solo and the guys in the band would applaud for him before the audience would. We didn't believe how good the band was. When we played Tuesday night, on Wednesday morning, we'd call each other: "Do you believe that band?" Mel Lewis would call me every time; "I can't believe the band!" If somebody was going to write a Hollywood style story about how a band hit it big overnight, that's what happened with us. Three hundred people every night, with a line waiting around the block to get in. That, in itself, is a Hollywood style story.

When critics around the country started to write about the band, they said that it was a kicks band and that most of the guys did studio work. Not true. Because of the fluke, we started out as a working band and had lots of kicks, but none of the guys except for Ray Triscari did any studio work. The contractors didn't know about the Frank Rosolinos, the Conte Candolis, and the Joe Mainis. In fact, the contractors would come in the club, look at the band and say to each other, "Look! Conte Candoli can read music! Frank Rosolino! He's reading music!" They didn't know the level of musicianship in the band.

Before we opened up at the Seville, I went to see Gene Norman, who owned the Crescendo and the Interlude clubs. I worked for Gene at the Empire Room when I was with Woody Herman's band in 1948 and by now, I was an established jazz name, so Gene knew who I was. I went to Gene and said, "I'd like to play your club with my quartet." Gene, who is a good friend of mine now, looked at me, and instead of saying something diplomatic like, "I don't have any openings right now," said, "Terry, who are you going to draw?" That really bugged me. That was like a slap in the face. He actually insulted me by saying that.

George Shearing was working for Gene Norman at the Crescendo at the same time we were working at the Seville. George heard about the band and had his valet bring him in between his sets on Tuesday nights. Sometimes he came in two or three times during the night. When we started playing five nights a week, his valet couldn't bring George in for this one set, so Gene brought him to the club. The club was packed and we had a line of people waiting to get in for the next show. Berrel came to me and said that George Shearing and Gene Norman were standing in line waiting to get in the club, so I said to Berrel, "You go out there and bring George in and then ask Gene Norman who he thinks I would draw." He brought George in the club and left Gene standing in line.

I always asked George if he would sit in with us but I actually think he was afraid to because the band was so powerful. Finally, one night, he got up enough nerve to sit in. George has a warped sense of humor, which I love. When he got up on the bandstand, the first thing he said was, "Terry, don't play anything too hard, I don't read music too well." Those were the wrong guys to tell that to because in the middle of the first song, somebody came over to him and said, "We're at letter B, George." There were all kinds of sick lines thrown at him, like, "Let's go hear a movie tonight, George." But he started it and he had the right guys to do it with.

The band sounded so good that I wanted to record it live. I heard about this recording engineer named Wally Heider, who used to go around the country taping big bands. Wally's father was a big attorney and Wally studied to be one also, but Wally stuttered very bad, and I don't think he would have made it as an attorney. I heard that he had good ears for recording live, so I wanted to hear what Wally could do. I asked him if he would sort of audition for me. I didn't know that he had been in the club a few times and had already heard the band. He was thrilled when I asked him if he would like to do a live recording.

The next Tuesday, Wally brought all his equipment in and recorded the band. I went back to the studio with Wally right after we got done working at about two o'clock in the morning and listened to what he had recorded. It was about 95 percent what I was looking for. I said, "Wally, that's great. But let me tell you what I want to hear. Number one. Do you hear how great the lead trumpet player sounds?" He said, "Yeah." I said, "Now, what I want to hear is the fourth trumpet player just as loud as the first trumpet player. In fact, I want to hear all four trumpet players on the same level. I want to hear a chord. I don't want anybody sticking out.

"Secondly, tomorrow I'm going to bring you a record called 'Jack the Bear' by Duke Ellington. Those days it was very hard to record a bass, especially with a big band. You'd hear boom, boom, boom. I want to hear notes. I want to hear bing, bang, boung, bong.

"Third thing: the drums. I don't want to feel them; I want to hear them. And I don't want them to sound 'distancy.' I want them to sound up front."

I wanted the band to sound like you'd hear it in the club. If you listen to the CDs that Wally engineered, it sounds like you were right there in the club. The band sounds like it's jumping right out at you.

The next night, after he heard "Jack the Bear," he came back and recorded the band again. The first Dream Band albums that came out were the audition tapes that I had in my house for twenty-seven years. If it weren't for Wally, the Dream Band CDs would have sounded like they were recorded in 1959. Instead, they sound like they were recorded yesterday.

Shelly Kasten, Joe Mikolas, and Skip Krask, who were from Chicago and were friends of Hugh Hefner, bought a club called the Mocambo, which was right next to the Crescendo. It was once the elite club of old Hollywood where all the famous movie stars used to frequent. It was completely mirrored and was once considered to be the classiest club in town. They renamed it the Cloister after another club they owned in Chicago.

They were a bunch of hip guys who loved our big band and they asked us to open up their new club along with Andy Williams and Frank Gorshin. Because of how Andy's music was written, we had to add sixteen strings to the band. Being that the walls were mirrored, when the band played, the sound bounced off all of the walls and made it sound louder than it really was.

Arlene Dahl, the movie actress, came in the club on opening night. She was sitting right in front of the band and every time the band played, she cupped her ears. That was very unclassy for such a pretty lady to do and it really bugged the hell out of me.

The band never got anything but positive reviews. We were the heroes of the town. The first negative review the band ever got was by Army Archerd from *Variety*. The Cloister was right next door to the Crescendo, so Army wrote: "Last night, the Terry Gibbs Big Band played dance music at the Cloister and six couples got up to dance at the Crescendo." That didn't get to me at all because it made it sound like we were playing too loud. I went to the three guys who owned the Cloister and I said, "Listen, if you want us to leave after the first week, we will." They said, "What happened?" I showed them the review and they said, "You know what? Play louder! Screw them all." They loved the band.

We stayed there two or three weeks, but I wasn't having fun. We were making more money, but we had lost that whole loose feeling of having fun playing music, drinking on stage, and carrying on. We had become a show band.

In the meantime, Jimmy Maddin, who owned the Sundown, asked me if I'd like to bring the band into his club. I went to see what the Sundown looked like and it was just what I was looking for. It was laid out just right for the big band. We could put the bandstand in the corner of the room because I wanted the band to play for dancing so that we could have more fun playing without everybody staring at us. We also agreed that there would be no cover charge. We wanted to make it a hangout. I went to the guys at the Cloister and gave them my notice. They were great guys; they understood what I wanted to do with the band. They did make me a great offer, though. Being that the band was only going to play at the Sundown one or two nights a week, they asked me if I would consider playing at the Cloister with a quintet the other five nights. I think they just liked hanging out with me. In fact, Shelly Kasten, one of the owners, and I became good friends. The guys would always invite me to their so-called Hollywood parties. There were always a lot of pretty girls and great food at these parties.

We played there for about four weeks and I used the same rhythm section that was in the big band at that time: Mel Lewis, Buddy Clark, and Benny Aronov. I had Joe Maini and Conte Candoli split the job as the fifth member of the quintet.

When we opened the Sundown, once again it was packed with movie stars. Johnny Mercer was there every night that we played. It was a one-of-a-kind band. It was so good and so much fun, that I didn't want to leave town. After that little experience of working at the Cloister, where I was making some money but not having fun, I went back to just having fun. We were having the times of our lives just playing music. I also think that the people who came in to see us were having more fun because with the band swinging so hard, they could now get up and dance and get something out of their system.

While we were at the Sundown, the band changed a little bit. We started with the same trumpets, Al Porcino, Ray Triscari, Stu Williamson, and Conte Candoli. After a few weeks, John Audino replaced Al Porcino, who went with Harry James. Then Bob Edmondson came in to replace Bob Enevoldsen on trombone. Vern Friley was still there and so was Frank Rosolino. We had a few replacements every once in a while for Frank because he would go out on the road, and then either Carl Fontana or Bobby Burgess would play in the band. There was always a heavyweight there to take Frank's place.

The original saxophone section had Joe Maini, Charlie Kennedy, Med Flory, Bill Holman, and Jack Schwartz. Bill Holman left after a few weeks because he got very busy arranging for Stan Kenton, so Bill Perkins took his place. Jack Schwartz got very busy with real estate so Jack Nimitz came in and stayed. Then Med left and Richie Kamuca came in. Mel Lewis was the drummer, Lou Levy was the piano player, and Buddy Clark played bass. That band stayed together for about a year. It was such a winner that even though I only made eleven dollars a night after I paid everybody in the band, it was worth it.

We played the Hollywood Jazz Festival at the Hollywood Bowl and it was great to see some of my East Coast friends at the Festival. I invited Sonny Stitt, Horace Silver, Paul Chambers, Wynton Kelly, and

Miles Davis out to the house for a pool party and jam session. Miles got lost because he wasn't used to taking all the side streets to get to my house and he never showed up. He must have called from about twenty phone booths. "Where the fuck are you?" I said, "Where the fuck are YOU?"

We jammed at my house and some of the guys from the big band were there. Al Porcino, who, along with Snooky Young, was probably one of the greatest lead trumpet players that ever lived, was at the same time one of the worst jazz trumpet players that ever lived. He was not even considered to be a jazz trumpet player because he couldn't play jazz. We started playing "Cherokee" and took it at such a fast pace that Sonny Stitt, even with his amazing technique, could have had a problem with it, but he didn't. Sonny must have played twenty-five or thirty choruses, and as he kept playing, we all shied away from our instruments. Nobody wanted to follow him. The only guy with enough *chutzpah* to follow him was Porcino.

Because the world was racially screwed up those days, black musicians like Horace Silver, Paul Chambers, Sonny Stitt, and Wynton Kelly were almost forced to be nice to the white musicians. They hardly ever said anything derogatory to them. After Al Porcino played, they said, "Yeah, man!" Yeah, man. Bullshit. They should have shot Porcino or at least lynched him for the way he played and I wouldn't have blamed them. That was not only the worst jazz trumpet playing, it was the worst ANYTHING I ever heard in my life.

Berrel was now living with Donna and me. He didn't have to pay us anything for rent or food. He almost became a part of our family and we used to hang out together all the time. I met him when we were in the army and always called him Berrel because that was his Jewish name but his real name was Bernie Siegel. Because he weighed pretty close to three hundred pounds, everybody thought I was calling him "Barrel," so that's what some people called him.

There was a restaurant called the Gaiety Delicatessen that was the after-hours hangout and was packed with all the celebrities in town. There would always be a line waiting to get in. Berrel and I would go to the Gaiety Delicatessen after the job and stand in line with the other people who were waiting to get in. Nobody knew how much money I was making at the Sundown. They probably thought that I was making a lot of money because the club was always packed. I started to get a reputation of being in the same class as Benny Goodman or Count Basie as a bandleader. Sid Garris or his brother-in-law, who were the owners, would always check the line outside to see if there was anybody important waiting to get in. I was starting to become a celebrity to them, so when they saw me standing in line, they'd say, "Hey, c'mon

Terry, you don't have to wait!" Give him a table!" When I saw the menu, I wasn't sure if I could afford anything that was on it. We were treated royally everywhere we went because the band was such a big hit.

A few months later, I hired Sid Garris and George Greif to become managers of the band. Besides owning the Gaiety Delicatessen, Sid was also a disc jockey. They used to call him Symphony Sid, just like Symphony Sid Torin in New York. George was a full-time manager. He and Sid also handled people like Jose Feliciano and bought the name the Christy Minstrels and were very successful. They both were very good businessmen.

Major Riddle, who owned the Dunes Hotel in Las Vegas, came into the club, heard the band, and flipped out. At the intermission, he came over to me and said, "I have an opening at the Dunes Hotel next week. I'd like to have your band play there." I told him he'd have to talk to my managers. They got together with Major Riddle, worked out all the details, and the next week we opened at the Dunes.

I called Joe Maini, who was working with Ray Anthony in Las Vegas making five hundred dollars a week, which was a gang of money back then. This must have been around 1962. Joe used to fly back to Los Angeles and work with our band on his night off. He just told Ray he was leaving tomorrow to go to another hotel. He didn't even give Ray any notice.

After paying out commissions, all I had left was enough to pay everybody 200 dollars each, and after I paid Berrel, I made about 111 dollars for myself. The hotel had a big publicity campaign for the opening where they crowned me the "New King of Swing." It was very embarrassing but fun.

I also hired Jimmy Witherspoon to sing with us. The only other singer that ever sang with the band was Irene Kral. Spoon was great, probably one of the best blues singers of all time. He had no arrangements, so what we used to do was, when he sang the blues, I'd have Joe Maini play behind him and the band would make up blues backgrounds, which were probably better than most arrangements anybody could write. Good jazz players can make up a background on the spot and it would sound like it was a written arrangement. One trumpet player makes up a riff, and then the other three guys in the trumpet section would jump in and find harmony parts. Conte would make up most of the riffs in the trumpet section and Frank Rosolino would make them up for the trombone section. When we got to the end of the song, everybody would find a harmony note and I'd cue them in for the last chord.

Mel Lewis really had it hard. He was on staff at ABC and had to fly to Hollywood every day to do a five o'clock show and then fly back to Las Vegas to play with the band. After making the trip every day for four days, I got a call from Mel telling me that they were going into overtime and didn't know whether he could get the next plane and come back in time for the first show. We never had another drummer ever play with the band. I didn't know what to do because not only was he the most important guy in my band, I didn't know any drummers in Las Vegas. Louie Bellson was working with his wife, Pearl Bailey at the Flamingo Hotel so I called him and said, "Louie, I'm in trouble. I'm stuck. Mel Lewis is not going to be here. He may make it for the second show but I don't have a drummer for the first show. Can you recommend somebody?" Louie heard the band many times and loved it. Being one of the nicest people I have ever known, plus a real good friend, Louie cut his part of the show short and had the house drummer play Pearl's act, came down and played with my band.

Louie could sight-read anything and as the saying goes, "He could sight-read fly shit." I don't know what his style of drumming would have felt like on the fourth night, because he had a completely different feel than Mel had. But for a one-shot deal, he came in and did a remarkable job. He played the heck out of the ensembles, made all the figures, and saved me from having a nervous breakdown. Everybody in the band stood up and applauded him after we finished the show.

We were breaking it up every night. All the hippest people in town were coming in to hear the band. Our third show was always packed with all the entertainers and showgirls who came there after they did their last show and we tore them up. We finished the two weeks and went back to Los Angeles a big winner.

Sid and George were trying to book the band on the road and make me a big time bandleader, which I really didn't want. I didn't want to go out with the band and travel, and also, some of the guys wouldn't be able to tour anyhow. They told me, "If you can't get Conte to play, get somebody else," but I said no, I wanted Conte, I wanted Mel Lewis, I wanted all the original guys there. Mel was on staff at ABC and couldn't go out anyhow, and I didn't want to go out without him. But they did book the band at the Avalon Ballroom on Catalina Island. We took most of the guys that went to Las Vegas, including Jimmy Witherspoon. After the second day in Catalina, one of the guys in the band came over to me and said, "Terry, we just tried to draw some money from your manager and he said that we could only draw money on a Friday." I went to George and Sid and said, "Listen, the guys need some money." They said, "Terry, we're running an organization now and the rule is you can only draw on Friday." I said, "I don't run a band that tight and I don't want to lose that loose feel that we have for each other. You guys are separating me from my band." They said, "That's how it's got to be. Just like all big bands do. It's a business." I said, "You do your business with another band. You're fired and I quit. We're going home after this week." They said, "Wait a minute. What do you mean?" I said, "I told you, I don't run my band like this." We left after the first week and went back to playing the Sundown.

Jimmy Maddin was real happy to see the band back at the Sundown because while we were gone, business had been terrible. Because we were playing for dancing at the Sundown and it was such a big success, I wanted to do a record album that people could dance to. It would still be high powered, but the people who bought the album could not only have fun listening to it, but just like they did in the club, they could also dance to it at home if they felt like it.

I was now dealing with Irv Green, who was the president of Mercury Records. I spoke with him in Chicago and he gave me the okay to get the arrangements written. After I got all the arrangements written and copied, I rehearsed the band and we were ready to record. I called Irv and he told me that he wanted me to record a small band album instead. I said, "But I've gotten all these arrangements written for a big band," but he didn't seem to care. I got bugged. I tried to reason with him but it seemed like I wasn't getting anywhere. So I thought about getting out of my contract with Mercury. I had been with Mercury for ten years and never had any problems before, so I went to the musicians union and told them my story. I asked them if they could help me get out of my contract and they said yes. I just wanted to make sure that the arrangements were paid for. So they wrote Irv Green a letter and told him that Mercury was out of line for what they did and that they had to pay for the arrangements.

In the meantime, I went to Norman Granz, who loved my band, and asked him if he would like to record us. He said yes and I said, "I may have something for you." I called Irv Green and said that since he didn't live up to his word, I wanted out of my contract. He already knew that he'd have to pay for the arrangements so he said, "Well, if I have to pay for them, either send me the scores or send me the music." I sent him the music and kept the scores so that if I ever lost any parts to the music, I could always go back to the score and get copies made. I had the arrangements copied and then called Norman who said, "When do you want to record?" I said, "Tomorrow." I had the arrangements copied, and the next day, we went into a studio and in two days, we finished recording.

Irv Green was a partner with Ralph Marterie. When he got my arrangements, he went into a studio and recorded Ralph playing the arrangements that were written for my band. He didn't realize that I had already recorded the arrangements with my band for Norman Granz's Verve label. Our album came out first and Mercury never released Ralph's records. If they had released them, there would have been no comparison in the bands anyhow. The album was called "It Might as Well Be Swing." Volume Two of the Dream Band albums has the same songs on it except that it was live and is called "The Sundown Sessions."

With big bands, you always have personnel changes. Benny Goodman had a lot of changes in his band, but the band that he had with Gene Krupa, Harry James, Lionel Hampton, Ziggy Elman, and Teddy Wilson was considered to be one of the greatest bands of all time. That's what I call a "one timer," because you're lucky that once in your life, you will have a band that's considered to be one of the greatest bands of all time. All of his other bands were good, but that band was a one timer.

Artie Shaw had one when he had Buddy Rich and Tommy Dorsey also had one when he had Buddy. Duke Ellington's bands always stayed the same. Count Basie had two; one when he had Papa Jo Jones playing drums and Lester Young and Herschel Evans playing tenor, and then later on with Joe Williams. Woody Herman also had two: the first and second Herds. I was very honored that the Dream Band was considered to be in that same class as one of the greatest bands of all time.

There was a big contractor in town called Ben Barrett who came to me and said, "Terry, if you let me contract your record dates, I'll get you a lot of studio work." I wasn't interested in studio work. The contracting was done by my baritone player, Jack Schwartz, who was one of my friends. I said, "I have my own contractor." I don't think Ben liked that because once he called my whole trumpet section to do a record date that he was contracting, which would have been on a Tuesday night when the band worked. The guys were making fifteen dollars to play with the band and a record date might have paid them 150 or 200 dollars apiece, which was a lot more money. One of the trumpet players told me that he got a call from Ben Barrett to do a record date on Tuesday night and didn't know what to do because we were playing that night. Then Conte said, "Hey, I got a call also." Then all of them said that they got a call from Ben Barrett. Finally, Al Porcino said, "Listen, it's not my band, but let's make a rule. If anybody takes the night off, whoever takes your place is permanently in the band." Nobody ever took off because nobody wanted to leave.

When we started playing at the Sundown, I had Wally come in again to check out the sound. It wasn't an audition anymore; I just wanted to hear how he'd pick up the band at another club. He came in and recorded the band at the Sundown and gave me the reel-to-reel tapes, which I also kept in my house for twenty-seven years. Those tapes eventually became all of Volume Two and part of Volume Three of the Dream Band records. The other half of Volume Three came from the Seville tapes.

We did a few concerts with Miles Davis when Cannonball Adderley and John Coltrane were in his sextet. Every time I worked with the big band, because of my yelling out little signals to the guys, at the end of the night, my voice would be hoarse and I sounded like Miles. After one of the concerts, Miles and I got to talking about when we first met. It was in 1949 and Miles had come into some club I was working at in New York and told me that he had heard Nat Cole's record of the song I wrote called "Peaches." He said he liked the song very much. Then out of left field, he said to me with his weird-sounding voice, "Terry, how come you got no niggers in your band?" I knew he was putting me on, so in my hoarse voice, which almost sounded like him, I said, "Miles, how come you got no JEWS in YOUR band?" Then we laughed and that was the end of that.

The first concert we played was at the Shrine Auditorium. On the end of my solo on "Prelude to a Kiss," I play a little obbligato and Joe Maini was supposed to just turn around, give the band a downbeat and then sit down. Then I would finish my obbligato and cut the band off. Before Joe turned around to face the band, he took his lob out and put it up on the outside of his shirt going up towards his chest with his jacket closed. Joe was very well endowed. When he turned around to give the band the downbeat, he unbuttoned his jacket and half of the band saw what he did. The guys that saw it tried to blow their horns but nothing came out but a "PHHFT" sound and they broke up laughing The guys that didn't see it played their notes and didn't have the slightest idea why the other guys didn't play their notes and were laughing. Joe sat down as if nothing ever happened.

The next concert was in Tucson, Arizona, and Stu Williamson could not make the job, so I hired Jack Sheldon. This was the first time Jack played with the band. He was really nervous because every guy in that trumpet section was like a god to him, especially Conte Candoli. The concert we played opposite Miles was outdoors in a ballpark. They built a bandstand on the pitcher's mound. It was nighttime and very windy and Jack was sitting at the end of the bandstand. We were in the middle of a song when the wind blew his music off the bandstand. He jumped down and kept playing his part, which was now on the ground. The wind kept blowing the music and Jack kept following it while continuing to play. By the time the band played the last chord, he was out in center field. That's when I found out that Jack marched to his own trumpet player.

Gerry Mulligan used to come into the Sundown practically every week with Judy Holliday to hear the band. After a while, he'd come in with his saxophone around his neck, wanting to play. He didn't want to play any solos; he just wanted to sit next to Jack Nimitz and play the baritone parts with him because he loved the band and the arrangements so much.

After playing at the Sundown for a few months, I got a call from Norman Granz, who asked me if I'd put a big band together and conduct for Ella Fitzgerald at the Apollo Theatre in New York. Ella was one of our frequent visitors to the club and flipped out every time she heard the band. I didn't want to stop the band from working on Tuesday, so I asked Gerry Mulligan if he'd like to front the band on the one Tuesday that I would miss when I went to New York. He was honored that I asked him and immediately accepted.

I called my friend Epstein to contract the band for me and took Mel Lewis with me to play drums. Epstein hired all the musicians I asked for. We had people like Kenny Dorham on trumpet, J.R. Montrose on tenor sax, and some other really good players. We were there for a whole week. Besides Ella, who was the headliner, there was the Oscar Peterson Trio with Ray Brown on bass and Ed Thigpen on drums. Sonny Stitt and Roy Eldridge were also on the show besides my big band. The quartet that played on a few songs for Ella wasn't too shabby either: Ray Bryant on piano, Gus Johnson on drums, Wilfred Middlebrooks on bass, and Herb Ellis on guitar.

It was really a lot of fun conducting for Ella and hanging out with her. She was such a great singer. We had some lengthy discussions about our private lives. She told me about the time she was in Europe with Jazz at the Philharmonic and had strong feelings for Jimmy Gannon, the bass player on the tour. Ella said that when they were in Europe, they got very close, but once they got back to the United States, he fluffed her off and she never saw him again. Then she said something that really made me feel bad for her. She said, "You know, Terry? I would give up my voice and all the God-given talent that I have just to be a person who is not famous, so that if some guy wants to take me out, he's taking me out because of who I am and not because I'm Ella Fitzgerald the famous singer." I could tell that she was very hurt about the scene that happened between her and Jimmy Gannon. I think that she probably had that feeling all her life about never being sure if she was being asked out on a date because of who she was rather than what she had to offer as a person.

When the week was over, I got a call from Norman Granz. He said, "Terry, I just got a bill from your contractor for nine dollars and eighty-seven cents." I asked him what it was for and he read the bill to me. "It says here, that on your first show, you went five seconds overtime and he charged me seven cents for the band. On the second show, you were nine seconds over which was eleven cents. Ten seconds, eleven seconds, seven seconds." He broke it down for every show. I broke up and I said to Norman, "That's funny." Norman said, "That's not funny." I said, "Where's your sense of humor, Norman? Epstein's putting you on. Who would charge twenty-two cents for sixteen guys playing five seconds overtime?" He didn't think it was funny. Norman didn't have a good sense of humor. Epstein scored again.

Jack Sheldon started to get comfortable in the band and would do and say funny things. He knew that so long as he didn't get dirty, that he had the freedom to say anything he wanted. When the guys would start to get up on the bandstand, Jack would go to the mike and introduce them as they sat down. He'd always have something to say that was out and funny and I liked it, so I let him do it any time he felt like it.

When I got back from New York and got to the club on Tuesday, I saw a strange face sitting in the trumpet section where Jack normally sat. I asked Berrel where Jack was and he said, "I forgot to tell you. Gerry Mulligan fired Jack." I said, "What do you mean, he fired Jack? Gerry was just subbing for me. It's not his band!"

If anybody knows anything about Jack Sheldon, you know that it's hard to keep him from talking dirty, except with me, because he knows he'd be fired right on the spot if he did. It so happened that when Gerry fronted the band on the Tuesday that I was gone, Jack said something that offended Judy Holliday and she told Gerry to fire him, which he did. I called Jack immediately and he came back that night. I explained the whole thing to the other trumpet player and paid him for the night.

Years later, when Jack became a TV star and even had his own band, he still played in the Dream Band. Jack has his own following, and those people expect Jack to get dirty, but never while he worked in the Dream Band.

Jack and I had a routine going. We were working at Disneyland in the Carnation Ballroom and I always gave Jack a featured spot in my show where I'd have him sing and play three songs. Every time I introduced him, a gang of people would come to the front of the bandstand because they were Jack's fans. Jack would come down from the trumpet section to the front of the stage, and he'd always start his spot by saying, "Ohhhh, it's so nice to be here in Disneyland with Mickey and Minnie Mouse!" While he was saying "Minnie Mouse," I would count off the tempo to the first song so what you'd hear was "Minnie Mouse" and then the band coming in with the introduction to his first song. His regulars always thought I did that to stop Jack from saying something dirty about Mickey and Minnie Mouse. But that wasn't the case. We worked it out that way. I can just imagine what would have happened if I let Jack say what he wanted to say at Disneyland. Fired immediately. Not only Jack, but the whole Dream Band.

I was losing so much money with the band that I was thinking about going back on the road. I really hadn't worked anything but local jobs. In fact, the most money I ever made on one of these jobs was forty dollars as a leader.

Frank Strazzeri worked for me a lot in my little band but he never had any money because he didn't do television or jingles; he just played jazz piano. Frank was one of the truest jazz piano players I ever had in any of my bands. He was also one of the most melodic piano players I ever worked with. I tried to use him a lot on my jazz jobs because he was fun to be around.

Musicians in my band always wore dark suits and I loved putting Frank on. I'd say, "Frank, how long have you had that suit? It's starting to walk by itself; it looks terrible." After about two months of working for me, I got a call from Frank. "Terry, I bought a new dark suit." That made me feel bad, because he had no money and here I was putting him on about this whole thing. When he showed up at the job, I made it worse. I said, "Well, why aren't you wearing the new suit tonight?" He said, "I AM wearing it!" I said, "You are? Well, you know what? It's not the suit, it's your body! The suit's good, your body's just weird."

I was getting into debt, so I called Joe Glaser and asked him to get me some work back east. Within a few weeks, he had booked a sixteen-week tour for me to go on the road. I asked Frank Strazzeri to go with me and Frank recommended a drummer called John Terrabaso and a bass player called Don Prell. I had two cars, so on September 9, 1960, we drove from California to Milwaukee where our first job was.

When we got to Milwaukee, everybody was so wiped out from making the long trip that the least I could do was to take the guys out to dinner. The money I paid everybody was good for those days; I think I paid Frank Strazzeri 195 dollars and the other guys 160 dollars.

The manager of the hotel recommended the best Italian restaurant in town. Prices were completely different then from what they are today. A bowl of spaghetti can cost you at least ten dollars today, but in those days it was a dollar or $1.25. I figured I'd take them to an Italian restaurant because John Terrabaso and Frank Strazzeri were Italian and I liked Italian food. We ordered drinks and looked at the menu and it said, "Spaghetti, $4.25." Frank said to me, "Hey Terry, let's get out of here." I said, "What's the matter?" He said, "$4.25 for spaghetti? Forget it." I said, "No problem, I'm taking you out to dinner." Frank said, "I make spaghetti at home; it costs me thirty-eight cents for four people. I'm not going to let you spend that kind of money." I said, "Frank, I'm taking you to dinner." He said "I don't care, I'm not going to let you spend that kind of money on spaghetti." So we had our drinks and went to some other cockamamie restaurant.

The rhythm section didn't sound good and I was having trouble playing with them. Frank felt terrible because he had recommended the guys. The next job was the Cloister in Chicago so we figured maybe the room in Milwaukee wasn't that good, so we would see what happened at the Cloister, which happened to be a nice, intimate room.

We got there and once again, it wasn't swinging, so Frank had a meeting with the two guys. After it was over, he came to me and said, "Terry, we don't want to hang you up, but we're not making it at all. If you want to get some other musicians from Chicago, do that, and we'll pay our own way back to California." So I hired Pat Moran, a girl piano player I knew from New York who was working in Chicago at the time. She and her rhythm section did the rest of the tour with me.

After Chicago, we went to Minneapolis; then to Kansas City, Cleveland, Baker's Keyboard in Detroit, and to New York City, where we played Birdland and the Jazz Gallery. Those were all two-week jobs. Those days, you played two weeks at a time in a club. Then we came back to California and went into the Summit.

By that time, Bob Gefaell had bought the Sundown from Jimmy Maddin and renamed it the Summit. We played three or four nights a week with the little group, and two nights a week with the big band. That was the first time that Pat ever played in the rhythm section of a big band.

Mel Lewis was really bugged with how she comped. He was used to hearing Lou Levy playing in the rhythm section. Jack Tracy, who was the producer on the album, brought a whole bunch of people connected with Mercury Records in to hear the band, which included Patrice Munsell, a very famous singer.

We played our first set, and I was talking with Jack and Patrice, and Jack was also introducing me to all these other people at Mercury who I had never met before. Mel Lewis ran over to me at the table and said real loud, "IF SHE PLAYS ON THE NEXT SET, I'M NOT PLAYING!" That embarrassed the heck out of me. I pulled him off to the side and said to him, "You know what? You're right. You're NOT playing! GET OUT OF THE CLUB!" He said, "Get out? Who's going to play drums?" I said, "GET OUT! I'M going to play the next set on drums," and actually, physically, pushed him out of the club. I threw him out. Like a little boy, he came back, begging Berrel to tell me to let him come back into the club. He knew he was wrong and apologized. Mel wasn't the classiest guy you ever met, but I think that he and Buddy Rich, who played completely different style of drums, were the two greatest big band drummers I ever heard.

We finally recorded two live albums from there using the same exact band for both records. Both albums were recorded early in 1961, about six months apart. The first was originally released by Verve Records as "The Exciting Terry Gibbs Big Band Recorded Live at the Summit in Hollywood" and the second was released by Mercury Records and called "Explosion." They were both out of print for about twenty years until Fantasy leased them from Polygram, who owned all the masters, and renamed them "Main Stem" and "The Big Cat." Those eventually became volumes 4 and 5 of the Dream Band albums. As I said before, volumes 1, 2, and 3 came from the audition tapes that Wally recorded at the Seville and the Sundown.

I was never going to put them out. They were just going to be for me and my friends to listen to. Buddy Rich and Shorty Rogers used to come over to my house and listen to the tapes, and indirectly, they were responsible for me putting out the Dream Band CDs because they kept saying, "Let the world hear that band! It's the greatest band in the world!"

In 1985, there were some big bands making some noise: Rob McConnell, Frank Capp and the Juggernaut, Bob Florence, and Bill Holman to name a few, had some albums out and were getting a lot of airplay. I still wasn't sure if I wanted to put them out, even though I had something on tape that was already a winner.

Gene Norman heard that I had some unreleased tapes of my big band. He called me and asked if I was interested in putting them out with his record company. I still wasn't sure if I wanted to sell the tapes to anybody but I agreed to meet with him at his office on Sunset Blvd. in Hollywood. He really flipped out over the sound and the performance of the band and made me a very decent offer for the tapes. I thought about it and told him that if he put out the tapes as a four-record set that I'd be interested.

The reason that I wanted a four-record set was that those were the days of albums and cassettes. If he put out one album at a time, there would only be one or two songs on each side because some of the songs were twelve minutes long. He told me that he could edit and cut the songs so that he could get about twenty minutes of music on each side, which meant cutting a lot of the solos out. Once again, I insisted on a four-record set. I saw his point when he told me that he couldn't make any money by putting them all out at one time. He was right, because he was going to pay me a good amount of money for the tapes but I passed on the deal.

In 1986, Dick Bock, who once owned Pacific Jazz Records, heard about the tapes from Buddy Rich. Dick was now producing for Fantasy Records. One of Dick's fortés was editing tapes. He had a great feel for splicing the tape in the right place so that you'd never know that a four-minute song was once a twelve-minute song. He was a very successful record producer and was very interested in getting me with Fantasy Records. Dick and I had a meeting and I told him the same thing I told Gene Norman about cutting the tapes. He asked me to lend him the tapes so that he could show me what kind of an editing job he could do without ruining the feel of the arrangements and the solos. I made him a cassette of "Opus One." He also asked me not to listen to the original take of "Opus One" for about a month so that I could get the original out of my head.

After a month went by, I met with him again at his office in Hollywood. He played me the edited version and even though he took a lot of the solos out, it sounded good. All of the band ensembles were there and that was the highlight of the band. It almost sounded like the original version we recorded in the studio when the band first started, except that this was live and all the fire of all the guys yelling and carrying on was still there.

We took the cassette that Dick put together up to Fantasy Records in Berkeley, California, where we met with Ralph Kaffel, the president of Fantasy. I was surprised when Ralph told me that he had been a big fan of mine for years. Ralph loved what he heard and wanted to buy the master tapes. The money he offered me was not as much as Gene Norman offered, but he gave me some other things that were even more important to me than the money. To start with, Fantasy Records was a major jazz label, so I knew their distribution would be good. I wanted to make sure that every disc jockey in the country was supplied with an album, so I asked Ralph for the use of Fantasy's phone number. Then I called every disc jockey and made sure that they had the album. If they didn't, then one would be sent to them immediately. There was a good feeling between Ralph, Dick, and I, so I made the deal. That turned out to be one of the smartest moves I ever made, because the Dream Band records are now known all over the world.

When the Dream Band albums first came out, it was the biggest success I ever had in my life. There were two jazz radio stations in Los Angeles then: KKGO and KLON. I turned on one station and heard four or five songs in a row from the albums. Then I'd go to the other station to see what was happening, and THEY were playing four or five in a row. This happened all over the country.

Chapter 14

When we were at the Seville, Wally Heider worked from his big truck, which was built like a small studio. There was no room to park the truck at the Sundown, so he ad-libbed a studio in the back room. What Wally did was something I've never seen any recording engineer do. He taped wires on the floor in front of the saxophone section, the trumpet section, and the trombone section. Then he put mikes all over the place. In the back room where he was with his equipment, he had light bulbs set up on the wall. There were four light bulbs on top for the trumpets, three light bulbs underneath for the trombones, and five light bulbs for the saxes. If you looked at the wall it looked just like a band set-up. When somebody had a solo, the moment they stood up, their foot hit a wire and the light bulb went on in the back room where Wally was. He knew exactly who and when somebody was going to play a solo. This was genius to me. That's why the solos sounded right up front. Berrel helped out a lot because he knew the arrangements and every once in a while, he could alert Wally when he thought there was a solo coming up.

Indirectly, I helped make Wally a millionaire. In 1968, I got him a job on the *Operation: Entertainment* show that I conducted. Wally didn't belong to the union so all he could do was get a balance for the band. Then all the engineer at ABC had to do was make the whole band louder or softer. If he thought the bass was too loud, it was none of his business; he couldn't touch anything. As it turned out, the sound of the show was so good, that the president of Filmways came to Wally and offered him a million dollars for his company. Wally traveled with us to all of the shows and on the last show, when we came back to Los Angeles, there was either a Mercedes or a Rolls Royce waiting for him at the airport. Filmways bought that for him to go along with the new job that he had as president of the Wally Heider Studios.

When you recorded those days, everything was two-track. If you were watching the band play and heard the trumpet solo, you'd hear it on the left side. When you heard the tapes, the trumpet was on the left side because that's where Conte sat. When I took the tapes to Fantasy in 1986, I brought them to their young hotshot engineers and they said, "What do you want us to do with it?" I said, "What can you do to make it better?" They said, "Nothing. It's perfect. All we can do is make it a little brighter." It was that good.

Sometimes the band almost looked like a comedy act. When I'd go make an announcement, everybody was talking and carrying on. Once in a while, if anybody had something silly to say, I would play straight man for them. All the guys had their own personalities and I would try to bring it out of them. Even with all the ad-lib talking and carrying on, they knew that when it came to playing the music, they "took care of business," which meant, don't fool with the music. Play the music like it's written and like we rehearsed it. When we were not playing music, if anyone had something stupid to say, they got up and said it. All of that added more spirit and more fun to the band.

Everybody loved Frank Rosolino. Before I counted off the first song I would say, "Here it is . . ." and snap my fingers. After two or three minutes of this, the audience became part of our act and they'd start saying, "Here it is" also. Then I'd say, "One, two, three . . ." stop, and say, "FRANK! How's your foot? How's your car?" Any question at all. Frank would jump up immediately and start rambling about whatever was going on in his brain. You never knew what he was going to do on stage. I liked that because it added a lot of spirit to the band.

Frank had these little silly things he would do. I'd be ready to tap off the tune, "One, two, three . . ." and before I could get to four he'd stop me. "Hey, T . . .T . . .Terry! Terry!" He did a great imitation of Wally Heider stuttering. I said, "What happened?" and he said, "You know who likes your playing?" I said "No, who?" and he said, "That's what I'm asking YOU! Do you know who likes your playing?"

One time he stood up, threw his music on the floor, and started running on top of it. I said, "Frank, what are you doing?" Frank said, "I'm running over my music." What this did was add more energy to the band. The guys would laugh and the audience would break up too.

Frank was a great yodeler. He would talk for about five minutes, and by the time he got done telling me about what was wrong with his car or his foot, he wound up yodeling. By that time, the band and the audience were in hysterics. That's when I would tap off the band and hit them in the head with our opening song.

Bill Putnam, who owned a recording studio and who was a great engineer, always came into every club the band played. When we got done with our set, Bill came over to me and said, "You know, Terry. I know why your band is so good. You never start out with a first set. You always start out with your third set."

Al Porcino could be the worst and the best for a band; it was all according to what mood he was in. When he was in a good mood, he'd just sit there and play the hell out of his part. But sometimes he could be a big pain in the ass. He always wanted to be a bandleader so he was always trying to tell me how to run my band. He was one of the best lead trumpet players I ever played with. Al and Ray Triscari both played lead and they were both equally as good. But Al was a little more aggressive than Ray, so he sort of took charge of the trumpet section.

Chapter 14

Most of the music we played was written for record dates so it was all very high powered. When we recorded, I wanted every tune to be a home run. The club was always packed with celebrities and I wanted to really knock them out. So I picked this set out where every song was like a closing song and we really tore up the place. One home run after another. The next night we had a gang of celebrities again, so I figured I'd play the same set. As I was calling out the numbers, Porcino said, "What are we doing? Playing all FLAG WAVERS?" Then the guys in the trumpet section all said, "What are we playing? All flag wavers? How about our chops?" I'd have to say something silly to get everybody back into the fun we were having.

Vic Schoen wrote a suite for two bands that was recorded with Les Brown and a band that Vic put together for the date. Les was the musical director of *The Steve Allen Show* at the time that my band was at the Seville. Steve asked me if I would do the suite with my band and Les' band. All the guys in Les' band heard my band play at the club a lot of times and were really afraid to play opposite us. It was almost like we were Mike Tyson in his prime. The only person who wasn't afraid was John Audino, who later joined my band. They all knew that our band was something else. I never saw and didn't know the music at all, so Les came to me and said, "Terry, do you want me to conduct it for you and show you how it goes?" Al Porcino, who talked very slow, said, "L-e-s! W-e h-a-v-e o-u-r O-W-N b-a-n-d l-e-a-d-e-r!" And that was it. Even though Al and I used to argue a lot, he had enough respect for me to let Les know that the band was our little family and that we didn't need any help from anybody. It was a great piece of music and it came off great. I think that was the first time that Les ever heard our band, and he was very impressed.

I believed in hitting a home run immediately. In fact, I may have picked that up from Woody Herman. I always started out with a closing tune so that the whole band is standing up at the end of the song. That is, whoever COULD stand up would stand up.

Even though the band knew that Wally was there, they didn't act like it was a record date, which it actually wasn't. Wally was just experimenting with different microphones. He was in the back room and didn't know if Joe Maini was lying on the floor or Frank Rosolino was standing on somebody's shoulders. He never knew if they were near their mikes. Luckily, on the takes I picked, they were all sitting in their seats. I have some takes where, all of a sudden, you don't hear the lead alto. Joe Maini may have been lying on the floor or going out to dance with one of the girls. He'd break up a couple and start dancing with both of them, and for laughs, he'd wind up dancing with the guy. You never knew what these guys were going to do. Everybody had a good time.

On volumes 4 and 5, everybody knew they were record dates, and so everybody sat in their seats. They still carried on, making all kinds of noise, cheering every soloist, or just having fun.

If you listen closely to the Dream Band CDs, there are a lot of times when I'm soloing that you can hear Frank Rosolino yelling, "Hammer, baby! Hammer, baby!" Conte's schtick was when I'd call out the number of the song instead of its name. I'd say, "All right guys, let's play number thirty-four," and then Conte would ask, "What number is that?" That's also on some of the CDs. On "Flying Home," which is on volume 3, when I'm soloing and really getting into it, Joe Maini yells out, "Ohhhhhhhhh, SHIT!" In the same chorus he yells, "JEEEESUS CHRIST!" We couldn't edit that out because Wally recorded those albums on two tracks and if you tried to make those few bars softer, then it would ruin the continuity of the solo. So "Ohhhhhhhhh, SHIT!" And "JEEESUS CHRIST!" are on "Flying Home." So when you listen to the records, you hear a lot of yelling, which really is just a bunch of guys having fun.

I conducted the band on a telethon for the blind, which had Florence Henderson singing. We had an intermission and some of the guys in the band went outside and smoked some pot. They must have gotten something completely different than regular pot. Florence was singing "Some Enchanted Evening." It was more of a concert arrangement than a jazz arrangement. In the middle of the song, Med Flory stood up and started to play bebop behind her. I didn't believe it because there was nothing written for him to play. This was all live and I didn't know what to do, so I said, "Sit down!" And he said, "I CAN'T!" I kept telling him to sit down and he kept playing through her song. Every time I'd tell him to sit down, he'd stop long enough to say, "I CAN'T!" She didn't know what was happening at all because she never heard the arrangement played like that. I couldn't stop Med and Med couldn't sit down, he was so stoned out.

We weren't working steady with the band, so when I got a call for a job on the road for the quartet that paid a decent amount of money, I took it. Joe Glaser's office booked us in Las Vegas for a few weeks and then we went on to San Francisco. I hired Pat Moran on piano, Ronnie Zito on drums, and Freddie Schreiber on bass. We worked opposite Harry James at the Flamingo Hotel.

Frank Sinatra and the Rat Pack were doing the movie "Ocean's Eleven" and were playing at the Sands Hotel. Frank loved Red Norvo and he'd always have Red play in the lounge when he'd work there. Every night when they got done with their last show, they'd always come over to the Flamingo, all five of them: Frank Sinatra, Dean Martin, Joey Bishop, Peter Lawford, and Sammy Davis, Jr. They really came over to see Harry James because Frank worked with the band in his younger years. Sammy would always come up on stage and play vibes with me, and he wasn't too bad.

There was a showgirl who danced in the showroom who I thought was the prettiest girl I had ever seen in my life. Every time she'd pass me, I'd say hello but she'd walk right by me, completely fluffing me off. We worked at the Flamingo for six weeks and for the first three weeks, every time she passed by me, I would try to talk to her, but it was always a cold hello and goodbye. I wanted to ask her out but she would never stop to talk to me.

On my day off, I wanted to see the show at the Sands so I called Red and asked him if there was anything he could do to get me a reservation. Red was great. He called me back and told me that he had gotten me a table for Monday night. I didn't know how he did that, because if you called and tried to make a reservation for any of the shows at the Sands with the Rat Pack appearing there, they would have told you that they were sold out. I didn't want to go alone, so I asked Pat if she wanted to go with me to see Frank and she said, "Oh, yeah! Without a doubt!" At that moment, the showgirl walked by me so just for laughs, I said, "You want to see Frank Sinatra tomorrow night?" She stopped, looked at me, and said, "Sure, I'd love to see him." I said, "Okay, I'll pick you up at six o'clock." Once again she walked away; fluffed me off completely.

I was in my car riding to the Sands Hotel with Pat and the showgirl, who didn't say one word to me in the car and hadn't even told me her name yet. When we got to the showroom, they had a nice table waiting for us not too far away from the stage. While we were watching the show, she was facing the stage with her back towards me. Frank sang about eight or ten songs and then, he loosened his collar, and they brought him some Jack Daniels. He started to talk to the audience about what a great city Las Vegas was. He talked about some of the attractions that were working at some of the hotels and finally, he said, "If you want to hear a great, swinging big band, Harry James is playing at the Flamingo, and playing opposite Harry is one of the greatest jazz vibists living, Terry Gibbs!" The moment he said my name, this girl turned around and looked at me like *I* was Frank Sinatra. She started talking to me and hitting on me, and when we went home that night, she and I wound up together. I couldn't lose her, I couldn't get her out of my room; in fact, I couldn't get rid of her.

Two nights later, when Frank came into the Flamingo, I told him what had happened and he said, "You should have told me you were going to be there. I would have given you a real good build-up." I said, "Forget about it! I can't get rid of her now! If you had said anything more than my name, she would have wanted to move into my house in Woodland Hills!"

We were really partying all the time. We used to stay awake for hours and sometimes even days at a time. I knew this doctor who gave me a pill called Preludin that he said would help us stay awake. He told us not to take any more than a quarter of a tablet. We were so wiped out that I gave Pat half and I kept the other half for myself. The pill didn't do much for her except pick her up a little so she could perform on stage.

After not sleeping for a day-and-a-half, I took the other half of the Preludin before I went on stage. When it hit me, it was hard for me to stand still. After I played my first tune, I couldn't keep one foot down and pick the other one up to get to my pedal. It looked like I was dancing. People were pointing at me and saying, "Look how good he is, he dances when he plays!" I talk fast as it is, and when I went over to the microphone to introduce the band, what came out sounded like total gibberish. What I said in those few seconds must have been the same as four or five minutes of regular talking. Besides introducing the musicians in the band, I told them the name of the song we just played and the name of the song we were going to play, but what the audience heard me say was "SCADGERBRAGOVOMIERHIHDTKES." After I finished my little speech, I thought, "What am I talking about?" *I* couldn't even understand what I said. After that, I didn't say one word; I just went from one song to the next. I might have said, "thank you," but if I did, nobody understood it anyway. Finally, at about five o'clock in the morning, the pill started to wear off and I think that's when I started to bomb with the audience because I wasn't dancing anymore.

Our bass player, Freddie Schreiber, would make up all these crazy names, like Oswald Mygum, Darrell B. Mordecum, and Herr Lip. When we got through playing at about six o'clock in the morning, we'd sit around trying to unwind, so for laughs, we'd call the paging operator and have all these names paged and sit there and laugh. We'd hear "PAGING SELMA CAR!" "PAGING OSWALD MYGUM!"

We did a terrible thing one night. We went over to the operator and gave her a piece of paper with the name Mike Hunt written on it and asked her to please page him. We were listening for the page and finally the operator said, "MIKE HUNT! MIKE HUNT! Uhh . . . MICHAEL HUNT! MICHAEL HUNT!" It took her a few seconds to realize what she had said.

After we got done working in Las Vegas, we opened at a club in San Francisco opposite a terrible comedian. He opened the show and we had to follow him. He did about a half-hour of no laughs, and when I say no laughs, I mean nobody laughed at all. For a half-hour, people were staring at him, waiting for some kind of punchline to what he thought was a joke. It never happened. Now we had to follow him, and that was hard. It's really hard to follow somebody who bombs. After the fifth night, Freddie Schreiber got so bugged, that after twenty minutes of no laughs from the audience, he went up on stage, put his arm around the comedian, who didn't have the slightest idea of what was going on, took out his list, and started reading, "Oswald Mygum, Darrell B. Mordecum, Selma Carr, Herr Lip, Herr Clipper," and people started to laugh. That was the first time this comedian heard any laughs while he was on that stage.

When we got back to Los Angeles, I put the band together again and we played at Shelly's Manne Hole for a few weeks. Those days, they allowed you to smoke in nightclubs in California. I never allowed smoking on the bandstand because I thought that it looked cheap. Drinking was different because the guys could put their drinks underneath their stands and they could sip on them. Ray Triscari was in the band longer than anybody was and one time, I caught him smoking on the bandstand. When the set was over, we went into the band room and I said, "Ray, of all guys, you know that I don't like smoking on the bandstand. I don't mind you drinking, but smoking really looks terrible." I was really bugged with him.

Now, like I said, you never knew what my band was going to do. Shelly wanted us to close at ten to two so he could get everybody out of the place. We always closed the night with "Billie's Bounce" at about twenty to two. I had it timed so that at whatever bar or letter it was, I'd play six choruses, the band would come in with a background, and then we'd play the ensemble on out, and it always came out perfect. Because the club was always packed and the band was swinging. I brought a bottle of cognac in on the first night and Conte, Ray, John Audino, and I would drink most of it. Then the next night, John would bring one in and I'd bring one in also. Then Conte and Ray would bring one in, and little by little, we'd have four or five bottles of cognac going around. The good thing about the band was that even though I allowed drinking on the bandstand, it never got to the point where they couldn't play their part.

On the night that I caught Ray smoking, we were playing our last song and, like every night, when I got to my sixth chorus, the band was supposed to come in and play a background. Nobody came in. I figured they were a little juiced and having fun, so I kept playing. I played my seventh chorus and my eighth chorus and still nobody came in. Now I was getting bugged because they were ruining my timing on finishing the song by ten to two when I got to my next chorus, nobody came in, but everybody in the audience started applauding. I figured they all loved me. Wonderful, I'll play another chorus. They still didn't come in and now I'm really bugged so I turned around, ready to give them hell, and EVERYBODY, all fifteen musicians, were puffing on cigarettes. There was so much smoke you couldn't see the band. All I saw was a cloud of smoke. They were bugged with me because half of them didn't smoke and they had to keep puffing on their cigarettes until I turned around.

I wrote a song called "It Might as Well Be Swing" which starts out with the band playing the melody and then I come in with a bell note on the fourth beat. We were only working one or two nights a week at the Sundown and I was playing at Jimmy Maddin's other club called the Sanbah five nights a week with a different rhythm section. When you play with a big band, it's a completely different feel than playing with a quartet, especially with Mel Lewis playing drums, because he sat on it rather than giving it a little edge, like you would play with a little band. With a little band, the rhythm section gives you that little edge and you play more on top. Now, after playing five nights a week with a little band, when I came to work with the big band, sometimes I would feel uncomfortable playing, because there was a difference in the time.

On the first set, I played "It Might as Well Be Swing" and was getting ready to hit my bell note on the fourth beat, but heard the band still holding their note. I thought, "This is going to be a weird night for me," because I was already having trouble with the time. After the next eight bars, I was ready to play the fourth beat again and the band was still holding their note. The third time this happened, I said to myself, "Wait a minute. I can't be THAT screwed up. There's something wrong here." What they did was, they were holding their note for four beats instead of three. So they were playing a 5/4 bar while I was playing in four, so I never came down with the note.

To me, Richie Kamuca was the most unheralded saxophone player of all time. I felt like he was in the same class as Stan Getz, Zoot Sims, and Al Cohn; he was as good as any of those guys. He could have been one of the Four Brothers and the sound wouldn't have changed. Everything he played was so melodic and beautiful. Richie and Bill Perkins were two introverted guys who became completely nuts on my band. Nobody could play in the band and be introverted. They couldn't help it.

Richie was also very handsome. I was standing in front of the band when I noticed this gorgeous blonde staring right at me. It looked like she was really hitting on me. She started to walk towards me, came to within three inches of me, and walked right PAST me to Richie and gave him the biggest kiss in the world. Fluffed me off completely. It was Richie she was looking at, not me.

Richie wasn't a big band lover. Even though he played a lot of solos, it was really never enough because we had so many great soloists and I had to let everybody play. What made the band so good was that it was an ensemble band. He loved little bands more than anything, but he loved our big band.

Every once in a while, it got so loose that I would get bugged and say, "I'm breaking up the band." What I meant by loose is that the guys had to be on time for every set. I didn't care if they showed up naked, just so long as they showed up on time.

In 1961, we were finally getting a chance to do a record date and get paid for it. After the first break, I sent Berrel out to find the guys so we could get ready to record again. He came back alone and said, "They're not here." I said, "WHAT DO YOU MEAN, THEY'RE NOT HERE? WE'RE IN THE MIDDLE OF A RECORD DATE!" He told me that they had all gone down to the Hollywood Palladium, a few blocks away, to hear Harry James' band. Richie and I were alone in the dressing room and I said to him, "You know, Richie, after we do this record date, I'm definitely breaking up the band." He said, "Oh, Terry, you can't break up the band. Don't do it. It's too good." Everybody finally came back and we got back up on the bandstand. On the song, "The Big Cat," at the end, the trombones just vamp and I noodle around for a while and then I cut off the band. While the vamping was going on—and this lasted about a minute—Richie knew I was serious about breaking up the band and he didn't want it to happen. So he started yelling behind me while I was playing the vamp: "GO GET 'EM, TERRY! GO AHEAD, TERRY!" which wasn't his bag because he was such an introvert. But he was egging me on. He was having a great time and didn't want me to break up the band. You can hear him saying that on the CD.

Bill Perkins, who everybody called "Perk," was also very introverted but not on this band. He was just starting to listen to John Coltrane and was getting a little bit influenced by him. Perk's style came out of the Lester Young school. When we recorded at the Summit, he had a solo on a song called "Soft Eyes." Being that we were a straight-ahead swing band, he came to me and said, "Terry, do you mind if I get a little out on my solo on 'Soft Eyes'? I've been listening to Trane and I love some of the things he's been doing." I never tell anybody how to play their solo, plus it wasn't really out, but it was a little different for Perk.

Charlie Kennedy was quiet and shy and had a funny sense of humor. In his younger days, Charlie worked with Gene Krupa and recorded a song called "Disc Jockey Jump" with Gene and played a solo on it that became very famous. Charlie's sound was closer to Charlie Parker than anybody in the band, even more than Joe Maini's. On Volume 2, called "The Sundown Sessions," Charlie played a solo on "It Could Happen to You" and you'd swear it was Bird.

Charlie was also a very humble human being and a very nice person, but he had to give up the music business because he couldn't be around it without getting in trouble with dope. In 1986, after the CD came out, I started up the Dream Band again and called Charlie to play lead alto because by then, Joe Maini had died. We were going to play at the Playboy Jazz Festival, and when I called Charlie he said, "Let me think about it." He called me later and said, "I don't want to do it. I can't play again; I haven't played in years." We had a few months to get prepared but he just wouldn't do it. I think he didn't feel that he could be around the jazz scene without getting in trouble.

Jack Nimitz took Jack Schwartz' place and he was nicknamed "The Admiral," I suppose, after Admiral Nimitz. Jack Nimitz was more of a soloist than Jack Schwartz was and got to be very much in demand doing studio work. The only guy in the original band who really did any studio work was Ray Triscari, but Ray would take off record dates to do our fifteen-dollar job. When Porcino left, John Audino took his place. John was doing the Hollywood Palace show and so was Ray. They loved the band so much that when we had a job to play, they both would take off that show. It wasn't just giving up the 200 and some-odd dollars that the show paid; they were giving up the pension fund money and the money that goes for their health and welfare benefits. They gave up a whole lot when they gave up those shows. The money wasn't important to them because they felt just like I did. It probably was the happiest part of their lives too.

I didn't name it the Dream Band. When the first CD came out, Ralph Kaffel, the president of Fantasy, named it that. The album was just titled "The Dream Band." I was against it because I hated names put on bands. Originally, we were called "The Exciting Terry Gibbs Big Band," but the name "Dream Band" stuck so much that every album was called "The Terry Gibbs Dream Band." When people talk to me about the band, they always address it as the Dream Band and leave my name out completely.

Joe Maini was, as the cliché goes, "one of a kind." Joe was also a street person. He'd use four-letter words even if he were talking to his mother. That was part of his vocabulary and he couldn't help it. When Bob Gefaell bought the Sundown from Jimmy Maddin, he renamed it the Summit. He loved the band so much, he decided he wanted to broadcast from there. Since it was his club, Bob decided he was going to be the announcer. The first broadcast was aired coast-to-coast on a show called *Monitor*. That day happened to be Joe Maini's birthday. I told Berrel to bring the whole band except Joe to the band room and I told them, "When we get to 'Cotton Tail,' and all the saxophones stand up on the saxophone chorus, go right into 'Happy Birthday.'" We played a few tunes and Bob Gefaell was announcing his heart away. We started "Cotton Tail," and when the saxophones stood up to play that great chorus that Al Cohn wrote, we went right into "Happy Birthday." Everybody in the band sang, and the audience did too. Everybody applauded, and Joe was really touched because he was a very warm guy. Then everybody stopped playing and were applauding him when all of a sudden Joe reached for the mike. Bob Gefaell, not knowing much about Joe, made the mistake of handing it to him. I thought, "Oh, NOOOO, not on the air!"

Joe's timing was perfect. He took the microphone and said, "Terry, this makes me feel so good . . ." then he paused a while and then said, ". . .that MY DICK IS TURNING PURPLE!" and handed the mike right back to Bob. Bob stammered and stuttered and didn't know what to say after that. He looked dumbfounded. I immediately said to the guys, "Take it from the sax chorus" and we went out swinging with Bob Gefaell looking like he was in shock.

One night, Harold Land played tenor sax with the band. For the first three sets we were playing mostly ensemble arrangements, but on the last set, I let him stretch out on one of the blues things and he played about thirty some-odd choruses. When he got done, Joe Maini had to follow him. Joe didn't own a clarinet, but there was one right next to him that Med used to play on two of the arrangements. After Harold played his thirty choruses and tore up the house, Joe didn't know what to play to follow him, so he picked up Med's clarinet and played Jimmy Dorsey's chorus from "Fingerbustin'," which had nothing to do with the blues. It was just a clarinet chorus that Jimmy made famous and it broke up the whole band. Joe was so talented. The title "Fingerbustin'" perfectly describes the type of a song it was, and it wasn't easy to play, especially when you played it on a strange clarinet.

I think that Conte Candoli was the favorite soloist of everyone in the band. When Conte played a solo, all the other trumpet players looked at him with admiration. Conte, who was married at that time, was seeing a Swedish girl named Kris who he eventually married after he got his divorce.

We were playing at a club called King Arthur's in Canoga Park and Kris came in with Conte. Conte was so in love with her that he was flipping out. Every once in a while, he would stand up in the middle of a number and throw kisses to Kris in the audience. Some of the people in the audience knew Conte's wife, so John Audino, who loved Conte, didn't want anybody to know what Conte was doing. So whenever Conte stood up to throw kisses to Kris, John stood up and also threw kisses to Kris. It looked weird to see two guys standing up throwing kisses to the same girl.

I was working in Toronto when I got a call from Jerry Lewis. Jerry liked to pantomime to big band records. I think that when Jerry started in show business, that was his act. He did it to a Count Basie record in one of his movies called "The Errand Boy" in a scene where he was sitting at a conference table. Jerry was a big fan of my band and loved a song we recorded called "Nose Cone" and wanted to do pantomime to it for another movie that he was now doing. I couldn't fly in so he asked me if I minded if somebody else played my solo. I said, "No, go ahead." They had my part written out and Larry Bunker played it. Playing somebody else's solo is the hardest thing in the world to do, especially mine, because I play four billion notes. Plus, I never know which mallet I'm going to use. In classical music, everything is usually right-left-right-left. But when you're playing jazz, who knows where your hands are going? Larry told me it was the hardest thing he ever had to read and he was one of the big studio players who could read anything. He did it but they never used it in the picture.

I was sitting at home when I got a call at about ten o'clock at night. It was Jerry, calling from the Sands Hotel in Las Vegas. He said, "Listen, I'm thinking about doing an after-hours show tomorrow after my last performance. Do you think you can get the band together? If you can, we'll fly everybody in." I was so elated, I didn't believe it. Jerry said, "I'll have a plane waiting for you at the airport. Catch the plane, come on in, we'll meet at three in the morning at the bar at the Sands Hotel and we'll talk about it." He sent a limousine to my house to take me to the airport. Money meant nothing to Jerry. Everything was first class.

I got to the airport, got on the plane, and when I got to Vegas, I went straight to the Sands Hotel. I didn't check in at all and went right to the bar. I didn't even know where I was staying. Jerry could be hot and cold. I waited at the bar for about a half-hour, sitting on *shpilkees* (pins and needles). He finally came over and sat on a stool next to me with his back towards me. After about two or three minutes, my temper got the best of me and I turned to him and said, "What the hell are you doing? What is this bullshit? You called me and got me so up; I'm sitting here waiting for you, and now you're fluffing me off? What's going on?" He said, "Oh, Terry, I just went through this whole scene with my agent. Do me a favor. I have a room waiting for you. Let me give you a call tomorrow and we'll talk about it." And he left. I was kind of bugged because I wanted to talk to him about it NOW.

A bellhop came and got my suitcase and took me not to just a room, but a SUITE of rooms. The next morning, I got a message. Mr. Lewis wanted me to come have dinner at six that evening and see his show at eight. I still didn't know what was going on. Jerry was such a big fan of my band that I gave him a copy of the arrangements of "Nose Cone" and "Sweet Georgia Brown" which he used in his show.

When I went down to dinner, they sat me down at a front table. After he did about an hour, he started to introduce celebrities in the audience and then went through a big speech about my band and finally, he introduced me. Just then, I saw them wheel a set of vibes out. I didn't know where he had gotten them from. He got me up on stage so I played "Nose Cone" and "Sweet Georgia Brown."

As I came off the stage, Jack Entratter, who was the entertainment director at the Sands Hotel said, "We have an opening coming up in the lounge in about three weeks. Would you like to play here?" I said, "I'd love to!" Jerry heard me talking to Jack and said, "Wait a minute. I'm his manager. You don't have anything to do with him. What are you talking to him about?" Jack told him that he wanted me to play in the lounge for six weeks. Jerry said, "What are you going to pay him?" Jack said, "$1500 a week." Jerry said, "No, you're going to give him $2500 a week." Jerry had all kinds of power at the Sands, so $2500 it was. And so Jerry got me that job.

For some reason, the after-hours show that Jerry was going to do never came off and I went back home the next day. When I got home, I couldn't remember when the job was supposed to start so I called Jerry to find out the dates that I was going to play. He yelled at me. "I GOT YOU THE JOB! WHAT ELSE DO YOU WANT? LEAVE ME ALONE!" And he hung up on me. If he had been next to me, I would have whacked him right in the mouth.

Jerry always wanted to hear the big band tapes before they came out. Berrel and I would go to Jerry's house and take the tapes with us. He had a room that had about ten reel-to-reel machines in it. He'd make copies of my tapes and give them to all of his friends: Tony Curtis, whoever his friends were, he'd give them all copies. They were all fans of the band.

He had a concert to do at UCLA and wanted the band to be on the show with him. Jerry had a guy that worked for him that weighed about four hundred pounds; a big ape. Jerry paid him five hundred dollars a week so that when Jerry got bugged, he would whack the guy in the arm. He'd just stand there and Jerry would beat up on him. We were about ready to go on when Jerry came up to me and put his hands up like he was ready to box. So I put my hands up too. Then he started throwing punches and I kept blocking them. He threw about three or four punches and every time I blocked one, it hit me on my arm, and it hurt. Finally, after I had enough, I faked a left and then threw a punch with my left. Luckily for Jerry, I opened up my hand and slapped him so hard that he fell over the saxophone section with all the stands flying right into the band. We had to stop the show for a while so he could go upstairs to put makeup on his face because he had my handprint with five fingers on his face. His ex-wife Patty said that was the best thing that ever happened to him. His piano player, Lou Brown, who was his conductor for many years and didn't really like Jerry, said that when I hit Jerry, it was the happiest moment in his life.

I appeared on *The Jerry Lewis Telethon* about three or four times, and when I'd go to rehearsal, he was always there. Every time he saw me, he'd purposely put his hands up, but playfully, and if I put my hands up, he'd say, "Forget it."

I was back east when I got a call from Ray Linn, who was contracting the Monterey Jazz Festival. He asked me to put the Dream Band together again to play at the festival. Cannonball Adderley, Oscar Peterson, Dave Brubeck, and Dizzy Gillespie were some of the people also playing on the festival. I gave Ray names of who I wanted to play in the band. I also wanted to make sure that they were all paid a decent amount of money so I told him that if he could work the money situation out for the musicians, he should call me back and we'd arrange a fee for me. About a week later, Ray called me back and said, "I got all the guys you asked for." He agreed to what I wanted and I said great. This was a hard job for the guys in the band. Not only did they have to play our music, but they had to be the house band also. This meant that they had to play Johnny Richards' arrangements and play music for other people, music that they really didn't enjoy playing. They were getting paid well and I suppose that's why they accepted the job.

I flew in and they called a rehearsal for three o'clock, the afternoon of the night of the show. Duke Ellington was the emcee and he was going to introduce the band, so I figured we'd open up with something he wrote, "Main Stem." I hadn't seen the guys in six months. Everybody came to our rehearsal: Dizzy, Oscar, Cannonball . . . They all came because they had heard about the band.

I tapped off "Main Stem" and the band played the heck out of the chart. You could have sworn that we had been playing together for the last six months. It was so perfect, that I said, "No rehearsal. See you guys in the dressing room tonight."

I put two bottles of cognac and gin in the dressing room. It was like old times and we were all glad to be together again. When we got on the stage, the curtain was closed. Duke Ellington was in front of the curtain introducing the band while Lou Levy, Mel Lewis, and Buddy Clark were playing the blues, which was the chord changes to "Main Stem." Duke had an eloquent way of speaking, and when he finished introducing the band, we could have played one chord and we would have been a winner. I had it planned so that when Duke said, "Terry Gibbs" and the curtain opened, I was going to go right into the ensemble of "Main Stem."

We were all on the stage with the curtain closed while Duke was introducing us and here is what was going on backstage. This was October and the World Series was going on. All four trumpet players had portable radios with their earphones in their ears, listening to the ballgame. They were just standing around, not even sitting in their chairs. Frank Rosolino was sitting on somebody's shoulders, just carrying on. Joe Maini was lying on the floor, kicking his feet, and the rest of the saxes were in hysterics because of what Joe was doing. The rhythm section was still swinging and Duke was still talking. It looked so disorganized that it didn't make any sense. The curtain was closed, so I didn't care, because nobody could see us anyway. When Duke said, "Terry Gibbs!" you'd think that everyone would sit back in their seats. The curtain opened up and everybody was still doing what they were doing. Joe was on the floor kicking his feet, Frank was still on somebody's shoulders, and the four trumpet players were yelling, "Hey! It's a home run!" It almost looked like Spike Jones' band.

With my dumb sense of humor, I let it go on for a while. Why not? They were all having fun. I knew the music was going to be good no matter what, so when the band finally came in, it was like a powerhouse. Not only did we break it up and get a standing ovation, they made us come back at the end of the show after Dizzy, Oscar, and everybody else had played. We had to play another half-hour. The only person in the whole place who wasn't shocked to see the band so disorganized was Duke Ellington, who was used to seeing a loose band. His band was loose, but this was ridiculous.

Lenny Bruce used to hang around my big band all the time. Lenny, Joe Maini, and Jack Sheldon were very close. After Gene Norman found out that I could draw people into a club, he hired me to work opposite Lenny at the Crescendo with my quartet. There were two writers in town called Abe and Belle Greenberg who wrote for the *Hollywood Citizen*. They used to put Lenny down because Lenny worked too dirty for them. Most of Lenny's language was just street talk. It didn't offend me because I used to talk that way growing up in Brooklyn. The "F" word was nothing at all because, growing up in Brooklyn, it was part of our language. But these two writers didn't like him because of that.

On opening night, Steve Allen came in with Jayne Meadows, Jackie Cooper, and Jackie's wife, Barbara. Lenny respected Steve and knew that Steve didn't like anything off-color, so he did the whole show without even saying the word "shit." He did all his great, out material. Lenny didn't tell jokes; he talked about situations that were really true and funny.

On the second night, before we went on stage to open the show, I noticed that Lenny was taking chairs and placing them in a certain way. I couldn't understand what he was doing. It looked like he was making an aisle from the back door to the stage. By that time, Lenny had already alienated all the police so that if he said the word "shit," they would bust him immediately. Those words weren't allowed to be said anywhere in public. Those days, "stinker" was a dirty word. If you said "shit" you could get thrown in jail. It got to a point where they had Jewish police there because he started saying Jewish things like "*schmuck*" and "*kish mir in tuchis*" and they would bust him for that.

Lenny's valet and chauffeur's name was Eric. Eric was sitting in Lenny's car while the car was running and was parked outside the back door. We played our part of the show and stuck around to watch Lenny do his show. This time, when he did his show, he used four-letter words all the way through. At the end, he introduced celebrities in the audience. Abe and Belle Greenberg were sitting right in front and Lenny said, "Ladies and gentlemen, I have two people sitting in front of me that aren't my biggest fans. But I appreciate them coming in to review my show tonight. How about a nice hand for Abe and Belle Greenberg!" He waited until they stood up and waited about five seconds. As they were starting to stand up, he said, "That's right, ladies and gentlemen, Abe and Belle Greenberg . . . TWO FUCKING KLUTZES!" As soon as he said this, he ran through that aisle that he had made and as he ran through it, like you'd see in the movies, he pushed the chairs over because the cops were chasing him. They couldn't get past all the chairs, Lenny got into his car, which Eric had running, and split.

It was one of the biggest shocks of my life when I heard that Joe Maini killed himself. I don't think he purposely did that. Joe was pretty wild, but there was no reason for him to do that. From what I heard, he picked up a gun that he thought was not loaded and pretended to play Russian Roulette. Unfortunately, there was a bullet in the gun. Joe was the type of guy that if people in a very small town in Iowa made a movie about what they thought a jazz musician was like, it would be Joe Maini's life. Jazz musicians back then had a reputation of being wild. He'd make love to his wife in the middle of the floor, but only if the band would watch. In his younger days, he was a junkie, but he knew never to fool with junk in my band. He was the type of guy who would stay awake for a week at a time just partying. But I honestly don't think that he killed himself. I can't think of any reason for him to have done that.

Frank Rosolino was another story. None of us could figure this out at all. Frank must have been hurting inside that bad when he went and shot one of his sons in the head, and then went into the other room, shot the other one, and then shot himself. After you shoot the first one and you see half of your son's brains coming out, you'd have to be that sick or hurting that bad to go over to another child and try to do the same thing. Luckily, the second son lived, but he was blinded for life. The biggest drag about that whole thing is that the mother of those two children had committed suicide four or five years before that ever happened.

Steve Allen wrote a great thing in *The Overture,* a magazine published by the Musicians Union, Local 47, called "A Tribute to a Fine Musician." We all loved Frank Rosolino but everyone hated him for what he did. No matter how bad things are, if things are that bad and you're that stupid, kill yourself, but don't kill your children.

Don Menza, a saxophone player and one of Frank's closest friends, also didn't know why he did it. There were different rumors going around like the girl he was going with was running around with another girl. If you feel that that's a problem, kill HER. Or if you're that dumb, kill yourself. To this day, we still don't why Frank shot his kids and committed suicide.

I talked to Frank two days before he died. I had a record company called Jazz A La Carte and I had an idea of recording him and Carl Fontana. This would have been different than what Kai Winding and J. J. Johnson did in that both Carl and Frank had tremendous technique. So instead of showing it off in their solos, what I was going to do was to have them show off their technique by playing the melodies to songs like "Tico Tico" and "Holiday for Strings." He was really up about it and wanted to do it so bad, but two days later, that whole incident happened.

People always ask me why the Dream Band wasn't much more successful. Actually, it was as successful as I wanted it to be. I was happy playing the Sundown and the Summit, making my eleven dollars a night. I didn't want the band just playing anywhere. That's why I left the Cloister. I just wanted to have fun. We were a complete winner. We played to a packed house full of celebrities every night. The club owner made money, and we had the times of our lives. Just listening to the band was the greatest thrill I ever had, and I had the best seat in the house. Sometimes when I was in front of the band, I would turn my back to them and cup my hands so I could hear them louder, if that was possible. As loud as they played, it was never loud enough for me. It was a great feeling. We were accepted by everybody in Hollywood. Even though every movie star came in to see us, WE were the stars. What could be better?

Chapter 15
The Coltrane Connection

Between working with the band and running on the road, Donna and I were back to living a very unsettled married life. We were both going in different directions. I met Carol Wadsworth at a club called P.J.'s in Hollywood and we started to run around together. Divorce seemed to be the only solution for Donna and me. The one good thing was that it wasn't a bitter divorce. Joe Glaser recommended an attorney called Jerry Pacht, who later became a very famous judge. There was no sense in both of us having an attorney because we weren't fighting over anything, so we hired Jerry. We told him what our assets were, which was not too much at that time. Jerry worked it out to where Donna got the house and some money, and I got the rest of the money that we had in the bank, the piano, all of the instruments, and my music library.

Divorce is never pleasant and I figured that I would go back to New York and try to start my life over again where it first started. When I got back there, I called Joe Glaser and he immediately booked a bunch of clubs for me to play at. I'd been away from New York for about six years and didn't know many of the new, young musicians. I called Herman Wright, the bass player that worked with my quartet back in the fifties, and he told me about another female piano player named Alice McLeod, who, like Terry Pollard, came from Detroit. Herman said Alice was great and that I would like her. Alice's brother was Ernie Farrow, the bass player who played in my quartet before Herman did.

I set up an audition to hear Alice play. I also spoke with Mel Lewis, who was now living in New York, and he recommended a drummer called Bobby Pike. I think we rehearsed at the old Nola's Studios on Broadway.

Right from the introduction Alice played on the first song, I knew that she was something else. She sounded just like Bud Powell. She played chorus after chorus, and every note was a gem. Bobby played real good, too, so now I had a good quartet.

Our first job was at the Metropole opposite Gene Krupa. I didn't know Gene well, but I found out what a sweet guy he was. The Metropole stage was laid out where you couldn't put any instruments in front of each other, but I could squeeze my vibes in front of the drums or on the side. After Gene got done with his set, in order for us to set up our instruments, my drummer and I had to move Gene's drums. The manager came over and said, "Wait a minute. You're not the star here. Gene Krupa's the star. The drums stay where they are." Gene happened to be standing there when he said that, and he told the manager, "Let me tell you something. When I'm on the bandstand, I AM the star. But when Terry plays with his group, HE'S the star. Please have somebody move the drums to the side." So on every show, they'd have two of the guys who worked there move Gene Krupa's drums. He was a real professional and a gentleman.

After we finished playing the Metropole, we opened up at Birdland opposite John Coltrane. I met John when he was working with Miles Davis. In fact, we worked together when Miles and my big band did those few concerts in California and Arizona. When I first introduced Alice to John, I immediately saw a puppy love romance starting. Alice was very shy and in a way, so was John. You'd never know it from the way John played, because his playing was very extroverted. It seemed like when he played, everything he was hearing in his head came right out of his saxophone.

I must admit that I didn't like his playing at that period in his life. I loved the music he played when he was with Miles Davis and up to the end of his "Giant Steps" period, but this sounded like he was just screeching. It sounded like he couldn't get to the highest note that he was looking for. It seemed like the melodic part of his playing was missing. That's what it felt like to me, but not to Alice.

There was a back booth in Birdland where musicians could sit, and every time we'd get off the stage, Alice would be there, just staring at John while he played. I think she was falling in love with him.

John was starting to get very popular. He started a completely new way of approaching jazz on the saxophone and was starting to become the next Charlie Parker to a lot of the young musicians. You had to know Alice to understand how beautiful she was as a person. John saw that and probably felt her inner beauty, for he fell in love with her too.

Alice's playing started to change a little. She was starting to incorporate some of John's harmonic structure in her playing, but she was still playing bebop.

While we were working at Birdland, we recorded an album for Mercury Records. Quincy Jones was now a vice-president of Mercury, so I went to him with an idea. I always wanted to do an album playing Jewish music, and play it almost like you'd play Latin jazz. We would play straight ahead, but instead of having the Latin feel from a conga drum and claves, I would have the other drummer play BAHH-bu-BAHH, bu-BAHH-bu, BAHH-bu-BAHH while we played jazz choruses. I also wanted to have an authentic Jewish band play part of the melody at the beginning and at the end of each song, so I hired my brother Sol. He got me the other musicians to play the Jewish parts: Ray Musiker on clarinet, Sam Kutcher on trombone, and my old friend Alan Logan on piano.

That record date was one of the most fun dates I ever did. Quincy loved the idea and he produced the date. I got to know Quincy fairly well when he was a young trumpet player with the Lionel Hampton band. Quincy always liked the way I played and when he'd hear me play, he'd always compliment me on my playing.

What made the date fun was that Quincy showed up wearing a *yarmulke* (skullcap) and a *tallis* (prayer shawl) that Jews wear when they pray in synagogues. What made it even more fun and authentic was that in the middle of the date, Lalo Schifrin, another friend of mine, brought me a box of *matzoh*.

The music turned out great. I played a bunch of songs that had never been written down on paper. The cliché, "you had to be there" was what was happening. All the Jewish musicians on the date were real *klezmers*. When they were hired to play a club date for different leaders, whether the jobs were weddings or bar mitzvahs, they never knew who the other musicians would be. But they did know all the old Russian folk songs, *bulgars*, and *freilachs,* and they didn't need any music for that. The only music I gave them were two original songs that I wrote.

Alice actually stole that date from me. She was starting to play runs she got from listening to John and all the musicians flipped out every time she played. She was making those Eastern-style runs on the minor songs and they sounded very authentic. I was the Jew and she was wiping me out.

I wanted to call the album *Jew Jazz* but Mercury wouldn't let me. The world wasn't too hip those days, and the album was eventually called *Terry Gibbs Plays Jewish Melodies in Jazz Time.* As I write about this now, *klezmer* music has become very big, and I just got word that Polygram Records is re-releasing the album that we did in 1963 on CD at the end of this year, which is 2002.

We played a few more clubs in the New York area, and then traveled to some other cities away from New York. Bobby Pike had other commitments and couldn't go on the road, so somebody recommended a young drummer named John Dentz. I had him come to the club we were playing at, and he sat in and sounded real good. He was under some real pressure because before we left New York, Mercury asked me to do another record date for them under their new subsidiary label called Limelight. That was the first job that John played with the quartet. I wrote all the music and arrangements and the only rehearsal we had was at the record date. John was very nervous but also played very good.

John Coltrane and Alice were getting a little tighter with each other. He'd come out on the road to where we were playing and was sort of courting her. At the same time that John was visiting Alice, Carol flew in from time to time to stay with me at some of the cities we were played. By this time, I taught Alice to play the vibes and she was a natural. Because the piano keyboard and the vibes were the same, all I had to do was teach her how to hold the mallets and how to do the hand movements. Every week she was better than the week before. After only a few months, she was becoming a good vibes player.

We played in Detroit, which was home for Alice as well as Terry Pollard. Terry came to the club to see us and I got her to play vibes with Alice and me. The people went nuts. A lot of the people in the audience remembered the famous vibes duets that Terry and I did when she worked with my quartet and they were knocked out to see another young lady from Detroit doing the same thing.

Joe Glaser had six weeks of clubs for me to play on the West Coast: four weeks in Los Angeles and two in Denver. I took Alice with me and picked up some musicians in L.A. that had worked for me before. When I got out to L.A., Carol told me that she was pregnant with my child. I felt happy but confused, for I didn't know what to do. My divorce papers from Donna hadn't been finalized yet. Those days, it took months to get divorced. After Alice and I finished the tour, we went back to New York and I got an apartment in Riverdale, which is about a thirty-minute car ride from Manhattan. Then I sent for Carol.

There was a club in Chicago called the London House that was owned by two brothers, Irving and Oscar Marienthal. It was really a high-class supper club that had great food but it was also a piano room. The only attractions that worked there were people like Oscar Peterson, Erroll Garner, Ahmad Jamal, and George Shearing. When Joe Glaser called and said that he had booked me to play there, I flipped out, for that was big time. I knew we'd break it up because besides the good music we'd play, I had the vibes duet with Alice, which always broke it up wherever we played.

About five days before we were to open at the London House, Alice came to me and said that John wanted her to go to Sweden with him and that they were eventually going to get married. I really got bugged because I had always wanted to play the London House. I was ready to call the union or my attorney. How could she do this to me? We had a winner and now she was going to leave me with an unrehearsed group. We had been together for almost one year. After calming down and thinking about it, I figured, to start with, how do you stop a woman in love from doing anything? Plus, Alice was one of the nicest people I ever knew. I lucked out by hiring Walter Bishop Jr., a very well-known bebop piano player, and we did very well at the London House. To this day, Alice and I are very good friends. She lives about five miles from where I live and we talk to each other from time to time.

By coincidence, Alice's son Ravi and my son Gerry are very good friends. Ravi worked in Gerry's sextet for a while and also recorded with him. They both lived in a two-story apartment house at the same time, one on top of the other.

In May 2001, I was booked to play a bebop festival in Los Angeles. The promoter, a good friend of mine called Ken Poston, told me that Roy Haynes was supposed to play on opening night but couldn't, because he was booked at another club in the same area at the same time. He asked me if I would put a little group together to play that day besides the day I was booked for.

I don't know why, but I thought I'd call Alice and ask her if she wanted to play some bebop. When I asked her, the first thing she said was, "Terry, I haven't played bebop in over thirty years." When she didn't give me an out-and-out "no," I kept talking more about us playing together, even using clichés like, "It's like riding a bicycle. Once you've ridden one, you never forget how." Then she said, "Why don't I call Ravi and see if he would like to play with us?" I knew that she was scared, but at least she sounded interested, so I said, "Great idea! I'll call Gerry, and if that works out, we'll have mother-and-son and father-and-son, not to mention a reunion between you and me." She called me back a few days later and said she'd do it.

I called Ken Poston and told him about what I had for him and he went nuts. We built up a little publicity campaign. Don Heckman, the chief jazz writer at *The Los Angeles Times*, came to my house and did an interview with me. Unbeknownst to me, Don was a big fan of mine, so he really gave us a lot of space in the *Times*. Ravi and Gerry both flew in and we met at my house for a short rehearsal. Since Alice hadn't really played the piano regularly, I picked out some of the songs that we had recorded back in 1963. I made her a cassette of the songs to take home so she could refresh her memory. I also wanted her to hear how she played back then. I wanted her to play bebop and everything I heard her play since she worked with me really sounded out. Ravi was more surprised than anybody was because he had never heard those records and didn't know that Alice could play that style. All he ever heard her play since he was born was mostly harp, and that sounded like she was out in Regooneeville.

With all the publicity we got, the place was packed. I added Larry Koonse on guitar and Darek Oles on bass, who both had played with Ravi and Gerry, and we really broke it up. Alice gave me everything I asked for. She played bebop and we got about three standing ovations and walked off the stage while the audience was standing and applauding. I brought everybody back on stage and asked Alice if she remembered "Giant Steps" and she said she did. We took it at a breakneck tempo, which meant that it was fast, and I do mean FAST. Once again, we walked off the stage to a standing ovation. We couldn't go back on again because nothing we would have played could have topped that. It was good to see Alice smiling and so happy because she had been leading a different lifestyle since John died, more of a reclusive style of living. We were a winner again.

Chapter 16
What's a Regis Philbin?

By the middle of 1964, I was having trouble keeping busy playing jazz. A lot of the clubs were starting to close, including Birdland, which was the biggest one of them all. We worked a little, but more clubs kept closing, and it was harder to keep the group going. I really lucked out, for I wound up writing and conducting music for television shows.

I had been on television many times before in the 1950s, but only as a guest. Even before I conducted for Steve Allen, I was a guest on the original *Tonight Show*. I played on a lot of shows like *The Mike Douglas Show* and *The Merv Griffin Show*, and anyone who liked jazz booked me on their show. I also got a chance to sit and talk with the hosts because they liked my out sense of humor.

I was sitting at home in my apartment in New York when I got a call from Dick Brill, a television producer, who asked me if I'd be interested in coming out to California and auditioning for *The Regis Philbin Show*. It wasn't a new show; it was really a replacement for Steve Allen's show that was sponsored by Westinghouse. Steve had a falling out with Westinghouse and quit. Since it was syndicated, they had to find a new musical director and an announcer so that it would look like a different show.

They only had about two weeks of shows in the can. They hired a young man who was hosting a local show in San Diego whose name was Regis Philbin. Dick, who was the producer of *The Steve Allen Show*, liked my sense of humor, so every time I was a guest on Steve's show, we'd hang out together. He wanted me to come and talk with Regis and see what kind of rapport we had, because besides being the bandleader, I would also be his second banana. I found out that Bobby Troup and Ray Anthony were also up for the job.

I flew in and met with Regis and Chet Collier, the executive producer of the show and after meeting with Regis and the staff, they offered me the job.

Regis Philbin was a complete unknown. He was so unknown that people didn't ask, "Who's Regis Philbin?" but "What's a Regis Philbin?" He was just a nice kid who had a local talk show in San Diego. This was going to be his first chance to host a major TV show.

Steve Allen had a nine-piece band, so they wanted me to have the same number of musicians that Steve had. I never conducted a band for a television show before in my life, but I'd been around talk shows long enough to be familiar with what other bandleaders did. When they asked me to put together a nine-piece band, I told them that I didn't want to do the show with nine pieces. I said that the show would be opposite Johnny Carson, who had Skitch Henderson, and Les Crane, who had Elliot Lawrence. Since both shows had sixteen-piece bands, I told them to either let me have a sixteen-piece band also or a sextet. If I had nine pieces, I would be forcing myself to make it sound like sixteen. With a sextet, we wouldn't be in competition with anybody. They asked me if I could make it work with six and I said I didn't think it would be a problem at all. I flew back to New York, took care of a few things, flew back the next week, found an apartment on Wilton Place in Hollywood, and we got started immediately.

When I put the sextet together for the show, I wanted to make sure I had an interracial group, just like I always had. In 1964, you didn't see much integration on TV. I asked Chet Collier if I could have a mixed group on the show and he said, "I don't care if you have six GREEN people, as long as they can play." That knocked me out.

I had the rhythm section all picked out because I worked with all of them before. Actually, the only one I really knew who could handle the job was Herb Ellis, because he worked on TV with Donn Trenner, the bandleader on *The Steve Allen Show*. I knew Herb when he worked with the Oscar Peterson Trio and he also recorded a few albums with me. I picked the rest of the rhythm section because of one job that each played with me. Mike Melvoin subbed one night at a club called P.J.'s, and Colin Bailey and Monty Budwig also subbed at a club I played.

What I wanted to add was a black musician who could play all the reeds. I knew a few black jazz reed players, but most of them were great on only one particular horn. I needed somebody who could play tenor sax, flute, and clarinet equally as well.

Although I lived in California in 1957, I moved back to New York in 1963 and didn't know many black musicians in L.A. who did studio work. I knew the guys who could just play jazz, people like Benny Carter, Gerald Wilson, and Buddy Collette, but not well enough to ask them about hiring a black musician without it sounding awkward. But I figured, the heck with it, I had a chance to do something that I thought was the right thing to do.

Buddy Collette was very much in demand but I called him anyhow and offered him the job first. He was too busy doing all kinds of record dates and film work and he turned me down. Then I called Gerald and Benny and told them I wanted to integrate my band and asked them for the name of a good black saxophone player. It turned out that I didn't have to rely on them because Buddy Collette called me back and gave me the name of Carrington Visor, who had played with Chico Hamilton. I called Carrington and hired him without even hearing him play, which is something I never do. He turned out to be great.

Now I had to write opening and closing themes for the show. When I composed music for my quartet or tried to write what is called a standard, I never had to picture anything in my mind. But when you write themes for television, you have to make them fit the mood of the show. You almost have to picture the stage both visually as well as musically.

As inexperienced as I was in writing for TV, it seemed to come easy to me. Jazz was changing, and just sitting down and writing a good song was getting harder, but seeing a picture in my mind made it easier to write. If you showed me a toilet seat, that's what I'd see and hear, so I'd write toilet seat music. I lucked out with the themes, but in a strange way. I only had a few days to write an opener and a closer for the show and a few more days in which I could rehearse before we had to film our first show. It took me at least ten hours to come up with a melody that I thought would fit the feel of the show.

The day before we went on the air, I was at home sitting at the piano, running over the two themes, and for some reason they didn't knock me out. So I started fooling around on the piano, and in about a half hour, I wrote two songs that became the themes for *The Regis Philbin Show*. It was like playing jazz; some nights you're more creative than other nights. I also wrote a bunch of play-ons and play-offs for different kinds of acts. There'd be one for comedians, another for actors, and another for male or female entertainers.

What was fun about writing for the show was I wrote jazz themes that fit the sound of our sextet. The sound of the flute and vibes gave us a different sound than the vibes and tenor sax or vibes and clarinet did. The most important thing in doing a show with a sextet is to have a good rhythm section. We didn't just have a good rhythm section; we had a great one. All the singers that appeared on the show had a ball singing with the group, and Regis always complimented us on the air.

Regis wasn't too hip about jazz musicians. What was unfair to Regis was that most of the acts that were booked on the first month of shows were acts that had been booked for Steve Allen. Steve loved jazz and always had jazz players and singers on the show. Regis had a different personality than Steve and it was hard for him to fall in with some of the acts that were booked for Steve.

Count Basie was a guest on the show, and if you didn't know much about him, he could be hard to interview. Basie could 'yes' and 'no' you to death. Here's how it sounded:

> **Regis**: How's it going, Count?
> **Basie**: OK.
> **Regis**: You enjoying your tour?
> **Basie**: Yes.
> **Regis**: Anything new with the band?
> **Basie**: No.

Regis was asking him all these questions and I could see that he was going into the toilet, so I said, "Regis! Can I come over there and ask Basie a question?" He said, "Yes, come on over, Terry!" I walked over to the set where Regis and Basie were sitting and said, "Say, Basie, remember when we were in Pittsburgh with the Birdland All-Stars? Tell Regis about that time when PeeWee Marquette accused you of stealing his red shirt." This didn't call for a yes or no answer, so he had to tell a story. Regis just loved me for that. The same thing happened when we had Dizzy Gillespie, Dinah Washington, or Sarah Vaughan on the show. He would always make me a part of the interview.

I wrote an arrangement of a song called "Our Day Will Come" that I recorded on the Roost label. At the rehearsal for our first show, I had a music stand in front of the vibes with my music on it. We rehearsed it and it came off great. The camera rolled in the right place and the director got his shots. About a minute before our spot in the show came, they took my music stand away so they could get a better shot of me. Now I didn't have my vibes part. I remembered most of the arrangement I wrote, but on the last chorus of the melody, I made a mistake and played two wrong notes. Since *The Regis Philbin Show* was syndicated, it wasn't going to be shown until two weeks later. Those two weeks, I was sick, waiting for that show to be aired because I made a mistake on our first shot on camera. When it was finally shown, our song went by so fast that I never even remembered where the mistake was.

In 1965, we were still living on Wilton Place in Hollywood, which was not too far from where they started the Watts riots. It might have been a mile away, and the rioters were getting closer, burning buildings, and shooting people. Carol was getting completely paranoid about it and kept saying, "We've got to get a gun." My friend, Joe Mandragon, the bass player, used to hunt. Joe was a full-blooded Indian. It was four in the morning and Carol said, "Call Joe Mondragon, we've got to get a gun!" I said, "I'm not going to wake him up, forget about it!" She was flipping out. "Just give him a call," she said. So I called Joe and woke him up. Joe always had a dry sense of humor so I told him, "Joe, Carol's flipping out. Do you have any kind of gun we can borrow?" He sounded bugged because I woke him up and said, "No, but I can give you a bow and arrow," and then hung up on me.

"Slapsie" Maxie Rosenbloom, the ex-light heavyweight, was a guest on one of the shows. Maxie was a punch-drunk ex-fighter who had retired from boxing and was doing an act, singing, dancing, and telling jokes. His singing was terrible, his dancing was terrible, and his jokes were even worse. Maxie was completely out there. We were rehearsing and Maxie stopped me all through the rehearsal and said, "Don't play those eight bars at letter B! It's out! I'm not singing it so don't play it!" When we did the show, he started singing the eight bars he told us to leave out at the rehearsal. Being jazz musicians, we were used to ad-libbing, so we picked up on it immediately and played it.

At the rehearsal, in the middle of one of his terrible jokes, he pointed to Carrington and yelled "Gimme a rim shot!" even though Carrington was a black SAXOPHONE player. "Hey, you! Gimme a rim shot!" Carrington looked around to see who Maxie was screaming at. It was him. Maxie thought that if you were black, you had to be a drummer.

Most of the artists' arrangements were written for a sixteen-piece band, so what I did with the sextet was to take the arrangements for all the acts on the show, and write introductions and endings to fit the sextet. Then I'd use the arrangements as a guide. Sometimes, in the middle section, I'd have Carrington play behind them for sixteen bars, then Herb Ellis would do the same, then me, then somebody else. When everybody went to lunch, I stayed behind and wrote introductions and endings for all the acts we had on the show.

Eartha Kitt was a frequent guest on Regis' show. I met Eartha when I was a young bandleader at Birdland. She was a big star and used to come in the club all the time when people like Count Basie, Dinah Washington, Sarah Vaughan, and Duke Ellington were playing there. The first time Eartha came on, she brought in music for a big orchestra. When she saw that I only had a sextet, she refused to sing. So

I asked her, "Why don't you try it with the sextet?" but I don't think she was listening to me because, to her, I was still the third attraction at Birdland. She made me feel like a little kid.

Finally, I said, "Listen, do me a favor. I know you have an arrangement for twenty-eight musicians. Let me try something. I think I know how you work. Try it once, and if it doesn't work, we'll forget about it. Let's start with Herb Ellis playing guitar by himself, rubato, and then when you go into the chorus, the rhythm section will come in."

She fought me on this, but finally let me rehearse it with the idea I had. When we did it, it worked so well that every time she was booked on the show, she'd come in without any music at all and say, "What are we going to do today, Terry?" I'd say, "What do you want to sing?" She'd pick a song and I'd make up an arrangement right on the spot. I had her down. In fact I wrote two different songs to play her on with. Since she was a great dancer, I wrote a straight-ahead easy swing kind of play-on that I called "Dance for Eartha" and a snake charmer kind of play-on called "Earthanova." Whatever song I played to bring her on with, she would go with the groove of the beat and either dance out or slink out.

Back then, Don Rickles was a completely unknown comic. He was working at Sardi's when Lenny Bruce opened at a place called the Slate Brothers Club. The Slate Brothers were dancers who retired and opened up their own nightclub. Lenny came out and opened with one of his dirtiest jokes and Henry Slate didn't even wait for the next one. He fired him right on the spot. He heard about this new young hip comic who was breaking it up at Sardi's and hired him to replace Lenny.

Don Rickles' act was insulting celebrities. He was starting to draw celebrities at Sardi's, and now they were coming to see him at the Slate Brothers Club. The more he insulted them, the more they loved it. One night, Vincent Price was there and Rickles introduced him and then said, "Vincent, stand up and take a bow!" Vincent got up and Don said, "All right now, sit down, you big faggot!" Vincent broke up laughing.

Nobody was off-limits, not even Frank Sinatra. Sinatra would be sitting there and Don would go after him: "Frank Sinatra, ladies and gentlemen. Okay Frank, stand up and hit someone." And Frank would break up, laughing.

I told Chet Collier that Don was one of the funniest comedians I had ever seen. By that time I had a little input on the show. Actually, I was more well known nationally than Regis was and the band was one of the hits of the show. When I took the job, my contract stated that my band would be featured on camera at least three times out of every five shows. It got to the point where I hated to play the three times because I had all of this other writing to do for all the acts that appeared on the show and didn't have enough time to write for my sextet.

Chet sent his staff down to check Don out and came back to me and said, "Terry, we can't use him. All he does is insult celebrities. We don't have celebrities in our audience. He'll bomb!" After I bugged him for a while, he finally said, "All right, we'll put him on the show, but we want you and Regis to sit in the audience, and if you see that he's bombing, yell something up to him so he'll pick on you. Otherwise, we're in trouble." This was recorded live on tape and you couldn't edit anything.

I had Herb Ellis conduct the sextet while Regis and I sat in the audience. When Don came out on stage and with no celebrities around to pick on, he had to pick on the audience. He was throwing lines all over the place and the audience was laughing so hard, I didn't have to yell anything up to him. All of a sudden he saw me.

". . . and YOU!"

I hadn't said a word. I was just laughing along with everyone else.

"YOU'RE ON TELEVISION NOW, PINOCCHIO, GET YOUR NOSE FIXED!"

I said, "Don, my mother's watching the show."

"WONDERFUL! HERE'S A COOKIE!"

He went through a whole routine on me. I got him the job and never said a thing, and he kept zinging me through the whole show. Whenever I go see Don perform, I sit in the back of the room because he always zings me, throwing lines like, "Hey, Terry, laugh it up. I laugh when YOU play!"

Freddie Blassie was a very famous wrestler. He was sort of the Hulk Hogan of the sixties; strong as an ox. But offstage, he was a pussycat. Once he got on stage, he wanted to rip your arm out of your shoulder and he became a maniac. He did our show a bunch of times, and after about the fourth time, he came over to me and said, "Terry, you know what we should do this time? When I come out, I'll pick up your vibes and throw them off the stage!" I said, "Wait a minute! What do you mean, pick up my vibes? Stay away from my vibes, Freddie! Don't even get close to them!" Show time came and when Freddie got out on stage, he went over to Regis, and started to act mean. He was getting vicious and was ready to pick up Regis' desk and throw it off the stage. He was foaming at the mouth. When he saw me, he ran over to my vibes. When I saw him come towards me, I lay down on top of the vibes so that he couldn't touch them. I keep four pairs of mallets on my vibes; two pair by the sharps and flats and two pair by the naturals in case I drop a mallet or break one. He couldn't get to my vibes with me lying on top of them so he took all my mallets out, put them all together, and broke them all in half. That maniac had to do something. Now, if I broke a mallet, I'd have to play with one instead of two. But that was Freddie Blassie.

When they asked me to move to California to do the show, I said I wouldn't go unless I got a twenty-six-week contract, which they gave me. When Regis' show was canceled after twenty weeks, I had six weeks left on my contract. So for the next six weeks I stayed home and got a weekly check for 860 dollars. That was a lot of money for 1964. It was the first time I was ever paid a salary without having to work for it.

Up to that time, I had never been on unemployment in my life. I never applied because all the jobs I worked were as an independent contractor and I never learned how to collect. In fact, I was ashamed to go down to the unemployment office. Everyone kept saying, "You're crazy! It's your money, go ahead and collect it!"

So I went to the unemployment office in Hollywood where all the actors went. I walked in there, making believe I was looking for somebody, glancing all over the place. I didn't know where to go or which line to get into. I was looking around and really didn't have the slightest idea what I was looking for when suddenly, a voice yelled out, "Hey, Terry! TERRY GIBBS!"

Real loud.

I didn't know what to do and got scared. For the last twenty weeks, I was featured on television, and now, I was in the Hollywood unemployment office and some idiot recognized me. I kind of looked over and saw that it was the producer of Regis's show, my friend, Dick Brill.

"HEY, TERRY! COME ON! GET IN LINE!"

Nobody really cared, because they were used to it. As embarrassed as I was, it felt good getting the money.

After that, I went back to playing jazz clubs and really didn't think about doing another TV show.

Chapter 17
Operation: Entertainment

I was starting to have fun playing jazz again. Of all the celebrities that came in to see me, Steve Allen was probably my biggest fan. It's weird how I started conducting for Steve. He was always a fan of mine. He'd come into a club and I'd have him sit in and play piano. I showed him a little bit about the vibes and taught him some hand schtick, and he picked up on it immediately.

Bobby Troup had a show called *Stars of Jazz* and he'd have the greatest jazz musicians on with him. I had my quartet on, and since Bobby knew that Steve was a good friend of mine, as a put-on, he had Steve come on as "Niles Lishniss." Steve used to make up weird names, but Niles Lishniss was a real person. Steve went to high school with him and used his name a lot in some of his sketches. He just thought that Niles Lishniss was a funny name.

Steve wore a bebop cap and talked hip. They did their little routine and then he played some vibes with me. This was before I ever worked for him.

Steve's agent booked him at the Sahara Hotel in Las Vegas and Steve asked me if I would like to work as an act in his show. I played "I Got Rhythm" where I played two-finger piano with Steve, did a ballad, and then he did the vibes duet with me. The money was right so I accepted the job. I asked him who was conducting the show and he said Nat Brandwynne, who was the house bandleader at the Sahara Hotel. I got the feeling that if he asked me to conduct the show, he would have felt like he was insulting me because then I would have to conduct all the acts as well as do my own spot. So I said, "It sure would be fun to conduct that show," and he said, "You really want to conduct the show?" I said, "Yeah, it would be fun. I know your dumb schtick that you do all the time." So he said great.

He always liked the drummer to give him rim shots when he made some of his silly moves, so what I did was to have a cowbell near me. Plus, I'd have whistles and bells so that if he said something out there, I'd blow the whistle and ring the bell. He loved that. Steve loved saying all his hip lines for the band. In fact, I think Steve did half his act for the band. It went great and the vibes duet was the highlight of the show.

After we closed at the Sahara Hotel, he told me that he might have another TV show coming up and asked if I would be interested in being his musical director. I told him that I'd love to and we left it at that.

When we got back to Los Angeles I went to the unemployment office to file a new claim to start collecting unemployment checks. After filling out the papers and putting the name of my last employer down, the lady behind the counter said loudly, "YOU WORKED FOR STEVE ALLEN?" I was still embarrassed about being in an unemployment office and said very softly, "Yes." She said real loud, "HE STINKS. I DON'T THINK HE'S FUNNY AT ALL!" Once again I said softly, "Okay, can we get on with this?" This time she talked even louder and kept saying, "I SAW THE SHOW AT THE SAHARA HOTEL AND HE WAS TERRIBLE! STEVE ALLEN IS NOT FUNNY!" Now I was getting really bugged. All of a sudden I found myself standing in an unemployment line defending Steve Allen to a complete idiot.

A few weeks later I got a call from Steve telling me that he was going to do a summer show for CBS called *The Comedy Hour,* and asked me to be the musical director for the show. Steve Binder, who used to direct Bobby Troup's *Stars of Jazz* show, was going to be the producer and director for the show.

At our first meeting, Steve Binder gave me a list of an all-star band that he picked out for me to use on the show. I looked at the list and told both Steves that I didn't want the job. They were both surprised and asked me what was wrong. I told them that I had my own band, and that the list they gave me had four lead trumpet players on it. There was not one guy on that list that had played fourth trumpet since he was in high school. You just don't give a guy any part to play just because he's a good trumpet player. It takes as much experience to play fourth trumpet as it does to play first trumpet. After discussing it for about an hour, it wound up with me using most of the musicians that had worked for me before, and the ones I used from their list were heavyweight players that I knew anyhow.

My regular bass player wasn't available, so how wrong could I go with Ray Brown? I never used guitar in my big band so their choice of

Herb Ellis would have been who I would have hired anyhow. Steve Binder said that since there were going to be a lot of contemporary acts on the show, he asked for Hal Blaine on drums. I knew Hal and even though he was the number one rock and roll drummer in the world, I knew that he had big band experience. I was surprised when Hal took the job because it only paid union scale and I heard that the Beatles once flew him to England and paid him 25,000 dollars to record one song.

Hal was a funny guy to be around and did a great job for me. He told me that the only reason he took the job was because besides being a big Steve Allen fan, he was also doing it for the prestige of working on a Steve Allen show. He only stayed for about four shows because he got too busy with his rock and roll record dates, so Frank Capp joined the band and took over as the regular drummer. Unfortunately, after we did the eight shows, the option was not picked up and the show was cancelled.

A few weeks later, I got a call from Bill Carruthers, who was the associate director of *The Regis Philbin Show*. He was now producing and directing TV shows of his own and asked me if I was interested in being the musical director for a new show produced by Chuck Barris for ABC called *Operation: Entertainment*. Bill knew me from *The Regis Philbin Show* and liked my work. He and Chuck also loved my big band and wanted to use it on the show.

The premise of *Operation: Entertainment* was to go to service camps around the country and do shows like Bob Hope did for servicemen when he went to Vietnam. But first, we had to do a pilot for ABC. If they thought it was good, then contracts would be signed for us to do a regular show.

We did the pilot in San Diego on a Navy cruiser. Rich Little and Vikki Carr were the headliners. The producers hired eight or nine girls who played instruments and sang, or at least they tried to play and sing. They were very pretty girls, but they were the worst singers in the world. They were really terrible. At the rehearsal, they played and then sang and danced with the sailors. The sailors didn't care how bad they were. And they WERE BAD.

Five minutes before the show started, Chuck Barris and Bill Carruthers came to me and said, "Terry, we're in trouble. These girls are terrible. They play terrible and they sing terrible." This wasn't a Vietnam army camp, where there weren't any girls. We didn't realize that in San Diego, these guys see prettier girls just standing around on street corners. He said, "What can we do?" I said, "I have an idea. First of all, shut off their mikes and pick up as little as you can of the audio." Then

I went over to the band and I said, "Trumpets, write this down." I gave them a little riff to play. Then I said, "Trombones, do this." And I gave them something. "Saxophones, I want you to do this." They all wrote it down. Now this bit had to last for eleven minutes. The girls would do their schtick, walk off the stage, grab sailors out of the audience, and dance with them. The girls were trying to sing and play a blues number. After the band played two choruses of what I gave them, Conte Candoli came up with another riff for the trumpets. Then Bud Shank made up a different riff for the saxophones. Then Carl Fontana came up with ANOTHER riff for the trombones. We were going from riff to riff and the band was really swinging. Finally, we got to the last chorus. That's where I put everything an octave higher and we went out shouting. I'm talking about SHOUTING. Because we didn't have a budget for arrangements, we used the Dream Band library to go in and out of commercials.

Before we did the pilot, Bill Carruthers and Chuck Barris asked me if I would mind if they hired Johnny Fresco to do the contracting for the band. Johnny was an ex-saxophone player that played with some of the name bands in the forties and was now the contractor at ABC. I didn't have any contractor in mind because I had never done a show like this before. On *The Regis Philbin Show*, we didn't need a contractor since we only had a sextet. I said that I didn't mind at all.

When we did the pilot, I had John Audino and Ray Triscari both play lead trumpet, but Ray was the main lead player. John and Ray were working on *The Hollywood Palace* with Mitchell Ayres as bandleader and Johnny Fresco as the contractor. Fresco started giving all the lead trumpet parts to John Audino. Even though he could play very good, John was the new kid on the block in my band, so I said, "Johnny, give Ray Triscari all the lead parts and he will give Audino the ones he wants him to play lead on." He said, "No, no! John Audino plays lead trumpet on *The Hollywood Palace*." I said, "Johnny, let me get something straightened out with you. First of all, this is not *The Hollywood Palace*. Plus, I run my band different than any bandleader you've ever worked with so don't question me on anything. Please do everything I tell you to do. Give Ray Triscari the lead parts." About two or three weeks after we did the pilot, I bumped into Ray, and he said, "Terry, you dirty . . ." I said, "What happened?" He said, "I've been relaxing playing third trumpet in *The Hollywood Palace* band and not worrying about anything. Johnny Fresco never knew that I played lead trumpet and ever since he heard me play lead in your band, now he keeps throwing all these lead parts at me. Thanks a lot!"

When the show got picked up, I asked for 2100 dollars per week plus all the publishing. They gave me everything I asked for. This was

1968 so that's like making 25,000-30,000 dollars a week today. The reason they did that was because we saved the show. Those eleven minutes could have been the biggest bomb of all time. If we had gone to Vietnam with that group of girls, the troops would have loved them, because over there, they didn't get to see pretty girls at all. But in San Diego, as soon as you walk off the gangplank, EVERYBODY is Marilyn Monroe.

Besides the money, what I really liked about the job as musical director was how important they made me feel. They gave me a large office and put in a baby grand piano and a great stereo system, so that I could listen to recordings of some of the acts that were booked on the show. It was great to have the piano there so that I could compose music when I felt like it.

Part of my job was to call some of the acts to find out if they needed new arrangements written and to find out what they were going to perform on the show. While I talked to the acts on the phone, I played Charlie Parker and Dizzy Gillespie records and was having a ball with the treatment that I was getting from the staff. I felt like the biggest winner of all time. This kind of a show wasn't new to just me, it was also the first time that Chuck Barris and Bill Carruthers had done a big network variety show, and they trusted me with everything I did.

I remember talking with the country and western comic team Homer and Jethro on the phone. I had my Charlie Parker record blasting in the background and in the middle of the conversation, Jethro said, "Is that Bird I'm hearing?" I didn't believe it. I didn't know that they were that hip. They knew all the records that they heard me play because they said that they also had them in their collection. When they did the show, we got along great.

I wrote all the original music for the show and had Bill Holman orchestrate it all. Bill was going through some hard times. He was trying to get rid of cancer in his jaw and needed money, so I tried to talk some of the acts into having new arrangements written so that Bill could make some extra money. Sometimes, if I needed Bill to write something overnight, I sang my song to him over the phone and then gave him half credit. One time I sang a fanfare to him that I wrote for a general, and when we played the arrangement, the melody was completely different from what I sang to him on the phone. I had to put him down as sole writer because what he wrote was so good, that I couldn't take any credit for something I didn't write.

We were contracted to do thirty-seven weeks of shows for the season. After we did the pilot, I wrote two new themes for the show and Chuck Barris liked them both. If we had the same host every week, my theme song could have caught on with the public. For instance, with *The Regis Philbin Show*, I wrote a theme for Regis, so after a while, when you heard it, you knew it was *The Regis Philbin Show*. When you heard *The Tonight Show*'s theme song, you knew it was Johnny Carson. But we had different hosts every week.

When we did the pilot, we used a song I wrote called "Pretty Blue Eyes," that I recorded with the Dream Band. When we were about to start shooting the regular shows, I was driving in my car and heard "You'd Be So Nice To Come Home To" playing on the radio. Since I was trying to be a team player, I thought that song would fit the show even better than the one I wrote.

I went to Chuck Barris and said, "Since we're playing for soldiers and sailors, how about using 'You'd Be So Nice To Come Home To' as the theme? The song is popular and the title fits the feel of the show." Chuck said, "That's a great idea, Terry. Let's use it." I didn't realize that I stood to lose 50,000-75,000 dollars because of my stupid idea.

I knew there was big money to be made when your songs are played on television, because I got little royalty checks for my theme songs that were played on *The Regis Philbin Show*. Network shows are shown on a few hundred stations around the country and Regis was on only about twenty stations. Then I got a brilliant idea. I wrote to the Cole Porter estate and told them we wanted to use "You'd Be So Nice to Come Home To" as a theme. I then asked them if they would give me a little taste for using it twenty to thirty times during the show. It was on ABC, so being a network show, it would bring in a lot more money for the publisher. A few weeks later, I got a letter back saying, "How dare you ask us for money! Not only won't we give you any money, but you can't use the song at all." Like an idiot, I wrote back and apologized to them. I begged and begged until they finally let me use it, so I screwed myself twice!

The publishing business in television was new to me. I didn't know that part of the business and didn't realize that theme songs paid a lot of money. That's where all the money is, not in all the little cues that we played between the acts. The theme songs, opening and closing, made all the money. I just didn't realize it.

We used to go out on the road for nine days and shoot four hour-long television shows. When you're doing a show in a studio, you'd rehearse all week for that one show, and then when you went on the air; sometimes you wouldn't have the slightest idea what was going on. The band never had enough time to rehearse. On our show, most of the time spent at rehearsal was for the director and his crew. The cameramen would have to get their shots and the director would be in the truck and make notes for which angle he wanted to shoot from. That took a lot of time. So the band only got to rehearse for about two hours. We'd rehearse one day and shoot the show the next day.

The day after that, we'd rehearse a completely different show and shoot that one the next day. Then we'd fly to the next camp. Rehearsal, show, rehearsal, show. It was the hardest thing in the world to do. Chuck Barris loved my band so much that after the rehearsals, he'd have somebody cart the instruments back to the hotel and the guys would have a jam session.

Every once in a while, an act would show up and their music would get lost, so Med Flory, Don Rader, and I would meet with the artist and sketch out an arrangement. Then Med would write the arrangement, Don would copy it, and they would have it ready the next day. Don couldn't copy the arrangement until Med wrote it, which meant that Don had to stay awake until Med finished jamming. It was funny to see Don, who was five feet tall, trying to get Med, who was six-foot-four, out of the jam session so that Med could write the arrangement. Don looked like a little kid pulling on his father's coattails.

I always went back to my room and memorized the show, because I was trusted with a job that not many musical directors were given. I hardly ever got any cues. I ran the stage. The only cue I ever got was a countdown to come back in after the commercial. This was done like a stage show. I had the best feel for what was going on because I was on the stage while the director was in a truck working from television monitors. I was honored that they trusted me with that responsibility.

I remember when the Lennon Sisters had to sing in front of the band. When they were through with their first song, while the sailors were applauding, they walked down the stage about ten feet and sat down on some steps. I had it timed out so the moment they sat down, BOOM, we went right into music. That's why I stayed in my room and memorized the show while the guys jammed.

I tried to keep the same feeling going that we had with the original 1959 band. I wanted it loose and fun, but at the same time, we had to take care of business. This was not a nightclub job; this was a television show. It didn't make any difference to my band. They carried on like they always did.

I happened to mention to Jim Washburn, who was one of the producers of the show that our band was much looser when they had a few drinks. I told him that they never got drunk, but that they just had more fun. I actually was talking about when we played in nightclubs.

We were getting ready to tape the first show and were on stage when I noticed a bottle of Scotch in front of each section and cups under each chair. When Johnny Fresco saw this, he said, "Hey, no drinking on stage!" I went over to Fresco and said, "John, let me tell you once again. All I want you to do with my band is tell them what time to show up. And even if they don't show up on time, don't you go and tell them off. You come to me and I'll take care of it." Eventually, he fell in with that whole thing, and went from being a very strict contractor to one of the guys in the band. He wasn't as uptight and I think he enjoyed the loose feeling that the band had. That was probably the first time that a band ever drank while playing on live television.

Jim Washburn was one of the nicest and hippest producers I ever worked with. He trusted me when I told him that nobody in the band would drink to the point where they couldn't play their music. They had too much pride to do that. They knew that if one guy screwed up, the band would sound terrible. I think that even Jim used to sneak in a little taste before the show.

Whether it was television or nightclubs, the guys in my band still had the same kind of nuttiness going on and I never knew what they were going to do next. I had my headset on and was getting ready to do the countdown for the opening. On this show we must have had about 20,000 soldiers in the audience. I got the countdown from the director and started giving it to the band: "Ten, nine, eight . . ." When I got down to "two," Med Flory stood up and yelled out, "WHOEVER CAN'T TAP DANCE IS A FAG!" Then the whole band got up and started to tap dance. Whoever was in the wings, the acts on the show, the crew, everybody broke up. They had to stop the cameras. Chuck Barris and Bill Carruthers came out of their trucks, laughing. That show turned out to be one of the best shows we ever did because it got everybody in an up mood. I still never knew what that band was going to do.

When we did the pilot for *Operation: Entertainment*, Bud Shank played lead alto and Carrington Visor, who played for me on *The Regis Philbin Show*, played tenor. Carrington wasn't as experienced playing with a big band as some of the other guys were. When we played a passage and Carrington wasn't playing his part right, Bud told him in a very nice way how to play it. Carrington was a beautiful guy and would listen to Bud. When we started doing the show regularly, Bud was too busy doing studio work and couldn't go on the road so Med Flory came in to play lead alto. Med wasn't as diplomatic as Bud was. If Carrington played something wrong, he would say, "Hey, you're WRONG!" That used to embarrass Carrington.

We just finished filming a show and after it was over, while we were still on the stage, Med and Carrington got into a big argument. It came as close to a fistfight as you have ever seen. Jim Washburn and all these heavyweights were all standing around watching and nobody was doing anything to break them up so I figured that I'd better do something before it really got out of hand. I leaped on Med, got him in a headlock, and got him away from Carrington. Med is six-foot-four and I'm about five-foot-seven, and I was the only one who tried to break up the fight. I honestly think that Carrington, being such a proud guy, would have wiped Med out, for as big as Med was, even if he knocked Carrington down seven times, Carrington would have gotten up seven times and won the fight.

Afterward, I was asked to come to Chuck Barris' hotel room. He heard about what happened on the stage and asked me what the problem was. I told Chuck that they were arguing about something in the music and that Med told Carrington something a little too strongly. I then said that if he wanted me to fire them, I would. Chuck said, "They were arguing about something in the music for the show?" I said, "Yeah," He said, "Well if they were arguing about some chick or something, I'd tell you to fire both of them. But if they're arguing about something to make the show better, that's great. Wonderful. Give them a raise!"

I had two great lead trumpet players: Bobby Shew, who played lead with Buddy Rich, and Dalton Smith, who played lead with Stan Kenton. I had Bobby Shew play the Bill Holman arrangements and Dalton played the arrangements that the acts brought themselves. After a few months of filming shows, I got stuck for a lead trumpet player. For some reason, Bobby couldn't make that trip, so I hired Conte Candoli. Conte wasn't known as a lead trumpet player, but I knew that he could handle the part because he occasionally played lead in the Dream Band.

Two days before we had to leave town, Conte called me and said that Al Lapin, the contractor at NBC wouldn't let him off *The Tonight Show,* and now I really was stuck. I bumped into Al Porcino, who didn't look good to me. He looked like he was chipping with junk. I really needed that kind of a lead trumpet player, so I took a chance on Al and took him with me for the nine days.

Some of the entertainers couldn't be there for the regular times we did our shows, so we had to rehearse the first show on the first day, then rehearse the second show the next day, and shoot both shows in a row. When we got on stage to rehearse the first show, Al was really shaking; he was really in bad shape. I didn't know what to do because he could hardly play at all, so I went to Chuck Barris and said, "My new lead trumpet player has a cold and is having trouble playing." Chuck said, "We don't need him for the rehearsals. Send him back to the hotel." He got Al a limousine to drive him back. He stayed in bed for two days, came back, and played both shows. I ran through the music with him before each show and he sight-read the heck out of them.

Al Porcino talked slower than Shorty Rogers did and he also had a quiver in his voice. On the third day when he felt better, we all had breakfast before the show and Al ordered two scrambled eggs. The waitress brought our food and put two poached eggs in front of Al. Al looked up and said, "W-a-i-t-r-e-s-s-s-s!" I o-r-d-e-r-e-d t-w-o s-c-r-a-m-b-l-e-d e-g-g-s! !" She said, "They are." He looked at the eggs and said, "A-m-a-a-a-y-y-y-z-i-n-g-!"

Bill Holman wrote the thirty-two bar arrangement of "You'd Be So Nice To Come Home To" that we used for the opening and closing themes. We never played the whole arrangement at the top of the show. In fact, we never played more than sixteen bars of it for any of the guest hosts we had on.

On one of the shows, Don Rickles was the guest host, and by this time, his career was really taking off. When Don was introduced, the soldiers gave him a five-minute standing ovation. The band was roaring that night and 50,000 soldiers were in the audience. They applauded so long that we had to play 64 bars of "You'd Be So Nice To Come Home To," which was TWO full choruses. That was the first time the band had a chance to get into that arrangement and they were really swinging. When we finished, Don waited for the applause to die down. When it got real quiet, he turned around, looked at me, and said, "That's by far the WORST band I ever heard in my life!" We all broke up laughing.

We flew in a soldier from overseas and were going to surprise him by bringing out his mother. We came out of a commercial and Don brought the soldier up on stage. We'd been hiding the mother for two days. She was in the wings and Don was talking to the soldier. The soldier told Don what he'd been doing overseas and how good it was to be back. As he was doing this, the mother looked out on stage and said, "That's not my son." We said, "What do you mean, that's not your son? Isn't your son's name Irving Schwartz?" or whatever his name was. She said yes, but we had the wrong Irving Schwartz. So they asked her, "Do us a favor. This is being taped live. Just go out there and give him a big hug. Would you do that for us?" She said sure. Meanwhile we went to another commercial.

They told Don Rickles not to say that this guy's mother was here but instead to say that there was a big surprise for him. We were afraid that when this lady walked out on stage, the soldier would take one look at her and say, "That's not my mother."

When the commercial ended, Don came out and said, "Irving, we have a big surprise for you . . ." The mother started to walk out on stage and before the soldier could say anything, she grabbed him and gave him a big hug. We went into music immediately and back into another commercial. We didn't give him a chance to give any kind of a reaction. The soldier looked completely confused. After the commercial, Don told everybody in the audience that the mother and the son were backstage, hugging and crying. Some of the staff got in a lot of trouble for that goof.

Merlin Olsen, who played for the Los Angeles Rams, was part of "The Fearsome Foursome" with Roosevelt Grier, Lamar Lundy, Deacon Jones, and Roger Brown. That's really five, because they added Roger Brown later. The Fearsome Foursome (Plus One) was also an act. They would sing and jump around and were really pretty good for football players. By the fourth jump, they were lucky not to go right through the floorboards because each of them weighed about 300 pounds.

Merlin was a defensive tackle and had a genius IQ. He told me that when he played football, he would go after the quarterback and try to rip his arms off and do anything he could to maim him. He didn't care what he had to do to get that quarterback out of the game. It's wild to hear a guy like him who has that kind of IQ talking like that.

Since it was like a vaudeville show, we even had a dog act. The guy who trained the dogs had about fifteen or twenty balloons filled with helium. What he would do was let a balloon go and a dog would leap after it and bust it. Then he would do some trick with each dog, and at the end of the act, he'd let all the balloons loose and the dogs would all leap at them, busting balloons in tempo as the band played "Scheherazade." I was conducting when he let the balloons go and the wind blew them right at me. The moment the balloons hit me, all the dogs jumped on me and knocked me down. I finished conducting while lying on my back. It was hard for the band to play because they were breaking up watching me trying to conduct. The show must go on.

Because I was making a lot of money on *Operation: Entertainment,* my accountant told me that I needed to find a way to lose money and have fun at the same time so that I could get a write-off on my income taxes. A friend of mine I knew from New York called Mel Zelnick was renting space in a piano store where he sold drums and guitars. Mel had played drums with Benny Goodman, Lenny Tristano, Boyd Raeburn, and a lot of small groups around New York. He was semi-retired and was now only running his store. I bumped into him at the musicians union and after talking to me, he said that he wanted to get a place of his own, but couldn't afford one. The music stores I knew weren't doing much business, because none of the young kids were

252   Chapter 17

playing horns. Rock and roll was starting to take over the music scene and every kid was buying either an electric guitar, an electric bass, or a drum set. Some of them would play for a few weeks and make a million dollars without being able to play at all.

I told Mel that I'd be interested in becoming partners with him in a music store, but only under certain conditions. He would have to run the place by himself because I was too busy but I'd be there when I could. The selling point for him would be the publicity the store could get from using my name. He agreed and we went looking for a good location.

We rented a store in Canoga Park in the San Fernando Valley next to a record shop called Pal's Records, which was owned by Paul and Pauline Levy, who I knew from selling my albums. In fact, they owned the building that the store was in. Finding a name for the store was hard but we finally came up with The Music Stop. Our sign looked like a stop sign. We had a gigantic lit-up sign made for us that we put on the roof that said, "Terry Gibbs and Mel Zelnick's Music Stop." Mel gave up his space in the piano store and we were now in business.

I was living in Canoga Park at that time and the store became my hangout when I wasn't busy with the show. We eventually hired my friend Berrel to manage the store. That worked out good because I hired Mel to play timpani on the *Operation: Entertainment* show, and he would have to be out of town for nine days a month. With Berrel, we had somebody we could trust to run the store.

Even though I was half-owner, I didn't have the slightest idea what was going on in the place. I never knew where anything was because I was too busy putting the music together for *Operation: Entertainment*. When I did show up, it was just to hang out.

Mel was really a good businessman. We had a front door that went BING when it opened and BONG when it closed. If we paid fifty dollars for a guitar and were selling it for a hundred dollars, Mel told me to take whatever we could get over fifty because we could always get another guitar. I couldn't haggle with people; that wasn't my bag. If somebody asked me how much a guitar cost, I'd say a hundred dollars. If they said, "I'll give you eighty dollars," I'd say, "Mel, I need some help. Please come over here and talk to this person."

One time I watched as Mel talked with someone. Mel quoted a hundred dollars for a guitar and the guy said, "I'll give you seventy five dollars." Mel came back and said, "Eighty-seven-fifty." The guy said, "I'll give you eighty-two dollars." Mel said, "No, that's not enough." The guy started to walk out. As he opened the front door, the moment it went BING, Mel said, "I'll tell you what I'm going to do for you." The guy stopped, came back, and they worked out some kind of deal. Mel would never let anybody leave. He would always get them between the BING and the BONG.

I happened to be in the store when a lady came in and wanted to buy three guitar picks, which cost three for a quarter. I happened to be behind the counter by myself and didn't know where anything was at all. I was trying to find the picks when some guy walked in, looking like he hadn't bathed in two years. We had a drum set in the window and this guy said, "Hey man, how much is that drum set without the cymbals?" I was bending down behind the counter looking for picks, so I made up a figure. "Twelve hundred dollars." I wanted to get rid of him so I could make twenty-five cents for the store.

I was still looking for the picks when the guy came over to me and said, "Hey, what if I add the high-hat cymbals? What would it be then?" I made up another dumb figure. "That'll be another hundred and fifty dollars."

I was still trying to make a quarter for the store and couldn't find the picks. This guy came over to me again and now he was starting to bug me. "What if I add that top cymbal?" I said, "Another hundred and fifty dollars." Finally he said, "How much is the whole drum set?" Once again I made up some dumb figure. "Eighteen hundred dollars." He whipped out a roll of bills from his pocket that must have had fifty hundred-dollar bills in it and said, "I'll take it." I stopped looking for the picks and said, "You'll take what?" He said, "I'll take the whole drum set, including the cymbals." I immediately called Mel over because I didn't have the slightest idea what the drum set sold for. I was actually quoting him much higher figures than what it should have been because I was trying to get him out of the store. Mel made the deal, and that scroungy-looking guy bought the drum set right out of the window. Back to clichés: "You can't tell a book by its cover."

I was hanging out at the store with Berrel when I got a call from Dizzy Gillespie. James Moody just had a Bell's palsy stroke and Diz asked me if I would play with him at a club in Watts for ten days. This was just a few years after the Watts riots and even though it could have been dangerous to go there, the thought of playing with Dizzy Gillespie was enough for me to go anywhere. I said I'd be out there in ten minutes. I remember that Mike Longo played piano and Candy Finch was on drums. I knew how great Dizzy was. Not only was he one of my idols, but I also knew every chorus he ever played on records. What made me feel good was that he must have liked my playing, or else he wouldn't have called me, because Los Angeles was loaded with great jazz players.

You actually have to play with somebody every night to really find out how creative they are. If you play the same songs every night and can't improvise a different melody on every chorus, then you're just okay. But I think that Dizzy was really impressed with my playing. In fact, every time I played a ballad and was really getting into it, he kept saying, "Goddam, Terry, you a MOTHERFUCKER!" He said it with love and admiration. Dizzy was so loved by everybody that he could get away with saying anything on stage. Another thing that made me feel good was that a lot of the black people that came into the club thanked me for coming to Watts because they said that they felt terrible about the riots.

We had so many commercial acts to play for, that when I found out that Ray Charles was booked to appear on one of the shows, it knocked me out. We all looked forward to finally playing some hard-swinging music. Ray's manager, Joey Adams, was an old friend of mine who used to be a disc jockey in California. We filmed the show in Port Hueneme, which was about an hour away from the San Fernando Valley.

When we rehearsed Ray's music, I don't think we got past four bars of the first song before Ray stopped the band. He had tremendous ears. "Third trombone, that's an A-flat in the fourth bar." Four more bars went by and he stopped the band again. "Hey, trumpet, that's a D-flat!" He kept stopping the band until I finally said, "Ray, your music is so marked up, let's go through it once without you stopping the band, and we'll have it down for you." He was starting to be a pain in the ass.

When he had to play a piano solo, they had put the piano way up in front of the band and he was having trouble playing. "Drummer, you're slowing down!" He kept picking on the band until I finally went over to Joey Adams and said, "Joey, we're only an hour away from Hollywood. The show isn't until tomorrow. Why don't you bring your own rhythm section in?" Then I said to Bill Carruthers, "You want to solve the problem? Put the piano in front of the band." We finally made Ray happy, but we were disappointed in how he acted. He may not have realized it, but he gave us a hard time and we were all looking forward to playing with him.

Florence Henderson was really a pain in the ass. She kept bugging everybody in the band, not just me. We couldn't seem to please her at all. We rehearsed her music over and over for no reason at all, and finally she looked happy. But we never felt too thrilled with her.

The next day, before the show had to be filmed, it started to rain. By the time Florence went on, it was down to a little drizzle, but the stage was still wet. During the commercial, while waiting to go on, she came over to the band and started to get a little friendly with us. We were still bugged with her for what happened the day before. She said,

"What if when I'm singing, the wires start to short out and I blow up?" I said, "Don't worry about it. If you blow up, I'll give you a B-flat chord." The band loved me for that.

Rodney Dangerfield was booked on one of the shows but couldn't be there for the rehearsal, so he sent his material in and we had one of our staff members read Rodney's lines. There must have been about six or seven minutes worth of material. When the guy read it, there wasn't one laugh. Nothing sounded funny at all, so we panicked. We tried getting Rodney on the phone but we couldn't find him anywhere. The show had to go on the next day and they didn't want to take any chances, so they called Louis Nye and flew him in immediately. Louis read his own material and it was very funny. The next day, Rodney came in and they were going to give him the courtesy of reading his material and then tell him that they were going with Louis Nye. When he read his material himself, we fell out. Whatever line it was, even if it was the straightest line in the world, it came out funny. It was his delivery and how he said the lines that made it funny: grabbing his tie, no respect, whatever he did and said was funny. Now we were stuck with two comedians and had to make room on the show for both of them, which we did.

Another show had Phil Harris and Martha Raye as co-hosts, two of the out-est people you ever met in all your life. Phil would drink all through rehearsal and Martha would swallow eighty-four bennies. When they rehearsed, they would change some of the lines and get a bit risqué. They were so funny, that we thought this would be one of the best shows that we ever did. When it came time to film the show, they played it straight and read the script like it was written, and they bombed.

We just finished shooting a show and the next one was the one that I was really looking forward to doing. We were going to have Louis Armstrong on. There were two reasons why I was thrilled to have Louis on the show. You would think that the main reason was to hear him play the trumpet. Although I wanted to hear him play, the number one reason I was glad to see him had to do with the fact that on the previous show, I had the stomach flu and didn't think that I would be well enough to conduct. I spent more time in the bathroom than any other place. Before we started filming, which was at about 8:00 in the morning, I drank about a half a bottle of Kaopectate, which didn't seem to do much good. It was strange to see what was happening on the show. It was a cold day. Every time it came time for the two-minute commercial break, everybody in the band was sipping either on some scotch or cognac while I was taking a few swigs of Kaopectate. By the time the show was over, I had finished a whole bottle, which still didn't do much good.

Now for the number one reason I was glad to see Louis Armstrong. Louis carried his own doctor with him whose name was Dr. Schiff. I met him a bunch of times through Joe Glaser. He was once the head of the New York State Athletic Commission. I immediately went to find Dr. Schiff and told him my problem. He said not to worry and fixed up some potion in a little bottle and gave it to me. I think it contained paregoric, which has opium in it. He told me not to take more than one drop every six hours. With what I went through the last few days, I figured that one drop would never do it, so I took three drops every six hours. Now to end this dumb story, Dr. Schiff was right, for after doing it my way, I didn't go to the bathroom for a week.

Back to the one and only Louis Armstrong. At rehearsal, the three songs that he played were all in the same tempo so I thought he should play some other song with a different tempo in the middle. After rehearsal, I was talking to Tyree Glenn, who was playing trombone for Louis, and who also was a good friend of mine. I casually mentioned that I thought a change of tempo on the second song could make a better program for Louis. Unbeknownst to me, he told Louis about it, and at about 6:00 that evening, the night of the rehearsal, my phone rang and that famous voice of Louis' said, "Hey Terry, I hear you'd like me to change the routine of my songs." I felt embarrassed and told him to forget about it and that anything he did would be great. Louis said, "Let's have dinner downstairs at the restaurant and talk about it." Even though I kept telling him that everything was okay, he kept on insisting that we have dinner.

We met in the dining room and I don't think I ever remembered what I ate, for I was so in awe of him. He was so humble. I think that if I told him that I wanted him to play "The Flight of the Bumble Bee" for his second song, he would have said okay. After being with him for a few hours, I found out why musicians loved him and stayed in his band for years. Why would anybody want to leave Louis Armstrong?

A funny thing happened while we were having dinner. A little girl about ten years old was sent over by her mother to get an autograph of Louis. There's a very famous picture of Louis sitting naked on a toilet seat; wearing a white bandana on his head. Louis took a copy of that picture out of his pocket and was going to autograph it for the little girl, until I reminded him that she was only about ten years old. He said in his growly voice, "Oh, that's right, Pops," and he autographed the table napkin for her. Before he put the picture away, I made him autograph it for me.

In dealing with the country-and-western stars who came on the show, I found out that some of them were very insecure. They always had to have somebody speak for them. Johnny Cash was on this one show, and at the rehearsal, we had some trouble with his music. I talked to some of the guys in his band and said, "Tell Johnny to come down to my room and we'll discuss it." Johnny came with his drummer because he didn't know what to say to me. I had to get everything straightened out with the drummer. Sometimes they would sing 6/4 bars or 5/4 bars because the songs were not so much about the music as they were about the lyrics.

Roy Clark was a country-and-western singer who was a very good musician. He was a pretty good guitar player. In fact, when we'd have jam sessions, he would come and play with us. He was also a sweetheart and a beautiful guy. I loved Roy Clark.

Jimmy Dean was another country-and-western star that I liked. He had a good sense of humor. He gave up show business after he started his sausage company. Jimmy told me a great story. He used to go out and play tent shows in little towns and had music for an eleven-piece band. He got to this one tent show and saw that there were thirty-one musicians sitting there: ten trumpet players, nine trombone players, eight saxophone players, and four in the rhythm section. He went over to the promoter and said, "Look, I only pay for eleven musicians. It's in my contract." The promoter said, "You don't realize that in this town, we don't have many professional musicians. These guys are doctors, lawyers, shoemakers, butchers, you name it. They don't play often, so after four bars, if the trumpet player's lip gives out, the guy sitting next to him jumps in immediately." They had a few guys playing each part.

I think that the show could have stayed on the air much longer if it wasn't for the war in Vietnam. The whole premise of the show was it was done for soldiers and sailors but there were too many people against the war. People were picketing and they were having marches protesting the war. It was a drag to see the show come to an end. The band and the staff, including Chuck Barris, had become like a little family. We all lived in the same hotel, ate, hung out, and partied together. You name it; we all did it together. To this day, when any of us who was connected to the show sees one another, all we talk about were the great times we had doing *Operation: Entertainment*.

Chapter 18
Hi-Ho, Steverino!

After *Operation: Entertainment* was canceled, I went to work for Steve Allen, but not as his bandleader. He had been doing a show for a month that wasn't a typical Steve Allen show. There was very little comedy. The premise of the show was to have Steve sitting around a table with about five people, trying to get them to argue with each other. The show was produced by Rick Rosner and the bandleader was Paul Smith. I bumped into Steve and we got to talking about his show. He said that he would like to have me on, but didn't know how to work it out because Paul Smith was the bandleader. I told him that Paul and I got along very well and that if I got billing, I wouldn't mind working as a featured artist. The billing would be "Paul Smith and his Sextet featuring Terry Gibbs."

Rick Rosner and I never got along very well. Sometimes he wouldn't tell the announcer to mention my name at the top of the show and that bugged me and we always wound up having an argument. Steve was starting to get bugged with the format of the show because I don't think he was having any fun. This was not his type of show. After a few weeks, he said, "We're going back to comedy." Paul Smith didn't like Rick Rosner either and going back to a variety show meant that the bandleader would have to go to staff meetings, and that was never Paul's bag.

In the meantime, Rick and I were still having problems with my billing situation. I got a call from Rick's office saying that they wanted to talk to me. I thought I was going to get fired because we just weren't getting along at all. When I got to the studio, my wife called me and said that she had just gotten a call from Paul Smith saying that he had quit the show. Paul said that they were going to offer me the job and that he wanted to play piano in the sextet as a sideman. They hired me and of course I hired Paul, because besides being a great jazz musician, he's without a doubt, the best piano player for television shows. We did about a week or two of shows and Rick, who knew as much about comedy as Adolf Hitler, was giving me all kinds of cues from popular songs to play going in and out of commercials. Most of the time I played Steve's songs because, first of all, it was Steve's show. Secondly, it was smart business because Steve was an ASCAP writer and there were royalties to be made. Plus, his music publishing company published most of his compositions and could give the show a good rate. The songs were just throwaways just to get us in and out of commercials.

During a commercial, Steve called me over and said, "Why are we playing all these songs that we have to pay out big royalties for?" I told him that Rick was telling me to play them and he said, "Don't pay any attention to him." Steve's mind went in so many directions, that if you didn't write a note telling him about something we just talked about, he wouldn't remember what you said to him at all.

Because it was a syndicated show, it was shown at different days and times around the country. About two weeks later, I got a letter from Steve saying the exact same thing we talked about on stage. "Terry, why are we playing all these songs that I didn't write?"

Even though it was a comedy show, Steve had other guests talking about other subjects besides comedy. For instance, he'd have a scientist or a politician. Steve was great interviewing anybody from all walks of life. One time we had a man who talked about the Irish Rebellion and how his parents were killed. In my earphone I got a cue from Rick Rosner to play him off with "The Irish Washerwoman." I said "Are you crazy? This man looks like he's going to cry any minute." Once again, he said, "I told you to play 'The Irish Washerwoman'!" I immediately answered him back, "KISS MY ASS! I QUIT!" and told Paul to play any kind of incidental music he wanted. Then I walked over to Steve during the commercial and said, "Steve, I just quit. Please have Paul take over for the rest of the show." He said, "What happened?" I said, "Your guest has just been crying, telling this story about his family getting killed in Ireland and this asshole Rick Rosner is telling me to play him off with 'The Irish Washerwoman.'" Steve said, "He did?" I said, "Yeah, but I wouldn't play it." And Steve said, "Well, we're firing him anyhow, so don't listen to anything he says anymore."

Working for Steve could be the easiest thing in the world or the hardest thing. When you're doing a talk show, *Tonight Show* style, it's easy. For example, when Steve would go out into the audience to talk to somebody, he'd ask them their name. If they said Rosie Machinski, or whatever their name was, immediately, he would make up a song using their name. We would then follow him and play along. No problem. It was all ad-lib anyhow. After working with Steve for a few months doing the talk show, we started doing a scripted show. Scripted shows are very tightly formatted. You could never ad-lib on a scripted show. You'd have forty-eight minutes of script and then commercials.

On the first show, Steve wrote a take-off on "The Taming of the Shrew." Every word was "thou art, thy, thith . . ." everything was t-h's. It got so silly that they even threw in the song, "Ith You Ith Or Ith You Ain't My Baby." There were sixty-three music cues in an eight- or nine- minute sketch. I'm usually good at remembering a paragraph or two ahead on the script, but in this case, I really had to have my brain open. Those lines were just flying by with stings, one after another. Bing. Bang. Boom.

At rehearsal, Steve never did the punchlines to the gags. Instead of the punchline, he said, "How's your bird? How's your fern? How's your Clyde?" on the ending of the real joke, which made the timing real hard for us to play the sketch off. The real punchline would be very funny and I got to see the punchline on the script. But the band would hear it for the first time when the show was live. It's almost impossible to play and laugh at the same time. As time went on, I got to know his timing and sense of humor and learned to anticipate him doing these funny lines.

The first show started with a skit and I was following along a paragraph ahead. The stings were flying. Bing, bang, boom. Steve was talking to Louis Nye when all of a sudden; I couldn't find what they were saying in the script. I was turning pages and looking for the cues and freaking out because I couldn't find them. After about thirty seconds of this, I realized that these idiots were ad-libbing on a scripted show and nobody did that because it was timed right to the minute: forty-eight minutes of show and twelve minutes of commercials. But it was Steve's show, so who was gong to tell him what to do?

I was looking for a place where I could come in and it was impossible, because I didn't know what they were ad-libbing. I have the same kind of sense of humor that Steve had so I sort of guessed where he was going to come back to the script. I waited for him and luckily came in at just the right time.

We were starting a new show with a new director and I got the feeling that he didn't like me because directors like to choose their own crew, and I was "Steve's boy." We went to the first meeting and were sitting at the table with the writers and the comedians, running through the script. As we left, Steve walked over to the director to say goodbye and I went with him. Steve said casually, "Oh, by the way, Terry doesn't take any cues from anyone," and walked away, leaving me with the director. I stumbled around and said, "Wait a minute, let me explain something. What Steve means is, he thinks I know his timing, but you count me down to the cues. That's no problem." I'm not sure how happy he was with that but at least he was back in charge of the show.

At the first rehearsal, this new director was getting hung up because Steve wasn't doing the punchlines. He and the other comedians were double-talking all over the place. There were ad-libs thrown all around the studio. "How's your bird? How's your fern? How's your Clyde?" Just funny, nonsensical stuff. By the time the actual show started, this director was becoming a nervous idiot. We did Steve's intro, then went into a commercial, came out, and went into the first bit. We were into it for about a minute and the first music cue was coming up when the director said into my headsets: "Okay, Terry, music coming up!" And he started to count me down. I knew damn well that Steve was not going to say the line in the script. I just felt it because if I was doing that bit, I also would have ad-libbed something right there. The director counted me down: "10, 9, 8, 7, 6, 5, 4, 3, 2, 1, MUSIC!"

I didn't come in with the music. Sure enough, Steve was ad-libbing. Now a good fifteen to twenty seconds went by and I heard a panicky voice scream into my headset, "*NO* MUSIC! *NO* MUSIC!" We hadn't even played a note yet. The director was flipping out in the booth. I waited for Steve to stop ad-libbing. He did the line in the script, I came in with the music, and we went to commercial.

During the commercial, I heard the director's voice in my headset again. It sounded like he was having a nervous breakdown. He said kind of quietly, "Terry, you've got it from here on in. It's all yours."

When you're doing a talk show, you hardly ever stop the camera from filming unless some catastrophe happens. The main reason is that if you go into overtime, it costs a lot of money for the executive producer, which is what Steve Allen was. Steve always had a lot of respect for jazz musicians and comedy writers and thought that they were the most talented people in the arts. We had the World's Greatest Jazz Band on the show, co-led by Bob Haggart and Yank Lawson. Steve wanted the director to superimpose each musician's name on the screen when he was soloing. I think Yank played first, but they didn't show his name. Then Billy Butterfield played and they didn't show his name either so Steve said, "Cut!" The cameras stopped and Steve said to the director, "I told you to superimpose their names when they're playing a solo." That little stop had to cost Steve five to ten thousand dollars, because Steve was the executive producer and he had to pay overtime to all eighty-four million people connected with the show. I really thought it was great that he respected jazz musicians that much that he would make sure their names were seen on screen, no matter what the cost.

Another thing that I admired about Steve was that if he believed in something, he didn't care who he alienated. He just came out and said what he felt. The show we were doing was a syndicated show and it was only shown in about forty cities. The producers told Steve to stay away from talking about anything controversial. One of Steve's bits was to take questions from the audience. A few of the questions were about intermarriage between black and white people. Steve completely forgot what the producer asked him what not to do and spoke his piece. The last question was "Would you want your son to marry a black girl?" I don't remember his exact words, but this is pretty close. Steve said, "I hope that people who are tuning in now will try to find out what we were talking about before they judge what I'm going to say. But to you people who have been tuned in and heard what the question was, my answer is no, I wouldn't want my son to marry a black girl, and the reason is, if they went down South, they wouldn't be accepted, and wouldn't be treated well. I love my son and want him to be happy." In the next few weeks, twenty stations down South canceled the show. I think if Steve had it to do all over again, I don't think he would have changed one word that he said.

Back in the 1950s, Benny Goodman was on Steve's show right after Steve played the part of Benny in *The Benny Goodman Story*. All Benny had to do was play one song and then Steve would go over, thank him, and say all these things that were written on the cue cards. He would say something like, "It was a pleasure having you here, Benny." Then Benny would put his hand out and say, "It was a pleasure working with you too, Steve." They'd shake hands, and go into commercial. They rehearsed that bit all week, sometimes five times a day so that the cameraman could get good angles on their shots and then the director would pick the shots he wanted.

After Benny played his song, it looked like Steve was touched by Benny being there, and when he had to read what was written on the cue cards, he got a little emotional, and told the cue card guy to put the cards down. He walked over to Benny, and I don't remember exactly what he said, but it was something like, "You know, Benny, the last six months have been the greatest thrill for me. Growing up in Chicago and listening to your music all my life, and now getting the chance to play you in the movie, plus hanging out with you for the last six months, has been the biggest thrill of my life." And he put his hand out and said, "Thank you very much, Benny." Benny put his hand out, looked around for a cue card, didn't see one, and said, "Well, it's been nice working with you too, uhh, uhh . . . Pops." Called him Pops on national television. Couldn't remember his name. El Foggo strikes again.

I think Steve liked me because I would never kiss his ass. If I had something to say about the music, I would speak up. Everything I did or said was to help Steve. I even taught him to play the vibes and wrote a vibes duet for us to play. Everything he played on the duet made him look like he could play as well as I could. After we finished the duet, people would come up to him and say, "Mr. Allen, I never knew you could play the vibes that good." That made me a winner.

When we did the summer show on CBS, we were in a studio far away from the stage, unlike *The Tonight Show*, where the band was right there on the stage. I worked by headset and television monitors. Steve was going to play a piano solo with the band. My rhythm section was Frank Capp on drums, Herb Ellis on guitar, Ray Brown on bass, and Mike Melvoin on piano. One of the best rhythm sections ever. We rehearsed all week and everything went great. The musicians all wore headsets so they could hear Steve while he was playing from the stage. We were taping the show and had a big audience in the studio. While he was playing his piano solo, Steve kept rushing. He was almost a bar ahead of the band. He stopped playing and yelled, "Hey, Terry! You're screwing up!" I turned my mike on, which went to the stage, and said, "Steve, YOU'RE screwing up and I'll come out there and tell you why!"

There was silence. You never told the star off in front of an audience. By the time I got over to the stage, the executive producer, the producer, the head of CBS, the makeup man, the caterer, you name 'em, were all waiting for me so they could fire me. I walked past them and went right over to Steve and said, "Steve, you're screwing up because of the way they've got the monitors set up. They're twenty feet away from you and you're getting the sound late! You can't play that way. Nobody can play that way. OSCAR PETERSON WOULD BE RUSHING!"

Steve realized that I was right. If I hadn't given him a valid answer, I'm sure he would have fired me right then and there. I did what I had to do. I'm no genius, but if it's not my fault, I won't take the blame for somebody else's mistakes.

People always ask me how good a piano player Steve Allen was. I really couldn't tell you because I don't know how good he really would have been if he had channeled all his energies into the piano. Steve's mind went in eighty-four directions at one time. I'll never forget the time we were going to play in Las Vegas. I was in his office and we were selecting music for the show. He had a guy there trying to transcribe one of his songs. Steve couldn't read music. Most of the songs he wrote he'd play on the piano into a tape recorder, and then have somebody write it out on music paper for him. I was asking Steve questions about the Las Vegas show and the other guy was trying to find out if the notes were right. At the same time, Steve was dictating a letter to his secretary to Vice President Hubert Humphrey. All at one time. Four bars of piano, four bars for me, four bars for the secretary. That's what he was like.

When he played boogie-woogie, he played it better than a lot of great jazz piano players. If he played in G or E-flat, he could play just about any song. I always wondered how good a jazz piano player he would have been if he just concentrated on music, which meant listening, playing, and jamming all the time. His potential was never reached.

Some of the most fun times I had with Steve were when we played nightclub engagements. When you spend time with somebody on the road; traveling, living at the same hotels, eating together, you really get to know that person. We laughed a lot and talked about personal things that men usually talk about. He loved when I told him funny jokes but Steve wasn't a joke teller. That wasn't his bag.

He did have his *mishigasses* and was strange in some ways. He went by what he thought was right by principle. In the 1970s we did a show at the Playboy Club in Milwaukee and the entertainment director, Sam Destifano, an old friend of mine who was a very good jazz pianist, said to me, "Terry, I sure would love to have Steve work here New Year's Eve. Do you think he'd want to work that night?" Most comedians don't work New Year's Eve because with all the screaming and yelling, who was going to listen to a comedian? So I went to Steve's room and told him that the Playboy Club would love to have him perform on New Year's Eve. "What would it take to get you to do the show and would you like me to handle it for you? No commission or anything." He said, "Yes, you can handle it. I'd like to have 10,000 dollars." Today that would be like 50,000 dollars. I said, "Good." I told him I always got 2,000 dollars for myself on New Year's Eve, which would leave him with 8,000 dollars. He said no problem.

I went to Sam and said, "Steve doesn't really want to work New Year's Eve, but if you make it worth his while, maybe he'll do it. I've got an idea. The ballroom holds about two thousand people. You hire a big band. We'll do a show at eight o'clock. Then the band can play dance music and ring in the New Year with music. After we get done with our show, we'll go to the theater next door where we do our regular show, which holds four hundred people, and we'll do a second show for them at ten o'clock. You charge twenty dollars a head for people to get in. You pay Steve Allen 15,000 dollars against 75 percent of the gross, whichever is better. We also need five first-class round-trip plane tickets and suites for all of us." The suites meant nothing to him. The food meant nothing to him and neither did the transportation so he said okay. Twenty-four-hundred tickets at twenty dollars each. There was a lot of money to be made. So we agreed.

I went to Steve and told him what the deal was. I was getting him 15,000 dollars instead of the 10,000 dollars he had asked for. He looked very happy. While I was talking to him, the phone rang. It was Sam. He said he wanted to talk to me. I told Steve I'd be right back. When I got to Sam's room he said, "Terry, we just had a meeting and went through the whole thing. We didn't realize something. The Playboy Club is in Milwaukee and people are going to be coming in from Chicago. If we have a bad snowstorm, we're going to be in for a lot of trouble. We'll give you everything you asked for, except the guarantee for Steve has to be 12,000 dollars." Steve had asked for 10,000 dollars but he's still making 2,000 dollars more than what he wanted originally so I figured it was still a good deal.

I went back to Steve and told him what the problem was and that now he would be getting 12,000 dollars, which was still more than what he wanted to start with. He said great. I went back to Sam and OK'd the deal. We did the Milwaukee job and went home to California. A few days later I got a letter from Steve. It said, "Dear Terry. Since you told me that I was getting 15,000 dollars and I ended up getting only 12,000 dollars, I'm giving you 1,800 dollars instead of 2,000 dollars." My temper got the best of me and I wrote an angry letter back to him: "I got you the job! No commission! You wanted 10,000 dollars and I got you 12! What kind of crap is this?" He wrote back, "Okay, I'll give you 1,900 dollars." I didn't believe it. I figured, "Where am I going with this dumb thing?" So I took the 1,900 dollars.

Four or five weeks later, Steve and Jayne made a big party for Rebekah and me when we got married at their house in Royal Oaks. They hired a band and bought more roses than you ever saw in your life. Jayne flew in about eighty-four pounds of lox from New York. The whole thing had to cost around 15,000 dollars, but he wouldn't give me that extra 100 dollars for the Milwaukee job out of principle. So I ate 100 dollars worth of lox to make up for it.

Steve and Gus Bivona, the clarinetist, were good friends. They met each other when Steve lived in California, and in fact, they were neighbors. Gus was getting up there in age and was having trouble getting work. Before we went back to play the Playboy Club, I told Steve about Gus's work situation and told him that Gus was at that age where nobody was hiring him. Even though they already hired a band that was being paid for by the Playboy club, Steve said, "Let's take him with us to Milwaukee. But don't tell him why we're doing it." We took Gus with us and Steve paid his salary. Throughout his life, Steve quietly helped a lot of musicians who were having career problems.

I used to collect soap from different hotels. One time I took a whole bunch of bars of soap from the Playboy Hotel. They had them all wrapped in fancy packages. I asked Steve's wife Jayne to do me a favor and bring the maid into her room and keep her busy by talking to her while I stole as many bars of soap off her cart as I could, which was always outside of the room. After the two weeks were up, with Jayne's help, I collected about three hundred bars of soap. When we went home, I gave Jayne half of the soap for helping me. At the wedding they made for us, Steve and Jayne gave my wife and me two presents, both beautifully wrapped. When we got home, I opened the presents. The first one was a beautiful piece of crystal and the other was a box filled with 150 pieces of soap, the other half of the soap that I gave Jayne.

We had an engagement to play in Japan and Steve was in China with his son Billy while Paul Smith, Frank Capp, and I were to meet him in Japan. Paul was going to leave a day after Frank and I did, so Paul called me and said, "Terry, I know it's not your business to do this, but please tell Steve that I've been to Japan before and sometimes they don't pick you up and forget about you. Tell Steve that if nobody picks me up an hour after I get there, I'm going home." Paul is that type of a guy. When Paul traveled, he traveled as light as you could go. He had one suitcase which had a wash-and-wear suit, a wash-and-wear shirt, a wash-and-wear tie, wash-and-wear socks, and wash-and-wear underwear. That and peanut butter and jelly. That's how he traveled to Japan. Sure enough, when we got to Japan, they never picked him up at the airport. If there had been a flight home right then, he would have taken it. Paul Smith did not look like a jazz musician at all. To the Japanese people, he looked totally unlike the other jazz musicians that they dealt with. He was about six-foot-four, had a crew cut, and looked like a Nazi storm trooper. Finally, because he was the only one left in the airport, they finally asked him if he was Paul Smith, and then they picked him up.

The reason we went to Japan was to open a new hotel in the city of Atomi, which was naturally called the Atomi Hotel. The owner's son went to Yale University and was a big fan of Steve's, so they booked Steve to be the first attraction to open the hotel. The hotel wasn't even finished yet. The rooms were done but the concert hall where we were playing wasn't. They had a wire fence around the auditorium where the walls were going to be so hardly anybody came in to see the show. People stood outside of the wire gate and watched the show without having to pay to get in the hall.

Chapter 18

On opening night, we must have had about twelve people sitting at the tables. This had to be the biggest mis-booking of all time. Steve didn't tell jokes; he just got out there and ad-libbed funny things. There wasn't one laugh. Nobody laughed at anything Steve said because nobody understood what he was saying. The only thing that went over well was the music. We had a sixteen-piece orchestra and the Japanese musicians were great. The vibes duet really tore them up.

A few days went by and it wasn't getting any better. Steve was still ad-libbing all these funny lines and nobody understood one word he said. Finally, somebody suggested getting an interpreter. They hired this little guy who was about five-foot-three. He was jive and was really full of shit. The guy kept saying how he and "Dean, Sammy, and Frank" used to hang out. Never mentioned second names, just "Dean, Sammy, and Frank." He knew everybody. On his first night, he stood on stage next to Steve. Steve's first line was, "Hello, ladies and gentlemen." Now the guy was supposed to translate that. This is what he said: "HUH-ROW, RAY-DEEZ AND GENTER-MEN!" He said the same thing that Steve said, but with a Japanese accent. Whatever Steve said in English, the guy repeated in English with a Japanese accent. We didn't believe it. They fired him after his first show.

We were there for two weeks and it was the biggest bomb of all time. Only the music went over, so after about four days, Steve stopped talking and played piano most of the time.

When Jack Kennedy was running for president in 1960, Steve asked me to get a group together to play for Kennedy. The first musician I called was Frank Butler. Frank was one of the greatest drummers I ever worked with. Unfortunately, he was strung out most of his life. But he knew that if he did drugs, he couldn't work in my band. For some reason, I had a way with guys who were screwed up. They enjoyed playing for me because I treated them good, I paid them a decent salary, and I let them play. I also called Al Viola and Teddy Edwards and we all went to the Coliseum where we had to clear security.

Jack Kennedy, Adlai Stevenson, Averill Harriman, Pierre Salinger, Robert Kennedy, and Steve were all standing around talking. They could have been talking about dropping the atom bomb for all I knew. I must have been about twenty feet away from them when I saw Frank Butler walk towards them. Before I could do anything, Frank tapped Steve on the shoulder and said, "Hey, man." Everybody stopped talking and looked at Frank. Steve didn't know who Frank was so he said, "What can I do for you?" He said, "Terry Gibbs called me for this gig and I was wondering: can I draw five dollars?" Nobody knew what to say. Steve looked embarrassed and finally told him to ask Terry Gibbs about that. I really felt bad for Steve.

Not long after that incident, Steve and I went to a methadone center that Frank was working at and talked with a bunch of kids who were hooked on drugs. After getting to know Frank a little better, Steve really got to like him.

Steve worked like a jazz musician. I think that he ad-libbed his way through life. One time during his act, a waitress dropped a tray full of dishes and Steve ad-libbed a bunch of lines that were absolutely hilarious. Then the same thing happened the next night. I tried to feed him some straight lines from what he said the night before, but he did completely different lines based on the same tray falling on the floor. Just like a jazz musician, Steve never said the same thing twice the same way.

Steve was such a big fan of mine that if one note was to be played on the vibes for anything, he'd always say, "Call Terry Gibbs," even though my grandmother could have played what he wanted. In 1960, I was working in New York and Steve was now doing his Thursday show for NBC on the West Coast. I got a call from one of the people who booked the talent on *The Steve Allen Show* asking me if I could come out to California on Friday. They wanted me to do a show with Steve on his Sunday show opposite *The Ed Sullivan Show*. The person I talked to said that Steve had asked for me personally. I was off until the following Tuesday so I told him that I could leave on Friday and be ready for a Saturday rehearsal. I didn't have the slightest idea what they wanted me to play. They also told me that I wouldn't have to worry about a vibes set and would have one there for me.

I immediately called Joe Glaser and told him about the call and he said that he would have his office alert all the club owners that they dealt with to watch the show. I also told my folks and they told every one of my relatives that I was appearing on *The Steve Allen Show* that Sunday. I got to Los Angeles on Friday and even though I lived there, somebody from the show's staff picked me up and drove me to a hotel near the studio. I also called Donna to let her know that I was in town for two days.

When I went to rehearsal on Saturday, I was told there was no rehearsal for me and that I would rehearse at the dress rehearsal on Sunday before the show. I figured Steve was going to jam just like we would do when he would sit in with me. On Sunday, when I came to rehearsal, there was a set of vibes there. They told me to go get made up and go to the costume room. I hadn't the slightest idea why I had to go to the costume room, and when I got there, they gave me a Hawaiian shirt to put on. Once again, I was pretty confused. They also asked me if I had more than one set of mallets. I told them that I always carried about five pairs with me. Then they told me that I was on for the rehearsal.

When I went over to the vibes, there was just a piano next to them. I was still confused. All the comics that worked on the show: Bill Dana, Louis Nye, Tom Poston, Don Knotts, and a few other funny guys, gathered around my vibes. Steve came out, said hello to me, and sat down at the piano. I saw Louis Nye walk out with a little pail of water and they asked me to hand out vibes mallets to the other comics. The stage manager yelled, "Quiet on the stage! Ready for the Martin Benny sketch!" What went down was the most embarrassing thing that ever happened to me. The "Martin Benny" sketch was a take-off on Martin Denny, the piano player who had those hit records of Hawaiian music with exotic bird sounds in the background. Steve started to play the song and everybody stood around my vibes making all these weird bird noises. Louis Nye was blowing into the pail, playing water. Somebody else was playing armpit and everybody was yelling, "SCHMUCK! SCHMUCK! SCHMUCK!" all over the place while banging on my vibes. Steve knew that Martin Denny had a vibes player in his band so he said, "Call Terry Gibbs." It was too late for me to call Joe Glaser or my folks because we were going on live to New York and they were three hours ahead of us. When I got back to New York, Joe made me come up to his office and he called me every four-letter word he could think of. He said all the club owners were watching the show to see and hear this great vibes player that he was bragging about, and now he was the laughingstock of all the agents. That wasn't as bad as my mother telling me that all my Jewish relatives couldn't believe that I would be on television yelling, "SCHMUCK! SCHMUCK! SCHMUCK!" which is a dirty word in Jewish.

When he wasn't doing a TV show or playing a nightclub engagement, Steve would always want to jam on the piano. Sometimes he'd come into the club where I was playing and sit in with me. The Joe Glaser office was going to book me back into the London House so I asked Steve if he'd like to play piano with me and my quartet. He said that he'd love to but he just wanted to play piano and not do any schtick or talking. He told me that I was the bandleader and that he would love working with me. He did, and he was the highest paid piano player I ever had in my band.

I worked it out with the Marienthal Brothers, who were big fans of Steve, that they had to give me an extra 10,000 dollars for Steve plus a suite of rooms and first class transportation. Joe Glaser didn't bug me for any commission for Steve; I just paid him for my little group. I also took Gus Bivona with us because Steve always liked to work with the clarinet and vibes sound. Plus, he and Gus were good friends.

As I said, Steve wasn't going to do any schtick, he was just going to play piano. Forget it. Once he got onstage, he couldn't help but be silly. We both worked well playing off each other. If I started to say something that he thought was off the wall, he'd jump in with something and be very funny. Plus, he was so hot those days that people were throwing questions up to him on every show, and he had fun answering them.

While we were there, Larry Flynt came in to see us and invited us to his place for food after the job. Nobody knew who Larry Flynt was in those days, including us. All we knew was that he was a young publisher. Every time we went to his place, there were always nice people there, a lot of a good food, and no hanky-panky. Because we didn't have any transportation to get around, he sent over a chauffeur-driven Cadillac to pick us up every night after we got finished working. This wasn't just an ordinary Cadillac. It was orange all over, even on the inside, which looked like a whorehouse. We enjoyed riding in that car because it was so out.

Steve happened to mention to Larry that he thought the car was great and Larry said, "It's yours. I'll have somebody drive it out to California. It's my gift to you." I think Larry was a big Steve Allen fan. Larry never talked about sex or anything dirty. In fact, he was pretty intelligent in his conversations. The engagement was a ball and we all went home happy. We got a chance to play and everybody loved us.

One night Larry told us that he had a new magazine that he was publishing and wanted to send Steve and me a free subscription for a year. The shock came about a month later when Larry's new magazine came to my house and to Steve's office. It was the first copy of *Hustler*, which made *Playboy* magazine look like the Bible. It wasn't as bad for me as it was for Steve, because the magazine came completely wrapped where you couldn't see the cover and Steve's secretaries always opened all his mail before he got to see it. I don't know how he explained the magazine to the secretaries, but it had to be funny. The biggest drag was that we couldn't stop the magazine from coming every month. What an honor we had. The first *Hustler* magazines.

The last two shows I did with Steve were both done for Disney Studios. One was called *The Music Room*, which had my big band and two or three musical guests. We did six shows, worked four days, and did three shows each week. They were done in November 1983. The other was called *The Comedy Room*, which was done in April 1984. Same routine as before, except we used a sextet with Frank Capp on drums, Gus Bivona on clarinet, Al Viola on guitar, Marty Harris on piano, and Bob Maize on bass.

Even though *The Music Room* was an all-music show, Steve hired a young comedian to be the announcer. His name was Bill Maher, who went on to fame and fortune with the *Politically Incorrect* show on ABC. Bill was a complete unknown and was very humble around all the celebrities on the show. The show needed somebody who, every once in a while, could bring a blurb about one of the guests to Steve while we were taping. Bill was perfect and he and Steve worked well off each other. No matter what, music or no music, Steve had to do and say silly things.

The first show was done with Steve Lawrence and Eydie Gormé. Steve's wife, Jayne Meadows, was the other guest. That was a fun show because most of Steve and Eydie's music was arranged by the late Don Costa, and it really swung.

Steve had a set of conga drums that he liked to play. It was set up on the side of the stage where the band was, about ten feet away from the band. Every once in a while, he liked to go noodle on it when the band was playing for one of the acts. He would be off-camera and just having fun. While Steve and Eydie were singing and the camera was on them, Steve Allen sneaked over to where the conga drums were and started playing. The moment the director saw Steve over there, he took the camera off Steve and Eydie and put the camera on Steve playing the congas. Steve didn't see any creativity in what the director did and after that show, he was fired. You never take the camera off the performer. The director got so nervous and was probably so in awe of Steve, that he lost control of the show.

Another show had Joe Williams, Paul Williams, and Melba Moore. The night before we had to do that show, I got a call from the producer who told me that Melba Moore's music was lost. She was in a hit show called "Pearlie" and wanted to sing the title song because her recording of it had become a big hit. I told the producers to get me a copy of the record and sixteen lead sheets of the song and get them to my house as soon as possible. I listened to the record and it was all strings and voices playing behind her, so I stayed up half the night and finally figured out what to do for her.

I used the lead sheets as an arrangement and where I heard strings, I had all the saxophones play flutes. Where there were voices, which were mostly whole note and half note chords, I had the brass play. Then I had them play the notes that were written on the piano lead sheet. When we went to rehearsal the next day, it came off so good that Melba asked me if she could have the music that the band marked up. That way, if she had to sing with a regular sixteen-piece band that didn't have any strings or voices, she could have that music for the arrangement. I think eventually she had it recopied so it would look clean.

Some of the guests on the other shows were Dizzy Gillespie, Sarah Vaughan, and Hank Mancini. The same thing happened with Dizzy; except that his music didn't get lost, he just forgot to pack the music in with his clothes. There was no problem there; I had him play on one of the Dream Band charts and then we did "A Night in Tunisia," which everybody knew. Dizzy told us how he wanted it done and we played the heck out of it. That was my favorite show.

The fourth show had Anthony Newley, Burt Bacharach, and Carole Bayer Sager. Show five had Lou Rawls, Rosemary Clooney, and Red Holloway.

Conte Candoli and John Audino both took off from *The Tonight Show* for two weeks to do our show. Doc Severinsen, Ann Jillian, and Patti Page were the guests on the last show we did. When Doc came to rehearsal and saw Conte and John, he said, "So THAT'S where you guys have been for the last two weeks!"

The Comedy Room was almost a throwaway for the band. All we did was laugh and jam for the audience when the tapes had to be changed. The premise of that show was Steve sitting around with three comedians, talking and ad-libbing about the past.

We did six shows with the greatest funny minds of all time. Here is the lineup for the shows that we did.

Show #1: Sid Caesar, Shecky Greene, Mort Sahl
Show #2: Louis Nye, Jack Carter, Dick Shawn
Show #3: Shelley Berman, Red Buttons, George Gobel
Show #4: Jan Murray, Danny Thomas, Bob Newhart
Show #5: Joe Baker, Tim Conway, Pat Harrington, Jr.
Show #6: Milton Berle, Carl Reiner, Billy Crystal

Just looking at that lineup of comics, you know those shows were hilarious. Steve played straight man for practically everybody and every once in a while would sneak in a funny line himself. He was sort of the moderator for a bunch of lunatics. It's hard to keep comics who are so great at ad-libbing in line, but that was always Steve's forté, hosting a talk show, and getting the best out of his guests.

I have been very fortunate. All of the television shows I did, I loved. To me, they weren't jobs, they were just fun. Regis Philbin helped me break into television and I learned a lot from doing his show. *Operation: Entertainment* gave me the chance to learn how to run a stage show. But working with Steve Allen was probably the most fun of all because he ad-libbed everything, even on scripted shows. When we played nightclubs, he let me jump in and ad-lib with him. But I knew when to do that so that I wouldn't step on his punchlines.

Steve was the master of television. He knew direction, he knew exactly where the camera should be, and he knew when the music should come in. I think that if it wasn't for Steve, all the non-scripted ad-lib shows, going back to Jack Paar, *The Tonight Show* with Johnny Carson and now Jay Leno, and David Letterman may not be on television. And that includes every style talk show that is ad-libbed, from Oprah Winfrey to Jerry Springer and from Larry King to Howard Stern. When you work with great people, the better they are, the better you are. It's much easier conducting with somebody good than with somebody bad. But the most important thing for me about being on television was that it was FUN! Once the red light went on, I was at my best.

Chapter 19
Phil Spector: Mr. Overtime

In 1973, I was sitting at home nursing a cold when I got a call from Frank Capp. He told me that Phil Spector, the famous rock and roll record producer, was recording John Lennon and they needed a vibes player. I told Frank that not only wasn't I feeling well, but I didn't do that type of work. I told him that there were a lot of guys who did studio work and as I was telling Frank all this, Phil got on the phone and said, "Terry Gibbs with Steve Allen!" And he started to sing Steve's theme song, "This Will Be the Start of Something Big." When he finished, he said, "Come down and I'll give you twenty doubles," which means that he would pay me the same as twenty times the normal rate.

Frank got back on the phone and said, "He's serious. He'll give you twenty doubles." I said, "Frank, I don't do that kind of date. I'll give him the names of some other vibes players." And we hung up.

Ten minutes later, Frank called back and said, "Phil doesn't want another vibes player. He wants you. Do you realize he's serious and will give you twenty doubles?" I didn't think about the money, I just thought that I would go to help Frank out. So I got dressed and went down to the Record Plant in Hollywood where they were recording.

When I walked into the studio, which was very small, I got stoned immediately from the smell of pot that everybody was smoking. I saw John Lennon surrounded by about nine Japanese girls and they were all listening to a playback of the last take they made. I walked over to the percussion section and Frank was the only one there. I went over to the vibes and asked Frank where the music was. He said, "There's no music." He had been playing vibes before I got there and he played these four notes for me that he had been playing. I said, "Frank, did you get me out of my sickbed to play four *fakacktah* notes? My grandmother could play that." He said again, "Phil's going to give you twenty doubles!" I didn't know Phil Spector but I did know about his reputation as one of the biggest hitmakers from the Beatles to every group that came out of Philadelphia.

Phil was in the booth and the moment he saw me, he turned on the P.A. and said, "Terry Gibbs with Steve Allen!" and started to sing "This Will Be the Start of Something Big" again, which embarrassed the heck out of me. Then he said, "Okay, take 45." After hearing some of the last take, I said to Frank, "Have you been playing this piece of garbage 45 times?" Anyhow, when we got to take 85, it was 4 a.m., which meant double money for everybody, and Phil called it a wrap.

When I was about to leave, I saw them wheel a cake out that was half the size of the room. It was Phil's birthday. Then I saw something I didn't believe. If you have ever seen an automobile accident, it happens so fast that you never see how it starts. All of a sudden, John Lennon ran towards the cake and dove into it like you would dive into a swimming pool. The icing on the cake flew all over the place. The moment John did that, Phil took out a gun and starting shooting into the ceiling. I got so scared that I dove under the piano. Hal Blaine, the drummer, came over to me under the piano and said, "Don't worry, Terry, they do this all the time." I had never been around heavyweight rock players before, but I heard how wild they could get.

Phil is known for what is called "The Wall of Sound" where every instrument blends together with the others. On that date, I did forty takes for him and never heard the four notes that I played on the vibes. I think he gave me all that money just so that he could say, "Terry Gibbs with Steve Allen!" and sing the first four bars of "This Could Be the Start of Something Big."

Phil Spector became the only person I did dates for as a sideman. He didn't do many, but when he did, he always called me. He loved to yell from the booth, "Terry Gibbs with Steve Allen!" and then sing, "This Could Be the Start of Something Big." He always hired jazz horn players on his dates. The only rock players on his sessions were drummers and guitar players. On the dates I did with him, some of the horn players he had were Conte Candoli, Don Menza, and Nino Tempo. The piano players included Pete Jolly, Joe Sample, Don Sherry, and Mike Lang.

When Conte and I were on the same session, you could hear Phil in the booth announce, "Terry Gibbs with Steve Allen!" sing "This Could Be the Start of Something Big," and then say, "Conte Candoli with Johnny Carson!" and sing *The Tonight Show* theme song.

One thing I learned about Phil is that he knew exactly what he's looking for. This one date he hired eight guitar players plus four horn players, three piano players, two bass players, two drummers, and four percussionists. Only seven guitar players showed up. We started to get a balance at 8 p.m. and Phil wasn't getting what he was looking for. He wanted eight guitar players but I didn't have the slightest idea what the difference would be. But he was so successful that he must have known why eight instead of seven.

At about 11:50, just before we went into overtime, he called it a wrap and asked us if we could all come back the next day. I think that everybody was available and said yes. Phil then walked out of the booth playing "The Anniversary Song" on the accordion and told Conte Candoli and Don Menza to follow him. He walked out to the parking lot, playing, with Conte and Don in back of him, playing along on trumpet and tenor. They went over to the security guard and Phil asked him to sing "The Anniversary Song" with them. The guard fluffed him off and walked away. Phil followed him, with Conte and Don still behind him playing, and wouldn't get off the guard's back until the guy sang the song with them. About twenty minutes later, the guard finally gave up and sang the song, probably just to get away from Phil.

Two weeks later, when I got my check for that session, I saw that he paid me for one hour overtime and I suppose he paid everybody for the hour that he was marching around the parking lot with Conte and Don. The strangest thing is that I never played one note because he never got to balance the percussion section. There's nothing like getting paid for doing nothing.

In the next few years, I did a few more record dates for Phil. On one date we recorded Leonard Cohen. We started about 8 p.m. and went till 3 a.m. Phil called it a wrap just as Bob Dylan and Allen Ginsberg walked into the studio. They wanted to hear the tracks that we just laid down. Phil said "Nobody go home." We stuck around until 5 a.m., just sitting around while Bob Dylan and Allen Ginsberg were in the booth with earphones on, listening to the tapes. That had to cost Phil a gang of money. There were four horn players, three piano players, two electric bass players, four guitar players, four percussionists, two drummers, a leader, and a contractor, all getting double overtime money, just for sitting around.

Something I never knew about Phil was that he was a big jazz fan. When Buddy DeFranco and I played Fat Tuesday's in New York, he came in to see us two nights in a row. One night he came in with Paul Shaffer, the bandleader on *The David Letterman Show*. The next night he came in alone and got juiced out. At the end of every song we played, he stood up on the chair that he was sitting on and gave us a standing ovation. He stayed until after we played our last show and then wanted me to hang out with him. He wanted to take me to this supposedly hip restaurant hangout. I told Phil that I loved him but that I didn't hang out. His bodyguard came and got him and they left.

About ten minutes later the bartender told me that there was a phone call for me. It was Phil, calling me from his car. He asked me if the waiter that served him had given the band the tip that he left for us. I said "What tip, are you putting me on? No, he didn't give us anything." About five minutes later he showed up at the club with his two bodyguards. He questioned his waiter on why he didn't give the band the tip that he left on his credit card. What he actually did was leave a hundred dollar tip for the bartender, the doorman, the five musicians in the band, and his waiter. The waiter gave him some feeble excuse and Phil wouldn't leave until everybody got their hundred dollars. I really got on him for that. I said that first of all, I didn't accept tips, and secondly, he was my friend. We argued for a short while and then he again tried to talk me into hanging out with him at that so-called hip restaurant. I passed.

As out as Phil is, he's no dummy. He knows exactly what he's looking for. I like him and I think that besides liking me he respects my talent.

Chapter 20
Three Women–
Four Marriages

I've already mentioned the names of my three wives but I haven't really talked about them because that could be a book in itself, especially my second marriage. Fortunately and unfortunately, my three marriages were meant to be. I'll try to be as brief as possible in explaining what part these three women played in my life.

I met Donna Hartsough at the Hollywood Palladium in California when I worked with the Buddy Rich band. Donna was seventeen and I was twenty-three. I think I fell in love with her at first sight. She looked like a combination of Elizabeth Taylor and Lena Horne. We got married in August of 1949 while I was with Woody Herman's band.

She was, without a doubt, the best first wife I could ever have because she let me have a career. We lived in the basement apartment of my parents' house in Brooklyn. I'd go on the road with my little group and leave her there for months at a time while I played music and partied. Donna was very knowledgeable about what was happening in the music scene. If Bird or Diz played a good chorus, she understood what they were playing. We also wrote about ten songs together. She wrote mostly lyrics, but she did write a few good melodies too.

When she was nineteen years old, she found out that she had a cyst on her ovaries and had a hysterectomy, so we could never have children. She would have made a good mother. We married twice and divorced twice. Donna was a fun person to be around and I owe her a lot for letting me go out and do my thing.

Now on to my second wife, Carol. That was the "unfortunately" part of my two fortunately and one unfortunately marriages.

I know that in a bitter divorce people have a tendency to say terrible things about each other and the cliché that it takes two to tango is the norm. Maybe the following will explain why everything I say about Carol will sound negative but is true. In this case it didn't take two to tango.

The reason that I married Carol was that Gerry was born out of wedlock and in those days, that was taboo. Gerry was about nine months old when I was conducting *The Regis Philbin Show*. Carol told me that if I didn't marry her, she would go to all the newspapers and tell them that Terry Gibbs, the musical director of *The Regis Philbin Show,* wouldn't marry her, even though we had a baby. I would have been fired immediately. Look what they did to Ingrid Bergman when she was carrying Roberto Rossolini's child. They had her deported from the U.S.

Besides being hooked on every kind of pill, Carol was capable of putting her head through a glass window and then calling the police and telling them that it was me who did that to her. Then they would come to where I was living and take me to jail in handcuffs. She would always do that at one in the morning of the day I had to film three TV shows with Steve Allen. Steve only wanted to work two days a week, so we started rehearsing the first show at ten o'clock. We rehearsed three shows and then at about 6:00 p.m., we shot three in a row. There's nothing like being in jail at one o'clock in the morning, getting bailed out, and then running down to do a show with Steve and trying to be funny.

In the early 1970s, if you got divorced, the husband couldn't get custody of his children, even if his wife was a hooker or a junkie. I'm not putting them down, for in my life I've known some nice hookers and some lovely ladies that unfortunately were strung out on dope. But no matter what, the wife usually got custody of the children. The only way the husband could get custody was to prove that she was mentally incapable of taking care of the children.

After all kinds of court battles about her not letting me see my children, and after having to go through fourteen lawyers that she had hired and fired, psychiatrists were brought into the case. After she tried many suicide attempts, I was awarded custody of my children. My son Gerry was 11 1/2 years old and my daughter Jerra was 7 1/2.

One of Carol's best lines when she was hiring and firing her fourteen attorneys was, "I don't care if I don't wind up with anything, so long as YOU don't wind up with anything." P.S.: We lost one million dollars, which all went to pay attorney and psychiatrists' fees. Neither of us wound up with any money after the divorce. As much as there is a tendency for me to want to call her all kinds of names, it boils down to one thing and that is that Carol was not a well person. If anything good came out of that marriage it was my two children, Gerry and Jerra.

As for my other fortunate marriage, actually my most fortunate marriage, I really lucked out because as I write this, for the last twenty-four and a half years I have been married to the most loving, caring, giving, and beautiful person I have ever known. I'm the luckiest person in the world to have her as my wife. As beautiful as she is on the outside, she's even more beautiful on the inside.

Rebekah Bergstresser and I met in Disney World in Florida when I worked there in November 1976. After Carol and I got divorced, I had been going with a young lady on and off, but when I got custody of Gerry and Jerra, she split. She was actually jealous of the love that I had for my children.

Rebekah was working in the lounge in Buena Vista in the Orlando area, which was part of the Disney World complex. All the hippest jazz musicians worked there: Clark Terry, Zoot Sims, Flip Phillips, Joe Venuti, Louie Bellson, and Kenny Burrell, just to name a few.

Jazz wasn't Rebekah's bag. When I first asked her out, she said, "I don't go out with musicians, Toby." I said "What, Toby?" and took her out to the lobby where there was a big picture of me with my name as big as can be and I said, "The name is TERRY, not TOBY." She didn't care and wasn't too impressed with my name or my picture. Rebekah was twenty-six and I was fifty-two when we met. I was twice her age and I thought that was the reason that she didn't want to go out with me.

I was working there alone with a very good house rhythm section that played for all the jazz artists who performed at the lounge. I asked her out five times and the excuses for not going out with me got more feeble each time. In fact, the last excuse was, "I MAY have a date tonight." I finally stopped asking.

I met some people who were very close to Rebekah and in talking with them, I told them what I had gone through to get custody of Gerry and Jerra. For some reason, they told that to Rebekah, and the night before the end of my engagement she said that if I wanted to take her out after the job, it was okay with her. I was shocked and said, "Was there something I played tonight that you liked?"

Rebekah has never laughed at any of my jokes and just like Benny Goodman did to me, she would walk away in the middle of me telling her a joke. What I didn't know about her was that this beautiful young girl was a family-oriented person. Rebekah would never have gone out with me if I didn't have a daughter. Unbeknownst to me, she also had a daughter, Kelly, who was fourteen days younger than Jerra.

She didn't care that I was Steve Allen's musical director. In fact, I don't think that she even knew who Steve Allen was. She wasn't too impressed with people in show business. When we went out on our only date, all we talked about were our children.

After seeing her that one night, when I got back to L.A., we had what you could call a phone romance. We talked to each other practically every night. If I didn't call her, she'd call me. On October 13, 2002, not only did I turn seventy-eight years old, but also, it was twenty-five years of marriage for Rebekah and me.

I was 25 1/2 years older than Rebekah when I married her, and believe it or not, I'm still 25 1/2 years older and I fall more in love with her as the years go on.

Chapter 21
My Friend, Buddy D.

Since 1980, besides doing some TV shows with Steve Allen, I worked a lot with Buddy DeFranco and also worked as a single doing clinics and playing colleges using the Dream Band library. Working with Buddy has been the most creative and musically fun thing that I've done in the last twenty years.

I first met Buddy back in the 1940s. I think I was with Woody Herman's band and he was playing clarinet with Tommy Dorsey. We both went on to become leaders of our own bebop quartets and always felt the same way about music, especially Bird and Diz. They were our gods.

It wasn't until 1980 that Buddy and I played together. We never even played opposite each other in clubs or festivals. Sometimes we would meet on the road when he and Tommy Gumina had their group.

I remember Tommy, Buddy, and I appearing on a talk show with three other guests who were scientists. The host of the show was pretty hip but also knowledgeable about various subjects. It was a funny show in that when he talked to the scientists, Buddy, Tommy, and I didn't know what they were talking about at all. Because this was our younger days, the three of us were being silly. We would purposely answer every question from the host with the hippest language ever used. WE didn't even know what we were talking about. We'd just say something stupid and break up laughing. I have a photo of us on the show with Buddy, Tommy, and I breaking up and the three scientists looking like somebody just died.

I think that from the 1940s until the time we worked opposite each other in England in 1980, I was only in Buddy's company about five times. Our friendship started at Ronnie Scott's club in London, England, where we were booked as two separate attractions. We met at the rehearsal where Buddy was going to play a half-hour with a rhythm section and I was going to follow him and do the same. The reason I was going to follow him was not that I was the main attraction, it was because Ronnie Scott mentioned to us that it would be nice if we played one song together at the end of the set. Being that I sweat a lot, Buddy was nice enough to let me go on last, so I wouldn't have to sit around all wet, waiting for the last song. The vibes that the club rented for me to play hadn't shown up for the rehearsal, so I rehearsed my part of the show playing two-finger piano. Buddy and I still hadn't played together.

After Buddy and I each played with our groups, I introduced Buddy and told the audience we were going to have a jam session. This was true because at the rehearsal, we never talked about what we were going to play. Buddy and I looked at each other on the stage and we picked "Lester Leaps In" for its "I Got Rhythm" chord changes, which we both knew. We also knew that the chord changes to that song wouldn't hang up the rhythm section. We thought that that part of the show was going to be a throwaway.

Immediately, we started to click, playing individual choruses, then eight bars each, then fours, twos, and ones. Then we played together and jammed for about three or four choruses. By the time we got to the end, the people in the audience were standing and cheering. We didn't believe it. Ronnie was so knocked out that he said, "Why don't you guys play two songs next time?" We did and broke it up again. This time we added Charlie Parker's "Now's the Time." We both knew the bebop songs so there was no problem there.

As the nights went on, we were playing less individually and more together. We weren't just knocking out the people in the audience, but also the guys in the rhythm section. But mostly, we knocked ourselves out. We were having the time of our lives playing together. Because Benny Goodman and Lionel Hampton made the sound of the clarinet and vibes so popular, you could take any two idiots who play those instruments and it would sound good. What Buddy and I found out was that we had something special. Buddy, being a little pessimistic, wasn't sure if it was just this engagement, but I knew that there was something special there.

When we got done at Ronnie's, we agreed that when we got back to the States, we should occasionally try to work together.

I don't know how, but word must have gotten back to somebody in the States because when we got home, I got a call from my old friend Jim Washburn, one of the producers on *Operation: Entertainment*. Jim was now in charge of entertainment at KCET, the PBS television station in Los Angeles. He wanted us to do an hour TV show, which of course we did. That was the first time that Buddy and I ever worked together in the United States.

We hired Frank Collette on piano, Andy Simpkins on bass, and Jimmie Smith on drums and the show came out great. Word was really starting to get out about us because we got a call from Herb Wong, a producer for Palo Alto Records, who wanted us to record an album. After meeting with Herb, we decided to record the album live, because Buddy and I played better before an audience. It was much looser; we'd have the freedom to stretch out more, and we wouldn't be restricted to how many choruses we could play.

We booked ourselves into THE hot club in L.A. called Carmelo's. It was the perfect place to play in and record because it almost reminded me of a Fifty-Second Street club. It wasn't too big or too small; the audience was right next to the stage and it was great for getting them involved in what we were saying and playing.

We recorded about twenty songs and were going to pick about nine or ten for the album. When he listened to the tapes, Herb Wong didn't know which ones to pick because they were all so hot. So he told us that since he couldn't make up his mind, he would pay everybody for two albums and put them out six months apart.

A few months after the album "Jazz Party—First Time Together" came out, we got a surprise call from *The Tonight Show* telling us that Johnny Carson heard our version of "Air Mail Special" and wanted Buddy and me to play it on the show. This knocked us out. They flew Buddy in from Florida and put him up in a nice hotel. It seemed like a lot of other people liked "Air Mail Special" also. John Wilson reviewed the album for *The New York Times*:

> Both he (DeFranco) and Gibbs are wild swingers, which they daringly establish by opening this, their first disc together with a Goodman-Hampton specialty, "Air Mail Special." Goodman and Hampton were pretty exuberant on this number, but DeFranco and Gibbs outdo them, neither one ever sounding like his Swing Era counterpart.

Those were very strong words coming from somebody who had never been one of my biggest fans.

We did *The Tonight Show* again about six months later. When we were on the first time, we didn't go on until near the end of the show. When we played our last song with the Doc Severinsen band, the show ended while we were in the middle of the song. I got to talking to Johnny before the second show and mentioned that to him. He said,

"Don't worry, I'll tell the producer to put you on first," which he did.

The Tonight Show helped us a lot, for we got booked into the lounge at the Sahara Hotel in Las Vegas for three weeks. We took Jimmie Smith with us and hired two local musicians who I had played with before to play bass and piano. We really broke it up and they asked us if we would like to play in the main room, using a big band. It was in a show starring Wayland Flowers, a ventriloquist who did an act with a puppet called Madame. We played there for five weeks and it was great.

Even though we had rooms at the hotel, they gave us the famous Jerry Lewis dressing room to change our clothes in. It was more of a suite of rooms than a dressing room. Every night, we'd have a lot of celebrities come backstage and tell us how much they enjoyed our playing. Playing the main room was much easier because we did two shows and would get through by midnight. In a way, the lounge was more fun because Las Vegas never had many jazz attractions play there, so after all the shows were done, we'd draw all the hip entertainers and showgirls. The people who were vacationing there would come in to see us and get a double treat by seeing a lot of famous people.

A piano player from Australia named Ron came in and told us that he could get us to play in his country. He said that his brother Stan, who was a very prominent attorney, was also a big jazz fan and was now promoting jazz concerts. He wanted his brother to hear us in person and asked us where we would be appearing in the near future.

After Las Vegas, we were on our way to Europe to do a tour for George Wein. We told Ron our itinerary and he told us that Stan would be in London at the same time and we could possibly meet there.

Buddy and I went by ourselves and George supplied us with a rhythm section. We told George that we didn't want any other horns to play with us because we had our arrangements down. All we had to do was give the rhythm section our little lead sheets that were not too hard. Any other horn would ruin the sound that we got with the vibes and clarinet.

We were starting to get known as the bebop answer to Benny Goodman and Lionel Hampton. You would think that the rhythm section of John Lewis on piano, Elvin Jones on drums, and Pierre Michelot on bass, who I didn't know, would be a ball to play with. In some ways it was okay, but they weren't made for each other. I never got to know how good Pierre was because when they backed us up, John was playing Chopin études, and Elvin sounded like he was starting World War VII. Maybe if they all had played the same style, we would have had more fun. We didn't know what style to go with; we just wanted to play some straight-ahead bebop.

Timing in life is everything. For example, if you are standing on a corner and move away and somebody else stands where you were and two minutes later gets hit by a car, that's bad timing. This may be a strange comparison to what happened to us, but it's all about timing.

As part of the tour, we were to play Ronnie Scott's club in London and Shelly Manne was to play drums with us. George Wein hired two English musicians to play in the rhythm section along with Shelly. Stan, the attorney from Australia, was to come into the club on our first night. He called us from his hotel in London and told us that the trip from Australia made him too tired to come in and see us and he would come the next night.

This is where the timing comes in. The first night was a catastrophe. It rained and there weren't many people in the club. The sound system was screwing up all over the place and Shelly was having trouble playing with the pianist and bass player. The next night, when Stan came in to see us, the place was packed. The P.A. system was working and Shelly had had a long talk with the other musicians. That night we swung our *tucheses* off and the audience gave us a standing ovation. We were a winner. That's what I mean by timing.

When Stan heard us and saw how packed the place was and the audience's reaction, when it came to talking about our fee, we were in the driver's seat. I handled the business for Buddy and me and got us a great deal. Besides the money that we agreed upon, I told Stan that we wouldn't go unless we could take our wives with us, have business class seats on the airplane, and our hotels and food paid for. He was still knocked out by our last show, so he agreed to everything.

We were to play three one-nighters in Sydney, Adelaide, and Melbourne, and he was going to try and book some more jobs, which we would be paid extra for. I also asked for a deposit on the signing of the contract. When we got back to the States and I got the contract from Stan, I couldn't understand anything that was written on it. Stan, being a trial attorney, had drawn up a contract that had "the party of the first part" and "the party of the second part" in every other sentence. I didn't have the slightest idea what this was all about. I wasn't sure who the party of the first part was compared to the party of the second part. So on any sentence that I didn't understand, I wrote "by mutual agreement" so he couldn't make us do anything other than what we first agreed upon without talking about it first. He called me from Australia and told me that I was the best attorney that he ever worked with.

Stan really treated us great. In fact, he gave us a credit card to use for food just in case we wanted to eat at some place other than the hotel we were staying at. I think that if I didn't have children and grandchildren that my wife and I would live in Australia, because it's so beautiful.

Before we left for Australia, Buddy and I got called to play in the band that did the music for the Burt Reynolds picture, "Sharkey's Machine." Burt handpicked most of the musicians and was a big jazz fan, which I didn't know. Bob Florence wrote the arrangements, and Joe Williams and Sarah Vaughan sang the theme song. Just to mention a few musicians on the date, Shelly Manne played drums, Ray Brown played bass, Art Pepper and Marshal Royal played alto sax, Conte and Pete Candoli and Harry (Sweets) Edison were on trumpets, Carl Fontana and Bill Watrous were on trombones, plus Buddy and myself. It was definitely an all-star band.

I wanted to meet Burt but didn't want to bug him. When I saw him talking with Pete Candoli, I walked over to them. Burt was standing there with a book under his arm and I saw that it was *The Encyclopedia of Jazz* by Leonard Feather. I didn't want to interrupt the conversation but it didn't look like I would be intruding, so I said, "Burt, my name is Terry Gibbs. I just want to say hello."

He looked nervous and started stuttering and fumbling, looking like he was in awe of me. "Are you kidding? I know who you are, I ASKED for you!" We talked for about a minute and then he said, "Would you mind meeting somebody?" I didn't know what he had in mind so I said sure. He took me over and introduced me to Sally Field, who ALSO had *The Encyclopedia of Jazz* under her arm. When Burt said, "Sally, this is Terry Gibbs," all of a sudden, SHE got flustered. Both of them seemed like they were in awe of every musician there. I felt like asking for a raise.

Buddy and I were really meant for each other. They say that opposites attract and onstage, we work completely different. Offstage, we were pretty much alike, but onstage, Buddy worked more routinely than I did. He would almost make the same announcement every time, where I never knew what I was going to say. One time when he started to make the same announcement that he had made the night before on the same song, I stopped him and said "This is jazz. You can't say the same thing that you said last night. We may have the same people that we had last night and they want to hear you say something different."

We were great for each other in that Buddy took no prisoners when he played. When you follow him playing, you'd better play good. He kept me honest and I kept him loose. My philosophy has always been that when you're playing music, you've got to be serious. But in-between songs, be like you are off the bandstand. Buddy has a great sense of humor and is very funny. So now, when we work together, whether it is a little club or a big festival, we have fun on the bandstand.

Buddy has a lavalier mike that he attaches to his tie so that it picks up the notes on the clarinet evenly. Sometimes if he's playing with a regular mike on a stand in front of him, and he moves to either side, some notes would get lost. That's why he uses that lavalier mike. I was going to make an announcement on a mike that was on a stand close to where Buddy was standing and when I went to talk, the mike wasn't working. So I went to Buddy's mike on his tie, which is near where his belly button would be, and made my announcement from his belly. Buddy just stood there and played straight for me.

I haven't taken my vibes on the road with me for the last twenty-five years. The promoter or club owner supplies a set of vibes for me wherever I play. I usually get to see the vibes and adjust them before I go on stage. I have a run that I make and if that sounds fairly good, then it's straight ahead. I never know what kind of instrument they're getting for me and even though they may all look alike, they're still all different. To start with, different companies make different sounding bars and some sets are taller than others are. There's always something that's not to my liking, but at least I get to see the set before we play.

We were on tour in Europe and were playing at the Cork Festival in Cork, Ireland. We got there about a half-hour before we had to play, but the vibes were already on stage, so I couldn't get a chance to adjust them. When we were announced, I went on stage and being that I work very loose, I made my usual run on the vibes to see what adjustments it needed. After I make that dumb run, I usually say, "And now for my second song . . ." This way, they think that I'm trying to be funny. I usually have to adjust the bars so that they're not pressing against the damper bar, which could make them sound dead. I usually have to loosen the damper bar so I can make them sound livelier. When I made my dumb run, every note rang into the next one. You couldn't tell one note from another. There is a metal tube about a foot and a half long that connects the damper bar to the pedal. That's what I would normally adjust. When I went to adjust that, I saw that instead of the metal tube, there was a piece of thread connecting the damper bar to the pedal. I was afraid to fool with that, because if it broke, the whole vibes set was liable to collapse, right on the stage. I played the whole concert like that, with every note ringing into the next one. If anybody is familiar with my playing they know that I play a lot of notes. The weirdest thing was that we got a standing ovation and I was never so embarrassed in all my life.

I don't really play for an audience. I want them to like what I'm playing but if I don't think that I played good, then I go home sick. I have to like what I'm playing first.

Now for the weirdest part of the story. About six months later, Buddy went back to Cork and played the festival with three clarinet players. Some man came over to him and said, "Would you please deliver a message to Mr. Gibbs when you see him? Please tell him that I enjoyed his performance so much when you were here together, I went and bought those vibes that he played on." That guy had to be either a complete idiot or he was in love with me.

Sometimes when Buddy and I were booked in Europe together, we wouldn't see each other until we got to the stage where we were performing. I live in Los Angeles and he lives in Florida so we get to Europe at different times. We met on stage in Germany for the Berlin Jazz Festival. When Buddy walked towards me, he looked strange. We hugged when we saw each other, but his face looked weird. He said, "Is there anything wrong with my face? It feels like I have a bump in my jaw." What bump? It looked like somebody added another face to his face. I didn't want to panic him, because at that time, cancer was starting to get to a lot of people and that's the first thing that came to my mind. I don't know how he played the concert, but he did and sounded very good. When he got home and took all kinds of tests, he found out he was allergic to a lot of different foods, including wheat, and he had to stay away from pasta for a few years. Can you imagine telling an Italian not to eat pasta? That's like telling Buddy not to play the clarinet for a year.

My Dream Band CDs were now out and doing very well and I wanted to record with Buddy because Palo Alto Records had gone out of business. We needed CDs out so we could get some work. I talked with Dick Bock, who helped me produce the Dream Band albums and thought we'd do another live date. We got a booking in Chicago at Joe Segal's Jazz Showcase. We were there for six days. Even though Buddy and I were co-leaders, he let me run the show.

We talked about songs we were going to record and then I wrote little arrangements for them. Buddy is a good arranger but he let me do them anyway. Plus, he liked the original songs that I wrote. I didn't want to just go in and jam, so after writing the melodies out with the little syncopations, I would always write interludes between the choruses. For the first three days we were at the Jazz Showcase, we played the songs that we were going to record. It was sort of a rehearsal, so that when we recorded the next three days, we wouldn't have to have our noses in the music.

Buddy was starting to remind me more and more of Benny Goodman. He was really into the clarinet and practiced every day. The clarinet was his life. Also like Benny, he was getting a little foggy. During those first three days, he kept forgetting the interlude that I wrote on

Horace Silver's song, "Sister Sadie." So I said to him, "After you finish playing your choruses, you have to play the interlude with me, because if I come in alone, it will sound like a mistake. I have an idea. I almost know when you're through with your choruses, so I'll lean over my vibes and to get your attention, I'll wave my right hand, and that will give you the cue for the interlude." He said, "Great. Wave your hand and that will remind me to come in with the interlude."

The next day, we started to record. We were playing "Sister Sadie" and when I figured that Buddy was about to finish playing, I leaned over my vibes and waved my right hand to cue him for the interlude. He saw me waving, stopped playing, got a bewildered look on his face, and said, "What do you want?" That broke up the band. He eventually got it all straightened out and the date came out great.

The band was getting tighter every night. We just finished playing "Fifty-Second Street Theme," the song that Bird and Diz closed their sets with, and we played it real fast. Neil Tesser, who wrote for one of the Chicago papers, was in the club to review us. When I walked by him to go to the dressing room, he stopped me and said, "When Buddy was playing his choruses on 'Fifty-Second Street Theme,' he played so good that when you had to follow him, I felt sorry for you. Then when you got into it, I felt sorry for John Campbell, who had to follow YOU."

I also took care of the business for Buddy and me, for Buddy was, without a doubt, the worst businessman I ever met. The reason I say this is because of a story he told me. He was at home when he got a call from a club owner in Montreal asking him if he was available to play his club on a certain date. Buddy, who can't remember where he is half the time, looked at his schedule and told the club owner that he was available. Then the club owner casually said to Buddy, "I heard that you played in Toronto last week. How did it go?" Buddy, who is the nicest and most honest man I ever met, said, "I bombed. Nobody came into the club to see me." The club owner immediately hung up on him. Never said another word. When Buddy told me this, I said, "Why did you tell him you bombed?" He said, "I DID bomb." I asked, "Didn't the audience like you?" He said, "Yes, they gave me a standing ovation." I said, "Why didn't you tell him that they loved you and gave you a standing ovation instead of telling him that you bombed?" That's Buddy being a little too honest for his own good. If anybody calls him and asks him if he and I are available, he always says, "Call Terry."

A few years later, we played Ronnie Scott's again. On our day off we had to fly to Edinburgh, Scotland, to do a TV show that Ronnie had arranged for us. Our wives were with us at the time. After the TV show, the producers took us to dinner at the Grand Hotel, one of the fanciest places in Edinburgh. A lot of people who saw the show were there and they applauded for us when we walked in. I think we had four different waiters serving us. We all ordered food and some wine.

For some reason I always thought it was phony when they brought you a bottle of wine, put some in a glass for you to taste, and then you would give them your opinion. Most people don't know a good wine from a bad wine. I always wanted to do this stupid thing but never had the nerve to do it. The waiter brought the wine to our table, poured a little in a glass, and handed it to me.

The only wines that I know the taste of are Manischewitz and Rokeach, two kosher wines that you drink on Passover. They're both so sweet that they can make you sick.

I took the glass of wine, shook it around a little (that's because I've seen people who think they're connoisseurs do it), took a sip, and for no reason whatsoever, went "Ecchh," and spit it out like it tasted terrible. Needless to say that even though Buddy and his wife broke up, Rebekah didn't talk to me the rest of the night.

We were called to do a tribute to Benny Goodman in Arvado, Colorado, and for that show, we had Louie Bellson on drums, Tal Farlow on guitar, plus a pianist and bass player from Denver, Colorado. Buddy and I always tried to stay away from doing tributes to Benny because we were starting to be compared to Benny and Lionel and wanted our own identity.

At first we were very negative about the idea, but the money was good and they told us there would be two parts to the show. Besides the Benny Goodman tribute, the second half would be a tribute to Duke Ellington because Louie Bellson played with Duke. We figured that was okay because we played a lot of Ellington songs and there was no other connection there.

It turned out to be so successful that now we were getting calls to do another tribute to Benny. Once again the money was good. All we had to do was play songs that Benny made famous and play bebop choruses on them. We were already playing "Air Mail Special," which was a big hit for Benny. An agent by the name of Bob Davis booked us to do a Benny Goodman tribute at a club in Berkeley, California, called Kimball's. He wanted to make it an all-star band and he added Herb Ellis on guitar, Butch Miles on drums, Milt Hinton on bass, and Larry Novak on piano. He also put together a tour to Japan to go with that job. I got Ralph Kaffel, the president of Fantasy Records, to let me produce a live album while we were at Kimball's. I picked all the songs and did the same routine that we did on our first album, "Chicago Fire." We played for three nights, worked out little head arrangements, and then recorded the next three nights. The people went nuts, because the Benny Goodman sound is a very exciting thing. We even used a lot of the routines that Benny did by jamming for two or three choruses on the end of each song to give it added excitement.

Butch Miles was the perfect drummer for that kind of a groove. Not only did we break up the audience, but we also packed the club every night. I think they set a record for the amount of dinners they served.

We left for Japan the day after we closed at Kimball's. I was going to mix and master the record when I got back. I was sort of the leader of the group and the guys in the band looked to me for leadership. When we recorded, being that I produced the album, I called all the shots. I tried to make each night a different concert so if Herbie played first on "Don't Be That Way" on Thursday, after we played the melody on that same song on Friday, I may have called on Buddy to play first. I called a lot of audibles on stage while we were playing. When you do that, it makes it hard to edit. You can't pick a chorus from a take on Friday and put it into a Saturday performance. To start with, the sound would be different in the club and also, the tempo would be different.

All I could do besides work with the engineer in mixing the album was to pick the best takes. As a producer, you can't pick the take that you played best on, even though there is a tendency to want to do that. You can't think as a performer; you have to put your producer's hat on. So I picked the takes that had the best group feel. After we made that long trip and arrived in Japan, everybody went to sleep except me.

The contract the Tom Cassidy Agency made with the Japanese promoter said that one quarter of the money would be sent to him a few months before the signing of the contract. When I got there, I had to pick up 20,000 dollars. I was really wiped out but I sat down with the promoter who gave me 20,000 dollars in American one-hundred-dollar bills. Even though they were packed in 1,000 dollar wrappers, I had to count it out in front of the man I was dealing with. That wasn't the hardest part of what I had to do. I didn't want to walk around with 20,000 dollars in cash, so I made packages and gave each musician part of their salary for the ten-day tour. Buddy, Herbie, and I made the same amount of money, so I gave most of the money to the three sidemen. I was so tired that after counting out everybody's money, I found that I was short a hundred dollars in one of the packages. Luckily, when I started to count each package again, I found out that I had miscounted the first one or I never would have gone to sleep.

I had been in Japan before with Steve Allen but never with a jazz group. The audience kind of scared me at the first concert. After we played the first chorus of "Seven Come Eleven," I came in and played the first bunch of choruses. When I finished and Buddy came in, nobody applauded for me. People usually applaud for the soloists after they play their solos. I thought they didn't like how I played and felt like I just bombed. They didn't applaud for Buddy, Herb, or anybody in the band until the song was over. Then they really applauded. I found out that the Japanese people are so humble and polite that they think they are insulting you by making any noise while the band is playing. When they didn't applaud for Buddy after he finished, I selfishly felt good.

At the end of the concert, the audience demanded two encores. I didn't realize until I checked the contract the next day that it said, "two fifty-minute sets with a twenty-minute intermission and two encores on the end." I think that the Japanese people were used to getting two encores at the end of every show.

On one of the concerts, after our two encores, I was already downstairs in the dressing room and had my tuxedo jacket and shirt off, both of them very wet with sweat. The Japanese people bang their feet on the ground when they want you to play more and they were banging so hard, you could hear it downstairs in the dressing room. The promoter ran down and asked us to please get back on the stage and play another song. I had to put my funky wet shirt and tux jacket on again and we did another encore.

Since the concert was a tribute to Benny Goodman, Buddy, Herb, and I took turns at the mike talking about Benny. I told more stories about him being a foggy idiot than about his great clarinet playing so it seemed like I was putting him down. But I always closed by saying that it was the thrill of my life playing with him.

When Herb spoke, he really put Benny down because Charlie Christian was Herb's idol and he thought that Benny stole all of Charlie's songs by putting his name down on the records as co-writer. Herb really didn't like Benny Goodman. Sometimes he would put Benny down for five minutes but he always ended by saying, "But Benny was one swell guy."

When Buddy spoke, the first thing he said was, "Is this really a tribute to Benny Goodman?" Then he would defend Benny by telling the audience that in the days of the big bands, when the bandleader commissioned you to write an original song for the band, it was protocol for the bandleader to put his name on the song as co-writer. But Herb never bought into that.

Amongst some of Buddy's *mishigasses*, he liked to buy luggage. I'm not exaggerating when I say that at one time, he had about thirty different pieces of luggage. Another *mishigass* is that he collected fake copies of famous watches. He once had about five different fake Rolexes that he bought for twenty-five dollars each. A strange thing happened to Buddy after one of the concerts. We played a private party and were in the band room. This Japanese guy was talking to Buddy and couldn't speak English too well. I was standing with Buddy while this guy was telling him, in very broken English, that he liked playing clarinet and that Buddy was his favorite clarinet player. He was so in awe of Buddy and was really nervous just being around him.

All of a sudden he said, "You're so good, I've got to give you something," took his watch off his hand, and gave it to Buddy. Buddy looked embarrassed and tried to give it back to him, but the guy kept insisting that it was a gift from him to Buddy. As he handed it to him, Buddy didn't even look at it. I took it out of Buddy's hand and walked over to Larry Novak and showed it to him. Neither of us could believe what kind of watch it was. Buddy also had a bunch of fake Patek Phillipe watches, but this one looked like a real one. When Buddy finished talking with that nice man, I showed Buddy the watch and he actually turned purple. It WAS a real one. The nice gentleman came to another concert the next night and brought the case for that watch to Buddy. We later found out that he was a multi-millionaire ship builder. When we got back to the States, Buddy had the watch appraised and was told that it was worth 10,000 dollars. Buddy hardly ever wears it. He's afraid he'll lose it so he wears the fake one most of the time. We had a very successful engagement in Japan and when we got back to the United States, we all went our separate ways. Japan was a ball.

I went back to Berkeley to mix the tapes from the date. The songs we mixed all seemed to be winners so we did the same thing that we did on the first album that Buddy and I did for Palo Alto. Ralph Kaffel and I couldn't figure out which were the best songs, so Ralph suggested that we put out two CDs and release them six months apart. Then he would pay everybody for two record dates.

The two CDs were called "Memories of You" and "The Kings of Swing." Buddy and I liked the name "The Kings of Swing" so every time we did a tribute to Benny Goodman, that's what we called ourselves. That's the second time that Ralph Kaffel put a name on one of my bands. He also came up with the name "The Dream Band."

Buddy and I continue to try and play together any time we are called. Unfortunately, we don't have an agent, so we haven't been playing together as often as we would like to. I think that besides my Dream Band, the most exciting and fun thing for me is playing with Buddy. We have been playing on and off as co-leaders for better than twenty years and have never come close to having an argument. I don't care who you are, when you get two people together, sometimes one person's ego can get in the way, or one of the wives can say something to her husband that can cause an argument. Our wives get along great and really like each other.

Buddy and I have become like brothers. I've been very fortunate to have worked with two of the greatest clarinet players that ever lived. In the thirties and forties, Benny Goodman and Artie Shaw were way ahead of all the other clarinet players. Everyone that played the clarinet either copied Benny or Artie. Then Buddy came along in the fifties and was the inspiration for practically every clarinet player since then, including Eddie Daniels, who came out of the Buddy DeFranco school, and who has now found his own voice. I was lucky to have played with both Benny and Buddy. They both were great instrumentalists and boy, could they swing.

Chapter 22
Goodbye for Now

It seems that when you get to a certain age, everybody starts to bestow all kinds of honors on you. I'm now called a living legend, even though I may have played better when I was younger.

In 1997 I had two honors bestowed on me. A young gentleman named Mal Sands, who worked for the Gas Company and is a big fan of the vibes, puts on a show called a *Vibes Summit* and honors a different vibes player every year. He rented the Ash Grove, a nightclub in Santa Monica, California, and invited about thirty vibes players from all over the country. Then, at the end, he introduced me and I played a solo and thanked Mal and all the other vibes players. Mal is not a rich man but he makes sure that there is never a cover charge, so the place would always be packed. After I finished playing, I was surprised because Steve Allen showed up and we finished the night off with he and I playing a vibes duet. They presented me with a plaque which was a great honor.

A few months later, the L.A. Jazz Society and the City of Los Angeles paid tribute to me by making me the main honoree among a group of talented musicians. Also honored were Joe Williams, Charlie Haden, Van Alexander, and Snooky Young. The City of Los Angeles also designated a "Terry Gibbs Day," which knocked me out more than anything. The thing about that award was that even though all the other musicians who were honored were very talented, just being the main honoree at the same time as Joe Williams was enough for me. My three favorite male singers of all time are Frank Sinatra, Nat Cole, and Joe Williams.

When I turned seventy-five years old on October 13, 1999, my son Gerry threw me a sit-down dinner party at the Ventura Club in

Sherman Oaks, near where I live. Everybody that came had to pay thirty-five dollars for dinner. The place held about 280 people but over 300 showed up. After the Dream Band played, with Larry Bunker and Emil Richards on vibes, I had to make my speech. I thanked everybody for coming and mentioned that if I played a free concert, this many people wouldn't show up to come see me. Steve Allen flew in from wherever he was to emcee the show and then flew back that night.

I don't know how my son arranged it, but he got Regis Philbin to do a video clip wishing me a happy birthday. This was the time when Regis was not only doing his regular morning show, but he was also the hottest thing on TV with his *Who Wants to be a Millionaire?* game show. Among the people who came to the party were Bill Holman, Horace Silver, Bill Henderson, Leonard Maltin, Lou Brown (Jerry Lewis' conductor), Gerald Wilson, Frank DeVito, Neal Hefti, Stan Levey, Howard Rumsey, Lou Levy, all the members of the Dream Band, and last but not least, the immortal Niles Lishness.

In 2000, the Percussive Arts Society inducted me into their Hall of Fame. The PAS, as it is known, has thousands of members all over the world and that award meant more to me than any other because it came from my peers. I think that I was the seventy-seventh musician inducted into the Hall of Fame in all the years they've been in existence. Three-quarters of the musicians in the Hall of Fame are symphony players and most of the jazz musicians are drummers. Besides me, Lionel Hampton, Red Norvo, Milt Jackson, and Gary Burton are the only vibes players in the PAS Hall of Fame.

When I was presented with my plaque at the banquet, I had to make a speech and I was a little nervous and didn't know how to get into it. The other inductees had their speeches already written and I couldn't do that so I just ad-libbed mine.

Three years before I was honored I was asked to play as a guest with the Navy Band at the Percussive Arts Society Convention at the Disneyland Hotel in Los Angeles. I must be honest: I had never heard of the PAS before and I never knew anything about the organization.

I rehearsed with the Navy Band for a program in which they would open the show and play for the first twenty minutes. Then I would close the show by playing the next forty minutes. The Navy Band was great and at the rehearsal they played the heck out of my music. One of the reasons was that every one of them was a big fan of the Dream Band and they were knocked out just getting a chance to play some of those arrangements. When it came show time, the Navy Band got carried away and played about forty-five minutes of high powered music and I had to follow them playing MORE high powered music.

I learned something from Steve Allen. He once told me that the best way to follow music with music was when you're first introduced, talk to the audience and let them rest their ears for about three to five minutes. I usually do that when I'm first introduced anyhow. When I follow another act, instead of going right into the music, I always use one of Steve's lines: "Are you enjoying the show?" Everybody usually applauds and then I say, "Well, I'll put a stop to that." I intended to do that but I thought that I would thank the Percussive Arts Society or PAS, as it was called, for inviting me to appear at their convention. Being unfamiliar with the organization, I started out and said, "I'd like to thank the PSA for inviting me to their convention" and before I had a chance to say the line that I stole from Steve Allen, everybody started to laugh. I didn't know why, so I said, "What's so funny?" Somebody in the audience yelled out, "PSA is a PROSTATE TEST!" Thank God for my fast brain. I said, "I'm sorry. I'm at the wrong convention," and walked off the stage. Of course, I came back and played my show. The people at the Hall of Fame dinner liked that story and it made it easy for me to thank everybody without being nervous about the whole affair. It really was an honor.

In 1994 we had an earthquake in Southern California and we were hit pretty hard. We had to move out of our house and rent another house for eight months. All of our belongings got all mixed up and had to be put in completely different places. When we moved back into the house, once again our belongings were put in different places in the house. About a year-and-a-half ago, I was rummaging through the top of my closet and found about twenty-eight reels of tape. In looking through them, the backs of some of the boxes said, "Seville/Sundown, 1959." I had my friend Rod Nicas take those tapes home and burn them onto CDs for me. When he brought them back, I found that they had unreleased tapes from the Dream Band on them. There were also different takes of some of the songs that we stretched out in the club where the soloists got a chance to play more. I then had Rod put together a CD for me. One plus was the great singer, Irene Kral, who died tragically at a very early age from cancer, sat in with the band on three songs.

I sent the CD up to Fantasy Records and Ralph Kaffel, Fantasy's president, immediately bought it. In July 2002, volume 6 of the Dream Band tapes, called "One More Time," came out. As I write this, it is getting all kinds of airplay in California. This will definitely be the last recording of the original Dream Band and there's no better way to go out than to swing that hard.

As I look back at my life, I've been very lucky and had a great time. I'm not through living yet. In fact, my next autobiography will start when I'm eighty years old and I intend to have as much fun as I had the first eighty years.

I'll say goodbye for now by quoting two clichés. One is familiar and the second I'll improvise on a little. I'm allowed to, because I am a jazz musician.

Even though we know that into each life a little rain must fall, all in all, I've been very fortunate for I've been able to laugh all the way to the bandstand.

Terry Gibbs Discography

This section contains a chronological listing, by recording date, of all of Terry Gibbs' most significant commercial recordings to date as a leader, co-leader, or major musician in an ensemble.

It is not the intent of this discography to itemize every label under which each of the recordings has been issued. In many cases, a variety of reissues on LP and CD were released. As a result, we are identifying only the original label these sessions were released on. In the interest of space, record catalog numbers and broadcast airchecks are also not included. Fortunately, most of Terry's work has been and continues to be made available in modern CD format.

Note: All single recordings (1946-53) are listed under the artist's name. Recordings made for Brunswick between 1952 and 1954 were issued alternately on 45, 78, 10" LP and 12" LP. All albums beginning with Terry's first 12" LP issue ("Terry" on Brunswick) list the major artist and album title directly beneath that.

Discography compiled by Cary Ginell and Rod Nicas with Terry Gibbs.

Aaron Sachs' Manor Re-Bops (Manor),
New York City; June 8, 1946
    Aaron Sachs (clarinet), Terry Gibbs (vibraphone), Gene DiNovi (piano), Clyde Lombardi (bass), Tiny Kahn (drums).
        Aaron's Axe, Tiny's Con, Sam Beeps and Bops, Patsy's Idea

Allen Eager & the Be Bop Boys (Savoy)
New York City; July 15, 1947
    Allen Eager (tenor saxophone), Terry Gibbs (vibraphone), Duke Jordan (piano), Curley Russell (bass), Max Roach (drums).
        All Night - All Frantic, Donald Jay, Meeskite, And That's for Sure

Chubby Jackson and His Fifth Dimensional Jazz Group (Cupol) (Sweden)
Stockholm, Sweden; December 20, 1947
    Chubby Jackson (bass), Terry Gibbs (vibraphone), Conte Candoli (trumpet), Frank Socolow (tenor saxophone), Lou Levy (piano), Denzil Best (drums).
    Lemon Drop, Crying Sands, Begin the Beguine, Crown Pilots
Same location; January 20, 1948
    Boomsie, Dee Dee's Dance

Woody Herman & His Orchestra (Capitol)
Hollywood; December 29, 1948
    Woody Herman (clarinet, alto sax, vocal); Ernie Royal, Bernie Glow, Stan Fishelson, Red Rodney, Shorty Rogers (trumpets); Earl Swope, Bill Harris, Ollie Wilson (trombones); Bob Swift (bass trombone); Sam Marowitz (alto sax); Al Cohn, Zoot Sims, Stan Getz (tenor saxes); Serge Chaloff (baritone sax); Lou Levy (piano); Chubby Jackson (bass); Terry Gibbs (vibraphone, lead vocal on "Lemon Drop"); Don Lamond (drums); Mary Ann McCall (vocals). Arrangements by Shorty Rogers, Ralph Burns, Johnny Mandel, Neal Hefti, Al Cohn. Harmony vocal on "Lemon Drop" by Shorty Rogers and Chubby Jackson.
    That's Right, Lemon Drop
Same location & personnel; December 30, 1948
    I Ain't Gonna Wait Too Long (logs list as I Ain't Getting Any Younger), Early Autumn, Keeper of the Flame.
Chicago; May 26, 1949
    Woody Herman (clarinet, alto sax, vocal); Ernie Royal, Al Porcino, Stan Fishelson, Charlie Walp, Shorty Rogers (trumpets); Earl Swope, Bill Harris, Ollie Wilson (trombones); Bart Varsalona (bass trombone); Sam Marowitz (alto sax); Gene Ammons, Buddy Savitt, Jimmy Giuffre (tenor saxes); Serge Chaloff (baritone sax); Lou Levy (piano); Oscar Pettiford (bass); Terry Gibbs (vibraphone); Shelly Manne (drums); Mary Ann McCall (vocals).
    The Crickets, More Moon
Hollywood; July 14, 1949
Same personnel except Joe Mondragon replaces Pettiford (bass)
    Jamaica Rhumba
Same location and personnel; July 20, 1949
    Lollypop
Same location and personnel; July 21, 1949
    Rhapsody in Wood, The Great Lie

Serge Chaloff & the Herdsmen (Futurama)
New York City; March 10, 1949

Serge Chaloff (baritone sax), Terry Gibbs (vibraphone), Al Cohn (tenor sax), Red Rodney (trumpet), Earl Swope (trombone), Barbara Carroll (piano), Oscar Pettiford (bass), Denzil Best (drums).

Chickasaw, Bop Scotch, The Most, Chasin' the Bass

Terry Gibbs' New Jazz Pirates (New Jazz)
New York City; March 14, 1949

Terry Gibbs (vibraphone), Shorty Rogers (trumpet), Earl Swope (trombone), Stan Getz (tenor sax), George Wallington (piano), Curly Russell (bass), Shadow Wilson (drums).

Michelle, T and S, Terry's Tune, Cuddles, Speedway

Benny Goodman & His Sextet (Columbia)
New York City; October 10, 1950

Benny Goodman (clarinet), Terry Gibbs (vibraphone), Teddy Wilson (piano), Johnny Smith (guitar), Bob Carter (bass), Terry Snyder (drums), Nancy Reed & Jimmy Ricks (vocals).

Oh Babe, You're Gonna Lose Your Gal, Walkin' with the Blues

New York City; November 24, 1950

Charlie Smith replaces Snyder; Ricks out.

Lullaby of the Leaves, Then You've Never Been Blue, Walkin', Temptation Rag

The Metronome All-Stars (Capitol)
New York City; January 24, 1951

Miles Davis (trumpet), Kai Winding (trombone), John LaPorta (clarinet), Lee Konitz (alto sax), Stan Getz (tenor sax), Serge Chaloff (baritone sax), George Shearing (piano, arranger*), Billy Bauer (guitar), Eddie Safranski (bass), Max Roach (drums), Terry Gibbs (vibraphone), Ralph Burns (arranger)**.

*Early Spring**, Local 802 Blues**

Benny Goodman & His Sextet (Columbia)
New York City; June 13, 1951

Benny Goodman (clarinet), Terry Gibbs (vibraphone), Paul Smith (piano), Johnny Smith (guitar), Eddie Safranski (bass), Sid Bulkin (drums), Nancy Reed (vocals).

Farewell Blues, Toodle-Lee-Yoo-Doo, By the Fireside, Who?

Terry Gibbs Sextet (Savoy)
New York City; August 28, 1951

Terry Gibbs (vibraphone), Hal McKusick (clarinet), Harry Biss (piano), Sal Salvador (guitar), Jimmy Johnson (bass), Sid Bulkin (drums).
Swing's the Thing, Begin the Beguine, Serenade in Blue, I've Got You Under My Skin

Terry Gibbs & His Orchestra (Brunswick)
New York City (Pythian Temple); July 11, 1952
Terry Gibbs (vibraphone), Howard McGhee (trumpet), Kai Winding (trombone), Don Elliott (vibraphone & mellophone), Horace Silver (piano), Chuck Wayne (guitar), George Duvivier (bass), Sid Bulkin (drums).
T And S, You Don't Know What Love Is
Same location & date; Billy Taylor replaces Silver
Flying Home

(The New) Benny Goodman Sextet (Columbia)
New York City; July 29, 1952
Benny Goodman (clarinet), Terry Gibbs (vibraphone), Teddy Wilson (piano), Mundell Lowe (guitar), Sid Weiss (bass), Terry Snyder (drums).
I've Got a Feeling I'm Falling, Bye Bye Blues, I'll Never Be the Same, Between the Devil & the Deep Blue Sea
New York City; July 30, 1952
Same location & personnel, except Don Lamond replaces Snyder
Under a Blanket of Blue, East of the Sun (and West of the Moon), Four or Five Times, How Am I to Know?, Undecided
New York City; October 22, 1952
Benny Goodman (clarinet), Terry Gibbs (vibraphone), Lou Stein (piano), Allen Hanlon (guitar), Eddie Safranski (bass), Don Lamond (drums).
East of the Sun (and West of the Moon), Four or Five Times

Terry Gibbs All Stars (Marshmallow) (Japan)
New York City (Birdland); October 6 & 13, 1952
Terry Gibbs (vibraphone), Fats Ford (trumpet), Don Elliott (mellophone), Allen Eager (tenor sax), Phil Urso (tenor sax), Harry Biss (piano), Gene Ramey (bass), Sid Bulkin (drums).
Jumpin' with Symphony Sid (Theme), Perdido, Tiny's Blues, Now's the Time, What's New, Perdido

Terry Gibbs & His Sextet (Brunswick)
New York City (The Bandbox); March 16 & 22, 1953
Terry Gibbs (vibraphone), Don Elliott (mellophone, vibraphone),

Claude Noel (piano), Kenny O'Brien (bass), Sid Bulkin (drums).
Out Of Nowhere, What's New, Now's the Time, Bernie's Tune

Milt Buckner Trio (Brunswick)
New York City; March 22, 1953
Milt Buckner (organ), Terry Gibbs (vibraphone), Bernie Mackey (guitar), Cornelius Thomas (drums).
Trapped

Terry Gibbs Orchestra (Brunswick)
New York City; April 8, 1953
Terry Gibbs (vibraphone), Al Porcino (trumpet), Johnny Mandel (bass trumpet), Don Elliott (mellophone & vocal with Gibbs*), Al Epstein (tenor & baritone sax), Claude Noel (piano), Turk Van Lake (guitar), Kenny O'Brien (bass), Sid Bulkin (drums).
Cheerful Little Earful, I May Be Wrong, Swingin' the Robert A.G. Lollypop*

Terry Gibbs Sextet (Brunswick)
New York City (Pythian Temple); April 13, 1953
Terry Gibbs (vibraphone, vocal), Don Elliott (mellophone, vibraphone, vocal**), Al Epstein (tenor sax*), Ray Abrams (tenor sax**), Claude Noel (piano), Kenny O'Brien (bass), Sid Bulkin (drums).
Trotting*, Bernie's Tune**, De Arango**, Lemon Drop**

Terry Gibbs Quintet (Brunswick)
Fort Monmouth, NJ; May 27, 1953
Terry Gibbs (vibraphone), Don Elliott (mellophone, vibraphone), Claude Noel (piano), Kenny O'Brien (bass), Sid Bulkin (drums), Jackie Paris* (vocal).
Perdido, These Foolish Things, Don't Blame Me, Cool Blues*, You Go to My Head*

Billy Eckstine with the Metronome All-Stars (MGM)
New York City; July 9, 1953
Billy Eckstine (vocal), Roy Eldridge (trumpet), Kai Winding (trombone), John LaPorta (clarinet), Lester Young, Warne Marsh (tenor saxes), Teddy Wilson (piano), Billy Bauer (guitar), Eddie Safranski (bass), Max Roach (drums), Terry Gibbs (vibraphone).
How High the Moon (part 1 & 2), St. Louis Blues (part 1 & 2)

Terry Gibbs Quartet (Brunswick)
New York City, September 8-9, 1953

Terry Gibbs (vibraphone), Terry Pollard (piano), Kenny O'Brien (bass), Chick Keeny [Louis Ciccone] (drums), Jackie Paris (vocal*).

Wednesday at Two, I Found a New Baby, Tea for Two, Exactly Like You, Blue Moon, My Friend Tiny, Terry's Blues, Vernerdi, That Feller McKeller, Fabulous Figs**

Terry Gibbs Quartet and Orchestra (Brunswick)
"Terry"
New York City; April 2, 1954

Terry Gibbs (vibraphone), Claude Noel (piano), Kenny O'Brien (bass), Sid Bulkin (drums), [Remaining musicians for this date probably similar to April 8, 1953 session: Al Porcino (trumpet), Johnny Mandel (bass trumpet), Don Elliott (mellophone), Al Epstein (baritone sax), Turk Van Lake (guitar),]

Where Are You?, That Feeling, Love Is Just Around the Corner

New York City; September 7, 1954

Terry Gibbs (vibraphone), Terry Pollard (piano), Kenny O'Brien (bass), Chick Keeny (drums)

Temporary, Tremendez, Old Man Newman, What Ho?, Fatty, Baby Doll, Peaches, Jazzbo Mambo, Trotting

Terry Gibbs Quartet (EmArcy)
"Terry Gibbs"
New York City; September 14, 1955

Terry Gibbs (vibraphone), Terry Pollard (piano), Herman Wright (bass), Nils-Bertil Dahlander ("Bert Dale") (drums).

King City Stomp, Pretty Face, Nutty Notes, Soupy's On, The Continental, Lonely Dreams, Dickie's Dream, Seven Come Eleven, Bless My Soles, Imagination

Terry Gibbs (EmArcy)
"Vibes on Velvet"
New York City, October 19, 1955

Terry Gibbs (vibraphone), Sam Marowitz (alto sax), Hal McKusick (alto and soprano sax), Ray Black (tenor sax), Frank Socolow (tenor sax), Al Epstein (baritone sax), Terry Pollard (piano), Turk Van Lake (guitar), Herman Wright (bass), Jerry Segal (drums), Manny Albam (arranger, conductor).

Autumn Nocturne, Lonesome Streets, Boulevard of Broken Dreams, Lullabye of Swing, For You, for Me, for Evermore, Mood Indigo

New York City, October 31, 1955

Smoke Gets in Your Eyes, The Moon Was Yellow, Leaving Town, It Might as Well Be Spring, Adios, Two Sparkling Eyes

Terry Gibbs Quartet (EmArcy)
"Mallets-A-Plenty"
New York City, June 15, 1956
> Terry Gibbs (vibraphone), Terry Pollard (piano), Herman Wright (bass), Jerry Segal (drums).
>> *Soupy's On* [recorded at September 14, 1955 session with Nils-Bertil Dahlander (drums)], *Then It Happens, Haunted, Gibberish, Er-Bee-I, I'll Remember April, Nothing to It, Mean to Me*

Terry Gibbs and His Orchestra (EmArcy)
"Swingin' with Terry Gibbs & His Orchestra"
New York, October 1, 1956
> Terry Gibbs (vibraphone); Bernie Glow, Al DeRisi, Ernie Royal, Nick Travis (trumpets); Don Elliott (mellophone); Bob Brookmeyer (valve trombone); Urbie Green, Tommy Mitchell, Chauncey Welsh (trombones); Sam Marowitz, Hal McKusick (alto saxes); Al Cohn, Frank Socolow (tenor saxes); Al Epstein (baritone sax); Terry Pollard (piano); Turk Van Lake (guitar); Herman Wright (bass); Jerry Segal (drums).
>> *Julie's Bugle, Let's Wail, Bewitched*

> Osie Johnson (drums) replaces Segal on remaining tunes.

New York, October 2, 1956
>> *Funky Serenade, Gubi, I Didn't Know About You, Slittin' Sam (The Saychett Man)*

New York, October 8, 1956
>> *Just Plain Meyer, Night Cap, Happiness Is a Thing Called Joe, Heads or Tails*

"Harry Babasin & the Jazz Pickers" (Mode)
Los Angeles; July 1957
> Terry Gibbs (vibraphone), Harry Babasin (cello), Dempsey Wright (guitar), Ben Tucker (bass), Bill Douglass (drums).
>> *Thou Swell, Wingo, Basin Street Blues, Pee Wee, De Ge, Hoppy, These Foolish Things, On Bear Hill*

Terry Gibbs (Mode)
"A Jazzband Ball – Second Set"
Los Angeles; September 1957
> Terry Gibbs (vibraphone, marimba); Vic Feldman, Larry Bunker (vibraphone, xylophone); Lou Levy (piano); Max Bennett (bass); Mel Lewis (drums).
>> *Just Friends, The Dipsy Doodle, Memories of You, Where or When, Broadway, I'm Getting Sentimental over You, Hollywood Blues, Tangerine, Softly as in a Morning Sunrise, Allen's Alley*

The Ex-Hermanites (Mode); **Terry Gibbs & Bill Harris** (Premiere)
Los Angeles, September 1957
> Terry Gibbs (vibraphone), Bill Harris (trombone), Lou Levy (piano), Red Mitchell (bass), Stan Levey (drums).
>> *Apple Honey, Everywhere, Your Father's Moustache, Laura, Woodchopper's Ball, Lemon Drop, Early Autumn, Blue Flame*

Terry Gibbs Quartet (EmArcy)
"Terry Gibbs Plays The Duke"
Los Angeles; December 4, 1957
> Terry Gibbs (vibraphone, xylophone, marimba), Pete Jolly (accordion), Leroy Vinnegar (bass), Gary Frommer (drums).
>> *Rockin' in Rhythm, I Let a Song Go Out of My Heart, Sophisticated Lady, Do Nothin' Till You Hear from Me, Caravan, Take the "A" Train, Don't Get Around Much Anymore, Johnny Come Lately, C-Jam Blues, Solitude*

Terry Gibbs-Steve Allen-Gus Bivona (EmArcy)
Allen's All Stars – Terry Gibbs, Captain
Los Angeles; March 24, 1958
> Terry Gibbs (vibraphone), Steve Allen (piano), Gus Bivona (clarinet), Al Viola (guitar), Red Mitchell (bass), Frank DeVito (drums).
>> *Pasternak's Blues, Rose Room, Velvet Eyes, Snacks at Pasternak's, Yours Alone, Baby, But You Did*

Steve Allen (Roulette)
Steve Allen At The Roundtable
New York City; June 1958
> Steve Allen (piano), Terry Gibbs (vibraphone), Gus Bivona (clarinet), Doc Severinsen (trumpet*), Mundell Lowe (guitar), Gary Peacock (bass), Gary Frommer (drums).
>> *Roundtable Boogie, Why Don't You Want to Go Home, I Got Rhythm, Even Stephen, I Thought About You, Baby, But You Did**

Various Artists (EmArcy)
Newport '58: Washington, Gibbs, Roach
Newport Jazz Festival, Newport, Rhode Island; July 6, 1958
> Dinah Washington (vocal and vibraphone*), Don Elliott (mellophone & vibraphone**), Urbie Green (trombone), Wynton Kelly (piano), Paul West (bass), Max Roach (drums).
>> *All of Me *, Backstage Blues, Julie and Jake ***

Terry Gibbs (EmArcy)
"More Vibes on Velvet"
Los Angeles; November 1958
>   Terry Gibbs (vibraphone); Charlie Kennedy, Joe Maini (alto saxes); Med Flory, Bill Holman (tenor saxes); Jack Schwartz (baritone sax); Pete Jolly (piano); Max Bennett (bass); Mel Lewis (drums).
>   *Moonlight Serenade, Blues in the Night, With All My Love to You, Don't Cry, I Remember, Lazy Sunday, Impossible, What Is There to Say?, The Things We Did Last Summer, You Make Me Feel So Young, Every Day Is Spring with You, At Last*

Terry Gibbs & his Orchestra (Mercury)
"Launching a New Band"
Los Angeles; February 17, 1959
>   Terry Gibbs (vibraphone); Conte Candoli, Al Porcino, Ray Triscari, Stu Williamson (trumpets); Bob Enevoldsen, Vern Friley, Frank Rosolino (trombones); Charlie Kennedy, Joe Maini (alto saxes); Med Flory, Bill Holman (tenor saxes); Jack Schwartz (baritone sax); Pete Jolly (piano); Max Bennett (bass); Mel Lewis (drums).
>   *Moten Swing, Opus #1, Stardust, Cotton Tail, Begin the Beguine, Jumpin' at the Woodside, Midnight Sun, Flying Home*

Los Angeles; February 18, 1959
>   (Phil Gilbert [trumpet] and Joe Mondragon [bass] replace Ray Triscari and Max Bennett)
>   *Let's Dance, Prelude to a Kiss, I'm Gettin' Sentimental over You, Don't Be That Way*

Les Brown & His Band of Renown (Coral)
"Jazz Song Book"
Hollywood; March 1959
>   Les Brown (clarinet, alto sax); Al Porcino, Dick Collins, Wes Hensel, Jerry Kadowitz, Mickey McMahan (trumpets); Dick Kenney, Roy Main, Jim Hill, Stumpy Brown (trombones); Ralph LaPolla (alto sax); Matt Utal (alto sax, flute); Billy Usselton (tenor sax); Abe Aaron (tenor & baritone sax); Butch Stone (baritone sax); Donn Trenner (piano); Bob Burteaux (bass); Mel Lewis (drums); Terry Gibbs (vibraphone).
>   *The Claw, Apple Honey*

Terry Gibbs Dream Band (Contemporary)
"Dream Band" (Volume 1)
Los Angeles (Seville Club); March 17-19, 1959
>   Same personnel as *Launching a New Band* above, except Joe Cadena (trombone) subs for Frank Rosolino.

Begin the Beguine, Don't Be That Way, Cottontail, Stardust, Opus One, After You've Gone, You Go to My Head, Let's Dance, The Subtle Sermon (bonus track on CD), *Kissin' Bug, Jumpin' at the Woodside*

Terry Gibbs Big Band (Mercury)
(45 rpm single only)
Los Angeles, exact date unknown, probably July 1959.
Exact personnel unknown. Probably similar to *The Sundown Sessions (Volume 2) below.* Add Jackie Paris, vocal*
*The Claw, I Can Hardly Wait Till Saturday Night**

Terry Gibbs Dream Band (Contemporary)
"The Sundown Sessions" (Volume 2)
Los Angeles (Sundown Club); November, 1959
Terry Gibbs (vibraphone); John Audino, Conte Candoli, Frank Huggins, Stu Williamson (trumpets); Bobby Burgess, Vern Friley, Bill Smiley (trombones); Joe Maini, Charlie Kennedy (alto saxes); Bill Perkins, Med Flory (tenor saxes); Jack Schwartz (baritone sax); Lou Levy (piano); Buddy Clark (bass); Mel Lewis (drums).
The Song Is You, Moonglow, The Fat Man, It Could Happen to You, Back Bay Shuffle, Dancing in the Dark, Blue Lou (bonus track on CD), *Softly as in a Morning Sunrise, No Heat, My Reverie, The Claw*

Terry Gibbs Dream Band (Contemporary)
"Flying Home" (Volume 3)
Los Angeles (Seville, Sundown, and Summit Clubs)
Personnel at Sundown same as Terry Gibbs Dream Band – Volume 2: The Sundown Sessions except as noted below.
Seville (March 1959) - Personnel same as *Terry Gibbs Dream Band – Volume 1*:
Midnight Sun, Evil Eyes, I'm Getting Sentimental Over You, Flying Home, Moten Swing (bonus track on CD)
Sundown (November 1959) - Personnel same as *Terry Gibbs Dream Band – Volume 2: The Sundown Sessions* except as noted below:
Airegin, Just Plain Meyer, It Might as Well Be Swing, Bright Eyes, (Benny Aronov [piano] replaces Lou Levy)
Wonderful You (Lee Katzman [trumpet] replaces Frank Huggins)
Summit (January 1961) - Personnel same as *Terry Gibbs Dream Band – Volume 4: Main Stem* or *The Exciting Terry Gibbs Big Band – Recorded Live at the Summit*:
Avalon

Terry Gibbs Dream Band (Contemporary)
One More Time (Volume 6)
Los Angeles (Seville and Sundown Clubs)
Seville (March 1959):
> Personnel same as *Terry Gibbs Dream Band – [Volume 1]*
> *The Fuzz, Opus One, Smoke Gets in Your Eyes, Prelude to a Kiss, Just Plain Meyer, Jumpin' at the Woodside*

Sundown (November 1959):
> Terry Gibbs (vibraphone); John Audino, Conte Candoli, Lee Katzman, Stu Williamson (trumpets); Bobby Burgess, Vern Friley, Bill Smiley (trombones); Joe Maini, Charlie Kennedy (alto saxes); Bill Perkins, Med Flory (tenor saxes); Jack Schwartz (baritone sax); Lou Levy or Benny Aronov (piano); Buddy Clark (bass); Mel Lewis (drums); Irene Kral (vocals).
> *The Subtle Sermon, Flying Home, I Remember You, The Fat Man, Slittin' Sam (The Shaychet Man), Sometimes I'm Happy, Moonlight in Vermont, Lover, Come Back to Me*

Steve Allen & Terry Gibbs (Signature)
"Steve Allen Presents Terry Gibbs at the Piano"
Los Angeles, ca. 1960
> Terry Gibbs (piano), Donn Trenner (piano), Steve Allen (piano), Herb Ellis (guitar), Buddy Clark (bass), Jack Sperling (drums).
> *Stretchin' the Blues, You Go to My Head, Fickle Fingers, Things Ain't What They Used to Be, Cherokee, Country Boy, For Keeps, Easy Blues, Shufflin' Blues, Lover Man, The Way You Look Tonight, Airmail Special*

Terry Gibbs & His Big Band (Verve)
"Swing Is Here!"
Los Angeles, February 23, 1960
> Terry Gibbs (vibraphone); Al Porcino, Conte Candoli, Ray Triscari, Stu Williamson, John Audino (trumpets); Bob Enevoldsen, Bobby Pring, Frank Rosolino or Tommy Shepard (trombones); Joe Maini, Charlie Kennedy (alto saxes); Bill Perkins, Med Flory (tenor saxes); Jack Schwartz (baritone sax); Lou Levy (piano); Buddy Clark (bass); Mel Lewis (drums).
> *Evil Eyes, Moonglow, Back Bay Shuffle, The Fat Man, The Song Is You*

Los Angeles, February 24, 1960
> *Dancing in the Dark, Bright Eyes, It Might as Well Be Spring, Softly as in a Morning Sunrise, My Reverie*

Terry Gibbs & His Quintet (Verve)
"Music from Cole Porter's Can-Can"
Los Angeles, March 10, 1960
>Terry Gibbs (vibraphone), Frank Strazzeri (piano), Herb Ellis (guitar), Al McKibbon (bass), Frank Capp (drums).
>>*You Do Something to Me, I Love Paris, Can Can, Come Along with Me, It's All Right with Me, Montmart', C'est Magnifique, Let's Do It, Just One of Those Things, Live and Let Live*

The Exciting Terry Gibbs Big Band (Verve)
Recorded Live at the Summit in Hollywood - later released as **The Dream Band, Volume 4: Main Stem**
Los Angeles (Summit Club), January 20-22, 1961
>Terry Gibbs (vibraphone); Al Porcino, Ray Triscari, Conte Candoli, Stu Williamson, Frank Huggins (trumpets); Frank Rosolino, Vern Friley, Bob Edmondson (trombones); Joe Maini, Charlie Kennedy (alto saxes); Richie Kamuca, Bill Perkins (tenor saxes); Jack Nimitz (baritone sax); Pat Moran (piano); Buddy Clark (bass); Mel Lewis (drums).
>>*Day In, Day Out, Summit Blues, Limerick Waltz, You Don't Know What Love Is, Sweet Georgia Brown, Nose Cone, Too Close for Comfort, Main Stem, Ja-Da, T and S*

Terry Gibbs Quartet (Verve)
"That Swing Thing!"
Los Angeles (Shelly's Mannehole); April 5 and 8, 1961
>Terry Gibbs (vibraphone), Pat Moran (piano), Jimmy Bond (bass), Gary Frommer (drums).
>>*Let My People Blow, Moanin', Stella by Starlight, Three Blind Mice, Blue Wednesday, Mannehole March*

Terry Gibbs & His Exciting Big Band (Mercury)
"Explosion!" – later released as **The Dream Band, Volume 5, "The Big Cat"**
Los Angeles (Summit Club); ca. June, 1961
>Personnel same as *Terry Gibbs Dream Band – Volume 4: Main Stem*
>>*Tico Tico, Big Bad Bob, The Big Cat, Soft Eyes, Billie's Bounce, Pretty Blue Eyes, I'll Take Romance, Do You Wanna Jump, Children?, Nature Boy, Jump the Blues Away, Sleep*

Terry Gibbs Quartet (Verve)
"Straight Ahead"
Los Angeles, January 30, 1962
>Terry Gibbs (vibraphone), Pat Moran (piano, organ), John Doling

(bass), Mike Romero (drums).
> *On Green Dolphin Street, Memories of You, Hippie Twist, You Go to My Head*

Los Angeles, February 1, 1962
> Max Bennett (bass) replaces Doling
> *Hey Jim, For Keeps, C.C. Blues*

Terry Gibbs (Mercury)
"Terry Gibbs Plays Jewish Melodies in Jazztime"
New York, January 11-12, 1963
> Terry Gibbs (vibraphone, marimba), Alice McLeod (piano), Herman Wright (bass), Bobby Pike (drums), Sam Kutcher (trombone), Ray Musiker (clarinet), Alan Logan (piano), Sol Gaye (drums, marimba).
> *Bei Mir Bist Du Schön, Papirossen (Cigarettes), Kazochok (Russian Dance), Vuloch (A Folk Dance), My Yiddishe Momme, And the Angels Sing, S & S, Shaine Une Zees (Pretty & Sweet), Nyah Shere (New Dance)*

Terry Gibbs Quartet (Vogue) (France)
"The Family Album"
New York, February 19, 1963
> Terry Gibbs (vibraphone), Alice McLeod (piano), Ernie Farrow (bass), Steve Little (drums).
> *Button Up Your Lip, Up at Logue's Place, One for My Uncle, Ballad for Barbara, Sherry Bossa Nova, El Cheapo, Henny Time, Many Moons Ago, Better to Be Richie Than Poor, Sunny Girl, Sol Right with Me, Half Stuie*

Terry Gibbs (Limelight)
"El Nutto"
New York, April 15, 1963
> Terry Gibbs (vibraphone), Alice McLeod (piano), Herman Wright (bass), John Dentz (drums).
> *Hey Pretty, El Flippo, The Nightie Night Waltz, Sleepy Head Blues, The Young Ones, Little "S," El Nutto, Lonely Days, Just for Laughs, Little "C"*

Terry Gibbs (Time)
"Hootenanny My Way"
New York City; 1963
> Terry Gibbs (vibraphone), Al Epstein (tenor sax, conga), Alice McLeod (piano), Jimmy Raney (guitar), William Wood (bass), Al Belding (drums).

Joshua, John Henry, When Johnny Comes Marching Home, Michael, Polly Wolly Doodle All the Day, Tom Dooley, Greensleeves, Boll Weevil, Down by the Riverside, Sam Hall

Gibbs/Nistico/Pierce/Van Lake/Andrus/Hanna (Time)
also released as **It's Time We Met** (Mainstream)
New York City; 1963

Terry Gibbs (vibraphone), Sal Nistico (tenor sax), Nat Pierce (organ), Turk Van Lake (guitar), Charlie Andrus (bass), Jake Hanna (drums).

We Three, Bathtub Eyes, 7F, Settling Down Slow, The Tweaker, Baby Blues, Big Lips, No Chops, Movin' In

Terry Gibbs Quartet (Impulse)
"Take It from Me"
New York City; January 16, 1964

Terry Gibbs (vibraphone), Kenny Burrell (guitar), Sam Jones (bass), Louis Hayes (drums).

Take It from Me, El Fatso, Oge, Pauline's Place, 8 Lbs. 10 Ozs., Gee Dad, It's a Deagan, All the Things You Are, Honeysuckle Rose, Tippie (Released only on "The Definitive Jazz Scene – Volume 1")

Terry Gibbs (Roost)
"El Latino!"
New York City; 1964

Terry Gibbs (vibraphone), Jerome Richardson (flute), Walter Bishop Jr. (piano), Bobby Rodriquez (bass), Willie Bobo (percussion), Candido Camero (percussion), Carlos "Patato" Valdez (percussion).

Hallelujah I Love Her So, Our Day Will Come, I Love You and Don't You Forget It, Mr. Something Else, Serenata, El Reigo, What Kind of Fool Am I?, Days of Wine and Roses, Kick Those Feet, Tenderly, If Ever I Would Leave You, Happy Baby

Steve Allen and Terry Gibbs (Dot)
"Rhythm and Blues"
Los Angeles; 1965

Terry Gibbs (vibraphone), Steve Allen (piano), Don Rader (trumpet), Jim Horn (sax), Mike Melvoin (organ), Donald Peake (guitar), Larry Knechtel (bass guitar, harmonica), Hal Blaine (drums), Frank DeVito (percussion).

Song for My Father, Watermelon Man, Let Go Sloppy, Let Go, Cloudy Monday Blues, Soul Stuff, Boss Groove, Wama Lama Joogie Boogie Shuffle, Scat

Terry Gibbs (Dot)
"Terry Gibbs Plays Reza"
Los Angeles; March 30, 1966
> Terry Gibbs (vibraphone), Russ Freeman (piano), Mike Melvoin (organ), Donald Peake (guitar), Dennis Budimir (guitar), Lyle Ritz (bass), Hal Blaine (drums), Julius Wechter (percussion), plus others.
>> *Missouri Waltz, Autumn Leaves, Secret Agent Man, Norwegian Wood, Canadian Sunset, Sweet and Lovely, Star Dust, The Shadow of Your Smile, Reza, Soon, Ebb Tide, That Old Black Magic*

Terry Gibbs (Xanadu)
"Bopstacle Course"
New York City, July 10, 1974
> Terry Gibbs (vibraphone), Barry Harris (piano), Sam Jones (bass), Alan Dawson (drums).
>> *Bopstacle Course, Body and Soul, Waltz for My Children, Softly, as in a Morning Sunrise, Manha De Carnaval, Do You Mind?, Kathleen, I'm Getting Sentimental Over You*

The Terry Gibbs 4 (Jazz a la Carte)
"Live at the Lord"
Playa del Rey, California (Lord Chumley's); March 12, 1978
> Terry Gibbs (vibraphone), Marty Harris (piano), Harvey Newmark (bass), Frank Capp (drums).
>> *Samba Wazzoo, The Fat Man, What Are You Doing the Rest of Your Life?, The Shadow of Your Smile, Take the "A" Train, Mean to Me, Masquerade, Blues for the Lord*

Terry Gibbs and the Jazz A La Carte Players (Jazz a la Carte)
"Smoke Em Up!"
Playa del Rey, California (Lord Chumley's); July 30, 1978
> Terry Gibbs (vibraphone), Conte Candoli (trumpet), Bob Cooper (tenor sax), Lou Levy (piano), Bob Magnusson (bass), Jimmie Smith (drums).
>> *Townhouse 3, Those Eyes, Those Lips, That Nose, That Face, That Girl, Chant of Love, Blues for Brody, Smoke 'Em Up, The Austin Mood, Nina, 4 A.M.*

Terry Gibbs/Buddy DeFranco Quintet (Palo Alto Jazz)
"Jazz Party – First Time Together"
Sherman Oaks, California (Carmelo's), October 4-5, 1981
> Terry Gibbs (vibraphone), Buddy DeFranco (clarinet), Frank Collett (piano), Andy Simpkins (bass), Jimmie Smith (drums).
>> *Air Mail Special, Yesterdays, Body and Soul, Samba Wazzoo, Love*

for Sale, The Austin Mood, Prelude to a Kiss, Triste

"Now's the Time" (Tall Tree)
Same location, date, & personnel
> *Now's the Time, In a Mellow Tone, Blues for Brody, Autumn Leaves*, Out of Nowhere*, The Man I Love*, Lover Man*, Show Eyes**

All titles included on the Contemporary CD "Air Mail Special" except *

Terry Gibbs Quintet (Atlas)
"My Buddy"
Los Angeles; January 14-15, 1982
> Terry Gibbs (vibraphone), Lou Levy (piano), Al Viola (guitar), Andy Simpkins (bass), Jimmie Smith (drums).
>> *There Will Never Be Another You, Please Let Me Play the Blues, Misty, All of Me, My Buddy, Waltz for My Children, You'd Be So Nice To Come Home To*

Terry Gibbs (Contemporary)
"The Latin Connection"
Berkeley, California; May 9-10, 1986
> Terry Gibbs (vibraphone), Frank Morgan (alto sax), Sonny Bravo (piano), Bobby Rodriguez (bass), Tito Puente, Orestes Vilato (timbales), Johnny Rodriquez (bongo, percussion), Jose Madera (conga, percussion)
>> *Scrapple from the Apple, For Keeps, Groovin' High, Chelsea Bridge, Sing Sing Sing, Kick Those Feet, Good Bait, Flamingo, Sweet Young Song of Love*

Tito Puente (Concord Picante)
"Sensacion"
San Francisco, California; 1986
> Gibbs featured on vibraphone on two titles:
>> *Guajira for Cal, Jordu*

Terry Gibbs/Buddy DeFranco Quintet (Contemporary)
"Chicago Fire"
Chicago, Illinois (Jazz Showcase); July 24-26, 1987
> Terry Gibbs (vibraphone), Buddy DeFranco (clarinet), John Campbell (piano), Todd Coolman (bass), Gerry Gibbs (drums).
>> *Rockin' in Rhythm, Please Send Me Someone to Love, Sister Sadie This Is Always, Cherokee, Giant Steps, Bopstacle Course, Stella By Starlight, 52nd Street Theme, Jitterbug Waltz*

Buddy DeFranco & Terry Gibbs (Contemporary)
"Holiday For Swing"
Berkeley, California; August 22-23, 1988
    Terry Gibbs (vibraphone), Buddy DeFranco (clarinet), John Campbell (piano), Todd Coolman (bass), Gerry Gibbs (drums).
        Holiday for Strings, Serenade in Blue, Seven Come Eleven, Yardbird Suite, Carioca, When the Sun Comes Out, Parisian Thoroughfare, Chad's Bad, Fickle Fingers, Doxy (CD bonus track)

Terry Gibbs/Buddy DeFranco/Herb Ellis Sextet (Contemporary)
"Memories of You"
Emeryville, California (Kimball's East); April 13-15, 1991
    Terry Gibbs (vibraphone), Buddy DeFranco (clarinet), Larry Novak (piano), Herb Ellis (guitar), Milt Hinton (bass), Butch Miles (drums).
        Flying Home, Rose Room, I Surrender Dear, Dizzy Spells, Don't Be That Way, Poor Butterfly, Avalon, Memories of You, After You've Gone

"Kings of Swing"
Same location, date and personnel as "Memories of You"
        Seven Come Eleven, Soft Winds, The Man I Love, Undecided, Body and Soul, Just One of Those Things, Stompin' at the Savoy, These Foolish Things (Remind Me of You), Air Mail Special

Terry Gibbs Quartet (Chiaroscuro)
"Play That Song"
Caribbean Sea, Cafe "S/S Norway;" October 23, 24, 25 and 27, 1994
    Terry Gibbs (vibraphone), Uri Caine (piano), Boris Koslov (bass), Gerry Gibbs (drums).
        Limehouse Blues, Play That Song, Penthouse Groove, My Friend Buddy, Give It All You Got, Moonray, The Fat Man, The Beautiful People, Sweet Young Song of Love

Steve Allen & the Steve Allen Big Band (Valley Entertainment)
Included in "Steve Allen's 75th Birthday Celebration"
Los Angeles (Bovard Auditorium, University of Southern California); September 4, 1997
    Steve Allen (piano, vibraphone), Terry Gibbs (vibraphone), Kim Richmond, Gene Burkert (alto saxes), Tom Kubis, Mike Nelson (tenor saxophones), Beverly Dahlke-Smith (baritone saxophone), Alex Iles, Kevin Bradley, Bob McChesney (trombones), Rick Bullock (bass trombone), George Graham, Wayne Bergeron, Frank Szabo, Dennis Farias (trumpets), Grant Geissman (guitar), Paul Smith (piano), Trey Henry (bass), Dave Tull (drums).

Here it Is, Hot Blues

Terry Gibbs/Buddy DeFranco Quintet (Chiaroscuro)
"Wham"
Caribbean Sea, Cafe "S/S Norway;" October 26, 28, and 29, 1997

Terry Gibbs (vibraphone), Buddy DeFranco (clarinet), Aaron Goldberg (piano), Darek "Oles" Oleszkiewicz (bass), Gerry Gibbs (drums) plus guest Flip Phillips (tenor sax).

Wham, Take Your Time, Sweet Georgia Brown, Rebekah, Lonely Dreams, Sweet and Lovely, Go Get 'Em, Early Autumn, Please Let Me Play the Blues, Here It Is

Terry Gibbs & Buddy DeFranco (Contemporary)
"Terry Gibbs and Buddy DeFranco Play Steve Allen"
Van Nuys, California; September 3, 1998

Terry Gibbs (vibraphone), Buddy DeFranco (clarinet), Tom Ranier (piano), Dave Carpenter (bass), Gerry Gibbs (drums).

I Used To Think That I Was Crazy, Sleepy Old Moon, Until I Left Chicago (I Never Had the Blues), Mister Moon, Lazy Days, Playing the Field, Alabama Baby, One Little Thing, South Dakota, Easy for You, Clarinet Lick, Nights in Madrid, In the Mornin' When the Sun Comes Up

Terry Gibbs Quartet (Mack Avenue)
Included in the anthology "The Legacy Lives On–II"
Los Angeles, California; August 2001

Terry Gibbs (vibraphone), Larry Koonse (guitar), Dave Carpenter (bass), Paul Kreibich (drums).

Dance for Eartha, Mean to Me, El Nutto

Terry Gibbs (Mack Avenue)
"From Me to You: Terry Gibbs' Tribute to Lionel Hampton"
Capitol Records Studios (Studio A), Hollywood, California; October 28-29, 2002

Terry Gibbs (vibraphone/piano/vocal*), Pete Christlieb (tenor saxophone), Mike Melvoin (piano), Anthony Wilson (guitar), Joey DeFrancesco (organ), Dave Carpenter (bass), Jeff Hamilton (drums), Barbara Morrison (vocal **)

*Midnight Sun, Blues for Hamp, Ring 'Dem Bells *, Moonglow, Gates Got Rhythm, On the Sunny Side of the Street *, From Me to You, Red Top, Evil Gal Blues **, Hey! Ba Ba-ReBop! *, Two-Finger Boogie Shuffle, The World is Waiting for the Sunrise, Star Dust, Flying Home*

Index

ABC (television), 198, 208, 243-244, 246, 272
Abe Gubenko & his Radio Novelty Orchestra, 5
Adams, Joey, 254
Adams, Pepper, 99
Adderley, Cannonball, 138-139, 201, 221
Adderley, Nat, 138-139
Adler, Larry, 134
"Air Mail Special," 285, 292
Albam, Manny, 21, 169, 188
Albright, Freddy, xiv, 14-15
Alexander, Irving, 41
Alexander, Van, 297
Alexandria Hotel (Chicago), 46
The All Stars, 111
"All the Things You Are," 49
Allen, Steve, xiii, 74-75, 152, 153-154, 177-178, 184-185, 189, 190, 210, 223, 224, 233, 234, 236, 241-243, 259-274, 275-276, 280, 282, 283, 293, 297, 298, 299
Allison, Tommy, 64
Amarosa, Johnny, 115
Ambassador Theater (Brooklyn), 4
Ammons, Gene, 88, 92, 103, 104, 107
"The Anniversary Song," 277
Anthony, Ray, 197, 234
Apollo Theater (New York), 64, 127, 202

"Apple Honey," 83, 88
Appleyard, Peter, 154
Archer, Tom, 36-37
Archerd, Army, 194
Armstrong, Louis, 51, 52, 151, 255-256
Aronov, Benny, 195
Arum, Bob, 144
ASCAP, 260
The Ash Grove (Los Angeles), 297
Associated Booking Corp., 111, 184, 186
Astor Hotel (New York), 114-115
Atomi Hotel (Japan), 267-268
Audino, John, 195, 210, 214, 217, 219, 244, 273
Auld, Barney, 181, 183
Auld, Georgie, 44, 127, 128, 151, 152, 181-183
Avalon Ballroom (Catalina, CA), 198

Babasin, Harry, 53
Bacharach, Burt, 273
"Back Home in Indiana," 42
The Back Street (San Francisco), 36
Bailey, Colin, 234
Bailey, Pearl, 198
Baker, Chet, 173, 175, 180
Baker, Joe, 273
Baker's Keyboard (Detroit), 185,

205
Ballard, Kaye, 132-133
The Band Box (New York), 136-137, 139
Banks, Danny, 115
Barnet, Charlie, 53
Barrett, Ben, 200
Barris, Chuck, 243-249, 257
Barton, Eileen, 77
baseball, 64, 106-107, 222
Basie, Count, 25, 27, 36, 63, 65, 68, 88, 139, 141, 159, 173, 174-175, 176, 177, 188, 189, 191, 196, 200, 219, 236, 237
Basin Street (nightclub-New York), 170-171
The Beatles, 243, 276
bebop, songs based on chord changes, 7, 35
The Beehive (Detroit), 155
"Begin the Beguine," 60, 61
Belafonte, Harry, 167
Bellson, Frank, 51-52
Bellson, Louie, 50, 51-53, 111-116, 120, 135, 198, 281, 292
Beneke, Tex, 187
Bengazzi Hotel (Washington, D.C.), 55
Bennett, Larry, 125
Bennett, Max, 183, 190
The Benny Goodman Story (film), 263
Benzedrine, 31
Berg, George, 133
Bergman, Ingrid, 280
Bergstresser, Rebekah. *See* Gibbs, Rebekah
Berigan, Bunny, 150
Berle, Milton, 185, 273
Berlin Jazz Festival (Germany), 290
Berman, Shelley, 273
Berman, Sonny, 90
Best, Denzil, 55, 59, 61
"Bewitched, Bothered and Bewildered," 172
The Big Cat (album), 206
"The Big Cat" (song), 216

"Billie's Bounce," 214
Billy Berg's (nightclub, Los Angeles), 105
Billy Reed's Little Club, 44
Binder, Steve, 242-243
Birdland (Miami), 171
Birdland (New York City), 10, 117, 118-119, 127-131, 136, 139-142, 157-160, 169-170, 176, 184-185, 205, 228-229, 233, 237-238
Birdland All Stars, 173-176, 236
Bishop, Joey, 212
Bishop, Walter Jr., 101, 231
Biss, Harry, 43, 44-45, 129
Bivona, Gus, 185, 266-267, 270, 271
The Blackhawk (San Francisco), 164
Blaine, Hal, 243, 276
Blake, Robert, 78
Blakey, Art, 14, 36, 120-121, 137
Blassie, Freddie, 239-240
Block, Bert, 125
The Blue Note (Chicago), 80, 81, 92, 149, 151; (Philadelphia), 126-127
bobby-soxers, 115
Bock, Dick, 207, 290
"Body and Soul," 136
"Boomsie," 60
"The Boulevard of Broken Dreams," 14
Bowes, Major Edward. See *Major Bowes' Amateur Hour*
"The Boy Next Door," 143
Boyd, Nelson, 112, 114
Brando, Marlon, 185
Brandwein, Naftule, 5-6, 154
Brandwynne, Nat, 241
Brehm, Simon, 57
Brewer, Harry, 14
Brill, Dick, 233, 240
Britton, Milt, 67-68
Brooklyn Dodgers, 8
Brookmeyer, Bobby, 103, 188, 190
Brown, Clifford, 127

Brown, Les, 107, 210
Brown, Lou, 221, 298
Brown, Ray, 63, 77-78, 202, 242, 264, 288
Brown, Roger, 251
Brubeck, Dave, 134, 164-165, 189, 221
Bruce, Lenny, 179-180, 222-223
Brunswick Records, 137
Bryant, Ray, 202
Buckner, Milt, 137
Budge, Don, 140
Budwig, Monty, 234
bulgars, 229
Bulkin, Sid, 125, 134-135, 141, 143-144, 147
Bunker, Larry, 219, 298
Burgess, Bobby, 195
Burns, Ralph, 80, 88
Burrell, Kenny, 177, 281
Burton, Gary, xiii, 89, 298
Butler, Frank, 268-269
Butterfield, Billy, 262
Buttons, Red, 273
Byas, Don, 36, 103

Cadillac Hotel (Detroit), 177-178
Caesar, Sid, 273
Café Society (Downtown) (New York), 28, 125-126
"Caldonia," xii, 83, 88
Callender, Red, 138
Campbell, John, 291
Candid Camera, 152
Candoli, Conte, 55-57, 59-60, 181, 188, 189, 190, 192, 195, 197-198, 200, 201, 208, 211, 214, 218-219, 244, 249, 273, 276-277, 288
Candoli, Pete, 88, 90, 183, 288
Capitol Records, 82-83
Capitol Theater (Brooklyn), 25, 170
Capp, Frank, 206, 243, 264, 267, 271, 275-276
Cappy's (Buffalo, NY), 185
Carbo, Frankie, 144
Carleton Hotel (Pittsburgh), 185

Carmelo's (Sherman Oaks, CA), 285
Carmen, Jackie, 79-80
Carnation Ballroom (Disneyland), 203
Carnegie Hall (New York), 152
Carr, Vikki, 243
Carroll, Barbara, 156
Carruthers, Bill, 243-245, 248, 254
Carson, Johnny, 78, 234, 246, 274, 285-286
Carter, Benny, 235
Carter, Jack, 273
Cash, Johnny, 257
Casino Gardens (Santa Monica, CA), 50
Catlett, Big Sid, 40
Catskill Mountains (New York), 13, 17-18, 30
CBS (television), 122, 242, 264
Cepeda, Orlando, 8, 185-186
Chaloff, Serge, 44, 80, 84, 91, 98-101, 102, 107, 182
Chambers, Paul, 136, 195, 196
Charles, Ezzard, 140
Charles, Ray, 254
Charles, Teddy, 89
"Cherokee," 50, 97, 196
Chicago Fire (album), 292
Christian, Charlie, 294
Christy Minstrels, 197
Ciccone, Louis. *See* Keeny, Chick
"Ciribiribin," 150
Clark, Buddy, 195, 222
Clark, Roy, 257
Clarke, Kenny, 35, 36
Click Club (Philadelphia), 68
The Cloister (Chicago), 205; (Hollywood), 194-195, 224
Clooney, Rosemary, 273
Cobo Hall (Detroit), 177
Cohen, Abe, 17, 30
Cohen, Leonard, 277
Cohn, Al, 21, 36, 47, 70, 80, 84, 90, 91, 96, 97-98, 107, 188, 215, 218

Cole, Nat "King," 94, 104, 201, 297
Cole, Natalie, 104
Coleman, Cy, 171
The Coliseum (Los Angeles), 268
Collette, Buddy, 235
Collette, Frank, 285
Collier, Chet, 234, 238
Colonna, Jerry, 10
Coltrane, Alice, xiv, 227-232
Coltrane, John, xiv, 201, 216, 228-232
Coltrane, Ravi, 231-232
Columbia Pictures, 77
The Comedy Hour (television program), 242
The Comedy Room (television program), 271, 273
Coney Island (Brooklyn), 10
Conway, Tim, 273
Cooper, Barbara, 223
Cooper, Jackie, 78, 223
Corabi, Teddy, 155-156
Corb, Morty, 134-135
Corcoran, Corky, 50
Corday, Barbara, 77
Cork Festival (Ireland), 289-290
The Corner House (Chicago), 149
Costa, Don, 272
Cottler, Irv, 14, 107, 180
"Cotton Tail," 188, 218
Cowan, Will, 71
Coward, Noel, 182
Cox, Wally, 185
Crane, Les, 234
Crawford's Grill (Pittsburgh), 185
"Crazy Rhythm," 66
The Crescendo (Hollywood), 191, 192, 194, 222-223
Crosby, Bing, 126
"Crown Pilots," 60
"Crying Sands," 60
Crystal, Billy, 273
Cupol Records (Sweden), 58
Curtis, Tony, 220
"Cute," 76
"Czardas," 5, 15, 17

D'artega, Alfonso, 121
Dahl, Arlene, 194
Dahlander, Nils-Bertil, 166-169
Dale, Bert. *See* Dahlander, Nils-Bertil
Dallas, Texas, 32
Dana, Bill, 270
"Dance for Eartha," 238
Dangerfield, Rodney, 255
Daniels, Eddie, 296
Darin, Bobby, 75
The David Letterman Show, 277
Davis, Bob, 292
Davis, Miles, 111, 136, 191, 196, 201, 228
Davis, Sammy Jr., 167, 212, 268
"Day In, Day Out," 76
Dean, Jimmy, 257
The Dean Martin Show, 180
DeArango, Bill, 42-46, 55, 80
DeFranco, Buddy, 277, 283-296
DeJohnette, Jack, 184
Denny, Martin, 270
Dentz, John, 230
Destifano, Sam, 265-266
"Detour Ahead," 90
Detroit Lions, 161
Detroit Tigers, 161
DeVito, Frank, 151, 159, 164-166, 298
Dibble, Dorne, 161
Dick Grove Music School, 184
DiMilo, Cardella, 167-168
The Dinah Shore Show, 180
Diner, Harold, 32
DiNovi, Gene, 55, 56
"Disc Jockey Jump," 217
Disney studios, 271
Disney World, 281
Disneyland, 72, 74, 203
Disneyland Hotel (Anaheim, CA), 298
"Donald Jay," 48
"Donna Lee," 42
"Don't be That Way," 76, 293
Dorham, Kenny, 202
Dorsey, Jimmy, 218
Dorsey, Tommy, xiii, 25, 27, 48,

49-54, 78, 101, 111, 113, 114-116, 117, 188, 200, 283
Down Beat, 43, 88-89, 100, 105, 125, 130, 131, 137, 155, 158-159; "Blindfold Test," 105
"Down by the Old Mill Stream," 144
Downbeat Club (New York), 122, 131-132, 134-137, 141
The Dream Band, xi, xiii, xvi, 75, 76, 169, 187-225, 244, 246, 249, 273, 283, 290, 295, 298, 299
drug abuse, 63-64, 70-71, 117, 143, 173, 182, 213, 217; in Buddy Rich band, 86; in Woody Herman band, 84-88, 98-99, 104
Duff, Howard, 98
Duffy's Tavern (Los Angeles), 179
Dumont network, 117
Dunes Hotel (Las Vegas), 197
Durante, Jimmy, 166
Duvivier, George, 131, 135, 137, 141
Dylan, Bob, 277
Dynasty, 77

Eager, Allen, 36, 47-49, 141
"Early Autumn," 82, 88, 93
"Earthanova," 238
Ebbets Field (Brooklyn), 8
Eckstine, Billy, 42, 136-137, 173-176, 177
The Ed Sullivan Show, 269
Edison, Harry "Sweets," 78, 174, 288
Edmondson, Bob, 195
Edwards, Teddy, 36-37, 268
Eldridge, Roy, 130-131, 202
"Eli, Eli," 170-171
Ellington, Duke, 25, 27, 68, 139, 188, 193, 200, 221-222, 237, 292
Elliott, Don, 130, 135, 137, 141, 142-144, 147, 150, 157
Ellis, Herb, 202, 234, 237, 238, 239, 243, 264, 292-294
Elman, Ziggy, 50, 51, 151, 152, 200
EmArcy Records, 166
The Embers (New York), 130
"Emily," 69
The Empire Room (Los Angeles), 81, 92, 95, 98, 105, 106, 192
The Encyclopedia of Jazz, 288
Enevoldsen, Bob, 190, 195
Entratter, Jack, 220
Epstein, Al, 44, 60, 93, 127-128, 144-145, 202-203
Epstein, Bubbles, 22
"The Errand Boy," 219
Evans, Herschel, 36, 200
"Every Day I Have the Blues," 176
The Exciting Terry Gibbs Big Band (album), 206, 217
Explosion (album), 206

The Fairmont Grill (Jamestown, NY), 185
The Famous Door (New York), 43
Fantasy Records, 206-208, 217, 292, 299
Farlow, Tal, 132, 292
Farmer, Art, 192
Farrow, Ernie, 157, 227
Fat Tuesday's (New York), 277
Faye, Normie, 39-40, 68
"The Fearsome Foursome," 251
Feather, Leonard, 137, 288
Federman, Peaches, 22
Feld, Morey, 148
Feliciano, José, 197
Ferguson, Maynard, 92
Ferrer, José, 56
Field, Sally, 288
Fields, Herbie, 141-142
Fields, Irving, 40
Fields, Jackie, 127
"Fifty-Second Street Theme," 138, 291
Filmways, 208
Finch, Candy, 253
"Fingerbustin'," 218

Finley, Larry, 184, 189
Fishelson, Stan, 30, 85, 94
Fitzgerald, Ella, 58, 202
Flamingo Hotel (Las Vegas), 105, 198, 211-212
Flanagan, Tommy, 177
Mrs. Fleck, 22-24
"Flight of the Bumble Bee," 15, 81, 118, 256
Florence, Bob, 206, 288
Flory, Med, 187, 188, 190, 191, 195, 211, 218, 247, 248-249
Flory, Pete, 155
Flowers, Wayland, 286
"Flying Home," 141, 170, 171, 188, 211
Flynt, Larry, 271
Fontana, Carl, 195, 224, 244, 288
Ford, Fats, 141
Fort Dix (New Jersey), 29
Foster, Frank, 173
Foster, Phil, 182
"The Four Brothers," 30, 84
Free the Fart (book), 102
Freeman, Russ, 188, 190
freilachs, 229
Fresco, Johnny, 244, 247-248
Friley, Vern, 189-190, 195
Frommer, Gary, 183, 184

Gage, Sol. *See* Gubenko, Sol
Gaiety Delicatessen (Hollywood), 196-197
Gaillard, Slim, 142
Galento, Tony, 131
Gannon, Jimmy, 202
Gardner, Ava, 98, 114
Garment, Leonard "Lenny," 17, 171-172
Garner, Erroll, 171, 230
Garris, Sid, 196-199
Gary, Johnny, 173
Gefaell, Bob, 205, 217-218
Geller, Uri, 126
Gershwin, George, 12, 35, 98
Getz, Stan, xiii, 36, 47, 80, 84, 88-89, 90, 91, 97, 98, 106, 107, 111, 142, 215
"Giant Steps," 228, 232
Gibbs, Carol (2nd wife), 72, 75, 151-152, 230, 237, 279-281
Gibbs, Donna (1st wife), 84-85, 101, 111, 113, 117, 133, 159, 163, 172, 177, 179, 181, 183, 184, 196, 227, 230, 269, 279
Gibbs, Gerry (son), 72-74, 231-232, 280, 297
Gibbs, Jerra (daughter), 72, 73, 280
Gibbs, Rebekah (3rd wife), xv, 266, 281-282, 291-292
Gibbs, Terry:
  attitudes towards: anti-Semitism, 31, 164; being a prodigy, 11; boxing and fighting, 8, 19; definition of "genius," 35-36; drug abuse, 27-28, 32-33, 45, 64, 86-88; 143; jazz labels, 180-181; jazz polls, 88; Judaism, 3, 11, 84; music critics, 43-44; race and racism, x, 60, 92-93, 157-158, 160, 167-168, 172, 174-176
  influences on: bebop, 34-35; Dizzy Gillespie, 34, 49; father, 5-7; Woody Herman, 81, 91
  personal life: 75th birthday party, 297-298; army, 29; auto accident, 165-166; becoming Terry Gibbs, 28-29; birth, 2; expulsion from high school, 22; first marriage, 84, 177, 227, 279; hyperactivity, 11-12; marriage to Carol, 151-152, 279-281; marriage to Rebekah, 266, 281-282; nickname, 11
  recording sessions: 42, 47-49,

Index   325

81, 88, 93, 168-169, 187-188, 193, 199-200, 206-208, 210-211, 217, 229-230, 275-278, 285, 290-291, 295, 299
Gillespie, Dizzy, xiii, 34-36, 58, 92, 105, 127, 137, 139, 155, 191, 221-222, 236, 245, 253-254, 273, 279, 283
Ginell, Cary, xv-xvi
Ginsberg, Allen, 277
Ginsburg, Ira, xiv
Giuffre, Jimmy, 84, 88, 107
Glabman, Herbie, 17
Glaser, Joe, 111, 125-126, 143, 147-149, 151, 155, 164, 170, 204, 211, 227, 230-231, 256, 269, 270
Glenn, Tyree, 256
Glow, Bernie, 30, 85, 93-94
Gobel, George, 273
Gonzalez, Babs, 42, 57
Goodall, Bill, 130
Goodman, Alice, 118
Goodman, Benny, xiii, 24-25, 27, 36, 50, 51, 52-53, 68, 101, 114, 117-124, 125, 126, 131, 134-135, 140-141, 145, 147-154, 188, 196, 200, 251, 263-264, 281, 284, 285, 286, 290, 292, 293, 294, 296
Goodman, Irving, 153
Gormé, Eydie, 272
Gorshin, Frank, 194
Gozzo, Conrad, 180
Grable, Betty, 106-107
Grand Hotel (Edinburgh, Scotland), 292
Grand Hotel (Göteborg, Sweden), 57
Granz, Norman, 142, 199-200, 202-203
Greco, Buddy, 144, 163
"Green," 73
Green, Irv, 199-200
Green, Urbie, 138
Greenberg, Abe, 222-223
Greenberg, Belle, 222-223

Greene, Shecky, 273
Greif, George, 197-199
Grier, Roosevelt, 251
Griffin, Chris, 151
"Groovin' High," 7, 35
Grove, Dick, 184
Gruber, Freddie, 76, 77
Gubenko, Abe (father), 1-3, 5, 6, 13, 172
Gubenko, Julius. *See* Gibbs, Terry
Gubenko, Lizzie (mother), 1-3, 7, 9, 13
Gubenko, Shirley "Sherry" (sister), 1-2, 7, 111
Gubenko, Sol (brother), 1, 7-8, 13-14, 229
Gubenko, Sonia "Sunny" (sister), 1, 7, 14
Gubenko, Nathan (Nat Gubin), 10
Gumina, Tommy, 283

Haden, Charlie, 188, 297
Haggart, Bob, 262
Haig, Al, 36, 101
Half Moon Hotel (Brooklyn), 10
Hamilton, Chico, 235
Hampton, Gladys, 53-54
Hampton, Lionel, xiii, 28, 51, 52-54, 63, 89, 104-105, 170-171, 188, 200, 229, 284, 285, 286, 292, 298
"Happiness Is Just a Thing Called Joe," 172
"Happy Birthday," 218
"The Happy Monster," 57
Harriman, Averill, 268
Harrington, Pat, Jr. 273
Harris, Barry, 177
Harris, Bill, 81, 85, 90, 91, 94-95, 133
Harris, Marty, 271
Harris, Phil, 255
Hartsough, Donna. *See* Gibbs, Donna
Haver, June, 190
Hawkins, Coleman, 36, 103, 130
Haynes, Roy, 42, 231

Heard, J.C., 102
Heath, Percy, 136
Heckman, Don, 231-232
Hefner, Hugh, 194
Hefti, Neal, 88, 103, 133, 183, 298
Heider, Wally, 193-194, 200, 206, 208, 209, 210-211
Henderson, Bill, 298
Henderson, Florence, 211, 254-255
Henderson, Skitch, 234
Herman, Woody, xiii, 7, 30, 55, 57, 63, 69, 71, 80-109, 111, 112, 115, 118, 149, 181, 192, 200, 210, 279, 283
The Hickory House (New York), 133
Hinton, Milt, 292
Hitler, Adolf, 126, 260
hockey, 163
Hoernschemeyer, Hunchy, 161
Hogan, Hulk, 239
Holiday, Billie, 90, 105-106
"Holiday for Strings," 224
Holliday, Judy, 202-203
Holloway, Red, 273
Hollywood Bowl, 195
The Hollywood Citizen, 222
Hollywood Jazz Festival, 195
The Hollywood Palace, 217, 244
Hollywood Palladium (Los Angeles), 63, 71, 216, 279
Holman, Bill, 103, 187, 188, 190, 191, 195, 206, 245, 249, 250, 298
Holtzfield, Frank, 149, 151
Homer & Jethro, 245
homosexuality, 96
Hope, Bob, 10, 243
"Hora Staccato," 5
Horne, Lena, 167, 279
"Hot House," 35
"How High the Moon," 7, 104, 148
Hubbard, Freddie, 191-192
Humphrey, Hubert, 265
Hustler, 271
Hutcherson, Bobby, xiii

"I Can't Get Started," 44, 105
"I Got Rhythm," xvi, 22, 49, 51, 83, 88, 156, 241, 284
"I Understand," 135
"If I Knew You Were Coming, I'd Have Baked a Cake," 77
"I'm in Love with You, Honey," 61
The Interlude (Hollywood), 192
"The Irish Washerwoman," 260
IRS (Internal Revenue Service), 108
"Is You Is or Is You Ain't My Baby," 261
"It Could Happen to You," 217
It Might as Well Be Swing (album), 200
"It Might as Well Be Swing" (song), 214

"Jack the Bear," 193
Jackson, Chubby, 55-62, 63, 80, 83, 85-86, 91, 94, 102-103, 106, 107, 133, 183
Jackson, Milt, xiii, 89, 298
Jackson, "Mom," 56-57, 61-62
Jacquet, Illinois, 40, 170, 188
"Jamaica Rhumba," 103
Jamal, Ahmad, 230
James, Harry, 102, 106-107, 138, 150, 151, 195, 200, 211, 212, 216
Jarrett, Keith, 184
Jazz A La Carte Records, 224
Jazz at the Philharmonic, 142, 202
The Jazz Gallery (New York), 205
Jazz Party-First Time Together (album), 285
Jazz Profiles (radio program), xiv
Jazztime USA, 142
The Jerry Lewis Telethon, 221
Jew Jazz (rejected album title), 229
Jillian, Ann, 273
Joe Segal's Jazz Showcase (Chicago), 290
Johnson, Gus, 159, 202

Index

Jolly, Pete, 190, 276
Jolson, Al, 56
Jones, Deacon, 251
Jones, Eddie, 173
Jones, Elvin, 72, 155, 286
Jones, Jack, 78
Jones, Jimmy, 177
Jones, Jo, 174, 200
Jones, Hank, 101
Jones, Quincy, 228
Jones, Spike, 222
Jones, Thad, 155, 173
Jordan, Duke, 48
Jordan, Louis, 127
"Jordu," 48-49
Jump Town (Chicago), 45
"Just Plain Meyer," 190

Kaffel, Ralph, 207, 217, 292, 295, 299
Kahn, Tiny, 20-22, 24, 28-29, 34, 39-41, 42, 44, 45, 46, 55, 66, 67-68, 86, 98, 102, 187
Kamuca, Richie, 195, 215-216
Kasten, Shelly, 194, 195
Kay, Monte, 131, 135, 137-138
Kay, Sammy, 41
Kay, Stanley, 65, 67, 70
Kaye, Danny, 51
Kayne, Judy, 28
KCET (Los Angeles), 285
Keeny, Chick, 155
Kelly, Wynton, 195, 196
The Ken Murray Show, 140-141
Kennedy, Charlie, 190, 195, 216-217
Kennedy, John F., 268
Kennedy, Robert, 268
Kenton, Stan, 195, 249
Kern, Jerome, 35
Kimball's (Berkeley, CA), 292-293
King Arthur's (Canoga Park, CA), 218
"King City Stomp," 166
King, Don, 144
King, Larry, 274
King, Peggy, 132-133

Kitt, Eartha, 237-238
KKGO (Los Angeles), 207
Klein, Dave, 50-51
klezmer, 229-230
KLON (Long Beach, CA), 207
Knotts, Don, 270
Koonse, Larry, 232
Kotick, Teddy, 120, 158
Kral, Irene, 197, 299
Krask, Skip, 194
Krupa, Gene, 66, 101, 150, 152, 200, 216-217, 228
Kutcher, Sam, 229

LaFaro, Scotty, 186
Lamond, Don, 80, 83, 85, 94, 101-102, 107, 130, 138
Land, Harold, 218
Lang, Mike, 276
Lapin, Al, 180, 249
LaPinto, Frank, 79-80
The Larry Finley Show (television program), 184
Las Vegas, 166-167, 197-198, 211-214
"Last But Not Least," 94, 104
Lawford, Peter, 212
Lawrence, Elliot, 234
Lawrence, Steve, 272
Lawson, Yank, 262
Layne, Bobby, 161-162
Lee, Peggy, 75, 152
Leeds, Charlie, 43, 46
Leesville (Louisiana), 30
Leighton, Bernie, 140-141
"Lemon Drop," 18, 57-58, 60, 81-82, 103, 115, 162
Lennon, John, 275-276
The Lennon Sisters, 247
Leno, Jay, 274
Leonard, Harvey, 42, 45
"Lester Leaps In," 174, 284
"Let's Dance," 25
Letterman, David, 274, 277
Levey, Stan, 36, 111, 180, 188, 298
Levy, Irving, 131-132, 137
Levy, Lou, 46, 56-57, 59-60, 80,

84, 85, 88, 90, 98, 99-101,
  108, 111, 113-114, 182, 183,
  190, 195, 205, 222, 298
Levy, Morris, 129, 130, 131-132,
  141-142, 171, 174
Levy, Paul, 252
Levy, Pauline, 252
Lewis, Jerry, 74, 78, 190, 219-
  221, 286, 298
Lewis, John, 286
Lewis, Mel, 21, 76, 187, 190, 192,
  195, 198, 202, 205-206, 215,
  222, 227
Liberace, 168
The Lighthouse All Stars, 180
Limelight Records, 230
Linn, Ray, 221
Lishness, Niles, 241, 298
Little, Rich, 243
Logan, Alan, 17-18, 229
Login, Abe. *See* Logan, Alan
"Lollypop," 94, 103
Lombardi, Clyde, 42
Lombardo, Guy, 50
The London House (Chicago),
  230-231, 270-271
Longo, Mike, 253
Loop Lounge (Cleveland), 163
Los Angeles Jazz Society, 297
Los Angeles Rams, 251
The Los Angeles Times, 231-232
Louis, Joe, 140
Lowe, Mundell, 141, 185
Lubinsky, Herman, 49
Lundy, Lamar, 251
Lyons, Jimmy, 147-148

MacMurray, Fred, 190
Maddin, Jimmy, 194, 199, 215,
  217
Maher, Bill, 272
Main Stem (album), 206
"Main Stem" (song), 221-222
Maini, Joe, 190, 192, 195, 197,
  201, 210-211, 217-218, 222;
  223-224
Maize, Bob, 271
Major Bowes' Amateur Hour, xiii,
  15-16, 27
Maltin, Leonard, 298
"Man, Don't be Ridiculous," 101
"The Man I Love," 56
Manaday, Irwin, 32
Mancini, Henry, 273
Mandel, Johnny, 21, 69-70, 79,
  103, 108
Manne, Flip, 106
Manne, Shelly, 98, 102, 106. 107,
  180, 214, 287, 288
Manor Records, 42
Mardigan, Art, 43
Marienthal, Irving, 230, 270
Marienthal, Oscar, 230, 270
marijuana, 27-28, 32-33, 39, 45,
  55, 57, 59, 68-69, 87, 173,
  275
Markowitz, Marky, 85
Marowitz, Sam, 84, 85, 96-97
Marquette, PeeWee, 10, 119, 158-
  159, 175, 236
Marsalis, Wynton, 192
Marterie, Ralph, 199-200
Martin, Dean, 212, 268
Martin, Tony, 181
Maryville, Kansas, 91
Matney, Bill, 157
Mays, Willie, 8, 182
MCA (Music Corporation of
  America), 28
McCall, Mary Ann, 89-90, 96-97,
  103
McConnell, Rob, 206
McGhee, Howard, 36
McKeller, Phil, 164
McKusick, Hal, 133
McLeod, Alice. *See* Coltrane,
  Alice
McPartland, Marian, 130, 133,
  156
McQueen, Steve, 190
Meadows, Jayne, 223, 266, 267,
  272
"Meeskite," 48
The Mel Tormé Show, 132
The Mellowlarks, 132-133
Melvoin, Mike, 234, 264

Menza, Don, 224, 276, 277
Mercer, Johnny, 190, 195
Mercury Records, 168-169, 187-188, 199-200, 205-206, 228-230
The Merv Griffin Show, 233
Metronome, 89, 100, 125, 131, 155
The Metropole (New York), 228
Mettome, Doug, 150
"Miami Rhumba," 40
Michelot, Pierre, 286
Mickey Mouse, 203-204
Middlebrooks, Wilfred, 202
The Mike Douglas Show, 233
Mikolas, Joe, 194
Miles, Butch, 292, 293
Miller, Bill, 50
Miller, Glenn, 68
Miller, Mitch, 117, 120
Mingus, Charlie, 132
Minnie Mouse, 203-204
Minton's (New York), 34
Miranda, Antonio, 22-24
Mitchell, Billy, 155
The Mocambo (Hollywood), 194
Modern Jazz Quartet, 89
The Modern Jazz Room (Cleveland), 185
Mondragon, Joe, 237
Monitor, 218
Monk, Thelonious, 35, 162
Monroe, Marilyn, 78, 245
Monterey Jazz Festival, 221-222
Montrose, J.R., 202
Moody, James, 253
Moore, Melba, 272
Moran, Pat, xiv, 205, 211-213
More Vibes on Velvet (album), 168, 184
Morello, Joe, 133-134
Moulin Rouge (Las Vegas), 167
Mulligan, Gerry, 180, 202-203
Mundy, Jimmy, 65
Munsell, Patrice, 205
Murder, Inc., 10
Murray, Al, 18
Murray, Jan, 273

Murray, Ken, 140-141
Music and Arts High School (New York), 30
The Music Room (television program), 271-272
Musiker, Ray, 229
"My Buddy," 78

Navy Band, 298
NBC (television), 157, 180, 189, 249. 269
New York Giants, 8
New York Philharmonic, 14
New York State Athletic Commission, 256
The New York Times, 285
Newborn, Phineas, 173, 174, 177
Newhart, Bob, 273
Newley, Anthony, 273
Newman, Joe, 173
Nicas, Rod, xvi, 299
"Night and Day," 60
"A Night in Tunisia," 273
Nimitz, Jack, 195, 202, 217
Nola's Studios (New York), 134, 228
Norman, Gene, 192-193, 206-207, 222
"Northwest Passage," 83
Norvo, Red, xiii, 28, 89, 132-133, 211-212, 298
"Nose Cone," 219, 220
"Not Really the Blues," 103
Novak, Larry, 292
"Now's the Time," 284
NPR (National Public Radio), xiv
Nye, Louis, 255, 261, 270, 273

O'Brien, Kenny, 155, 157
"Ocean's Eleven," 211
Oles, Darek, 232
Olsen, Merlin, 251
"One More Time," 299
Operation: Entertainment, 208, 243-257, 259, 273, 284
"Opus One," 207
"Ornithology," 7
Ott, Mel, 8, 185

"Our Day Will Come," 236
"Out of Nowhere," 91, 128-129
The Overture (magazine), 224

P.J.'s (Hollywood), 227, 234
Paar, Jack, 274
Pacht, Jerry, 227
Pacific Jazz Records, 207
Page, Patti, 273
Paich, Marty, 188
Palermo, Blinky, 143-144
Palo Alto Records, 285, 290, 295
Pal's Records (Canoga Park, CA), 252
Palumbo, Frank, 68
Paramount Pictures (studio), 71-72
Paramount Theater (Brooklyn), 25, 64, 150
Parisian Room (Los Angeles), 168
Parker, Charlie "Bird," xiii, 34-36, 42, 48, 49, 70, 86, 92, 98, 112, 117, 128-129, 137, 138, 139, 158, 159, 169, 191, 217, 228, 245, 279, 283, 284
Parsons, Louella, 190
Passover, 7, 292
Payne, Sonny, 173
PBS, 285
"Peaches," 104, 201
Peacock, Gary, 184, 186
"Pearlie," 272
Pellegrini, Al, 132-133
"Pennies from Heaven," 97
Pep, Willie, 140
Pepper, Art, 288
Percussive Arts Society, 298-299
Perkins, Bill, 195, 215, 216
Peterson, Oscar, 63, 105, 202, 221-222, 230, 234, 264
Petrillo, James C., 34
Pettiford, Oscar, xiii, 35, 36, 91, 92, 103, 107, 111-112, 136
Philbin, Regis, 233-240, 273, 298
Phillips, Flip, 90, 281
Piccadilly Hotel (New York), 28
Pierce, Nat, 138
Pike, Bobby, 228, 230
Pincus, "The Mayor of 52nd St.," 41-42
Pizzarelli, Bucky, 138
Playboy (magazine), 271
The Playboy Club (Milwaukee), 265-267
Playboy Jazz Festival, 217
Politically Incorrect, 272
Pollard, Terry, xiv, 151, 155-158, 160-161, 167-168, 170-174, 176-178, 227, 230
Polygram Records, 206, 230
Porcino, Al, xii, 103, 189, 190, 195, 196, 200, 209-210, 217, 249-250
Porter, Cole, 246
Porter, Roy, 36
Poston, Ken, 231
Poston, Tom, 270
Powell, Bud, xiii, 35, 36, 49, 101, 129-130, 173, 176-177, 228
Powell, Mel, 51, 118
Prell, Don, 204
"Prelude to a Kiss," 201
"Pretty Blue Eyes," 246
Price, Vincent, 238
Putnam, Bill, 209

"Queer Street," 65

racism, 91, 92, 160, 172, 174-176, 196, 263
Rader, Don, 247
Raeburn, Boyd, 27, 39, 251
Ramey, Gene, 42
"The Rat Pack," 211-212
Rawls, Lou, 273
Raye, Martha, 255
The Record Plant (studio-Hollywood), 275
Reed, Billy, 44-45
Regal Theater (Chicago), 65
The Regis Philbin Show, 233-240, 243-244, 246, 280
Reig, Teddy, 47-49, 135
Reiner, Carl, 273
Reles, Abe, 10
Reynolds, Burt, 288
Rich, Buddy, xiii, 21, 47, 63-78,

80, 84, 86, 98, 101, 105, 115, 138, 144, 200, 206-207, 249, 279
Rich, Elaine, 77
Richards, Emil, 298
Richards, Johnny, 221
Richardson, Beans, 155
Rickles, Don, 238-239, 250-251
Rico, Joe, 142-143
Riddle, Major, 197
The Ridgecrest (Rochester, NY), 185
Roach, Max, 35, 36, 47-48, 66, 163-164, 180
Roberts, Don, 148
Roberts, Johnny, 131-132
Robinson, Sugar Ray, 140
Rodney, Red, 83, 85, 86, 90, 91, 93, 127-128, 129
Rogers, Shorty, xii, 22, 30, 76, 80, 81, 82, 85, 88, 91, 92, 94, 96, 100, 103, 104, 142, 180, 206, 250
Rollini, Adrian, xiii, 28
Roost Records, 236
Rosenbloom, Maxie, 237
Rosh Hashanah, 7
Rosner, Rick, 259-260
Rosolino, Frank, 181, 190, 192, 195, 197, 209, 210-211, 222; 224
Rossolini, Roberto, 280
Roth, Sid, 22
Rouge Lounge (Detroit), 160
The Roundtable (New York), 184-185
Royal, Ernie, 80, 81, 85, 91, 92, 93, 103, 107
Royal, Marshall, 288
The Royal Nevada (Las Vegas), 166
The Royal Roost (New York), 81, 86, 92, 118, 181
Royal York Hotel (Toronto), 108
Rugolo, Pete, 188
Rumsey, Howard, 298
Russell, Curly, 48, 111, 143

Sachs, Aaron, 42, 47
Safranski, Eddie, 141
Sager, Carole Bayer, 273
Sahara Hotel (Las Vegas), 241-242, 286
Sahl, Mort, 273
St. Vitus' dance, 11
Sales, Soupy, 162-163, 190
Salinger, Pierre, 268
Salvador, Sal, 133
Sample, Joe, 276
San Francisco Giants, 185
The Sanbah (Los Angeles), 215
Sands, Mal, 297
Sands, Nick, 69
Sands Hotel (Las Vegas), 105, 211-212, 219-220
"Santa Claus is Coming to Town," 112
Sardi's (Los Angeles), 238
Saunders, Berrel, 36, 74, 75, 189, 192, 196, 203, 206, 208, 216, 220, 252-253
Savitt, Buddy, 83, 104, 107
Savoy Records, 47, 49
"Scheherazade," 251
Dr. Schiff, 256
Schifrin, Lalo, 229
Schiller, Alice, 188
Schiller, Harry, 188-189, 191
Schmidt, Joe, 161-162
Schoen, Vic, 210
Schreiber, Freddie, 211, 213-214
Schwartz, Jack, 32, 183, 189, 190, 195, 200, 217
Scott, "Crying" Jimmy, 135
Scott, Ronnie, 284, 287, 291
Scott, Tony, 129
Scully, Vin, xiii
"September in the Rain," 158
"September Song," 61
"Seven Come Eleven," 294
Severino, Frank, 184
Severinsen, Doc, 273, 285
The Seville (Hollywood), 188, 190-193, 201, 206, 208
Shad, Bobby, 168-169, 187-188
"The Shadow of Your Smile," 21,

69
Shaffer, Paul, 277
Shank, Bud, 244, 248
Sharkey's Machine (film), 288
Shaughnessy, Eddie, 73, 158
Shavers, Charlie, 50, 51, 111-114, 116
Shaw, Artie, 25, 27, 36, 68, 78, 188, 200, 296
Shawn, Dick, 273
Shearing, George, 27, 43, 104, 129-130, 135, 158, 192-193, 230
Sheldon, Jack, 201-202, 203-204, 222
Shelly's Manne-Hole (Los Angeles), 214
Sherry, Don, 276
Shew, Bobby, 249
Shrine Auditorium (Los Angeles), 201
Shu, Eddie, 134
Siegel, Bernie. *See* Berrel Saunders
Siegel, Jerry, 187
Silver, Horace, 142-144, 195, 196, 291, 298
Silvers, Phil, 185
Simpkins, Andy, 285
Sims, Zoot, 36, 47, 80, 84, 90, 91, 97, 106, 107, 129, 173, 174, 175, 215, 281
Sinatra, Frank, 14, 15, 77, 78, 114-115, 126, 180, 211-213, 238, 268, 297
"Sing, Sing, Sing," 21, 150
"Sister Sadie," 291
Slate Brothers Club (Los Angeles), 186, 238
Small's (New York), 34
Smith, Charlie, 122, 131
Smith, Dalton, 249
Smith, Jimmie, 286
Smith, Paul, 74, 134-135, 259-260, 267
Snyder, Terry, 122, 141
Socolow, Frank, 21, 27, 32, 39, 55-58

"Soft Eyes," 216
Soldier Meyers (club-Brooklyn), 111
"Some Enchanted Evening," 211
A Song Is Born (film), 51-52
"Song of India," 50
Southern, Jeri, 173, 175, 176
Spector, Phil, 275-278
Springer, Jerry, 274
Stalavitzky, Whitey, 13
Stanley Theater (Pittsburgh), 16
"The Star Spangled Banner," 161
Star Time (television program), 117, 125
"Stardust" or "Star Dust," 36, 161, 171, 188
Stardust Hotel (Las Vegas), 166
Starr, Eve, 188
Stars of Jazz, (television program), 241-242
Steirs Hotel (Catskill Mountains, NY), 17
"Stella by Starlight," 49
Stern, Howard, 274
The Steve Allen Show, xi, 159, 209, 233-234, 259-274
Stevenson, Adlai, 268
Stitt, Sonny, 142, 195, 196, 202
Strand, Pete, 162
Strand Theater (New York), 25, 114
Strazzeri, Frank, 204-205
"Summer Sequence," 88
The Summit (Hollywood), 205-206, 216, 217, 224
The Sundown (Hollywood), 194-195, 196. 199-201, 202, 205-206, 215, 217, 224
The Sundown Sessions (album), 200, 217
Supack, Nate, 182
Supersax, 36
"Sweet Georgia Brown," 220
Swift, Bob, 85, 94
Swope, Earl, 80, 85, 90, 94, 95-96, 106, 107
Symphony Sid. *See* Sid Torin

"T & S," 94, 142, 166
The Taming of the Shrew (play), 261
Tatum, Art, 28, 35
"Taxi War Dance," 174
Taylor, Billy, 131, 135, 137, 141
Taylor, Elizabeth, 279
telethons, 74
Tempo, Nino, 276
"Temptation Rag," 119
Terrabaso, John, 204
The Terrace Lounge (St. Louis), 169
Terry, Clark, 281
"Terry Gibbs & Mel Zelnick's Music Stop" (Canoga Park, CA), 252-253
Terry Gibbs & the Woody Herman All Stars, 138
"Terry Gibbs Day," 297
Terry Gibbs Plays Jewish Melodies in Jazz Time (album), 229-230
Tesser, Neil, 291
"That Feller McKeller," 164
"That's Right," 81, 82, 93, 103
Thiele, Bob, 142
Thielemans, Toots, 134
Thigpen, Ed, 202
"This Will Be the Start of Something Big," 275, 276
Thomas, Danny, 273
Thompson, Lucky, 103
The Three Deuces (New York), 34, 41, 45
"Tico Tico," 224
Tilden High School (Brooklyn), 10, 22
Tin Pan Alley (nightclub-New York), 128
Tjader, Cal, xiii, 185
Tom Cassidy Agency, 293
The Tonight Show, 72-73, 180, 233, 246, 249, 260, 264, 273, 274, 276, 285-286
Torgman, Irving, 19-20
Torin, "Symphony Sid," 48, 197
Tormé, Mel, 71, 78, 132-133, 160-161
The Town Tavern (Toronto), 185
Tracy, Jack, 205
Traubel, Helen, 166
Trenner, Donn, 234
Triglia, Billy, 120
Triscari, Ray, 189, 192, 195, 209, 214, 217, 244
Tristano, Lenny, 251
Tropicana Hotel (Miami), 172
The Troubadour (New York), 44
Troup, Bobby, 234, 241-242
Tucker, Bobby, 42, 177
Turchen, Abe, 107-108
Turkus, Burton, 10
Tyson, Mike, 129, 210

UCLA, 220
"Unforgettable," 104
Urso, Phil, 93, 135, 141, 143

Variety, 16, 194
Vaughan, Sarah, 139, 173, 174-175, 177, 236, 237, 273, 288
Ventura, Charlie, 82
The Ventura Club (Sherman Oaks, CA), 297-298
Venuti, Joe, 281
Verve Records, 200, 206
Vibes on Velvet (album), 169
Vibes Summit, 297
Viola, Al, 78, 268, 271
"Violets for Your Furs," 160-161
Visor, Carrington, 235, 237, 248-249
"Viva Cepeda," 185

Wadsworth, Carol. *See* Gibbs, Carol
"The Wall of Sound," 276
Wallington, George, 57, 111
Warrington, Tom, 78
Washburn, Jim, 247-248, 284-285
Washington, Dinah, 139, 236, 237
Watrous, Bill, 288
Wayne, Chuck, 27
The Weavers, 125-126
Webster, Ben, 36, 188

Wein, George, 286-287
Weiss, Sid, 134, 147-148, 150, 151
Wess, Frank, 173
west coast jazz, 180
Westdale Hotel (Toronto), 185
Westinghouse, 233
WFAA (Dallas), 32
"What Is This Thing Called Love," 35
"What's New?", 95, 108-109
"Whispering," 7, 35
Who Wants to Be a Millionaire?, 298
Wilkins, Ernie, 138
Wilkinson, Dave, 167
Williams, Andy, 194
Williams, Joe, 173, 176, 200, 272, 288, 297
Williams, Paul, 272
Williamson, Claude, 2, 184, 185
Williamson, Stu, 189, 195, 201
Wilson, Gerald, 235, 298
Wilson, John, 285
Wilson, Nancy, xiv
Wilson, Ollie, 85, 95
Wilson, Shadow, 65, 102
Wilson, Teddy, 122-124, 129, 135, 140-141, 200
Winding, Kai, 111, 142-143, 224
Winfrey, Oprah, 274
Winter, Jerry, 111, 114
Wisotski, Marty, 41

"Witchcraft," 171
Witherspoon, Jimmy, 197, 198
WLTH (New York), 18
Wolverine Hotel (Detroit), 161
Wong, Herb, 285
"The World Is Waiting for the Sunrise," 140
The World's Greatest Jazz Band, 262
Wright, Herman, 151, 157, 161, 165, 167, 171, 227

Xylophone, 5

Yale University, 267
Yoder, Walt, 89
Yom Kippur, 24
"You Don't Know What Love Is," 156
"You Go to My Head," 66-67, 70, 99
"You'd Be So Nice to Come Home To," 246, 250
Young, Lester, 36, 47, 49, 103, 106, 142, 173, 174, 200, 216
Young, Snooky, 196, 297
Young, Terry, 24

Zelnick, Mel, 251-253
Zito, Ronnie, 211